QUEBEC

THE REVOLUTIONARY AGE

HILDA NEATBY

QUEBEC

THE REVOLUTIONARY AGE
1760–1791

The Canadian Centenary Series

McClelland and Stewart Limited

Reprinted 1971, 1977

0-7710-6658-9

DESIGN: FRANK NEWFELD

The Canadian Publishers
McClelland and Stewart Limited
25 Hollinger Road, Toronto 16

THE
CANADIAN
CENTENARY
SERIES

A History of Canada

W. L. Morton, EXECUTIVE EDITOR
D. G. Creighton, ADVISORY EDITOR

VOLUMES STARRED ARE PUBLISHED

†ALSO AVAILABLE IN PAPERBACK

CONTENTS

Quebec: The Revolutionary Age

MAPS

The Canadian Centenary Series

Half a century has elapsed since *Canada and Its Provinces*, the first large-scale co-operative history of Canada, was published. During that time, new historical materials have been made available in archives and libraries; new research has been carried out, and its results published; new interpretations have been advanced and tested. In these same years Canada itself has greatly grown and changed. These facts, together with the centenary of Confederation, justify the publication of a new co-operative history of Canada.

The form chosen for this enterprise was that of a series of volumes. The series was planned by the editors, but each volume will be designed and executed by a single author. The general theme of the work is the development of those regional communities which have for the past century made up the Canadian nation; and the series will be composed of a number of volumes sufficiently large to permit adequate treatment of all the phases of the theme in the light of modern knowledge.

The Centenary History, then, was planned as a series to have a certain common character and to follow a common method but to be written by individual authors, specialists in their fields. As a whole, it will be a work of specialized knowledge, the great advantage of scholarly co-operation, and at the same time each volume will have the unity and distinctive character of individual authorship. It was agreed that a general narrative treatment was necessary and that each author should deal in a balanced way with economic, political, and social history. The result, it is hoped, will be an interpretative, varied, and comprehensive account, at once useful to the student and interesting to the general reader.

The difficulties of organizing and executing such a series are apparent: the overlapping of separate narratives, the risk of omissions, the imposition of divisions which are relevant to some themes but not to others. Not so apparent, but quite as troublesome, are the problems of scale, perspective, and scope, problems which perplex the writer of a one-volume history and are magnified in a series. It is by deliberate choice that certain parts of the history are told twice, in different volumes from different points of view, in the belief that the benefits gained outweigh the unavoidable disadvantages.

The writing of the history of the years covered in this volume was a task that required courage as well as Professor Neatby's special qualifications and talents. The period has long been a controversial one, provoking debates distinguished often for learning and occasionally for acrimony. It is now almost forty years since the intensive research and penetrating interpretations of A. L. Burt first provided a fundamental study of the history of the old province of Quebec; the work was long out of print but is now happily available in a two-volume edition in the Carleton Library series. New accounts of the old province have had to grow up in the shadow of that monumental work. It is good to know that Professor Burt, now no longer with us, lived to welcome a new study by a former pupil, as fresh and original as it is a model of historical thinking and writing.

W. L. MORTON,
Executive Editor.

D. G. CREIGHTON,
Advisory Editor.

Quebec: The Revolutionary Age

The editors have explained the nature and general purpose of this work. No one need emphasize the importance of this critical thirty years in the history of the French-speaking Canadian community. I need only say that my re-examination of this period in our history has afforded me an enjoyment which I hope may to some degree be shared by my readers.

Nearly thirty years ago I prepared a study on the administration of justice after 1775 at the suggestion and under the direction of Professor A. L. Burt of the University of Minnesota. Many Canadians and others have grateful memories of this most generous of "advisers." Perhaps only I can testify to even greater kindness at the latter end than at the beginning. *The Old Province of Quebec* has been my constant companion and unfailing helper in my research.

The kindness of the Board of Governors of the University of Saskatchewan, the co-operation of my colleagues in the history department, and the generosity of the Canada Council in granting me a fellowship made it possible for me to have two years' leave of absence from teaching during which I was able to devote myself to the completion of the book. For this exceptional privilege I am most grateful.

I remember with pleasure the kindness of the archivist of the Archbishopric of Quebec, who gave me every facility for examining the ecclesiastical records for the period. The archivist of the Collège Ste Marie in Montreal also received me with the distinguished courtesy at once of his nation and his order. That most hospitable of institutions, the Public Archives of Canada, where most of the materials for this period are available, gave me every possible assistance. I am grateful to the Chief Archivist and to all his staff, especially to Miss Barbara Wilson of the Manuscript Division. The reference staff of the Library of the University of Saskatchewan borrowed rare material for me on several occasions. The staff of the Provincial Archives arranged loans of microfilm and provided reading facilities over periods of many months. To all of these I offer my sincere thanks.

My colleague, Professor Jean E. Murray, read a part of my manuscript and gave me valuable advice. Professor W. L. Morton has performed the sometimes thankless task of editor with unfailing kindness and patience. I am grateful for his good counsel at all times and especially for invaluable assistance in the work of revision. In this final stage I am also indebted to Professor D. G. Creighton for helpful suggestions. Together they have greatly reduced the number of errors and infelicities of style, leaving, I can only hope, a comparatively small number for which the author accepts sole responsibility.

Finally I wish to express my gratitude to Miss I. D. Parrott who deciphered my original manuscript with unexampled patience and skill and to Mrs. Janet Saunders for her care and vigilance in the preparation of the final copy.

HILDA NEATBY

CHAPTER 1

Introduction

The great river was the centre and heart of all life in the old province of Quebec. Over its surface moved all those ships identified by names now mere memories of a forgotten age: sloops and schooners, snows and shallops, brigs and brigantines; to say nothing of the purely local craft, the canoes, the heavy bateaux, and the ferries. From far down in the gulf, where sailors first sighted the rocks of Bic, the ships moved up past the seal-fishing stations of Anticosti and its neighbours, past the noble hills and mountains of the north shore, by the Ile aux Coudres to the Island of Orleans, cultivated like a garden, into the basin, and the anchorage of the King's Wharf under the great rock of Cape Diamond. Some went beyond, up and up past the despised but energetic little town of Three Rivers, through Lake St Peter and into the narrows, passing on the left that other highway, the Richelieu, or Sorel, until at last they reached Montreal, the second capital, offering to the waterfront its narrow, bustling streets and market place, the wooden houses interspersed with fine stone ones, and the pleasant orchards beyond already beginning to climb the lower slopes of the mountain.

The whole rhythm of the country's life, economic and political, was governed by the habits of the river, habits reasonably but not entirely predictable. The fundamental fact then, as now, was the winter ice. Although the "bridge" at Quebec was reliable only during January and February, navigation was impracticable from some time in November until May. Early in May transatlantic ships, some great, some unbelievably small, began to appear in the Quebec basin, while the river schooners were moving on the reach between Quebec and Montreal. From May until November the direction of the wind became a subject of absorbing interest; tacking was difficult or impossible in the treacherous St Lawrence channel.

No doubt, in the thousands of little strip farms that ran back from the river, seedtime and harvest followed their own rhythm independently of the movements of wind or water. The 76,000 or so Canadians were chiefly small farmers living in rural parishes, just beginning in 1760 to be conscious of what Ontario later would call "back concessions" and centring their social life in the church and the presbytery. Originally, however, these rural parishes had been a by-product; the colony of the St Lawrence had been founded by a trading country penetrating the interior of the continent for furs, and by a country at a moment of vast missionary enthusiasm seeking converts among the fur-trading nations. Trading France refused to risk depopulation in order to swell the settlements on the supposedly inhospitable banks of the St Lawrence, and trading England conquered the country, and took over the community for purposes of trade.

The year 1760 was the beginning of a slow economic revolution. England's successes in the Seven Years' War enabled her to break the French Empire in North America. The long economic-political rivalry of the St Lawrence and the Hudson became for the moment an economic rivalry only, in which the St Lawrence had an undoubted advantage. But another and equally fierce rivalry was developing between the St Lawrence and Hudson Bay in the competition for furs. The courage and enterprise of the St Lawrence fur-merchants united with the skill and endurance of Canadian canoemen and traders to overcome the enormous handicap of distance and to bring the precious pelts from the far Northwest out through the St Lawrence. The first thirty years saw only the beginnings of a rivalry that was to last for another thirty years of increasing harshness and bitterness. The river in the end was defeated; but the slow processes of evolution had mitigated the harshness of defeat. The community that had begun as a by-product of the fur trade was now asserting its identity as an integral part of the trading empire with its own exports of wheat and timber, exports at first insignificant but sustained in their hesitant beginnings by those enterprising and needy Quebec traders who of necessity turned their attention to any saleable object.

If in material matters the old province saw a slow revolution after 1760, in the less tangible human activities, social, religious, and political, it was struck sharply and repeatedly by revolutionary changes. First the conquest itself cut off connections which through more than two centuries had been growing up at each end of the river. The French Empire was dissolved; the fragile lines which had united Quebec and New Orleans were severed, and forever. Men still went up country, but the merchants and voyageurs at Montreal, the wilderness end of the river, could no longer contemplate the vast interior and think that, but for the interlopers from Boston and New York, it was effectively theirs. They had become instead a part, and only a part, of a new and strange continental system. If France had won the war and established its own continental system, the shock to Canada would have been less, but there would still have been a shock.

But France had not won the war. The links at the Quebec end of the river also were cut. The ties with the mother country, so much more and completely a mother than Britain had been to any of her active and sometimes ungainly offspring, were severed. One more journey direct to France could be taken, by British permission in a British ship, and then no more except by special permit from London and London officials, separated from the Canadians on the St Lawrence by many barriers of which language was only one.

During fifteen years some progress had been made in adjusting to these new transatlantic and continental connections when the next revolution struck. The continental system fell to pieces. The St Lawrence colony emerged as the most important of Britain's remaining American colonies, and the key, perhaps, to a possible reunion. To the west, along the upper river and the lakes, there were the beginnings of new communities of New Yorkers and others; they and the Bostonians appeared in the gulf provinces as well. The river community was now the central and largest element, and yet only an element, in a British North America, a series of settlements from the lower lakes down river to the gulf and the great island which guarded it.

During eight years of war and the ensuing eight years of peace the Canadians and their British rulers were absorbing and adjusting to the shock of this revolution. Before the second eight years had passed there began, although only a few realized it, the greatest revolution of all, this time centred neither in London nor in Boston, but in Paris. The impact of that revolution on the Canadians of the St Lawrence was felt only slightly in 1791. It is curiously reflected in the anguished cries of expatriate Canadians in France who, after a quarter of a century spent pleading with their St Lawrence friends to return to civilization, now exclaimed in bewilderment that civilization was collapsing.

In 1760 Britain faced for the first time the government of a considerable community deriving from a civilization and culture which she recognized as at least equal to her own and like her own, and yet also unlike and antagonistic. The British cabinet and British administrators looked at the task with their accustomed phlegm; indeed, at first they hardly looked at it at all. After all, it was not Paris they had conquered; it was Quebec, a remote and primitive province. There was no reason why the new subjects and the old should not in happiness and harmony devote themselves industriously to producing such raw materials as would make Quebec an advantageous market for British merchandise.

This complacent viewpoint would certainly have been modified by contact with reality and might have been modified gradually and without tension, had it been possible for British ministers and administrators, in that portion of their leisure which they were able to devote to the affairs of the state, to look on the St Lawrence community as a community – an integral part of the Empire, a branch business, certainly, but still an entity in its own right.

Such an approach was impossible in this period of war and revolution. Out of the thirty-one years with which this volume is concerned Britain was at war for eleven; and during the whole of this time Quebec was either under military occupation, or under immediate threat of armed invasion. During the years 1760-63 it was uncertain whether Canada could be retained; the first responsibility of the military governors was security. In the ensuing years there were constant fears of French and Spanish intrigues from across the Mississippi, and this was natural, for the great Anglo-French duel was only suspended. During this same period the not unexpected showdown with Atlantic colonies was foreshadowed. The St Lawrence colony from being a fortress to be held against Frenchman and Spaniard became, in over-optimistic eyes, a citadel from which Boston and New York might be reminded of their duty. During the war years it became again a beleaguered city, in fact for a time, and always in imagination. After the war there were two new elements to cope with: one was the visible and tangible body of Loyalists camped in the upper part of the province; the other was the continuing contest between monarchism and republicanism in America, a war which might yet be won for monarchism if things were rightly ordered on the St Lawrence.

All this is reflected in the social and political development of the period. Almost all government policies were a by-product of changes and pressures outside the province. It was inevitable that the fate of Quebec should be inextricably involved in the American Revolution and the continuing Anglo-French duel.

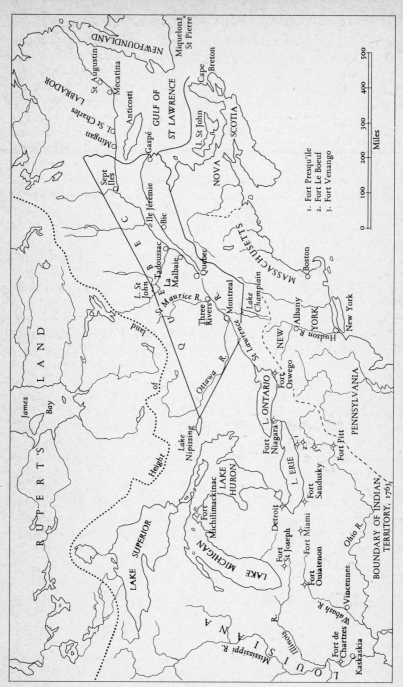

British North America after the Treaty of Paris and the Proclamation 1763

CHAPTER 2

Subjects of the King

It was in September 1760 that the Comte de Vaudreuil, governor of New France and commander of the French troops, signed with General Jeffrey Amherst, the British commander in North America, the articles of capitulation which surrendered to the British the whole vast area of the river and the lakes, from the lowest islands of the gulf to the remote trading post of Michilimackinac at the junction of the three upper lakes.

Vaudreuil had no choice. Caught between Amherst advancing along the lower lakes and General James Murray coming up from Quebec, he could look for no further help from France. Resistance would have been of no military advantage. Vaudreuil negotiated with Amherst, asking certain privileges, including the honours of war for his army and for the garrisons of the up-country posts. Amherst's refusal of these amenities of surrender angered the French officers who urged further resistance by their army, comprising upwards of 10,000 men, chiefly French troops.[1] Vaudreuil wisely refused, contenting himself with ensuring essential matters: the disposition of his regular troops, who were to be sent to France in British ships with an engagement not to serve again in the present war; good treatment for the sick and wounded who must be left behind; arrangements for government officials returning to France; and some provision for the inhabitants of the conquered colony.

Protection for militia men who returned home was granted as a matter of course. For the Canadians Vaudreuil also asked specific undertakings for freedom of worship, for the enjoyment of their property, and for the right of all to remain unmolested in their own homes. The last was no mere formality, for the expulsion of the Acadians must have been in the thoughts of every Canadian. All this Amherst granted, although not in every detail. Two other requests followed: that no Canadian or Acadian should be obliged to take up arms against the French king, and that

6

Canadians should continue to enjoy their customary law. To these requests Amherst made the terse reply, "They become Subjects of the King." No other reply could have been made in the circumstances. Although Amherst's king was a parliamentary one and Vaudreuil's was not, they both worked within the general context of the centralized monarchical state. Amherst knew that he could promise what a humane and civilized eighteenth-century ruler would grant – reasonable security for homes and property and freedom from religious persecution. More than this he could not promise, and Vaudreuil could hardly have expected it.

Amherst's words expressed precisely what had happened. The war being fought in North America was not a war over Canada. The conquest of Canada was only one episode, if a very important one, in the duel of two commercial empires presided over by two kings. The St Lawrence branch of the French Empire was, on September 8, 1760, transferred to the successful rival, the English king, and the people who lived there became his subjects. It was inevitable that they should be viewed not primarily as a community, and certainly not as a potential nation, but as an economic factor. As an economic factor this community must be adjusted to numerous other economic factors in North America and in Britain. It was the immediate duty of His Majesty's ministers to see how these new subjects of the king could be fitted profitably into the king's trading empire. If they could not be fitted in profitably, they should not be kept.

There was, indeed, some question in 1760 whether Britain should keep Quebec. In spite of important British successes in every theatre of war France was not totally defeated. In the prolonged and complicated peace negotiations Britain had an advantageous position but she could not keep all the territory that she had occupied. Within Britain the existence of parliamentary government and of a number of pressure groups such as the "West Indian interest" made the question of what to keep and what not to keep so much a matter of public discussion and conflict of special interests as to give rise to the story of the great Pitt leaning forward at the cabinet table and saying, "Some are for keeping Canada, some Guadaloupe. Who will tell me which I shall be hanged for not keeping?"

The final decision to keep Canada was, however, based on rational grounds.[2] Britain's war aim in North America had been to secure a satisfactory frontier for the American colonies. This would not necessarily involve the cession of all of Canada. Even after the capture of Quebec in 1759 there is evidence that British ministers would have been satisfied with a boundary running south of the St Lawrence and the Great Lakes. These ideas were, however, soon changed. Although from the viewpoint of direct and immediate trading profit the West Indian islands were of paramount importance, Jamaica alone buying as much as Virginia and

Maryland and more than all the New England colonies together,[3] the fundamental question became one of security. "We should keep Quebec and Canada as preventatives of a future war," said the Earl of Chesterfield. By March 1761, when peace negotiations began, Pitt, at least, had decided that all of Canada must be retained for "the Security of our Colonies." It would not indeed be difficult to decide that the loss of potential profits from a sugar island or two might well be set against security from the risk of another series of costly campaigns in the North American wilderness. Even though there was a murmur in the cabinet about the cost of garrisons to control the French population, it was agreed that the whole of Canada must be retained.

There was some brisk discussion about the boundary between Canada and Louisiana, but the further progress of war and negotiations finally secured to Britain, in the general settlement with France and Spain, all territory to the east of the Mississippi. France, compensating her ally by renouncing her claims to all territory west of the river, was confined in North America to the little islands of St Pierre and Miquelon which proved to be of importance not only to fisherman but also to smugglers. Britain's now apparently satisfactory boundary in North America was, however, soon to be marred because of a slip attributed to the ineptitude and double-dealing of Lord Bute who, without the knowledge of his colleagues, agreed that the boundary line should pass along the easternmost outlet of the Mississippi by Iberville River, Lake Maurepas, and Lake Ponchartrain. As this channel was not navigable, the British did secure the use of the regular channel, but because, unlike the French, they had no right of depot at New Orleans on the west bank, this concession was of little value. Bute's unfortunate slip gave an important advantage to French traders on the Mississippi and Illinois and, increasing the general British sense of insecurity in the interior, had an inevitable impact on the attitude of the conqueror towards the "subjects of the King" in the St Lawrence colony.[4]

Although after the spring of 1762 there was little doubt that Canada would be retained by Britain and that Canadians would be permanently subjects of the English king, it was to be many months before the formal signature of the treaty, and many more before all who might be called Canadians became aware of the fact. Nevertheless, in broad outline, the new arrangements for their government and for all the lands of the interior that they were accustomed to think of as theirs were already settled in the minds of the authorities in Britain. Here again the particular arrangements to be made for the government of the king's new Canadian subjects were necessarily subordinated to the much greater task of defending North American possessions as a whole, of administering the new territory south of the lakes and west of the Allegheny Mountains, and of maintaining peaceful relations with the Indian peoples who inhabited them. How to deal with the lands in the Ohio Valley and beyond, claimed by the British and French alike, occupied by Indians, travelled by fur traders, and coveted by settlers and speculators, had engaged the attention of officials on both sides of the Atlantic before the outbreak of the Seven Years' War. The experience of the war and the nature of the peace treaty, leaving the problem more urgent than ever, had also suggested some of the principles of settlement. These were embodied in the document known as the Proclamation of 1763, certainly the most significant as well as the most famous of royal proclamations in that and many another year.[5]

The proper conduct of the fur trade, of defence, and of relations with the Indians in general had been a matter of discussion in the summer of 1754 when the Earl of Halifax, then President of the Board of Trade, presented a project of mutual defence for the colonies. He suggested a single authority to control forts and command troops and to direct Indian affairs. The general project collapsed with the failure of the Albany Conference, which should have implemented it, but Britain did send out a token frontier force under General Edward Braddock in 1755. Britain also appointed two imperial officers, one for the northern colonies and one for the southern, to be responsible for political relations with the Indian tribes. During the war, however, it became clear that no system could be effective so long as it depended on voluntary contributions and voluntary co-operation from the colonies. Governors, Indian superintendents, and the Board of Trade periodically urged the need for a common authority. Meanwhile the Indian tribes were growing bitter over the alienation of their lands. Whether or not the tribe or any individuals in the tribe had received adequate compensation was almost irrelevant; the conception of a permanent alienation of land by the same process that covered the sale of a beaver skin was foreign to the Indian's way of thought, and appeared to him substantially unjust. Moreover, the general relations of the American traders with the Indians were bad.

All these considerations contributed to the development and clarification of a threefold policy by the British government: a temporary prohibition of settlement beyond a given line, the suggested line being the watershed between the Atlantic and the Mississippi; the organization of defence of the frontier by twenty battalions of troops under a British commander; regulation and control of the fur trade through the Indian superintendents. This policy, the fruit not of mercantilist or of free trade theory, but of practical experience, over a decade, of the facts of frontier relations, was agreed on in the spring of 1763. In spite of changes of ministers in Britain and alarming events in the summer on the western frontier, it was issued, unaltered, in the form of a proclamation in October.

This Proclamation of 1763 was an inclusive document, dealing with the administration of the western lands, and also defining the boundaries of, and providing constitutions for, all the newly acquired colonies in North America.[6]

While this policy was being developed, events on the frontier were offering a sensational demonstration of the need for a just and firm policy with special understanding and conciliation of the Indian peoples. In the spring of 1763 the Indian war known as "Pontiac's Rising" was spreading terror along the lower lakes and over to the Ohio. Little is known of Pontiac's origin, character, or career, apart from the brief episode of this Indian war.[7] He was a member of the Ottawa tribe of Indians who, with the Chippewas and Potawatomis, had hunted and traded along the Ottawa and north of the lower lakes until, after 1648, they shifted south and west to the Michigan peninsula. Later, some went to the area about the fort known after 1763 as Detroit.

Detroit was the key fort in the group affected by the sporadic outbreaks initiated by Pontiac but not caused or even fully controlled by him. The others were Michilimackinac to the north at the confluence of the three upper lakes; Miami and Ouiatenon to the southwest; Presqu'ile and Niagara on the lower lakes, linking Detroit with Montreal; and Le Boeuf and Venango, the two small forts which linked the northern posts to the strong post at Fort Pitt on the Ohio. All these forts except Fort Pitt had been taken over from the French by Amherst following the capitulation of Montreal in 1760.

An Indian outbreak on the frontier was not unpredictable, and had even been predicted a year or two earlier. Sir William Johnson, the Indian Superintendent for the Northern Colonies, and his assistant George Croghan had tried to explain to Amherst the importance of following the French system of granting ready hospitality at the forts, making presents from time to time, and ensuring to the Indians in one way or another an adequate supply of ammunition and a prompt re-opening of the trade under favourable conditions. In none of these matters were the Indians satisfied. Amherst had been urged to be economical, and he instructed the Indian agents accordingly. Giving Indians food, he said, encouraged laziness, a too plentiful supply of ammunition could be dangerous, wholesale giving of presents to secure friendship was costly and unwise: "When men of whatsoever race behave ill, they must be punished, not bribed." [8] In September 1761 Sir William Johnson did open the trade again at Detroit with a ball for the ladies, and presents for the Indians, to the satisfaction of all. He confided, however, to Colonel Donald Campbell, the commander, that these were to be the last presents.

Campbell was alarmed, believing, as he did, that gifts and especially supplies of ammunition were necessary to prevent trouble. The Indians were grumbling about trade prices, and the young men about the shortage of rum, which had flowed more freely when the English feared the rivalry of the French. Moreover, there was a constant nervousness among the Indians about their lands, a nervousness increased by the fact that Amherst had actually granted lands without proper authority in the neighbourhood of Fort Niagara. Meanwhile French traders on the Mississippi, it was said, were promising that the French father would return and drive out the British. As the news of the signing of the peace did not reach the Illinois country until the autumn of 1763, such operations would be an entirely legitimate form of warfare. Nothing happened for a time, beyond a restlessness among the Senecas, the westernmost tribe of the Iroquois. Seneca restlessness might have found no outlet had it not been for the gradual change of temper about Detroit. There Pontiac had become vehemently anti-English, and, determined to promote the return of his French friends, had employed his considerable personal gifts and energy in securing an ascendancy over the Ottawa and other Indian villages near Detroit, as well as over Indians who came there to trade. These provided the force which, acting independently under Pontiac at Detroit, touched off the violence which spread from there in every direction, north, southwest, southeast, and east. These outbreaks were largely spontaneous. "There is no documentary evidence of a conspiracy headed by Pontiac. No contemporary British officer gave such an interpretation of the war." [9] Moreover, it was apparently by pure chance that Pontiac touched off the war at a time when the British were singularly unprepared for it. The troops victorious in 1758, 1759, and 1760 had been gradually drawn to other theatres where the war was still active.[10] The departures added to Amherst's embarrassment in dealing with the vexatious and, indeed, infuriating frontier incident, for to him it was no more.

To the active participants it was alarming and tragic enough. By the spring of 1763 Pontiac, with an ingenious adaptation of the visions of a famous "Prophet" of the Delawares, had convinced most of the Detroit Indians that God had decreed that all white men who wore red coats must be eliminated. The first step was to be the surprise capture of the key fort at Detroit. A small party of Indians paid a courtesy visit to Major Henry Gladwin, commandant of the fort, in order to reconnoitre, on May 1. Detroit was less a fort than a tiny fortified town surrounded by a wooden palisade some fifteen feet high, within which the various military buildings, and also shops and private houses, were ranged along four little streets running parallel to the river. The whole had the disadvantage, being built on a slope, of being completely overlooked by the rising ground on the opposite side of the river. It had also the important advantage of direct access to the water.

Having made his preliminary visit, Pontiac matured his plan of returning on May 7 with a considerable number of Indians carrying sawed-off guns under their blankets. His preparations were too careful and his instructions too explicit for that isolated, gossip-loving community. The sudden demand, without explanation, for files, needed to deal with the guns, would have been enough to invite comment. Gladwin heard the news, perhaps from several sources. When Pontiac appeared at the gates on the appointed day he was admitted and courteously received, but the doubled sentries and the troops drawn up under arms told him all he needed to know. He left the fort in anger, opened hostilities officially by murdering some English traders unlucky enough to come his way, and, contrary to all law, Indian and European, detained officers sent by Gladwin, at his request, for a parley.

After this both sides prepared for a siege. Gladwin was able to lay in ample supplies from the friendly Canadian trader, Duperron Baby. Moreover, he had vessels available to bring up supplies from below, and his communications were maintained throughout the campaign, although not without difficulty. Pontiac also realized that his warriors must be fed; he rationed supplies and persuaded the habitants, some of whom were cooperative, to allow the squaws to plant their fields with Indian corn.

Meanwhile the war was spreading, and much to Pontiac's satisfaction. He sent his own Ottawas and Hurons to Sandusky where Ensign Christopher Pauli, entirely unsuspecting, admitted them on May 16 for a parley, only to see his garrison massacred around him. Pauli was carried to the neighbourhood of Detroit where after having suffered torture he was allowed to make an Indian marriage. From this modified captivity he escaped into the fort itself early in July. On May 25 some visiting Potawatomis, once more on the pretext of a visit of courtesy, surprised and overwhelmed Ensign Francis Schlosser at St Joseph on the southeast of Lake Michigan. Encouraged by Sandusky, Pontiac also astutely planned and carried through, late in May, the capture of reinforcements and provisions on their way up to Detroit. At the same time, ignorant of the signing of the peace treaty, news of which reached Gladwin on June 2, he sent a delegation over to the French in the Illinois country. On the way the Indians captured Fort Miami through the carelessness and folly of the young officer in command who had been warned of trouble. Ouiatenon was secured by surprise during a peaceful parley.

The Chippewas at Michilimackinac, acting on their own, secured the fort on June 4 by the picturesque ruse of a lacrosse game played on the sandy beach before the fort with visiting Sauks from the west. While the officers stood outside looking on, a calculated shot sent the ball within the fort, pursued by the players, changing as they went sticks for sawed-off guns concealed under the blankets of their squaws. It was a very neat coup, admirable from the point of view of the Indian who, believing that men were never expendable, adapted his tactics to the bloodless victory. It was proportionately odious to the English, who believed that war was a game to be played by European rules. The victory was followed by a slaughter of some thirty expendable English traders and soldiers and the appropriation of considerable plunder, including invaluable powder and lead. This bloody affair was observed by the young fur trader, Alexander Henry, sheltering in the attic of a friendly Canadian.

While these events were passing in the western and northern forts the Delawares about Fort Pitt, the key fort on the Pennsylvania frontier to the southeast, heard the news and themselves prepared for action. They did some looting and murdering in the neighbourhood, but the fort itself with sixteen cannon and two hundred and fifty men was impregnable to them. The neighbouring Senecas to the north were more fortunate. The small blockhouse of Venango fell to them in mid-June and no white man survived to tell the story. The commander, Gordon, was allowed to live until he had recorded the Indian complaints of the scarcity of powder and the threat to Indian lands. Then he was killed by slow torture, as a calculated act perhaps the most shocking incident of the war. Le Boeuf, the other blockhouse connecting Fort Pitt with Presqu'ile, was evacuated after being attacked with burning arrows and a number of the garrison were able to make their way to Fort Pitt.

The fort at Presqu'ile, in the key position on Lake Erie, had been carefully constructed by Colonel Henry Bouquet in 1760, and was considered sufficiently strong to be safe against any attack. The commander, Ensign John Christie, had also received warning and so was fully prepared. He was besieged by two hundred Indians sent by Pontiac from Detroit, who joined with the Senecas from the east. His own account is that he made a courageous and resourceful resistance to the shower of burning arrows that threatened the wooden blockhouse, digging a fresh well to secure water, as he was cut off from the regular one. The Indians, however, had the help of an adopted Englishman who showed them how to approach the fort under cover of a trench. Christie stated that, as the walls were undermined and the fort became indefensible, he yielded on the promise of life and liberty for his garrison. The promise was broken, the four tribes, Ottawas, Chippewas, and Hurons from Detroit, and the Senecas, dividing the prisoners between them. Some were taken immediately to Detroit where Christie was turned over to Major Gladwin. On July 6 Gladwin held a formal inquiry into the capture of the forts at Sandusky, St Joseph,

Miami, and Presqu'ile. Most of the accounts give the impression that a good deal was left unsaid, and that the junior officers at these posts had been careless and overconfident. Only Christie's account sounds convincing.[11]

The general situation by the end of June was that the two strongest places, Detroit and Fort Pitt, were resisting and were probably not in serious danger. The smaller tributary stations had fallen, as might have been expected. Presqu'ile – a link between Montreal and Fort Pitt to the south and Detroit to the west – had fallen when from its strength, position, and importance it might have been expected to stand.

It was on June 6 that Amherst in New York heard of violence about Fort Pitt from Colonel Bouquet in Philadelphia. The rumours from Detroit and Sandusky he did not believe until he received a letter from Gladwin on June 21, showing for the first time that this was no local affair in Pennsylvania or New York, but that the western Indians had risen. He made light of the matter in letters home, but did send reinforcements to Gladwin and, with Colonel Bouquet, tried to prod the reluctant provincials into assisting in their own defence. After much delay Bouquet reached Fort Pitt from Philadelphia early in August, and on August 5, a few miles east of the fort at Bushy Run he engaged a considerable force of Indians, some from local tribes – Shawnees, Delawares, and Mingoes – and Hurons from Sandusky. He dispersed them after heavy fighting in which some fifty of his five hundred men were killed.

The event was, however, typical. The Indians were prepared to operate by surprise when they could reasonably count on a bloodless victory. They had not the manpower for battles in the open. Neither had they the supplies for a long campaign, still less for a series of campaigns. By September many of Pontiac's following at Detroit were discouraged. All had to leave for the hunting by October if their families were to live. All were suffering and likely to suffer more from the cessation of trade. And Pontiac himself on October 29 received a heavy blow in a letter from Neyoude Villiers, the French commander at Fort Chartres on the Illinois. Word had reached him at last of the signing of the peace treaty in February. He informed Pontiac that he could not help him; the French and English must henceforth be friends. He wrote to Gladwin of his formal recognition of peace and willingness to surrender. And he instructed the Canadians at Detroit that there must be no more collaboration with the Indians.

And so, although there was a bloody ambush of the English by the Senecas near Fort Niagara in mid-Stepember, the war was effectively over. Pontiac did not give up hope of renewing it in 1764, but he got no encouragement from the French. As for the Indians, trade was a necessity to them, and much of their trade was now dependent on the English, as many of them had aways recognized. In 1764 to complete the pacification of the country two military expeditions were sent west. One under Colonel John Bradstreet, by Lake Erie, relieved the weary Gladwin, who retired thankfully and honourably to the life of an English country gentleman. The other under Bouquet, who knew the Indians and their country, accepted no superficial protestations of peace, but moving west from Fort Pitt insisted on surrender of all white prisoners before he would make a treaty or admit any end to hostilities. The Indian agents Johnson and Croghan joined their peaceable efforts. By 1765 even the Illinois country was reasonably secure. The "incident" had been sustained and costly; perhaps four hundred and fifty British soldiers, eighty or ninety Indians, and many more civilians had lost their lives.

Although there was no more talk of substituting punishment for presents to the Indians, there was no major change of policy on the frontier. The policy of the Proclamation, already determined, was put into operation even before peace was made. The scheme of the Proclamation seemed simple enough. Out of the "extensive and valuable acquisitions in America" secured by the peace treaty the four new governments of Quebec, East and West Florida, and Grenada were erected and the boundaries of the first three were defined. The government of Quebec was not the old colony of Canada, but a rough quadrilateral comprising a broad strip on either side of the St Lawrence from its upper reaches down to the river St John and the west end of Anticosti. The settled parishes and the towns of the river were politically severed alike from the fur posts up country and from the fishing and sealing posts below. The gulf and the gulf islands were confided to the care of the Governor of Newfoundland, Newfoundland being the centre of the fishing industry. St John, later Prince Edward Island, and Cape Breton were attached to Nova Scotia. Within the new governments, governors were authorized to grant lands to retired officers and men of the army and navy who had seen North American service, and to others who chose to apply for them.

So far the Proclamation read like a speedy and special arrangement for the new settlements acquired by treaty. The second half, however, put in force the policy so long matured, of imperial definition and control of a fixed boundary line between the colonies and the western tribes of Indians. No governor of any colony was to make any grant of land or issue any warrant of survey "for the present, and until our further pleasure is known" beyond the sources of rivers falling into the Atlantic from the west and northwest. For the time being this was to be a reserve for "the several nations or tribes of Indians with whom we are connected, and who live under our protection." Land belonging to Indians within the limits of any colonial government might be purchased, but only by the governor, acting for the purchaser, and at a public meeting of the Indians called for the purpose. Trade was to be free, but every trader must take out a licence with a guarantee to observe regulations made by the imperial government or its agents.

This was the legal enactment of the policy of an Indian reserve. It should have been accompanied, as agreed, by an imperial defence force of twenty battalions, and a system for regulating and supervising the fur traders, all to have been under the control of the central government. Practical experience over many years on the frontier showed that this would have been the most effective way of keeping peace. But practical experience was also to show two major obstacles in the way: the difficulty of raising the necessary money, and the difficulty of securing the consent of all the colonies.[12] In the meantime, the frontier forts with their little garrisons were maintained and Indian superintendents were supported as before from the military chest.

The Proclamation of 1763, like Pontiac's rising, may seem to belong rather to American than to Canadian history. The Indian war occurred almost entirely on what is now American soil; by far the greater part of the territory covered by the Proclamation is now in the United States; and the efforts to carry through the policy of the Proclamation precipitated the financial disputes which occasioned the Revolution. But the Proclamation happened to give to the province of Quebec its first civil constitution under British rule, and also to make a drastic change in its ancient boundaries. In order to establish peaceful and just relations between the American colonies, seen as entities, and the Indians now officially recognized as "Nations or Tribes . . . under our protection," the new "subjects of the King" on the St Lawrence lost their ancient historic links with the lakes and the Mississippi Valley above, and the gulf and its islands below, to be constitutionally penned into a parallelogram on the middle St Lawrence. And, incidentally, in a mere parenthesis, the reduced province was endowed with British law, and promised an elected assembly. From the viewpoint of London, and even of New York, this was natural and not unjust. The new subjects transferred by solemn agreement from the care and control of Louis to the care and control of George could expect just and humane treatment as individuals. They could also expect that measures would be taken to integrate them as smoothly and profitably as possible as a trading unit into the great trading empire of which they were now a part. They could not expect much attention to their moral rights as a collective entity. Probably few of them were conscious of the existence of such rights.

CHAPTER 3

The Dictates of Clemency

When Amherst and Vaudreuil signed the capitulation of Montreal in September 1760, English government had already been going on for a year under James Murray, in the district of Quebec. It was Murray, more than any other one person, who, as first military governor of Quebec and first civil governor of the whole province, established the traditional attitude of the early British governor to the Canadian people.

"I shall follow," he said, in a letter to Amherst, "the natural disposition of my heart which dictates clemency." [1] Murray always did follow the natural disposition of his heart, sometimes with embarrassing results. The younger son of a Scottish peer, he described himself as "a soldier of fortune" and without influence. He was not quite without influence, and he did not disdain to use it, as his letters abundantly show, but he never attempted to use it as a substitute for hard work and integrity. In 1759 he was in his thirty-ninth year and had done some twenty years' service as an officer in the British army. Murray was a contentious figure in his day. Vain, ambitious, hasty, rash, overconfident, with a quick and violent temper; kind, generous, compassionate, affectionate, with a scrupulous sense of justice, he was a man who made both friends and enemies easily. Often lacking in prudence, and sometimes in consistency, he was yet steadfast in his pity and affection for a conquered people, and in his generous desire to make them happy under their new rulers. This desire was strengthened by his sincere conviction of the infinite superiority of the British system which, properly administered, must, he thought, make any people happy. ". . . the inhabitants," he wrote, shortly after the capitulation, "want nothing but that plenty which the ravages of war have deprived them of to make them entirely happy." [2]

But it fell to Murray to initiate British rule under conditions in which it was far from easy either to follow the dictates of clemency or to make people happy. Wolfe having died in battle, and two other senior officers, Monckton and Townshend, wishing to leave the country, Murray found himself in command of Quebec on October 23, 1759. The city, distinguished for the natural beauty and strength of its position, for its fine public buildings and churches, for the gaiety and prosperity associated with the military and political capital of an important province, was in a pitiful condition. Winter was coming on, many houses were destroyed and more were damaged, many people were already impoverished, and there was a natural fear of the encroachments of a conquering army, in spite of the promise of protection to persons and to property made on the surrender of the city. Murray, on his side, had his own fears. He occupied a city called a fortress, but a fortress in name only. The surrounding districts were hostile or untrustworthy, not conceiving themselves included in the Quebec capitulations, and, willingly or otherwise, co-operating with the Chevalier de Lévis, commander of the French troops who constantly menaced the city. Behind his insecure walls Murray was responsible for seven or eight thousand troops, many of them sick or wounded, and for as many civilians. Troops had to be accommodated in barracks, hospitals, or billets; buildings essential for the needs of government and administration had to be found, and supplies of fuel and other necessaries ensured from the surrounding country.

Winter proved a bitter enemy. The men's clothing was neither adequate nor appropriate to the climate. Murray and his staff did what they could with the available army supplies, but in December Fraser's Highlanders were still without trousers to replace the picturesque but inadequate kilt. Gradually, however, costume was adapted to climate. "We find the mogosan with a double frize sock much warmer, and in all respects more consentaneous to this country in winter, than a thick, hard, or stubborn-soled shoe," said Captain John Knox, who also remarked feelingly that iron stoves were "a most incomparable invention."[3] But iron stoves had to be fed, and this alone would have forced Murray to bring the country parishes to terms. The British held that the capitulation of the stronghold of Quebec involved the submission of the whole district. On September 22 all the Canadians were invited by proclamation to lay down their arms, take an oath of fidelity, and resume the peaceful enjoyment of their homes, property, and religion. Murray followed this in November and again in the spring with renewed threats and promises: threats of severest reprisals, destruction of property, even expulsion from the country; and promises which went beyond anything contained even in the final capitulation of Montreal. On May 22 he promised in the king's name "to maintain the communities and private individuals in all their property, laws and customs," if they would submit to his orders.[4] Murray also sent army officers down river to sequester and, after an interval, carry off or destroy all the livestock and farm produce of those who were still serving with the French.

Where prominent individuals were concerned Murray endeavoured to make a striking example. Thus it was decreed that as Duchesnay, the seigneur of Beauport, remained obstinately with the French army, his lands and possessions should be confiscated and granted to two British officers, Captain William Johnston and Lieutenant Richard Nugent, to use or dispose of as they pleased. Such a procedure was not clement, nor was it legal; as Duchesnays remained for many years in possession of Beauport it was evidently a threat without a sequel.

Canadians outside Quebec probably believed that their obligations to the English would begin only when they could be afforded security from the French. Security Murray could not offer. The unhappy habitant from the Lévis shore captured by the French carrying provisions over to Quebec, brutally beaten, and then sent as an "exhibit" to Murray, was an example of the kind of thing that many had to fear.[5] Murray struggled through the winter, his men cold, and, if not hungry, suffering increasingly from scurvy. On April 28, being threatened by the advance of Lévis, he rashly went out towards Ste Foy to meet him with a decidedly inferior force,[6] and suffered a nearly disastrous defeat. Only the arrival of a British fleet in the first weeks of May forced Lévis to retreat and allowed Murray to advance at last with confidence, commanding the inhabitants to remain peacefully in their homes, on pain of destruction of their property or worse.[7]

Within Quebec Murray was noted for humanity and consideration, although he did abruptly turn the Jesuits out of the city, commandeering their college for the use of the army. To the communities of nuns he showed unfailing goodwill.

The goodwill was acknowledged in a substantial fashion, for the nuns provided the men of Wolfe's army with the nearest approach to professional nursing that the age could produce, almost certainly the first that these Protestant soldiers had ever known. The sisters regretted only that, by the orders of Murray and the commands of their own bishop, they were allowed to minister to bodily needs alone. Religious instruction was strictly forbidden. Murray showed his appreciation for the nuns' services by putting them, as well as the wounded, on army rations, and also by supplying them with firewood. His assistance to the nuns from government stores was needed and was generously given long after their nursing duties were completed. His friendship for them lasted throughout his stay in Canada.[8]

Murray was equally conscious of his obligations to the rest of the community. With an army suffering from cold, in arrears of pay, conscious of victory after a long and hard campaign, it was not easy to keep the pledge of security for private property. Clearly it was not always kept. In a proclamation of November 15 Murray acknowledged that "in the first moments of confusion we are but too fully persuaded that wrong was being done to many poor inhabitants," an admission which might have done something to dispel bitter feelings if not to restore lost goods. From that time, however, Murray invited immediate complaints of injuries or insults by soldiers, and, in fact, on the day following a soldier was court-martialled and executed for "notorious robbery" of the house of a Canadian.

An important gesture of confidence in the "new subjects" was the appointment of Canadians to positions of responsibility in the rudimentary administration which Murray established shortly after the surrender of the province. Jacques Belcourt de La Fontaine became a kind of general administrator for the South Shore. The corresponding position on the North Shore was given to Joseph Etienne Cugnet. Jean Claude Panet was made clerk of the "superior council" of officers in Quebec. Cugnet and Panet continued in public office throughout the period. La Fontaine later incurred Murray's displeasure and earned a veh~ment public rebuke. Murray was often mistaken in his judgement of individuals, but his obvious friendliness and goodwill did much to conciliate a proud and sensitive people, who knew how to make allowances for irascibility and even for harshness when the necessity was obvious, but who resented coldness and arrogance.[9]

On September 22, 1760, Amherst established British rule by proclamation. He then quitted the province, leaving military administrators in charge of each of the three districts: Murray in Quebec; Thomas Gage at Montreal, with headquarters at the Chateau de Ramezay; and Ralph Burton in Three Rivers at the imposing governor's house, "the only tavern for the whole army between Quebec and Montreal." [10] All three, from prudence and principle, followed the policy of conciliation laid down by Murray, a policy the more welcome to Canadians because they had been led to expect something very different from their heretic enemies.[11] They recognized the comparative clemency of their new rulers, some perhaps with positive gratitude, and all with relief. The transition period was helped by relatively informal relations with the military governors, and by the fact that the same men remained in their districts throughout most of the period. Murray returned to Quebec after making contact with Amherst on the eve of the capitulation of Montreal, and remained there until, four years later, he inaugurated the first civil government. Gage remained in Montreal until, late in 1763, he succeeded Amherst at New York as commander-in-chief for North America. He was succeeded at Montreal by Burton, who moved up from Three Rivers. Burton's successor was Frederick Haldimand, a Swiss officer who had seen much service in North America, benevolent, diligent, and methodical. All these men were served by French-speaking secretaries. French was accepted, and even imposed on some reluctant English, as "the language of the country." [12]

The first responsibility of the military governor was military security. The army must be maintained, equipped, supplied, and always ready for action against enemies from without in the unsurrendered portions of French North America, or from within. The task was simplified by the nature of the community and its former government. Habitants were accustomed to having their services and equipment commandeered, and they welcomed the prompt cash payments ordered by Amherst. The safety of the upper country posts, now the responsibility of the governor of Montreal, was secured by the forwarding of supplies coming in from Britain and the colonies by the regular routes; and by careful arrangements for licensing all traders going up country. These men were strictly prohibited from traffic with the Mississippi colonies still in possession of France.

But the essential condition for the security of the army was the establishment of just and orderly government of the civilian population, a policy dictated by prudence and happily lightened by benevolence and generosity. Murray in Quebec was immediately faced with a threat of famine for want of wheat to sow the farms devastated in the campaigns of 1759 and 1760. Gage and Burton in their districts acted promptly, requiring the habitants to sell their surpluses at a reasonable fixed price, and urging the compassionate to give what they could in charity. There was a certain reluctance to renounce a profitable speculation, but after additional and sterner exhortations, and a substantial donation from the Montreal seminary, Quebec was supplied with wheat for the spring sowing. Suffering during the winter of 1760-61 was severe; ". . . to describe it is beyond my power," said Murray. He, his officers, and the soldiers joined with the merchants in raising a fund for the distressed, while necessary measures were taken in all three districts to keep prices down.[13]

Meanwhile some scheme of orderly government had to be devised in accordance with Amherst's capitulations. The question of religious toleration gave no trouble. Religious processions passed through the streets as usual, and Protestant officers were required, from prudence and courtesy, to show the ordinary marks of respect. Rights of property, oddly, were rather more difficult as they involved the question of Canadian civil law, which Amherst had specifically refused. Murray had incautiously promised the people their "laws and customs." The others avoided any specific statement, but following the general principle that a conquered people keeps its own laws until the conqueror issues new ones, they accepted former practices "not inimical to the King's service."[14]

For the punishment of crime and the settlement of civil disputes all districts used a system of military courts, based on the local Canadian captain of militia. Under France, the militia in each parish had been organized under captains, lieutenants, and sergeants, who had been entrusted with a variety of local duties. The English found these men most serviceable. Lacking the education of the priest and the social standing of the seigneur, they were yet intelligent enough to carry out orders and not too proud to receive them. The captain of militia was indeed so useful that he must sometimes have thought his seat of honour in the church dearly earned by his labours outside. He had to provide men for the various needs of the army: fuel, straw, transportation; he had to help with billeting troops; he had to receive and forward the weapons surrendered to the English, and then to receive back again those returned for redistribution; he had to administer oaths of fidelity, supervise repairs to roads and bridges, apprehend deserters and other offenders, and give his help when a census of surplus grain must be taken, or a charitable collection made. And, finally, he was the base of the administration of justice, being authorized to settle disputes by conciliation or judicial decision, or to pass them on to the local English officer. Such vague and ample powers were open to abuse and were occasionally abused. It is not surprising that new and more precise regulations had to be made as some militia officers were accused of petty exactions and of undue exercise of power. It is, however, remarkable that for four or five years a small group of English officers should have administered the province peacefully and with reasonable efficiency through the agency of these men who, with all their native ability, were sometimes unable to read or write.[15]

Serious cases, or appeals from militia officers, passed up the hierarchy from the local officer to military courts sitting in the towns of Quebec, Three Rivers, and Montreal. Only Murray, apparently, followed the practice of employing Canadians by commissioning a Canadian as a senior judge. The system worked well enough although, as the officers later learned, it was irregular. Three years after the military courts had come into operation, Murray was casually informed by the authorities in Britain that these courts had no right to impose the death sentence on citizens. Murray in reply thanked the writer for the "tenderness and delicacy" with which he was preparing to "cover" the illegal operations. He went on to remark with understandable frankness that it was fortunate that they had not been informed earlier of their limited powers, as people would have gained a curious idea of their government had they been unable to mete out appropriate punishment, even for a notorious murder. Capital sentences had been imposed on civilians in Montreal as well as in Quebec.[16]

The mildness of military rule and its general similarity to the government which had preceded it were valuable in softening the impact of the Conquest. Those who spoke of the capitulation as "the late revolution" gave an accurate picture. Even before the rupture of the Proclamation of 1763, the community on the St Lawrence suffered a shock which was bound to be painful in its violence. Each of the two civilizations now brought into intimate relations had cherished as fundamental certain special social values. Each tended to misunderstand and to underrate those of the other. Meanwhile the people did not know their own fate. Every group in society was waiting in uncertainty. The most perplexed were the seigneurs. Probably most of those who could afford it returned to France. During the years following 1763 many letters crossed the Atlantic from the little Canadian colony of Loches in France, urging relatives and friends to sell their goods and leave a heretic country, although there were occasional warnings that the cost of living was higher in France. Some families maintained sons in the French army while the parents remained in Canada. The Canadian seigneur was vulnerable in that the land which gave him rank gave him neither adequate income nor an assured place in society. Most of the more wealthy and ambitious seigneurs were not country dwellers. They lived in Quebec and Montreal, or in little towns like Boucherville or Terrebonne, near enough to Montreal to enjoy the best of both worlds.

Looking to the future, these men had to rest their hopes either on the return of the country to France, or on some compromise which would enable them to retain under the British not the position of country magnate, for this they had never had, but the fruits of office through public service, government pensions, or government contracts. Although the seigneur attached much importance to rank and status, there was inevitably considerable mingling with the merchant class in the towns. A seigneur might be a merchant, or married into a mercantile family; some were the merchants' needy relations and dependent on their bounty.[17]

As a class, the Canadian merchants were optimistic. Before the Conquest trade had attained respectable proportions apart from the boom which, it was said, had made twenty Canadians millionaires during the closing years of the war. It was not, however, the millionaires who influenced the outlook of the merchant group, for they did not stay. The lesser folk who remained hoped to take the places of the wealthy in the commercial and social life of the colony. They were busily adapting to the new regime. The elder Lanaudière, a seigneur, was at La Rochelle as early as 1762 attending to his own business and to that of a widowed sister. Others, some very young, were also in France. Pierre Guy, little more than a boy, was at La Rochelle in 1762, as agent for his widowed mother in business at Montreal. François Baby of Quebec, not yet thirty, was in La Rochelle from about 1761, doing business for himself and for his brother at Detroit. Guy and Baby were making arrangements to shift their business from France to London. Their letters show that, thanks to arrangements between bankers and authorities of La Rochelle and Bordeaux, and French merchants settled in London, the principle that there could be no trade with the enemy in wartime was taken lightly.[18]

Canadian merchants were harassed by the uncertain value of the paper currency of Quebec.[19] They were also anxious about their goods purchased in the years 1757 and 1758 and held for them in France because the risks of shipment were too great. The Canadians thought it reasonable that they be allowed to bring this property into the country. The British, anxious to send their own goods into the new possession, also had an idea that while the Canadians were pleading only for the camel's nose, the entire animal in the shape of continued trading and political relations with France was ready to insinuate itself into the tent. The islands of St Pierre and Miquelon, retained by France for the benefit of the fishing industry, were obviously also useful for smuggling.

These suspicions were justified. Baby's French correspondents informed him that the English ("there is no nation as industrious as the English when it is a question of smuggling and cheating the customs") had already worked out a system, sometimes picking up wines from Guernsey, at other times clearing openly from London with British goods which were slipped into France in exchange for a cargo which they hoped to dispose of in Canada. Baby was advised to organize a centre at Miquelon, with English merchants as well as French in the enterprise.[20] This method was favoured, especially for French wines, which were sadly missed. "Vous savez, Monsieur, qu'il faut boire et qu'il est triste de le faire avec amertume." So ran the petition of Canadian merchants, praying relief from British "brandy." [21]

In spite of anxieties and some losses, the outlook of the young merchants was, on the whole, cheerful. If they had no very large resources, neither had many of the English who were moving in from Boston, New York, and London. Guy returned from London in 1763 well satisfied with his purchases, while Baby showed not only confidence in his business prospects but something of the political ambition justified by his education and social experience.

Very difficult to determine is the impact of the Conquest on the mass of the people, the habitants. Records are wanting, as few were able to write, and fewer still wrote anything likely to be preserved. The habitant in 1760 looked back on a hard life where he had survived by endurance and toughness. Although freer and better off than his counterpart in France, he had, during the recent wars, been called on increasingly for military service and unpaid *corvées* of all kinds, and he had been compelled to surrender his agricultural surpluses at the demand of the government and at a fixed price. During the invasion many had suffered in person and property. The English rule was a change. The habitant received more money, and punishment was, on the whole, less severe than under his old rulers. And the English rule brought peace. The new government being tolerable and in some ways advantageous, he gave up his arms when obliged to do so, obeyed orders when he had to, and retained his natural courtesy and good humour.

It was, however, natural for him to exploit the advantages of a favourable situation while he could. He resisted as long as possible Gage's demand in 1760-61 that he surrender his wheat on the mere promise of four livres a minot, to say nothing of the ridiculous suggestion that he should give it away. He might also try to evade unpaid work on the roads by removing the wheels from his carts and selling them to some merchant or pedlar.[22] The shock of the Conquest, the change from accustomed authority and discipline, was strengthening in the habitant the tendency to indepen-dence and "indocility" which, in fact, had always characterized him. For a decade or so the circumstances that were encouraging his emancipation were not fully understood by authorities in the state or even in the Church.

No other body felt the revolutionary impact of the Conquest as the Church did; and in none was the response so significant for the future of the community.[23] The Church alone drew its members from all classes and maintained intimate associations with all classes; the Church contained the only substantial body of French who remained in Canada after the Conquest; and among the clergy and the religious communities were to be found most men and women of education and culture. And, if no group felt the shock so much, none had to adapt to it so rapidly and yet so cautiously. The work of the Church had to go on; there was more need than ever for its ministrations to the faithful. And yet in spite of the promise of toleration, every aspect of its life and work was affected by the war, by the break with France, and by Protestant rule.

The Canadian clergy at the capitulation comprised about one hundred and sixty persons, including some seventy parish priests. The regular clergy, many of whom as priests served parishes, were divided among the large and wealthy establishment of the Seminary of St Sulpice at Montreal, the Quebec Seminary, the Jesuits, and the Récollets. Half of the total num-ber, including half of the parish priests and most of the Récollets, were Canadian in origin; the leaders, the men of education, and those who con-trolled most of the property, were French. The death of Bishop Pontbriand, a Frenchman, at Montreal, June 8, 1760, left the Church under the direc-tion of three grand vicars, Jean Olivier Briand of Quebec, Etienne Mont-golfier, head of the Sulpicians of Montreal, both Frenchmen, and Joseph François Perrault of Three Rivers, a Canadian.

The Church suffered materially by the war and the Conquest. About a dozen French priests and one or two Canadians went to France. Damage to property in Quebec, if not crippling, was embarrassing. Some 60,000 livres in allowances made by the French government were necessarily withdrawn.

The great shock to the Church, however, and the one that compelled the most difficult and delicate adjustments, was caused by a complete change in its legal and official status in the community. Under France the Roman Catholic Church had enjoyed great power and prestige; Protestants had been admitted into the colony but with no right even of public worship. By the capitulation of Montreal Roman Catholics had been promised freedom of worship; by the courtesy of the military governors this was interpreted to include full protection for public processions, which would have been impossible in England.

The conquerors were, however, Protestant, with a strongly anti-Roman historical tradition, softened by eighteenth-century urbanity, but kept alive by the Jacobite risings consistently supported by Roman Catholic France. The English service of thanksgiving held in the Ursuline Chapel on September 14, 1759, and attended by Huguenots who understood no English, was a sign that henceforth the government was officially Protestant and Church of England. Toleration for Roman Catholics did not imply a neutral state or voluntary churches. Such a conception would have been as foreign to the English official of the day as it was to the French. Whether the state was the arm of the church or the church the moral and spiritual aspect of the state, all would have agreed that they belonged together and that each must respect, assist, and supplement the activities of the other.

What, then, was to happen to the Roman Catholic Church in this Anglican state? With bare toleration, with no official countenance, with no government grants, with no authority to discipline priests or to collect tithes would it be possible to maintain the traditional authoritarian and hierarchical structure, and above all to maintain the necessary contacts with Rome? Would it be possible to retain the loyalty and obedience of a people ignorant and totally unused to a divided allegiance in a situation where there would almost certainly be material and social inducements to go over to the official church? The situation put a strain on the military governors and on the vicars general, neither group fully understanding the responsibilities of the other. In Montreal and Three Rivers the vicars general remained courteous and aloof, obeying somewhat grudgingly instructions which, if occasionally tactless, were never intended to offend.

Only in Quebec was there a positive policy on the part of the Church towards the British government. If Murray was, perhaps, the most demanding of the military governors, Briand was the most co-operative and complaisant of the vicars general. Briand began his association with Murray and the English fearing, as the former Bishop Pontbriand had, the outrages of which this heretic army would be guilty. He soon changed his mind. A kind and affectionate man himself, he soon observed and appreciated those qualities in Murray. With his flock, he was prepared to thank God who had sent them not the horrors that they heard of in devastated Germany, but a governor "moderate, just, humane, tender and compassionate toward the poor and unfortunate." [24]

He was therefore able the more heartily to preach to his priests and their flocks obedience to the civil power in accordance with the oath of fidelity taken, and in obedience to the teaching of Scripture. Following these principles, Briand rendered immediate and willing obedience to Murray in everything permitted by conscience, although his pride and sometimes his judgement might have chosen another course. Murray was not merely informed of the appointments of priests; he was requested to approve them. When Murray from a charitable motive asked for a lay person to be admitted to a cloistered area, Briand agreed to relax the rules at the Governor's request. When he asked why the sacraments had been refused, Briand answered courteously; he explained that neither bishop nor pope could come between a priest and a penitent. When he chose to recommend or require a nomination or a transfer, Briand might accept although the choice would not have been his own.

When Murray, like the other military governors, ordered prayers for the king to be offered, Briand obeyed explicitly the spirit as well as the letter, refusing the compromise of Montreal and Three Rivers, where the prayer was offered only from the pulpit, and not during the mass. It was not an easy decision, and it was not approved by Henri François Gravé of the Quebec seminary, one of the *"bons Patriottes"* of the colony, or by a number of his clergy. Briand was prepared to defend a course which, he admitted, he had been reluctant to take:

> I think that it would be wrong not to name George in the Canon if it can be done, just as it would be wrong to do it if it cannot be done. It should not be refused without reason, any more than it should be admitted against the rules. Therefore I concluded that if the church did not forbid it, which they have not been able to prove to me, one should name him, and not to do so would be a trick in which there would be more prejudice than reason. . . . I could not admit that I should be given as a reason that it is very difficult to pray for one's enemies. They are our rulers and we owe to them what we used to owe to the French. Does the church forbid subjects to pray for their Prince? Do the Catholics in the realm of Great Britain not pray for their King? I cannot believe it.[25]

This passage sums up Briand's position. He was accused of weakness and servility, but this is rather the letter of a man clear-headed enough and humble enough not to confuse conscience with the impulses of ecclesiastical or racial pride. Broadly speaking, clemency on one side and cautious co-operation on the other resulted in a military occupation surely exceptional, if not unique, in the friendliness and forbearance exhibited by both sides. The English did not forget that they were conquerers, nor the Canadians that they were conquered, but the ground was laid for mutual co-operation and respect in the four years that preceded the introduction of civil government.

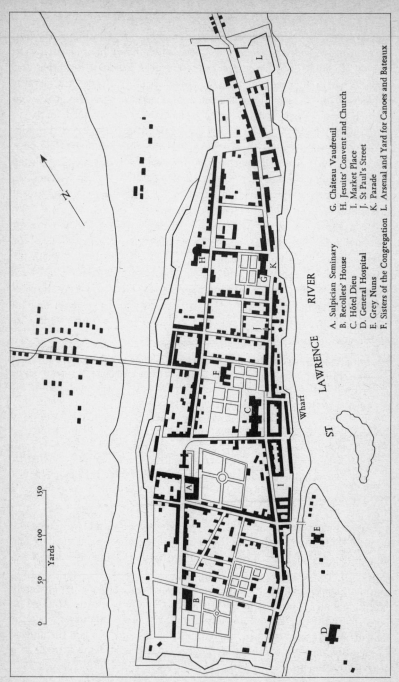

ST LAWRENCE RIVER

Wharf

A. Sulpician Seminary
B. Recollets' House
C. Hôtel Dieu
D. General Hospital
E. Grey Nuns
F. Sisters of the Congregation

G. Château Vaudreuil
H. Jesuits' Convent and Church
I. Market Place
J. St Paul's Street
K. Parade
L. Arsenal and Yard for Canoes and Bateaux

Plan of the City of Montreal

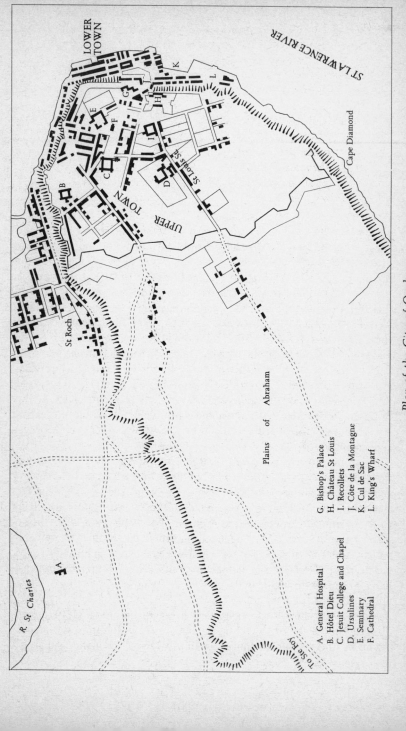

ST. LAWRENCE RIVER

LOWER TOWN

UPPER TOWN

St Louis St

Cape Diamond

R. St. Charles

St Roch

Plains of Abraham

To Ste Foy

A. General Hospital
B. Hôtel Dieu
C. Jesuit College and Chapel
D. Ursulines
E. Seminary
F. Cathedral

G. Bishop's Palace
H. Château St Louis
I. Recollets
J. Côte de la Montagne
K. Cul de Sac
L. King's Wharf

Plan of the City of Quebec

CHAPTER 4

Civil Government: Vexation and Confusion

As it happened the first and most bitter quarrelling in the St Lawrence colony was not between Canadians and English, but among the English themselves. Although Canadian interests were involved and the presence of the Canadian population influenced the course of the struggle, the conflicting parties were all English : James Murray, the civil governor of the province; Ralph Burton, commander-in-chief of the troops with headquarters in Montreal; and the English merchants of both cities. There were few clear-cut issues between the parties. The fundamental causes of the trouble were personal jealousy and dislike between Murray and Burton and conflict and resentment between army officers and merchants. More important, there was divergence of the political viewpoints of Murray and the merchants as the ideas of each party became clarified. A barbarous attack by some soldiers on one of the merchants in Montreal was both a result and a contributing cause of the continuing factious disputes which disturbed and entertained the public during the two years of Murray's civil administration.

It was unfortunate that an interval of a year and a half elapsed between the cession of Canada to Britain by the Peace of Paris signed in February 1763 and the inauguration of civil government in August 1764. The Proclamation of 1763 defining the boundaries of the province and authorizing civil government was issued in October. Not long after this Murray learned that he was to be appointed governor, but he had to wait, impatient and embarrassed, for ten months before his commission arrived. For nearly a year he was governor-elect, with a kind of imputed responsibility for affairs throughout the province, but no power outside his own military district.[1]

Murray was, however, delighted with his appointment. He wrote enthusiastically of the St Lawrence, the finest river in the universe, producing on its banks abundant timber for ships and iron "enough to supply all

Europe," and providing an immense and secure harbour. This glowing picture, succeeded as it was by a more sober official report, was typical of Murray's warm optimism, typical also of his tendency to form judgements hastily before all the facts were in. Equally characteristic was the childlike vanity which led him to order a handsome coach, and table silver (in sets of six dozens), and to urge his wife to get "a large stock of magnificent clothes." "The people here love show – I hate it, but I must not starve the cause," he explained, rather unconvincingly. With all his enthusiasm, however, Murray was aware of some of his problems. He greatly liked the Canadians and was prepared to be their champion, but he dreaded the close connection of the upper classes with France. He hoped the Canadian merchants and seigneurs would return to their mother country, leaving the habitants, a supposedly docile peasantry, to be presided over by a benevolent oligarchy of English merchants and squires. He himself purchased land in several parts of the province, and he looked forward to farming: "I have every book which has been wrote on husbandry since Virgil's time." [2]

Murray's commission arrived at last. He was formally proclaimed governor on August 10, 1764, the troops drawn up under arms in the square before the Château St Louis, in the presence of a numerous concourse of people. Cannon fired from the ramparts, men-of-war answered from the harbour below, the troops joined in with volleys of small arms, and, according to the Quebec *Gazette*, "the day ended with demonstrations of joy and universal satisfaction." It is to be hoped that the Governor, having quitted the parade ground and passed to his comfortable house on St Louis Street, where he sat, perhaps with his friend Captain Cramahé, talking over the events of the day, did share for a time these feelings of joy and satisfaction. They were not destined to last. He was almost immediately confronted with a situation that was to him as unexpected as it was unwelcome, and that caused him much disappointment and bitterness. He was "Captain General and Governor in Chief of Quebec" but, he gradually learned, in spite of these high-sounding titles, he was not commander of the troops in the province, perhaps not even of those in the city of Quebec. This was in accordance with American precedent. British troops in all the colonies were simply a detachment of the British army serving abroad; they were generally sent for a special purpose and there could be no thought of placing them under the command of governors with civil appointments, and often civilians themselves.

Murray had not even thought of losing his military command. At first incredulous, he protested to Gage in New York, to his old chief, Amherst, and to many other influential friends at home. His efforts were fruitless; early in 1765 a letter from the Secretary of State, Halifax, informed him that his was a civilian appointment, and that North American troops would remain under the commander-in-chief and his two brigadiers. Murray's resentment was not based solely on his personal disappointment. He was the victim of the imperial attitude that saw Quebec as only another colony. He maintained, vehemently and convincingly, that Quebec was a special case, and that he was no ordinary civil governor. A soldier by choice, he had accepted a civil appointment in a province where a military form of government was traditional, and where military authority for the governor was, at the moment, a necessity.

> It is by military force we are to govern this lately conquered Province in which there does not exist above 50 Protestant subjects exclusive of the troops, and by my instructions of these 50 Protestants must be composed the Magistracy; but what force, what weight can such a Magistracy have unless the Supreme Magistrate has authority with the troops? It is evident that the Brigadier must, in fact, be the Governor. . . .[3]

The efforts of the civil governor "can be productive of nothing but vexation and confusion."

Murray's case was almost unanswerable. He was vindicated by the fact that not for a generation was another governor appointed in a civil capacity only. Unfortunately, having proved that his commission could not be fulfilled in the circumstances, he did not decide on what would now appear to have been the prudent course : resignation, and a return to Britain to make his report with all the force of a man who no longer had any personal interest to serve. His failure to do this may be attributed to vanity, or to natural ambition. He was still in his early forties and as he now knew, there were no immediate prospects for him in the army. And he may still have believed that he was better fitted than any other to reconcile the Canadian people to British rule and to plead their cause with the authorities at home. While Murray's decisions were often imprudent, generosity was almost never absent from the sometimes inextricable tangle of motives that produced them.[4]

Unfortunately the Brigadier of the Northern Department, who, as senior officer, was to command the troops in the province from his headquarters in Montreal, was the one man whom it was impossible for Murray to tolerate in that position. Ralph Burton, the former military governor of Three Rivers, had been Murray's second in command in Quebec during the hard winter of 1759-60. At the disastrous battle of Ste Foy, Burton, leading the right wing, had been driven back by Lévis in some confusion. Rightly or wrongly, Murray blamed Burton for the disaster and, although at the time he shielded him, later he remarked bitterly that Burton should have been court-martialled.[5] His anger and frustration when he discovered, in October of 1764, that the promotion he longed for had, according to Gage's wish, gone to his junior, to Burton whom he thought he had saved from disgrace, were freely expressed. He accused Gage and Burton of having revenged themselves for their failure to secure the governorship by endeavouring to drive him from the army; he made no attempt to maintain even the appearance of friendly relations. [6]

It was during this unhappy period that Murray had to address himself to the task of inaugurating civil government under the constitution provided by the Proclamation of October 7, 1763. Murray, who was no lawyer, professed himself at first entirely satisfied with the constitutional arrangements which were shortly to engage constitutional lawyers in a lively debate. With apparent confidence, he set about the immediate task of creating legislative and judicial institutions for the whole province. The Proclamation and instructions assumed that Quebec was to have the usual pattern of British colonial government, governor, council, and assembly, with a system of law courts headed by a chief justice, and resting on the solid administrative and judicial base of the local justice of the peace. Murray's instructions, however, allowed him a slight discretion, acknowledging that it might be "impracticable" to form an assembly immediately, and therefore authorizing government by council alone. Murray was fully in accord with this view. Believing that Roman Catholics could not hold office he preferred a council which he might hope to control to an assembly of Protestants. He inaugurated what came to be called crown colony government, government by an appointed council with executive and limited legislative powers. Intended by Britain to be allowed in Quebec as a temporary expedient, it lasted for thirty years.

Murray's council lacked the strong official element which characterized later crown colony councils. Under him and under most of his immediate successors, because of officials absent or offices left vacant, the official element was very small. During Canada's crown colony period the governor depended chiefly on the advice and assistance of ordinary citizens. In 1764, Roman Catholics being automatically excluded, there were few citizens of reputation and experience who qualified for a seat on the council. Murray's first council did include three merchants who did good service. One of them, Thomas Dunn, survived to become a trusted senior member and judge in the colony. The leading members of this first civil council were, however, the military officers who for nearly five years had been responsible for administration and who had knowledge, experience, and leisure possessed by no others.

Murray's most trusted adviser and assistant was Hector Theophilus Cramahé, who had been with him during the hard winter of 1759-60 as intelligence officer, and from the fall of 1760 as secretary. [7] A second military appointment was Paulus Aemilius Irving, who was to become administrator of the province on Murray's departure.

The third and most junior of the three military men, Adam Mabane, had appeared in Quebec with the army as surgeon's mate in 1759. In that winter of cold and sickness even a surgeon's mate would come to the attention of the governor, and Mabane was a man whose energy, ability, and force of character were such as to make him remembered. Murray, in the absence of Mabane's senior, in 1762 secured an acting appointment for him, and later had him confirmed as surgeon to the garrison. Although his professional qualifications were probably slight, he was a kindly man and he pleased his patients. As councillor, judge, and close personal friend of three successive governors, he was to remain for thirty years one of the best known characters in the city of Quebec. Like Murray a man of strong affections and strong prejudices, he made enemies as well as friends.[8]

Murray and his little council began work on August 7 and laboured diligently through the autumn, re-enacting much of the routine legislation of the military regime. A difficult and contentious ordinance was the one establishing courts of law; here, in his endeavour to adapt the system to the Canadians, Murray began to realize the problems inherent in the new constitution. He also, in following the English and colonial tradition of placing local government in the hands of unpaid magistrates, the justices of the peace, realized fully the extreme difficulty of establishing Protestant civil government in a place where there were very few civilians even nominally qualified. Inevitably, at the circumference, as at the centre, the government retained something of a military flavour. In Montreal Murray chose a retired officer and fellow Scot, Captain John Fraser, to head the quarter sessions, and later appointed him judge of the court of common pleas. The choice was criticized; Fraser, like Mabane, was strong willed and prejudiced, but he appears to have been honest and reasonably competent, and his marriage to a Canadian lady, a Deschambault, gave him a useful insight into the attitude and needs of some Canadians.[9]

Murray faced immediately two problems that it was not in his power to solve, and he made one serious error. First, the original plan of the home government to continue something of the old administrative pattern by appointing lieutenant-governors of Montreal and Three Rivers who would be *ex officio* members of the council was given up.[10] The resulting situation in Montreal was particularly unfortunate, for Burton had his military headquarters there, and in the absence of any senior official, the civil authority was only too likely to be ignored. Moreover, the absence of any full-time civil official in Montreal left too heavy a burden on the justices of the peace, who needed help and guidance.[11]

Murray's second problem was the want of character and capacity in two officials on whom he had to depend for assistance in setting up the institutions of civil government, the chief justice and the attorney general. No province ever needed a good chief justice more and few can have had one less qualified. William Gregory's appointment can only be described as a particularly bad eighteenth-century job. He was a needy man of doubtful background, slack in his attendance at council, and given to gossip in public about what went on when he did attend. He was also careless in his judicial work. He wanted, said Murray, both head and heart. The Attorney General, George Suckling, was not a member of council, but was frequently called on for legal opinions, and for help in drafting ordinances. Suckling was abler and more conscientious than Gregory, but his inexperience led to embarrassing slips in drafting. Resenting the deficiencies of the Chief Justice, he could forget himself so far as to criticize and dispute with him in public. A more experienced administrator than Murray would have been hampered by the deficiencies of such men. Neither had any knowledge of French law or of the French language. [12]

Striving to better his position, Murray made what proved to be a serious mistake. In October 1764 he sent Cramahé to England, hoping that he would be able to lay before the authorities the lamentable state of the province, and especially that he could persuade them of the need for a governor with a military command, and for a lieutenant-governor at Montreal. Cramahé carried, in addition to a letter to Lord Halifax, the gift of "the model of a . . . French man of war . . . made by a Canadian Recollet who never saw salt water," but this offering availed him nothing. Lord Halifax "had no time at the moment but would look into the matter when he had leisure." [13] By July, 1765, there was a change of ministry and Cramahé had to begin all over again. There is no evidence that he did Murray or Quebec the slightest service in England and, at the time, his knowledge, patience, and tact were much needed in Quebec. The only person he was able to serve was himself, for during this period he became the friend and protégé of Murray's successor, Guy Carleton. [14]

Meanwhile antagonism between Murray and the English merchants of Quebec and Montreal was developing into a personal feud. "The most cruel, ignorant, rapacious fanatics who ever existed," [15] Murray called the merchants. Their indictment of him was more precise, and no less damaging. They accused him of innumerable acts of despotism and of enriching himself from public funds.

In the beginning the relations had been satisfactory enough. The merchants' party was composed of individuals ranging in substance and standing from the large wholesale importers, through the ranks of agents working on commission and retail traders, down to the humble discharged soldier turned innkeeper. They had come into the province, some with the army, others year by year from New York, New England, and across the Atlantic, to exploit the possibilities of the new colony. In Quebec and Montreal together there were about two hundred English-speaking house-holders in 1764.

Their relations with Murray, and the army generally, had not been all bad. There had been trouble over military regulations, over selling liquor to the soldiers, over illegal trading operations of various sorts. In the early days of his military rule, however, Murray had praised the merchants for their services to the troops and for the risks they were prepared to run to build up trade. [16] He endeavoured, as he said, to please them, and believed that he had succeeded.

The merchants, however, were restive under military rule and eager for the beginning of civil government. During the early part of 1764, after Murray's appointment as governor was announced, but before he had received his commission, they became increasingly critical. This was natural, as he was no longer the soldier who happened to command in Quebec, but their future governor. He levied taxes as under the French regime, even issuing the proclamation in his own name; he detained ships arbitrarily on suspicion of smuggling, and even imprisoned the owners; he took in large sums of public money, and issued no public accounts. He was even openly accused of peculation. [17] Murray was, indeed, often arbitrary and informal; he was not corrupt. He did try to govern justly and to show consideration to the merchants. When, for example, he detained a ship and its owners, it was because he thought it would cause less loss and inconvenience to the owner than to refer the case to the district admiralty court at Halifax. He, for his part, was increasingly resentful of the merchants' criticism and of their conduct, especially of what he considered their unscrupulous attempts to traffic in the depreciated paper currency of the province.

Apart from their opinion of Murray the trading classes had their trials in 1763 and 1764 in the interruption to the Indian trade. Gage, as military governor in Montreal, absolutely forbade traffic into the Indian country in order to deprive the Indians of ammunition and to prevent possible French intrigues. The regulations were necessary and reasonable, but irritating to the merchants. They were tired of military governors and they resented the superior airs of military officers. They looked anxiously for the fulfilment of the Proclamation of 1763: an elected assembly and "the enjoyment of the benefit" of English law.

They were proportionately disappointed and angered when Murray established a council but showed no intention of summoning an assembly. This was not his only offence. In preparing the ordinance for setting up courts of justice he seems to have realized for the first time that there would be some hardship in following the apparent meaning of the Proclamation and introducing English law wholesale. In his inferior civil court, therefore, although with doubt and hesitation, he allowed Canadians to practise as lawyers and Roman Catholics to serve on juries. His reference to the law was ambiguous, but he seems to have made it clear to the Canadians that he intended this to be their court where their customs could be followed. As two of the judges of the court, Adam Mabane and John Fraser, were warm supporters of Murray's policy of conciliating the Canadians, it was likely that his intentions would be carried out. The merchants, in the simplicity of their selfishness having clearly given no thought to the needs or interests of the Canadians, were exasperated. They were the more angry with Murray because he had, in theory, accepted the policy of anglicization. Murray never fully understood the complexity of the Quebec legal problem, and so he seemed to the merchants to be acting against his own expressed views and theirs, when he intended only a simple and obvious act of justice to the Canadians.

Hostilities with the merchants began immediately after Murray had approved the ordinance setting up the courts of justice. The merchants of Montreal sent him an address of congratulation on his appointment as governor, apparently for the sole purpose of regretting his arbitrary imprisonments in the past. The next unhappy incident was the presentment of the grand jury of Quebec at the autumn quarter sessions. Through the influence of one Conyngham, a lawyer, a friend of Chief Justice Gregory, and an incorrigible mischief-maker, the grand jury was so chosen as to include, along with some Canadians, certain English merchants who felt very strongly about Murray's supposedly arbitrary and "pro-French" tendencies. The presentment, while including a number of practical suggestions for regulating the markets, street-cleaning, chimney-sweeping, and the like, was obviously intended as a sharp criticism of Murray and his administration. In default of an assembly it was suggested that the public accounts should be laid before the grand jury as the only "representative body in the province." The ordinance on the courts of justice was criticized, with a special emphasis on the responsibilities laid by it on ill-qualified justices of the peace. A clause added as an appendix, and signed by the English members only, objected to Roman Catholics serving as juries on causes between Englishmen, and suggested that the use of Roman Catholics at all was contrary to English law.

The presentment was ill-judged and impertinent in tone. Apart from the claim to review the public accounts there was nothing very objectionable in the substance. Murray, however, was infuriated. Not content with a severe lecture read to the jurors by the presiding justice, he considered prosecuting them for libel. As the Canadians who had signed the present-ment offered their apologies, explaining that they had not fully understood what they signed, the story got about that the English members had deliberately tricked them. The Canadians made no such accusation and their inability to follow a discussion carried on in English and hastily translated is easy to understand. Murray believed the story of trickery and added it to his score against the merchants.[18]

His anger on this occasion can be explained only partly by the fact that his policy was criticized. He was seeing more and more clearly the difficulty of making Quebec, as he wished, into an English province, without hardship and injustice to the Canadians. He was anxious to conciliate them, not only as an act of justice, but also because he hoped by gentle means to convert them to Protestantism. At the same time he feared Canadian disaffection and Canadian intrigues with France. His whole Canadian policy depended on the loyalty and goodwill of an increasing English civilian population. Agricultural immigrants, however, were not coming into the country as he had hoped, and now the merchants' turning against him added greatly to the trials of a difficult period.

From the fall of 1764 the merchants took every opportunity of attacking Murray publicly and privately. They sent agents over to England, merchants who would use what influence they could with their corres-pondents to have Murray recalled; they drew up a public petition to the king asking for the recall of Murray and the grant of an assembly; and they engaged, in the spring of 1765, a competent lawyer in London, Fowler Walker, as their permanent agent.[19] In addition to numerous distorted and extravagant accusations, they charged Murray with an "unexampled rage and rudeness of demeanour." This charge was un-doubtedly well founded. Murray called it "natural vivacity of manner" and insisted that he tried to restrain it. No doubt he tried.[20]

Meanwhile the dangerous dissension and ill-feeling in the province was stirred up by the mysterious incident of Walker's ear. This case involved the whole complex tangle of enmities between Murray and the merchants, Murray and Burton, and the merchants and the army. It also revealed the incompetence of Murray's law officers and the general weakness of the provincial administration. The origin of the affair was a dispute over billets in Montreal. A Captain Payne had moved into quarters in a house used by the army for billeting officers. As the house was now rented by a justice of the peace, who was exempt from billeting, Payne was told that he must move. He refused persistently, and finally, by a warrant signed by all the Montreal justices, including John Fraser,

Murray's unofficial agent, he was committed to jail. No doubt the magistrate, Thomas Walker, one of the more substantial merchants, took a leading part in this assertion of civil authority. Murray had been warned, when he appointed him a justice, that he was a difficult character. Murray's retort had been that Walker was clever and ambitious, and that, properly handled, he could be very useful. He had forgotten his own previous insistence that he could not, from Quebec, adequately control people in Montreal. Now, shocked at this excessive display of civil power, he ordered the whole bench of magistrates down to Quebec to explain their conduct. It was agreed later that their action, though unnecessary and provocative, was not illegal. Long before there could be any official report, however, members of the army took unofficial action.

On the evening of December 6, 1764, Walker was sitting at supper with his wife in the large front room of their house on St Paul's Street. Suddenly the door flew open and a number of men with blackened faces rushed in. They set upon Walker, who, defending himself vigorously, retreated into an inner room where he kept his pistols. After a few minutes' struggle the men made off, leaving Walker severely beaten and wounded in the head. A little later a freshly severed human ear, flung onto the table of the adjutant of the 28th Regiment, with the remark that "that was for his supper," revealed the nature of poor Walker's wound. It later appeared that the men involved – about twenty in all – were of the 28th Regiment. [21]

Walker was convinced that his attackers had intended to kill him and he spent the ensuing winter counting his numerous wounds, bruises, and scratches – two hundred, he said – and fancying that he and his servants were being dogged about the streets by would-be assassins. Only in his own house, "locked up in my room with a bar at my outer door . . . a sword by my side, a brace of pistols in my bosom, one of my large ones with ball and buckshot lying on my table . . ." could he feel tolerably safe. [22]

Walker was not alone in his alarm. Shortly after the news reached Quebec Murray learned that there was danger of serious rioting between the soldiers and townspeople. He hurried up to Montreal with the members of his council. Murray and Burton dealt with the immediate danger by arranging to send the 28th Regiment down to Quebec, bringing up some of the Quebec garrison in exchange. Murray also used every resource at his disposal to bring Walker's assailants to justice, but in vain. In spite of the difficulty of getting evidence, a number of men were indicted. In due course they were brought to Quebec for trial. Blundering on the part of the Chief Justice and the Attorney General resulted in a technical fault in the empanelling of the grand jury. The members took advantage of the fact to evade what, in view of the temper of the 28th Regiment, now at

Quebec, they probably thought of as a dangerous duty, and refused to find a true bill. At the same time Walker, somehow persuaded that the trial ought to have been held in Montreal, refused to appear to prosecute the suit or give evidence. In the summer of 1765 a new trial was arranged and held at Three Rivers. Walker and his wife again refused to appear, convinced that Murray was their enemy and that they would not get justice. The prisoners were discharged. Later the council was informed that the junior officers of the 28th knew very well who the culprits were and had shielded them. The informant named certain men, stating that as the collusion of their officers had made it difficult to maintain discipline over them, they had all been sent home, or discharged from the army. But little, however, could be done on the word of one tardy witness and Murray had had enough of the state trials. The Walker case rested for a time. [23]

This affair only increased the tension already existing between the army and the merchants at Montreal and between Murray and Burton. Burton, inexperienced in complex commercial cases, had got himself into some trouble with the merchants during the military regime. After August 1764 Murray suspected that he continued carelessly to irritate the merchants and at the same time to encourage them to blame Murray, as governor, for any regulations that might injure them. It was in these trying circumstances that Murray and Burton were forced to co-operate in two difficult problems involving the military and the civil power: corvées and military billets.

The corvée was the compulsory paid labour imposed on the Canadian habitant in order to ensure necessary services for the army. It was Burton's responsibility every spring and fall to see that supplies went to Detroit, Michilimackinac, and other up-country posts. For this purpose men with their horses and carts, or sleighs, were needed to carry goods above Montreal beyond the rapids to the point of embarkation at Lachine or Ste Anne. At these points the canoes and their crews must be ready, each man trained for his own place in the boat, and each man equipped with his paddle, kettle, and provision bag.

Under the military regime these men had been secured through the captains of militia and, by Amherst's orders, although they had no choice but to serve, they had been adequately paid for their services. The introduction of civil law changed all this. The army could no longer command the services of civilians. Colonel Gabriel Christie, Quartermaster General, aware of the problem, applied to Murray as civil governor for a general warrant authorizing him to impress the men he needed. Murray at first refused the warrant and told Christie to ask the justices of the peace when he needed men. Later he decided that this procedure was not legal and he therefore issued special limited warrants to Judge Fraser to supply

Christie with men in the spring of 1765. There was a delay for which each man blamed the other; Christie complained bitterly that the roads to Lachine had become impassable before the men could be impressed.

Through the summer Christie and Fraser quarrelled, and Christie, ignoring Fraser and the law, proceeded to impress men as before through the captains of militia, and to use them occasionally, also as before, for his own private purposes. He was an enterprising purchaser of seigneuries and no doubt, like other landowners, was embarrassed by the shortage of labour. [24] By September Christie had reached an *impasse* with Fraser, and, as there was a real danger of the supplies not going up to the posts for want of men, a frantic correspondence ensued with Murray, involving also General Burton, General Gage, commander-in-chief in New York, and even the authorities in London.

There was no disaster, the men were found, and the supplies forwarded, but this prolonged quarrel lasted through the first fifteen months of Murray's civil government. An ordinance was passed in the fall of 1765 formally disbanding the militia and releasing militia captains from any duties or responsibilities in the parishes. Henceforth the bailiffs and sub-bailiffs, provided by the ordinance which established civil courts, would attend to local business. Unfortunately, the unhappy wrangling among his betters and the inevitable breach with the past had increased the spirit of indiscipline in the habitant, never noted for docility, without giving him any increased sense of social responsibility. In the summer of 1765 militia captains had reported to Burton that the men were insolent and demanding, asking not only higher pay, but the unheard-of luxury of a tent to sleep in. The bailiffs fared even worse. The inhabitants of one parish threatened to beat the unhappy man who was required to press them for the king's service. Army officers blamed Boston merchants for corrupting the habitants with ideas of liberty; they might have considered the influence of their own undisciplined conduct. It was unfortunate that Murray even drew the Attorney General into the quarrel. On several occasions when Suckling foolishly injected into his legal opinions sharp criticisms of Christie's conduct, Murray accepted the statements instead of returning them to be presented in proper form. He was corrupting a subordinate, and as all the correspondence went back to London, he was injuring Suckling's reputation and his own. [25]

Murray's handling of the situation in Quebec suffered, probably, from the absence of the cautious Cramahé and the presence of Mabane, who was a warm partisan, too ready to help him discover how wrong Burton and Christie were. To have bent the law a little and granted Christie a general press warrant under proper safeguards would not have injured the habitants. They had to give their services in the end. Maintaining due respect for authority in the disorderly colony would have furthered, not injured, the cause of law and of civil rights.

A second difficulty was the provision of billets for the troops. Billeting was a chronic problem in the American colonies. It was not a serious matter in the city of Quebec where most of the men were in barracks, although finding accommodation, even for officers, in the recently bombarded town could be a burden. In Montreal, in addition to officers, four or five hundred men had to be provided with rooms, beds, and cooking facilities, no light task in a town of some five thousand people, including many who were poor. Moreover, in Montreal there was a special source of irritation. Under the military regime billeting and all other administrative duties had been done by militia captains under the direction of army officers, militia captains in the town being the more substantial of the Canadian merchants. After the introduction of civil government, billeting was the responsibility of civil magistrates who were all Protestant. And so the Canadian merchant, who had acted as a kind of military justice of the peace, now lost his power and prestige, and perhaps also the privilege of being himself left free from unwelcome guests. His duties were taken over by a few justices of the peace, newly arrived English merchants, who, if they were conscientious, found their privileges a poor exchange for the burden of their unpopular task.

The billeting problem, like the problem of corvées, became acute in the summer and early winter of 1765-66. On May 18, 1765, a disastrous fire beginning near the waterfront at Montreal destroyed 121 homes. Soldiers and civilians alike were made homeless and many whose houses had been spared asked to be freed from billeting in order to take in relations and friends.

Not long after, news came from Britain that, by an act of Parliament passed the previous March, private citizens could no longer be compelled to provide billets for troops. Murray ordered the justices in Montreal to hire houses. He also sent up an officer, Major Carden, with authority to provide for the troops as he thought best, drawing on the home government for the cost. Carden got on well with the magistrates, took over a large building that had been used by the French as a government storehouse, and had it almost ready for occupation when it was burned down, the evidence pointing strongly to a deliberate act of incendiarism. Thereafter general panic or general ill-will took possession of the citizens. Professing to fear for the safety of any house in which a soldier lodged, they threatened to turn them all into the streets, even though by this time winter was closing in. The situation would have been easier but for Burton's unwillingness to move soldiers out to the suburbs. He did not think his forces should be dispersed, and his military decision had to be accepted. Finding billets was now a civil affair and he cheerfully left Murray, who had criticized him for meddling in civil affairs, to find his own solution.

In this emergency Murray sent Mabane to Montreal and also Hertel de Rouville, a seigneur from Three Rivers. People said that it was an act of folly to send a Three Rivers man to tell Montreal what to do, but Mabane and Rouville together acted quickly and competently. Mabane arranged proper compensation, including insurance, for those who would let their houses; Rouville conciliated the people, explaining the good intentions of government; and both put such gentle pressure on the Seminary, the Récollets, and the Jesuits, whose houses the government might have commandeered, that the clerics in turn put pressure on the citizens, who graciously consented to shelter the troops at least until April, when the worst of the winter would be over.

The billeting problem was more than a minor and irritating affair of military housekeeping. Military discipline in those days was harsh, five hundred or even a thousand lashes being common penalties. It could also be extremely lax. Soldiers in Montreal muttered resentfully that they could not have been worse treated had they been a defeated instead of a conquering army. No responsible officer could discount the danger of a mutinous attack on the unco-operative civilians. Mabane reported with indignation the irresponsible conduct of English merchants who had made a scene at the meeting of citizens called to discuss the matter, and had even induced a number of young Canadian merchants to join them. [26]

All this time Murray suffered peculiar irritations in Quebec. He knew the merchants were complaining and intriguing against him, but he could dismiss the "licentious fanatics" from his mind. His special trial came from the 28th Regiment, sent down to Quebec after the attack on Walker. Murray insisted that although not in command of troops in the province, he was military commander of the city of Quebec, subject only to Gage, Commander-in-Chief in North America. His claim was not admitted by Major Brown, commander of the 28th, and there were public clashes of authority. When Burton visited Quebec he showed his displeasure to the Governor by entertaining officers and merchants together, and sending Murray no invitation.

Murray, unhappily, could not conceal his resentment. Burton as commander in the province had ordered Adam Mabane, surgeon of the garrison, to make an estimate of his expenses for the coming year. Mabane referred the order to Murray who answered that Burton had no right to give such an order, and that if he had, no one could tell how many sick there would be in the coming year but "to please the General, I would have you imitate the almanac makers and guess at it. I give you leave to indulge his curiosity. . . ." This letter Mabane was ordered to show to Burton. Very foolishly Mabane did so, with the result that Burton reported his impertinence to Gage, who ordered Mabane to make his peace with Burton as best he could, on pain of the severest penalties. Murray complained of the persecution of poor Mabane, forgetting that he was himself largely to blame for once more bringing a junior officer into his own quarrel. [27]

It was not surprising that the new ministry in England which took office in July 1765 asked him to return to give an account of his administration. At the end of June 1766 he sailed from Quebec. He was received kindly by the king, and by the following April had fully vindicated himself of all the truly disgraceful charges against him.

Although he was vindicated and although he remained governor until 1768, Murray was not asked to return to Quebec. He had failed in the primary task of maintaining order and of doing justice. The fact that he had been asked to work under impossible conditions, that he had been given no help or advice, and that Henry Conway, Secretary of State in the government which recalled him, was grossly ignorant of Canadian affairs, could not cover the simple fact of failure. [28]

Nor is it likely that Murray would have been a great administrator under any conditions. Although able and astute enough, he was emotionally incapable of coming to terms with a difficult situation and adapting himself to it. Having correctly stated in 1764 the difficulty of governing Quebec without a military command, he should have avoided occasion for conflict with Burton. Deprived of military pomp he might have exploited more effectively the dignity and even the terror of the civil authority. Murray was defeated partly by his own temper, vanity, lack of dignity, and above all by his failure to judge men soberly and accurately. The squalid Walker affair revealed a situation for which Murray was not primarily responsible, but which steadily deteriorated through the personal weaknesses and limitations of the governor.

And yet it is hard to wish that any other man had been called to govern Quebec at this time. If Murray was not an effective governor he was a good man. His very faults were appealing; there was nothing petty or mean about them, and they harmed no one as much as himself. The Canadians first met English rule in the person of this conscientious, lovable, impulsive, simple-hearted man; they responded warmly to his unaffected kindness and concern for them.[29] If his faults were too ready weapons in the hands of his English enemies, they also helped to show clearly the impossible nature of the task that had been laid upon him.

CHAPTER 5

The Benefit of English Law

The apparent conflict of laws precipitated by the Proclamation of 1763 raises a difficult question. How could Murray have approved of the Proclamation since it appeared to establish conditions of government which he found impossible and unjust? The answer seems to be that, as seen in the previous chapter, although his task was rendered more difficult by the confusion of the law, the first strife in the colony was between different groups of English rather than between English and Canadians. Moreover Murray, although at times he was anxiously and even stubbornly legalistic, was no lawyer. He had no real grasp of the complexity of the situation. He always assumed that his friends, the Canadians, and all worthy English merchants, could be satisfied by some compromise that would lead ultimately, by easy stages, to an English colony. So casually, indeed, had the new colony been received, so light-heartedly had responsible officials accepted sixty-five thousand unknown people as "subjects of the King," and as an integral part of the North American empire, that only gradually did it dawn on the authorities at home that Quebec offered problems for the constitutional lawyer rather than for the administrator or statesman. Before Murray left the country, however, it had become clear that fundamental to discussions of what should be done was a determination of what exactly had been done. What law did prevail in the colony and where lay the power to change or add to it? [1]

Lawyers when consulted could only go back to the completely safe ground of the French regime. Safe, but not simple; the law of France under the old regime, based as it was on a multiplicity of local codes or "customs," was not easy to define. For Canada Louis XIV had specified the custom of Paris; this was supplemented by some other local customs, by the Roman civil law, and by edicts of the king. Decisions of the governor and council and of the intendant also had the force of law. The fact of conquest changed automatically only the public law, that is, the law regulating the relations of the king to his subjects. In accordance with the law of nations the great body of law would remain until specifically altered by the conqueror in accordance with accepted constitutional practice.

Since the capitulation two almost independent processes had been taking place. First, France having surrendered the colony on conditions, the acceptance of these conditions as at least morally binding on the administration [2] seemed to dictate the preservation of much of the existing civil law of the colony. On the other hand, as this colony had been retained for the purpose of securing and developing Britain's American possessions, it was to be expected that such changes would be made as seemed necessary for the well-being of the empire and of imperial trade. Failure to identify these two processes and to reconcile their potential contradictions caused the confusion in the laws of Canada after 1760. The change from a typically French to a sufficiently English system could never have been simple. It was rendered peculiarly difficult by the intrusion of imperial concerns in the shape of agitation in the thirteen colonies destined to lead to revolution and partial dissolution of the empire.

The articles of capitulation of the province signed at Montreal in 1760 granted Canadians, with certain minor limitations, the enjoyment of their property and freedom of worship. Enjoyment of property implied, at least for a time, the continuation of certain laws, especially those relating to land tenure and inheritance. It seems clear, however, that these concessions were meant to be limited. Amherst refused to promise the continuation of French civil law; the peace treaty in 1763 granted freedom of worship but only "so far as the laws of Great Britain permit."

It looks, therefore, as if the Canadians, far from receiving any pledge or guarantee of the continuance of their own law, had been given pretty clear warning that Canadian law would soon be English. On the other hand it was soon obvious that justice required something like permanent retention of the laws of real estate at least. There were also very important differences between the English and French laws of inheritance. The Englishman was proud of the law which allowed him the the fullest possible right of bequeathing all property, real and personal, apart from entailed estates. Many a Canadian was equally proud of the protection afforded to his family by the law which secured four-fifths of his real property to his natural heirs. The same difference in the attitude toward the family is discernible in the laws relating to the property of married women. In English law, effectively, the married woman was always a minor under the guardianship of her husband, and the power of the husband to dispose of his wife's property could be limited only by elaborate settlements placing the property in trust. French law, on the other hand, recognized a community of property between husband and wife, the rights of the husband being superior in management only and not in ownership or in the power to alienate.

The laws, in fact, reflected different economic interests and different social values. The English merchant was conscious of the utility of a system which made for free exchange of land, ensuring, presumably, that it would fall into the hands of those best able to exploit it profitably. He was also attached to a law which put the maximum power and responsibility into the hands of the individual businessman, compelling him to support his engagements to the full extent of his property, and making it as difficult as possible for him to use the rights of his family as a protection from the consequences of his own mistakes or misfortunes. The Canadian, on the other hand, valued the regard for the community and for all human rights which limited the power of a man to risk the total property of his family in the pursuit of his business.

It was some time before this problem, which looks obvious now, presented itself clearly to the authorities in London or even to the governors in Canada.

The first civil constitution of Canada, and therefore the first formal statement of the law and of law-making powers,[3] was framed not specifically to meet the needs of Canada but as a general settlement for the whole of the territory extending from the St Lawrence Valley to the Gulf of Mexico, now formally secured to Britain. The Proclamation of 1763, apart from its extensive regulation of Indian affairs, did three things: it enabled land-seekers to move to the newly acquired colonies, including the mainland colonies of Quebec and the Floridas; it promised them elected assemblies to make laws and levy taxes; and until such assemblies could be summoned it promised prospective settlers that they could rely on "the enjoyment of the benefit of the laws of our realm of England."

It seems certain that the precise constitutional and legal impact of this law on the province of Quebec was not understood or even considered. The wording of the Proclamation implied that in the newly acquired provinces English law was already in force and that, therefore, all who moved into those provinces might rely on it for protection. Assuming, however, that English law was not yet in force in the conquered province, had the king the constitutional power, merely by proclamation, to sweep away a whole legal system and replace it by another, and that not by a direct statement but by inference only? The general although not the unanimous view of English jurists after the event was that if the king had any such right, he could not have used it in so general and casual a fashion. Therefore the Proclamation had made no change in the law which, being French and Canadian before October 7, 1763, remained French and Canadian thereafter, precisely as if the Proclamation had not been issued.

There was, however, a further complication. Even if the Proclamation had made no change in the laws, the promise of an assembly was entirely unambiguous. It was the opinion of Lord Mansfield, expressed ten years later in the case of *Campbell* v. *Hall*, that the king had the power without Parliament to transfer legislative power to the people of the colony but that, once having made this transfer, he could not withdraw the grant except by act of Parliament. According to this theory, after October 7, 1763, only the British parliament or an elected assembly had the constitutional right to legislate for the colony. The royal instructions, authorizing Murray to legislate by council only, were invalid since they directed the governor to use a power that the king had already given away.

All the legal analysis of the Proclamation, commission, and instructions, all the learned discussion of the rights of the king over a conquered colony took place only after Murray had established his civil government, and after experience had shown the difficulties of reconciling the two legal systems, each of which had an undoubted claim to some recognition in the colony. Moreover, it was not until March 1768 that Lord Hillsborough, who had been President of the Board of Trade in 1763,[4] insisted that there had been no intention of doing away with Canadian laws and customs, repudiating any such idea with pious horror. In 1764 Murray was in possession only of the Proclamation, which seemed to assume the validity of English law and to promise an assembly, and of his instructions, which gave him leave to defer the assembly and to legislate by council. In the face of this and other evidence only an able and confident lawyer would have been bold enough to challenge the power of the Proclamation as infringing on "natural rights" and on the rights conceded by capitulation and treaty to a coherent community of civilized people. Murray had no such lawyer at hand: he had, instead, Gregory and Suckling. Even if he had had better lawyers he would have been puzzled by the theory which dismissed his council, and every one of his ordinances, as unconstitutional. One may be thankful that with all his other troubles he was spared additional torment. He was happier not to know that in the province over which he presided, to put it bluntly, no one knew what the law was, or who had the right to define it.

Untroubled by doubts, therefore, Murray constituted his council and in the course of a few weeks produced the ordinance of September 17, 1764, which gave the province a system of regularly established law courts, following, roughly, the English pattern. With some minor amendments and one important change, this ordinance remained in force until 1775.[5]

The ordinance established three levels of judicial administration. The lowest and broadest was that of the local justice of the peace, a typically English institution. The justices could hear and determine police and minor criminal cases and some civil suits. On the highest level was the court of king's bench, hearing both civil and criminal cases, presided over by the chief justice, keeping the regular English law terms, and holding sessions in each of the two judicial districts of Quebec and Montreal. This high court, like the lowest courts, usually heard cases in English and determined them by English law.

In between these two levels came a court for civil causes only, the court of common pleas, designed by Murray, as has been shown, to serve the Canadians. Canadian lawyers could practise in it, and on the bench were local amateur judges who spoke French and who shared Murray's benevolent attitude towards the Canadians. This court could deal with cases involving amounts as low as ten pounds, and up to any sum, with an appeal to the court of king's bench. In civil matters there was also a right of appeal from the king's bench to the members of the council, sitting as a court of appeal, and from there to the Privy Council in Britain in cases involving five hundred pounds or more.

Such was Murray's ordinance for the administration of justice, a subject of bitter complaint from Canadians and English; from Canadians because, officially, all courts might apply English law and because they found this new system elaborate, costly, and slow; from English because the system was ambiguous, offering, even in theory, concessions to the Canadian law which, they feared, the pressure of custom would render even more ample, thus destroying their dream of "the enjoyment of the benefit of English laws," and perpetuating military rule.

Most writers have given their sympathy to the Canadians, and understandably. They had been accustomed to the simple and cheap justice provided by a competent and benevolent despotism. French law, both civil and criminal, was expressed in general maxims, interpreted and applied by the judge to the particular case. Courts sat weekly or oftener under the eye of the intendant who was prepared to intervene at any stage if he disapproved of the proceedings.

In contrast to this method and approach the English system must have appeared extraordinarily cold, heavy, and brutal, with its rigid substantial and procedural laws, its elaborate machinery, and above all its terrifying impersonality, its apparent dedication to method and form with complete indifference to the results. Any reader of Dickens will sympathize with Canadian bewilderment at English reverence for venerable institutions preserving, so it seemed, the mediaeval faith in trial by combat, in defiance of modern rational analysis. It was difficult for them to understand the stubborn tradition which associated the sacredness of the written law, of clearly defined customary procedure, and above all of trial by jury, with the liberty of the individual; it might have been still more difficult for them to understand why this abstract liberty was more precious than speed, economy, simplicity, and a reasonable chance of an equitable decision. It was equally impossible for the English to understand how anyone could prefer the former Canadian system.[6]

The British system was not much commended to Canadians by the lawyers who first introduced them to it. Probably Gregory and Suckling were no worse than could have been expected in a remote colony where the small remuneration was not sufficient to induce an able man to bury his reputation, although it might be very welcome to a man who was only too anxious to bury his past. The judges of the common pleas, Adam Mabane, John Fraser, and Francis Mounier were more acceptable in some ways. Mounier was a respectable merchant, a Canadian Protestant. Mabane and Fraser have already appeared as Murray's chosen and trusted assistants. None of these three men had any legal training, but Mabane in the course of a long career collected a small law library and a considerable store of legal knowledge. His great offence in the eyes of English merchants was his increasing tendency to adopt the attitude of his French predecessors on the Canadian bench, concerning himself less with the strict letter of the law than with the equitable application of a general principle. The greatest tribute to Mabane and Fraser, and to Murray who selected them for their posts, is that the English merchants, who opposed their politics and hated their arbitrary methods, never in the course of prolonged and skilful attacks convicted either of them of any act of corruption or shameless self-seeking; yet both were poor men, on low salaries.[7]

The greatest weakness in the judiciary, apart from Gregory at the summit, was the justices of the peace who formed the base of the pyramid. The province did not possess enough men of substance and education, independent enough to be judges, and yet willing to take directions from the central government. Murray made a bad situation worse by assuming, naturally, that he had no right to appoint Roman Catholics, who, by "the laws of England" mentioned in the proclamation, were not capable of holding office. As, to his disappointment, English from the other colonies did not come flocking in to acquire seigneuries and settle on new lands, he had to employ English and American merchants. Some did good work; others were deficient in ability or character, or both. The good ones were likely to be busy men. The Attorney General, ordered to instruct them in their duties, at least showed commendable caution in declining to compress into a few simple directions the accumulated English practice of four centuries. The conscientious justices depended on the manual of the day,

Burns' "Justice," but one troubled and faithful soul had to write from a remote district asking for help in a complex case that should not have come before him at all, and complaining that he had been unable to procure "a Burns." [8]

The justices were authorized to determine cases up to five pounds singly, up to ten where two sat together, and up to thirty pounds in quarter sessions. In 1764 these were substantial sums. Only in cases over ten pounds was an appeal permitted. Murray's purpose, expressed in the ordinance, was to suit the "ease, convenience and happiness of His Majesty's loving subjects." He was very sensible of the need to reduce the delays and costs of the higher courts, but he might have realized that apparent ease and convenience could be bought too dearly at the cost of happiness and security. The justices were assisted by bailiffs appointed by the governor from parish lists, each man serving in rotation. These officials seem to have been an inefficient substitute for the captain of militia, whose office was suppressed until 1775. Some, however, preferred them as less prone to petty tyranny. [9]

A source of irritation to successive governors and of confusion, if not of actual hardship, in the province was the system by which eighteenth-century officials at home and abroad were appointed and paid. Payment was by fees plus a salary, or by fees alone. Appointments were made through influence, as a favour to the supporters or friends of those in power. A further abuse of the system was that the official holder of the office, the "patentee," often did not perform the duties himself, but appointed a deputy, who paid him for the privilege. Moreover, one man might hold several offices and deputize them all. Murray complained that James Goldfrap, who was deputy provost marshal (sheriff), registrar, clerk of the council, provincial secretary, and commissary of stores and provisions, could not read a word of French. [10] Having collected all these offices from the two English patentees, Henry Ellis and Nicholas Turner, Goldfrap had to deputize in his turn, appointing sub-deputies to act as provost marshal in Quebec and Montreal. After some unfortunate choices – one of his Montreal agents increased his income by selling hunting licences to the habitants through the former captains of militia for ten shillings apiece [11] – he found honest and adequate men.

Much depended on the man acting for the provost marshal, who was the executive agent of civil and criminal courts, responsible for summoning juries and executing all writs and sentences of the courts. The appointment of this important official was in the hands of Goldfrap, deputy of the patentee. Murray could advise against a bad appointment, and he could suspend a man who had proved himself unfit, but he could do no more.

The man ultimately appointed in Montreal in 1765, who filled the office creditably for over forty years, was Edward William Gray, at that time twenty-three years old. He had arrived in the province some five years earlier and, while making his way as a merchant, served also as Goldfrap's sub-deputy in his numerous other offices. The apparent necessity of making only Protestant appointments thus placed a heavy responsibility on a very young and busy man. The provost marshal had no salary and received his compensation entirely in fees, of which he could retain only a part, as the deputy and the patentee would each claim his share.

Canadians and their governors complained of the heavy cost of justice and the rapacity of officials. Such unaccustomed burdens must have been trying, and it seems to the modern mind odd to procure in such a clumsy fashion pensions for English gentlemen who had earned the favour of government. The Canadians, however, paid no other taxes and it is possible that the costs of justice were generally not much heavier than under the traditionally lenient military regime. Such abuses as occurred were naturally resented the more from being unfamiliar and coming from alien hands.[12]

As far as Murray and his legal advisers knew, the ordinance of 1764 carried out the intention of the Proclamation of 1763, the constitution of the country. They had done all in their power to mitigate the inevitable hardship and injustice by the "middle court," the court of common pleas, intended especially for Canadians. This laudable effort received scant recognition from the English law officers. In April 1766 the Attorney and the Solicitor General of Great Britain, Charles Yorke and William de Grey, criticized sharply the judicial system in Quebec:

> the attempt to carry on the administration of justice without the aid of the natives, not merely in new forms, but in an unknown tongue, by which means the parties understood nothing of what was pleaded or determined, having neither Canadian advocates or solicitors to conduct their causes nor Canadian Jurors to give verdicts, even in causes between Canadians only, nor judges conversant in the French language to declare the law, and to pronounce judgement. . . .[13]

This astonishing passage contains five false statements, two of them clearly at variance with the wording of the ordinance itself. No doubt Canadians taken before justices of the peace or into the king's bench might have their causes heard in English; and although Canadians might serve as jurors in any court, their use in the king's bench where the Chief Justice knew no French would have to be limited to those with some knowledge of English. The common pleas court, however, was "the Canadian court." Although the ordinance was cautiously worded, the judges in this court are to determine agreeable to equity, having regard nevertheless to the laws of England as far as the circumstances and present situation of things will admit . . .

the judges of the court noted the word "equity" and decided that this meant Canadian civil law. In this court Canadians could have their own law in their own language with Canadian pleaders and Canadian jurors. The Canadians considered this their own court and resisted attempts on the part of the Chief Justice to demand the transfer of mixed cases out of it into the court of king's bench.[14] There is indeed every reason to suppose that Canadian civil laws and customs remained practically undisturbed. People continued to have deeds and contracts drawn up by their own notaries, commissioned by the new government but working on the old forms. Evidence from deeds of land transfer shows careful attention to Canadian law.[15] There is also evidence that English purchasers of seigneuries assumed that they possessed every right recognized by Canadian law, and that the courts would support them.[16] There were cases in the common pleas where Canadians pleaded English law even against French suitors and the English pleaded French law, leaving the judges, no doubt, full scope for the practice of "equity."[17] On the whole, however, it seems clear that Murray and his law officers had, in the court of common pleas, achieved for the Canadians roughly the kind of general recognition for their property laws that they had enjoyed under military rule.

It was, therefore, hard on Murray that the law officers in Britain, ignoring the facts, should achieve a fine humanitarian flourish by accusing him of doing the very things he had avoided doing. Placed in a difficult situation and provided with no help from Britain, he had produced a tolerable compromise for which he, and even Gregory and Suckling, might have been given more credit. They were, indeed, placed in between two fires, with the Quebec merchants complaining that English laws forbade even the empanelling of Roman Catholic jurors, whereas the opinion of the law officers of Britain, offered too late to be of any help to Murray, was that Roman Catholics in the colonies should be subject to none of "the incapacities, disabilities and penalties" of those in the United Kingdom.

Murray's ordinance, however, was no more than a creditable attempt to make the best of an impossible situation. The common pleas might be effectively a "Canadian court" but its power to apply Canadian law was necessarily limited, first, by the right of justices to settle cases up to ten pounds, and second, by a right of appeal to the king's bench in all cases of twenty pounds or over. In the king's bench, officially, English law prevailed, and, if rigidly applied, might alone cause a reversal of decisions in the common pleas. After 1766 when Hey replaced Gregory as chief justice, and perhaps even before, the king's bench settled cases appealed to it from the common pleas by the law used in that court, that is, by Canadian law. In mixed cases, however, the situation might be very different, as English suitors would naturally prefer to take their cases to the king's bench in the first instance.[18]

Moreover, at best, Murray's Canadian court could do no more than cushion the shock of change to the Canadians. His ordinance had specifically introduced English law and, by implication, allowed the parallel application of Canadian, thus sanctioning two legal systems in one community. There was nothing inherently impossible in this; most modern countries had inherited a number of collections of mediaeval customs, especially in relation to land tenure. Canada, however, had been developed as a commercial colony. In the towns of Quebec and Montreal Canadian and English merchants were increasingly doing business with each other and with firms in London, Boston, and New York. At the same time Canadians were inevitably involved in liquidating the close commercial ties that had bound them to France. As business grew, and the groups mingled, the two streams of law would increasingly flow together. Some definite statement of the laws of property was necessary.

Lord Mansfield, Chief Justice of England, on hearing that Canadian law had apparently been swept away, was said to have cried out in horror at "so rash and unjust an act," and to have called urgently for "a speedy remedy." The remedy, agreed upon between the Board of Trade and the law officers, was Canadian law for cases of real property and of inheritance, and English law in criminal cases. As for commercial law, "the substantial maxims of law and justice are everywhere the same." No doubt, with this easy dismissal of what became a major issue in the province, the law officers assumed that the council would legislate on commercial matters. What merchants needed was the translation of "substantial maxims" into precise regulations governing, for example, the complicated dealings associated with bills of exchange.

The government of the day approved of the proposed remedy. Appropriate instructions were prepared to be sent to the governor in Quebec. Instructions also authorized the governor to admit Canadians to any office except that of judge in the superior court. London expressed its sense of the injustice of their exclusion up to that time. These instructions should have gone to Quebec in the summer of 1766. They were, however, not sent at all. The proposed changes were the work of Charles Yorke who, energetic and ambitious, had irritated the gouty Lord Chancellor Northington, who suspected Yorke of wishing to succeed him. Northington persuaded the cabinet to postpone any change until it had been shown a "code" of the laws of Quebec. Later in the summer, sensing continued opposition, he contrived by resigning his office to overturn the weak ministry, and the Quebec plan was set aside.[19]

Thus, apparently, but for the impatience of ambition in Charles Yorke and of gout in Lord Northington, Quebec might have had relief from the conflict of laws ten years before the Quebec Act came into force. This attractive explanation is, however, too simple. Lord Northington shared the doubts, later hardened into a judicial decision by Lord Mansfield, whether, after the promise of an assembly in the Proclamation of 1763, the king could continue to legislate by council. Already the lawyer Fowler Walker, the merchants' agent in London, had expressed this view.[20] The instructions were, therefore, filed away until an appropriate bill could be presented to Parliament.

An act of Parliament, however, is no light matter. Although the claims of Canadians to equitable treatment might seem clear and uncontestable, there was still the awkward question of adapting the colony to the empire, the empire which was becoming, increasingly, a special cause of anxiety. It was no wonder that year after year went by, leaving the people of Quebec still in uncertainty as to what was the law, the benefits of which they were, or ought to have been, enjoying.

In the fall of 1766 Colonel Guy Carleton, a soldier of reputation, a friend of Wolfe who had served in the 1759 campaign and who knew America, arrived in the province as lieutenant-governor. While taking the keenest interest in the knotty problems of the laws and the constitution, he was also prepared to listen to the particular woes which the merchants were very willing to relate.

CHAPTER 6

Profit and Loss

The exasperated Murray thought of Quebec merchants as needy New Englanders, New Yorkers, and others, out for what they could get; and he was right. They looked at provincial matters generally, if not exclusively, in terms of profit and loss – their own profit and loss. Their representations to the government emphasized their contribution to commercial growth, but also harped continually on the sad theme of loss. This fact, and the disparaging and even abusive comments of the governors, can give the impression that after the Conquest commerce languished in the hands of traders who were a shabby lot of schemers.

Such an impression is a distortion of the truth. In spite of serious problems the province achieved a modest level of prosperity during the fifteen years between the Conquest and the war of the American Revolution. The English and American merchants concerned represented in their own estimation the energy and enterprise, and the national interest, of England. It was their view that Canada had been retained only as a positive economic asset, to be developed by individual enterprise with the approval and support of government. There was confirmation for this view in the searching inquiries directed from Britain to the military governors in 1760 on the natural resources and commercial possibilities of the country. Young Lieutenant John Marr, who liked the Canadians and disliked any suggestion of English arrogance, still took it for granted that Britain's purpose in the colony was the exploitation of its economic resources. Governor Murray was in full agreement. The London merchants trading to Quebec expressed these views at length. They formed a "Quebec interest" no doubt, but an interest that in the councils of the empire would be opposed by none but a rival "interest" bent upon economic exploitation elsewhere.[1]

The only limitations which merchants could be expected to feel on their right to exploit the economic possibilities of the new possession would be necessities of defence and security and, perhaps, considerations of humanity and justice to the inhabitants. If the merchants were inclined to brush aside too lightly the claims of inhabitants, it is apparent that Murray, and even Carleton, failed to achieve any sympathetic grasp of the viewpoint of the merchant. Both were ready in principle to protect commerce; neither could see the source of Britain's wealth and power in the "Quebec traders," whom they met in the council chamber and passed in the streets. The merchants were represented as rude hecklers of the humane governor and would-be oppressors of the Canadian. It is fair to see them also as they saw themselves, building their own fortunes, but also enriching the community and the nation by seeing life steadily in terms of profit and loss.

I

Farming and Fishing

Agriculture, the occupation of the great majority of the inhabitants of Quebec, was much in the minds of imperial statesmen. Their conviction that the province was capable of great agricultural expansion did much to shape the first constitution, the Proclamation of October 7, 1763. Some parts of this document suggest that, in the minds of those responsible for it, Quebec was to replace the Ohio country as the American farmers' Mecca, leaving the true fur trader of the Hudson River to pursue his calling, free from the interference of the land-seeker and from the rivalry of the St Lawrence. The fur traders, however, whether Canadian or English, had no intention of quitting the St Lawrence, and Quebec was not at that time attractive to the land-seeker. The settlement line was moving west to familiar and fertile lands. There was nothing to draw the ordinary farmer to the remote and unknown back concessions of the St Lawrence, and there were no wide stretches of land there to tempt the speculator. Nevertheless, those obliged to come to Quebec on other business, military governors, army officers, and merchants, looked with interest on the land and its possibilities, for land rightly used could turn a trader into a gentleman, and could help a gentleman to solvency.

From the beginning the English officers looked with admiration and affection at the picturesque countryside, the gentle rhythm of the strip farms, the snug houses, the church spires, the wind and water mills, all so reminiscent of the French countryside, standing in strange contrast to the immensity of rock and river and the wild darkness of the forest beyond. The romantic and tender feelings inspired by these scenes expressed themselves in the charming sketches and water colours which still survive; and the occasional illusion of having found Rousseau's ideal country was re-

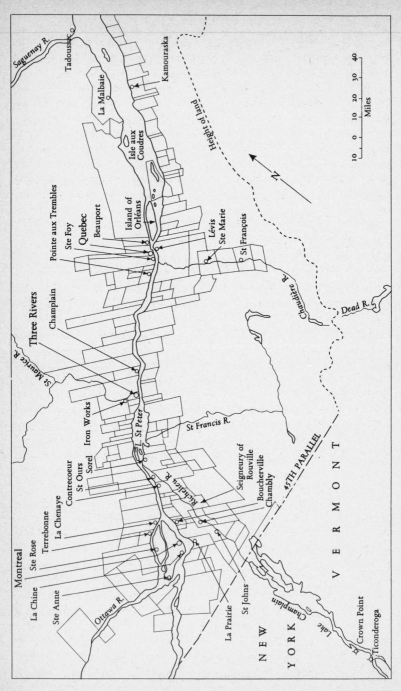

The Seigneuries of Quebec. (This small map inevitably suggests boundaries more precise than those recognized at the time)

inforced by the discovery that the Canadian habitant often united with the language of the peasant something of the unaffected courtesy and dignified bearing of the gentleman.

And yet when called on for a practical opinion of Canadian farming the English had to subscribe to the general view of visitors from France and elsewhere; judged as farming, it was very bad. The Canadian habitant was idle and without ambition. He kept too many horses in order to drive about the country in cariole or calèche, instead of staying at home and attending to the breeding of good cattle which would at once cultivate and manure the land. Such manure as he had was not spread over the land, but dropped on the frozen St Lawrence to be carried down when the ice broke, an unsightly harbinger of spring. Meanwhile, the habitant smoked tobacco from the generous patch which could have been planted with wheat, and smoking, eating, drinking, driving, dancing, and visiting, he passed the winter, if not in idleness, at least in occupations almost wholly uneconomic. Not that he despised money; he could be sharp enough if a piastre was within reach or even within sight, but he did not spend his days dreaming of how many more he could make next year.[2]

The Canadian farms at this time occupied only the river front and, at most, one concession behind, beginning on the stretch of river a little above Montreal and fading out a little below the Island of Orleans, with the rich valleys of the Richelieu and a few other tributary rivers serving as side streets to the main thoroughfare of this gigantic village. These farms showed only the leisurely face of Canada. Those who frequented the wharves of Quebec or Montreal in spring and fall could catch glimpses of the other side. From the tranquil farms of the middle river came the seal hunters, the canoemen, and the fur traders, who, on the upper lakes and down in the gulf, showed almost incredible powers of endurance, strength, and sagacity. Farming, on the contrary, did not seem to make great demands on vigour and initiative, and the Canadian easily persuaded himself that it was of little advantage to produce a surplus beyond the minimum needed for the essential supply of brandy and for such desirable articles as coffee and molasses, red caps for the men, and gay cottons for the women. When hunting and fishing produced such good food so pleasantly it seemed pointless to labour for surplus bread.

Murray attempted no such psychological analysis, merely noting regretfully that the habitant was a poor farmer and inclined to be lazy. While hoping that the province would attract many English small freeholders, Murray also sought to draw in men of education and substance who would purchase land from departing Canadian seigneurs, and set an example of good management and good farming. His own purchases comprised some seigneuries in the neighbourhood of Quebec, including his country house, which bore the inapposite name "Sans Bruit," and less developed but potentially valuable holdings on Lake St Peter and in the Champlain district.[3] Murray's friends, however, did not join him in Quebec. As he was not invited to return as governor when cleared of the charges against him, he eventually sold his lands and retired to a farm in Sussex.

Murray's agricultural enthusiasm did bear some fruit in Canada. Like other English officers he sent home samples of seeds, shrubs, and trees, and ordered seeds to be sent in return. His own gardener was brought out, and remained in Quebec as a dealer in seeds and plants. Murray's special gift to Canada was the potato, hitherto almost unknown. He spared neither time nor cost in importing seed potatoes and teaching proper methods of cultivation. His success was remarkable. Within a few years of his departure the potato patch rivalled the tobacco patch on every habitant farm, while on the Island of Orleans, conveniently near to the city of Quebec, potato farming had become a business.[4]

Other Englishmen bought land. Ten years after the Conquest there may have been two hundred English landowners, of whom thirty held *en seigneurie*, some of them estates of considerable size.[5] Colonel Christie, Murray's Montreal opponent, early invested £1,200 in land on Lake Champlain. He extended and improved his holdings until, a dozen years later, they were described as "a small kingdom," valued by Christie at £20,000 and admitted by a detached observer to be worth £15,000.

This type of estate was not, however, agricultural, in the modern sense. In England Arthur Young, George III – "Farmer George" – and many others were interesting themselves in the cause of better farming; but it would have required much faith or folly to make an Englishman believe that he could persuade the habitants to use methods approved in England and France, even if he thought that such methods in Canada would pay dividends. Murray's enthusiasm was exceptional, and it was not lasting. Those who bought seigneuries bought them to exploit them as the Canadian seigneur did by making the most of the rent rolls, the banalities, and the timber rights. Colonel Christie, for example, having been persuaded that the custom of Paris was in full force, endeavoured to apply it with surprising precision. His habitants of La Chenaye, he conceded, need not all come to bake bread in his oven; they could contract out by paying a fee. But when they took their wheat over to Terrebonne to be ground he pursued the offenders, and made them pay him mill dues and a fine in addition. He even instituted a suit against the refractory in the common pleas, refusing to allow them to make their peace. "All the talk of the habitants of La Chenaye of their prescriptive rights is the greatest folly," he declared grandly. Within a few days, however, he had changed his mind. "I thought it better to arrange with the habitants, as long as they confessed their faults and promised to pay better in future." All fines were to be returned and any legal expenses incurred by the habitants paid. Christie had, no doubt, received a hint, perhaps from Judge Fraser, not only that the law was doubtful but that such arbitrary behaviour was hard to justify by any law. His claims and his mode of enforcing them are however an interesting example of the attitudes of certain seigneurs in Montreal and elsewhere. His neighbours, the seigneurs Rouville and St Ours, could also be arbitrary and exacting.

Christie did not depend on rents and fines. His valuable timber holdings were developed and exploited with a careful eye on possible poachers. With all these preoccupations he still found time to think of the welfare of the Church, and to regret that the priest of La Chenaye should have "his heart and mind attached to the good things of this world." [6]

Although the English did not do much to stimulate agriculture directly, wheat production increased for many reasons. After 1760 the province had fifteen years of complete peace, farmers were no longer called from their farms except for the *corvées* which, legal or not, were not burdensome, and favourable weather resulted in a series of good or excellent crops. The wheat market revived, and the habitant, once he was conscious of a marketable surplus, not only increased his area of cultivation but proved himself a shrewd enough bargainer. Even before the war raised prices, wheat was becoming a significant commodity. Gathered onto river schooners from the docks at Montreal, and from many little towns on the Richelieu and upper St Lawrence, it was taken down to Quebec to be loaded onto the ocean-going ships for Europe. The grain business could be highly profitable. A short crop in Europe might mean a price of six or seven shillings a bushel; a plentiful crop in Quebec could cause prices to drop momentarily as low as two livres, although the average price was nearer four, for the much larger French bushel. News of market and crop conditions travelled slowly and always reached the merchants first. It was, therefore, theoretically possible to buy at Sorel for a shilling or so what would sell in London for six shillings, and the bare possibility was quite enough to tempt the merchant in London or Quebec, as well as the local trader, to speculate.

The wheat was harvested in August and laid away for the winter threshing, one of the occupations that did interfere with the winter leisure. The habitant could take his grain or flour to the open market at Quebec or Montreal, but it was often more convenient for him to trade grain to the local storekeeper for merchandise or cash. Often the wheat had been pledged months before in return for credit. Where there were rival storekeepers it required a nice calculation to know how much and for how long credit should be given in order to retain a customer, especially one who would pledge his grain at a fixed low price. As the wheat trade grew, merchants of Montreal sent out buyers who worked for a commission, and who strove to undercut the storekeepers, who paid in goods, by offering money, along with a tempting advance in cash. Even a slight difference in price meant much to the habitant, and to the parish priest who received a substantial part of his income in tithe grain. Prudent merchants, however, conscious of the long interval between purchase and delivery in London or Spain, bid cautiously until the approach of war encouraged speculation on all sides.[7]

The market was not the only cause of harassing uncertainty in this trade. The owners of the river schooners which were to bring down the wheat from Montreal liked to wait at Quebec for the arrival of the ships from Britain in order to secure an up-river cargo. If they delayed too long contrary winds and the ebbing of the spring flood in the Richelieu, from which much grain came, might make loading difficult. Ideally, wheat purchased for shipment down river should have been brought to wait at the loading places, but for want of public granaries the habitant usually agreed to store it until it was needed. The result was that, if the ships arrived late, the storekeeper might be beset by farmers wanting to get rid of the grain; if early, he might have to hunt the countryside to gather a cargo for the impatient shipmaster. Where a storekeeper had his own granary at the loading point matters were eased, but fragments of acrimonious correspondence which survive show something of the strain imposed on merchant, shipmaster, and storekeeper even by the apparently simple business of sending wheat down river to Quebec.[8] For these reasons it needed the combination of a series of good harvests in Quebec and good markets in Britain to make it worthwhile to develop a regular organization of the wheat trade. Cramahé wrote home in 1772 that the colony had exported 180,000 bushels in 1771, 150,000 during the current year, and, following an abundant crop, he expected 200,000 to 300,000 in 1773.[9] In the spring of 1773 Thomas Walker, on a visit to London, observing that Canadian merchants had invested rather heavily in merchandise in advance of the fur sales, which proved disappointing, wrote immediately to his wife to buy up quantities of wheat at the lowest possible price. He foresaw that in the fall returning ships would be looking for cargoes and merchants with remittances to make would pay a good price for anything acceptable on the London market.[10]

It is not possible to say how often Thomas Walker or any other merchant made large profits from speculation in wheat. It is clear that the habitants were never their helpless dupes. Often the merchants feared that they must lose the chance of a good sale in Europe because the habitant, following the example of the local priest, might hold his grain for a higher price than the buyer dared to pay.[11] With all its uncertainties, however, the wheat trade was sufficiently developed and organized for habitant and merchant to take full advantage of the heavy demand and high prices in 1775 and the war years that followed.[12]

Increasing interest in grants of public lands brought up the important problems of registration of land titles and of accurate surveys. Many of the existing seigneuries represented not one but a series of grants. After the Conquest, as the seigneur was trying to make the most of the land which might henceforth be his sole resource, it became apparent that there were doubts about the limits of his property. When Carleton required a precise description of seigneurial holdings, the best that his Canadian assistant could do in one instance was to report that Mr St Ours held land on the St Lawrence next to Mr de Contrecoeur and Mr de Contrecoeur next to Mr St Ours. No doubt even moderate investigation would have produced more information. The English merchants asked and secured the remedy, to them the obvious one, of requiring an accurate survey of lands and provincial registration of all land titles. This was intensely disagreeable to the seigneurs. It was a vulgar substitute for the seigneurial custom of claiming lands by an act of foi et hommage at the Château; it might involve costly surveys, and difficult research into various notarial deeds. "Le Registerre" appears very early in the list of seigneurial grievances against the government; prejudice against the law was general and it seems not to have been enforced.[13]

Essential as land was to the permanent prosperity of the province, the first interest of Quebec merchants was in commodities that would bring in quick returns. Of the considerable number who came in hoping to establish themselves by supplying the troops, and to build up a general prosperity on that foundation, some did succeed as merchants in Quebec and Montreal; others, less fortunate, or with less influence, settled as local storekeepers in the smaller towns and villages.[14] The city merchants who kept their footing in Quebec were attracted very quickly by the gulf fisheries and particularly by the sedentary seal fishery, a highly specialized industry developed by the Canadians with peculiar skill. Seal could be caught in the gulf and along the Labrador coast only during the very short seasons when they were migrating in fall and spring. The success of the catch depended on precise observation of their nature and habits. When migrating they were accustomed to hug the shore, even passing through the very narrow passages formed by the offshore islands in the gulf in preference to moving into open water. This habit gave the seal fisher his opportunity. Nets were fixed across the bottom of the narrow channels with one end anchored to the island and the other fastened to a capstan on shore. As the seal were seen to approach, the nets were tightened, one after another along the channel, so that those who escaped the first ones would be caught in the end.

The seal fishery in any one place was a natural monopoly, and the whole industry could be ruined by free competition. Nets and other equipment were costly, and had to be prepared especially for the particular channels in which they were to be used. Moreover, the channel and the adjacent shore must be guarded and maintained with scrupulous cleanliness as any unusual sound or smell might frighten away the highly sensitive and timid animals. The preparation of the seal oil and the skins was done in permanent huts on the shore. The merchant usually outfitted a ship in the spring or summer and sent it with equipment and provisions for the winter down river to his own concession where huts and copper kettles for trying out the oil were in readiness. In spring the ship would return to Quebec with perhaps a thousand pounds' worth of oil and a thousand or more seal skins which would sell at a few livres apiece to make winter moccasins for the habitants. As the success of the fishing depended so much on the care and skill of the men, they were generally paid not in fixed wages but with a proportion of the profits.

The English merchants found that this industry had been stopped altogether during the last years of the war by the menace of the British fleet in the lower St Lawrence. Formerly it had engaged large numbers of men, variously estimated at from three to six hundred. The French government, recognizing the character of the industry, and with no fixed ideas in favour of free competition, had been accustomed either to grant the fishing areas *en seigneurie*, including exclusive fishing rights, or to grant the fishing rights separately on condition that the fishers paid the landholder 3 per cent of the catch. It was usual to grant or lease the rights for a period of from seven to nine years and when a lease changed hands the new occupier was accustomed to take over the equipment and installations at a valuation.

At the time of the Conquest a number of Canadians had claims in the form of grants *en seigneurie* or unexpired leases. The territorial vagueness of the grants, and the frequent subdivision through inheritance and dowry provisions, made this one of the most complex pieces of property guaranteed by the capitulations and the treaty. The status of this property was rendered even more uncertain by the Proclamation of 1763 which, defining and greatly curtailing the provincial boundaries, left most of the seal-fishing posts within the jurisdiction of Newfoundland. Before 1763 Murray had received requests for a recognition of seal-fishing rights. He allowed his Canadian judicial officer, La Fontaine, to go down river and resume the fishing. Later he came to distrust La Fontaine, and he was reluctant to let any Canadians go down river except as employees. He did give leases to a number of English merchants to take over the fisheries on paying to the Canadians compensation for installations and a yearly rent. Shortly after the signing of the peace treaty, but before the provincial territory was reduced by the Proclamation, he made an outright grant of land at St Charles to Daniel Bayne and William Brymer.

It was Bayne and Brymer, isolated and exposed at the eastern extremity of the line of posts which ran from Anticosti along the north side of the gulf and on toward the Straits of Belle Isle, who met the brunt of an attack on the Canadian seal fisheries launched by Hugh Palliser, the new governor of Newfoundland. Palliser was aware of the danger of smuggling and of the possibility of French intrigue in the lower St Lawrence. He was also an exponent of the free fishing policy, designed to help the English fishing ships in their competition with New England. He refused to recognize any property rights in the shape of leases or installations, and announced in April 1765 that the first comer each spring might claim any right on any shore. In August 1765 two summer employees at the post of Bayne and Brymer were violently expelled, and the property at the post destroyed or sequestered. One of the men, William Lead, determined to make his way to Quebec to turn back the ship coming down with supplies for the coming winter, and so save his employers from yet further loss. Forced to make the journey alone in a small open boat, he reached the island of Anticosti where he met the supply boat, and told his tale of disaster.

Bayne and Brymer, bitterly resenting this treatment and their losses, had the stubbornness and the capital to fight back. Maintaining that Murray's grant of land, made before the Proclamation, was valid, and that Palliser had not only violently trespassed but had wantonly destroyed property, they petitioned against him to the Board of Trade and the Privy Council, and finally sued him in the king's bench in Britain for £5,000. In the end the case was settled out of court, the government providing Palliser with £600 from army contingencies to pay Bayne and Brymer, and £400 for his own legal expenses.

This was in 1770. After having their business operations suspended it took Bayne and Brymer four and a half years to secure £600 damages in a case that had cost their opponent at least £400 in legal expenses, and themselves, presumably, no less. As they had ventured on the seal fishing in good faith, with the full permission and approval of Governor Murray, it is easy to understand their profound dissatisfaction and that of their group with government policy in Quebec. This does not excuse the merchants' persecution of Murray, who did all he could to defend their rights to the seal fisheries, but it does explain the general sense of frustration which might lead the merchants to make Murray, often in manner as arbitrary as Palliser, a scapegoat. Compared with the fur trade the seal fisheries were a small business, but they were so situated as readily to become a monopoly of Quebec merchants and £12,000 to £16,000 worth of business meant much to young men who were starting with little or nothing.[15]

This was one of the serious economic grievances met by Carleton on his arrival in the province in 1766. He resumed Murray's protests and spoke eloquently of the hardship to the Canadian proprietors, and to the Canadian seal fishers, accustomed to make their living by the industry. Forwarding also a memorial from the merchants, Carleton remarked that the industry was most necessary for redressing the unfavourable trade balance, and that but for his determination to discourage numerously signed public petitions he could have had the signature of every merchant in the town. Ostensibly London yielded nothing to Carleton's representations, even though they were reinforced by those of Murray, now in England, and by the tenacious pursuit of Palliser carried on by Bayne and Brymer. There is, however, evidence that the seal fishery was resumed during this period, even within the bounds of Palliser's government, and even by Canadians. François Baby, the Quebec merchant, stated in 1775 that he and his partners at St Augustine, beyond the boundaries of the province, had been in the business twelve years and that it brought them in £1,400 a year. Palliser's regulations, in some places at least, must have been harassing rather than crippling.[16]

II

The Fur Trade

The great commercial interest was, as always, the fur trade. There, if anywhere, fortunes were to be made. Nearly every merchant and trader, whatever his other concerns, was in some fashion involved in the fur business. Some trading went on within the province, even within the narrow boundaries set by the Proclamation of 1763. Tadoussac, where Champlain first traded, and neighbouring posts, were a government monopoly, known as the king's posts, leased for a yearly rent. During the war trade had languished; early in 1760 Murray turned the posts over to his friend the merchant Thomas Ainslie, with instructions to inspect their accounts and take over the furs. If he hoped for a little revenue for his penurious government he was disappointed; this part of the province had not yet surrendered, the navy reached the posts first, took the furs, and secured them as lawful prize.[17]

By 1762 Murray had control of the posts, five in all, Chicoutimi, Malbaie,

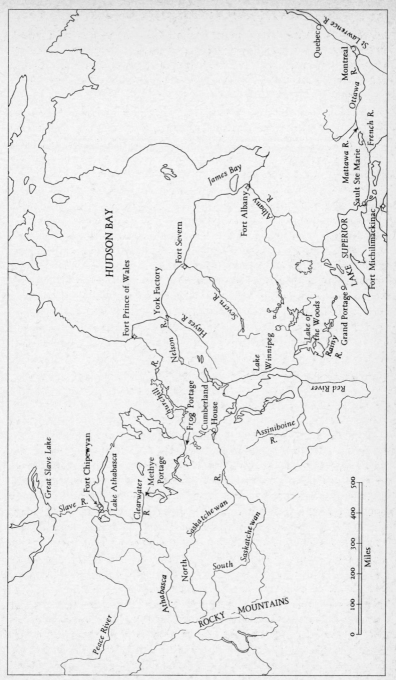

The Fur Trade in North America

Tadoussac, Ile Jérémie, and Sept Iles, and had leased them to the merchants Thomas Dunn and John Gray for £400 a year. The fact that this was £100 more than the French had ever received and that the excluded merchants spoke bitterly against monopoly even in this relatively poor area is evidence of a profitable and expanding trade.[18]

In one other place in the province the fur trade was carried on directly with the Indians, not as a government monopoly, but under close supervision. The little town of Three Rivers, a modest canoe- and ship-building centre, and the source of the best melons in the province, also profited from the annual visit of the Tête de Boule Indians with their furs. Any travelling up river to "forestall" the market was strictly forbidden. The Indians having first settled their accounts with those who had given them credit were invited to display their furs at an appointed place "opposite Mr Francheville's house" where the merchants and traders met them. No alcohol could be given or sold until the trading was over. Necessary supplies of gunpowder were brought in by the governor and distributed equitably among the merchants. Such were the arrangements approved by Burton and Haldimand during the military regime, clearly a continuation, in principle at least, of the French custom.[19] It would greatly have eased the burden of government, French and English, if all fur trading could have been conducted in this simple and orderly way.

These, however, were incidental operations, divorced from the great stream of the trade. The best furs would not flow down river so long as traders were sufficiently enterprising to go and look for them. Canadians had suffered long from the rivalry of the English on the Hudson, less favoured geographically but offering better and cheaper goods. Now the triumphant English with their goods found themselves on the St Lawrence, the best road to the fur country, peopled with folk who from generation to generation had been following that road in the birch canoes which they made and handled with unparalleled skill. The English lost no time in exploiting their advantage. From 1761 passes were issued for the upper country, and at the moment when the peace treaty was signed in February of 1763 the fur sales in London showed as many furs from Quebec as from Hudson Bay.[20] This promising business was interrupted completely for one season, and hampered for another, by Pontiac's rising. Only in January 1765 was Murray able to declare the upper country once more open to merchants, traders, and voyageurs from Quebec.

The permission, however, was hedged with such conditions that it caused more anger and resentment than rejoicing. The most obvious fact about the fur country, extending in a vast sweep north, northwest, southwest, and south of the Great Lakes, was that there were so many doors of entry, the Mississippi, the Hudson, the St Lawrence, and their innumerable tributaries from the Wabash to the Ottawa. Of the three main groups seeking entry at this time, the English on the Hudson, the French on the Mississippi, and the English on the St Lawrence, the last two were the real rivals in the highly competitive trade. The French, with no territorial possessions on the mainland, had been granted full privileges by the Spaniards west of the Mississippi. Their traders, maintaining an uninterrupted traffic facilitated by the friendly Canadian settlements on the Illinois, were able to send large cargoes of furs down the Mississippi to the market at New Orleans. The English on the St Lawrence could easily match them, and outstrip the English on the Hudson, by taking full advantage of their position and resources. They found to their annoyance that their economic operations were hampered by political considerations. The fur country belonged to no province or colony. West of the Mississippi, the shadowy claims of the Spanish from the south approached, but did not meet, the shadowy claims of the British in Hudson Bay. East of the Mississippi the great reserve envisaged by the Proclamation of 1763 was under the control of the commander-in-chief of the British forces in New York, assisted and advised in Indian affairs by the two Indian superintendents and their commissaries, officials stationed at the trading posts to interpret and administer all the regulations. There was, however, no government in the country. Traders there came under the jurisdiction of their respective colonial governments.

As Murray had no instructions from London, he issued passes to traders in exchange for a bond, to the amount of double the value of the goods taken up country, that they would keep such regulations as might be made. Once beyond the narrow boundaries of the province they were to proceed to one of the forts, Niagara, Detroit, or Michilimackinac, and there follow the directions of the commander. The fort commander was guided by orders from his own chief, General Gage in New York, and by Sir William Johnson, Superintendent for the northern district. Pending instructions from London, Johnson issued on his own discretion directions intended to ensure fair trading practices and justice to the Indians. In practice they proved harassing even to the well-intentioned trader.[21]

The principal regulation was that the trader must operate only at the posts, under the eye of the commanding officer and the commissary. Later, prices came under control, according to a tariff established by the commissary. Apart from this, trade was free, much too free for the trader, for he learned that he could not compel even the Indian indebted to him to turn over his furs. Any credit that he chose to give was at his own risk.[22]

It is easy to imagine the abuses that might have inspired such regulations; it is equally easy to understand the bitter complaints of the merchants. They made it clear that Johnson's rules for the protection of the Indian could ruin the trade and the Indian who depended on it. Trade could not be confined to the posts. Traders had to go among the Indians to gain their confidence, to encourage them to hunt, to advance goods as necessary, and particularly to provide ammunition and to replace the all too unreliable guns. At Michilimackinac trade depended entirely on the men who wintered with the Indians. Elsewhere, if remote tribes tried to come to the posts, they would at best lose a season's hunting, and at worst starve on the way, for they were not allowed to hunt on the territory of another tribe. But Indians south and west of the lakes would not come to the posts. They would simply turn over their furs to the friendly, ubiquitous French, leaving the Quebec trader with his goods, loitering at the fort, while his rivals captured the business.

The Montreal merchants did acknowledge the need of regulating the trade. Their vigorous spokesman in the west, the Ranger, Major Robert Rogers, commandant at Michilimackinac, developed an ambitious plan of setting up a totally independent fur-trading colony with its capital at Michilimackinac and its governor responsible directly to king and council for the conduct of the trade and the traders. Although Rogers was later accused of ambition and self-interest and even of treasonable dealings with the French, it was yet a clear statement of the need for authority by a responsible and well-informed individual on the spot. Another plan, suggested by some of the merchants and approved by Gage, was the adoption of a system that had been used by the French, the division of the country into districts each of which would, for trading purposes, be leased to a responsible merchant who would be compelled by the natural competition of his neighbours to give fair prices and good treatment. Others suggested that regard for their own safety would ensure tolerably good behaviour among the traders and that a strict limitation of the quantity of spirits taken up country would be a desirable additional precaution. All, however, were agreed that the regulations as interpreted at the posts must ruin the St Lawrence trade. The regulations were not even equally enforced. Commandants and commissaries alike were accused of abusing their power of extending favours to those who would assist their private trading operations by ensuring that the best furs should come their way. Where there was no deliberate injustice it was still considered a grievance that traders were not furnished with a written copy of the regulations they had engaged to keep, but must learn them verbally and piecemeal from the commissary at the fort.[23]

As soon as Murray had declared the fur trade open in 1765, the merchants presented their grievances to him and also, through their agent, to the home government. Murray was sympathetic, but his representations on their behalf had no effect. When Carleton arrived at

Quebec in 1766 he was already well briefed on the merchants' case. He wrote vigorously to Johnson, who repudiated, rather vaguely, the idea "of any injury to the trade," and insisted that Canadians were not to be trusted in the upper country. Carleton commented sharply to the Board of Trade:

> ... through this province is the most favourable access to that country, the Canadians are well acquainted with it, as well as with the genius of its savage inhabitants; and though it would be highly improper not to watch with the greatest attention both their words and actions I am confident that if not prevented by the jealousy of their rivals in that trade, they may be made useful instruments to wrest it out of the hands of our antagonists . . . for the benefit of Great Britain and the detriment of its natural enemies.[24]

In short, Canadians were reliable subjects and, if not shackled by regulations dictated by the jealousy of New York traders, could easily meet the rivalry of the Mississippi French. It was not, said Carleton, New York that would benefit from the regulations, but the same Mississippi French who two years earlier had carried off furs from within twenty leagues of Detroit almost under the eyes of the Canadians who had advanced credit on these furs that they hoped to buy. If French from New Orleans could be allowed to move about so freely, why not Canadians from Quebec? And, if all traders must take out bonds for good behaviour, why not ask bonds also from commissaries?[25]

Carleton, although he showed some want of charity for Johnson and for his commissaries, presented a good case. Lord Shelburne, the new secretary for the colonies, answered in a dispatch which implied that Carleton could use his own discretion with the traders. Gage, too, was by now convinced that each province should take the chief responsibility for its own traders. Although the merchants continued to complain of the regulations until 1768, when the commissaries were withdrawn from the posts, it is probable that from 1767 they enjoyed considerable freedom of movement away from the posts. At Michilimackinac the regulation had never been completely enforced.[26]

In spite of all hindrances and frustrations the fur trade flourished. Every year in the early spring traders prepared to move up country as soon as the ice should break. The birch canoes were stored for the winter at Montreal. Those who needed new ones would order them at Three Rivers, perhaps asking Mgr St Onge, the obliging Vicar General, to keep an eye on the leisurely workmen. The heavy canoes were worked by paddle and sail with a crew of eight to ten men; those for the far west were smaller. While the trader secured from the merchants English "strouds," point blankets, guns, powder, shot, kettles, knives and tomahawks (*casse-*

têtes), the pleasant miscellany of needles, scissors, thread, beads, and other small articles known as "haberdashery," and a plentiful supply of rum, women in Montreal would be cutting and sewing shirts and petticoats, while silversmiths worked on the brooches, bracelets, and crosses, which were among the luxury articles of the trade.[27] Tobacco could be got from Three Rivers. Cash, needed for the goods, for the work people, for beef, pork, peas, and biscuit to provision the canoes, and for wage advances to the voyageurs, was often forwarded by the merchant known as "the last outfitter." Canoes ready and the crew engaged, it remained only to secure the pass from the governor or his deputy. This document set out in detail the name and place of origin of the trader, the canoemen, and the guide, along with a list of the trade goods and a statement of their value. The pass had to be shown to officers commanding at all posts reached by the trader. Traders to Niagara and Detroit might sell their goods and return in one season. Those bound for Michilimackinac would go with the intention of wintering up country. In 1767 one hundred and twenty-one canoes with nearly £40,000 in merchandise cleared at the fort of Michilimackinac and went off to winter at traders' outposts on Lake Superior, Lake Huron, Lake Michigan, and "La Baie." Fourteen of these went beyond Lake Superior to the far northwest.[28]

In a trade organized in this fashion the "outfitter" who gave credit had to wait long for his profit. The goods that he furnished to a trader leaving in April or early May must have been ordered from Britain early in the previous year, probably before the merchant could know what profit he had made on the furs sent home. Traders wintering up country could leave later, taking up goods carried out in the ships of that spring, but they would not be back with furs for over a year. Either way the Montreal merchant had to order goods from London at least two and perhaps three years in advance of the sale of the furs which he secured in return. He was thus committed to a long-term investment and also to considerable risk as fur prices and yields both varied. The trade, therefore, had to be organized in such fashion that, if all went well, profits would be large. Some merchants, instead of advancing the £500 needed for equipping a large canoe, would arrange to buy beforehand at a fixed price the total take in furs. If the yield was good the merchant might be able to make a speedy profit, shipping his furs to London with the fall ships, and at the same time making a small premium by selling bills of exchange on his consignees to the unlucky merchants whose furs or other goods were insufficient to meet their London payments.[29]

The fur men fell naturally into three groups, the voyageurs with their "guide" who manned the canoes; the trader who went up country to do the actual buying and selling; and the merchant who supplied the goods for cash or for some form of credit. The groups, however, were fluid. Some of the very able pioneers among Canadian traders came from the voyageur group, employed by or working for the merchants; and often a merchant might be his own trader, at least for a time.

Although the day of the great fur companies had not yet arrived, partnerships or less formal associations for various purposes were numerous and often transitory. The Baby family, however, co-operated in the fur trade for at least fifteen years. François Baby at Quebec was in charge of affairs down river.[30] He attended to orders from England and kept his own schooner on the river between Quebec and Montreal. In the early spring he travelled to Montreal to equip and dispatch the canoes to his brother Duperron at Detroit. Their sister, Mme Benoist, meanwhile, was supervising the sewing of clothing for the trade. Back at Quebec, Baby occupied himself with supplying retail traders and buying wheat. By early fall he would be corresponding with Pierre Guy in Montreal who would be asked to receive and forward the furs coming down river, to arrange storage for furs and grain, to collect debts from returning traders, and to pay off the voyageurs. All this Guy did very readily except for the last; the voyageurs he found so unruly and violent that he dreaded having to deal with them.[31] Having received the furs François Baby forwarded them to correspondents in England, and issued orders for next year's goods, often adding astringent comments on goods already received. Whatever was the nature of the arrangement between these competent Babys, it seems to have worked smoothly, foreshadowing the methods and relationships of the great companies of the decades after the Quebec Act.

One man might combine the function of trader and merchant or outfitter, as when James Morrison, a Montreal merchant, made a journey to Michilimackinac by way of Niagara and Detroit and back by the Ottawa River, in the spring and summer of 1767, the first year that traders went freely to winter out from Michilimackinac. Morrison endeavoured to buy furs on his way up from Indians about Lake Ontario; he also purchased flour and tobacco at Detroit to take on to Michilimackinac. A more important purpose was probably to look into the possibilities of the trade and to make contacts with those who might stay permanently up country, the "wintering partners" of later years. That year Morrison sold goods to fur traders at Michilimackinac, accepting their note for the invoice price plus 35 per cent payable in furs at Montreal the following June.[32]

Furs might be brought down by traders or sent under the care of the voyageurs and the guide, who were paid their wages only after a strict accounting for all fur packs and equipment. A very important item of trading equipment was the paint or ink used to mark every pack with the owner's brand mark.[33]

Once the furs of a trader reached Montreal, the last outfitters had to be paid, and they could move very rapidly if a man showed signs of dealing with another merchant. These claims satisfied, there was keen competition and hard bargaining for the rest of the furs. Those who bought for overseas shipment, following the urgent advice of their correspondents in London, tried to accept only the choice furs. Duperron Baby sorted all his at Detroit and sent down only the best for export. The ordinary small trader, however, was stubbornly opposed to any examination of his packs, insisting on selling all in bulk; probably, in his turn, he had been obliged to purchase without much discrimination in order to keep his Indian customers. Buyers complained, but might have to yield, hoping that they could dispose of inferior furs by selling them to provincial consumers, or sending them to New York by Albany, thus saving on insurance and freight charges. Sometimes, although all furs were bought at a uniform price per pound for each kind – beaver, fox, cat, marten, mink, raccoon, bear, elk – a rough classification of quality might be made and a heavy deduction applied to the weight of the poorer furs.[34]

The scramble to get the canoes up in the spring, the strain of waiting at Montreal for their descent in the fall, the fierce competition to get sufficient furs for remittances home, the hurry to get them down river in time for the last ships bound for London, the eager expectation of the results of the winter fur sales which would tell the merchant what chance he had of liquidating his debts or making some provision for next season's goods already ordered: these marked the seasons of the year for the fur merchant. He might do very well but he could also lose disastrously. During the generation following the Conquest many, if not most, merchants lived precariously, but keenly and hopefully. They might be ruthless with each other and with the traders indebted to them. They insisted, however, with much truth, that their services were of value not only to Britain but to the colony and to the Indians living beyond. If, as they admitted, it required some skill and perseverance to convince the Indian that he needed a broadcloth coat, it required none to persuade him that he must have a new gun, or his wife that she needed scissors and needles and a brass kettle. The trade was also rooted in the community on the river. Most trade goods came from England, but little subsidiary industries developed in Montreal and elsewhere. Not only were dressmakers, tailors, and silversmiths needed; coopers and blacksmiths also helped to stock the canoes. According to an estimate of 1767, for every canoe that went up to Michilimackinac, £178 was spent in the province on wages of all kinds and on provisions, without counting local trade goods such as tobacco or the local manufacture and maintenance of the canoe itself.

As for the individuals involved, all the voyageurs and most of the traders were Canadian. Of the merchants who petitioned in December 1766 against the rule confining traders to the forts, thirty-six were Canadian and thirty-four English.[35] Merchants can also be identified by the names of men who went bond for the traders. In 1767, out of thirty-nine names of guarantors on the passes of men trading out from Michilimackinac, twenty-nine were Canadian. The English were the larger investors, although fewer in number; together they accounted for as much as half the value of the goods that went up. English capital was coming in from Britain and from the American colonies, whereas after 1760 the wealthier Canadians had returned to France, taking their capital with them. In these early years, however, Canadians remained active in every branch of a trade dependent inevitably on the metropolitan market, but rooted also in the province itself, in its natural resources, and in the skill of its people.

During the years following the Conquest the combined skill and enterprise of Canadians and English showed remarkable results. In 1766 they were still struggling to get permission to leave the shelter and restraint of the three main forts; ten years later they had fanned out south, west, and north of the Great Lakes. By 1771 merchants in Montreal were commenting on the superiority of the furs from the the the far north.[36] By 1774, when the Hudson's Bay Company established Cumberland House on the Saskatchewan to contain the "pedlars" from Montreal, these men – voyageurs, traders, and merchants – were already on their way across the watershed to the basin of the Mackenzie. Disagreeable they may have been; despicable they were not.[37]

III

Auxiliary Operations

Another obvious article of export and one sure to find a ready sale in Britain was timber, and timber was plentiful – "oak, ash, hickory, walnut, birch, beech, maple," as Murray reported. Unfortunately, freight costs were high and it was only with the heavy demands of war at the end of the century that the timber trade of Quebec came into its own. Already, however, many owners, especially those about Lake Champlain, were prepared to exploit their stands. Within the province there was always a market for firewood, and a special stretch of beach at Quebec was customarily reserved for the vendors. Thanks to the repeated devastations of fire, and to the growth of population, there was also a good sale for oak planks and building materials of all kinds. Cut planks were sent abroad, but the chief article of export was barrel staves, needed in enormous quantities for the innumerable pipes, puncheons, casks, barrels, and kegs in which most overseas freight was carried.

Cutting oak staves was a common winter occupation on Lake Champlain. In early spring the cutters prepared a kind of raft on the ice, thirty or forty feet long, with a plank bottom and sides of woven twigs. As the ice broke up, with the raft piled high with staves and linked to other rafts fore and aft, the men began the long chill journey down to Quebec, their sole comfort the broad bed of packed clay in the centre of the load, on which fires could be built for cooking and warmth. Passing the rapids in the Richelieu and the St Lawrence was risky. The unlucky might have to desert their cargo and take to the canoes; the rest landed in coves above Quebec in order to put the finishing touches before transferring the staves to the merchants. The normally heavy freight rates were reduced when a plentiful harvest brought many ships to Quebec. Then the holds were filled with wheat and staves were piled on the deck. The Canadian product found a ready market in London but the pressure of Baltic merchants, it was said, prevented the amendment in the law which would have qualified it for the bounty paid on staves from Europe. The extensive wood-cutting alarmed the deputy surveyor, John Collins, who claimed the king's right to all trees fit for masts, a claim protested by English owners who found it convenient for this purpose to stand on what they claimed to be French law.[38]

Most other industries in the province were purely local or auxiliary to the fur trade and fisheries. Enterprising merchants early ventured on a distillery in Quebec city, hoping to save the drain of specie to the other colonies for rum. The first attempt failed and not only because the distiller was unskilled. Capital and other essentials were wanting: what was needed, said a disgruntled promoter, was a man who could distil without yeast, molasses, corn, or money. By 1771, after some initial loss, another distillery was producing 70,000 gallons, not much more than a quarter even of the amount cleared at Quebec, without counting what came in by Albany, but still hailed as a hopeful beginning. During the next twenty years this industry saw a steady expansion.[39]

The St Maurice iron-works, belonging to the Crown, were, like the king's posts, leased to a company of merchants, English and Canadian. They employed as manager one Pelissier, who produced iron stoves and kettles for the local trade, axes and hatchets, which also went up country, and pig iron for export to England. His Canadian career came to an end after he consented, perhaps under pressure, to make cannon balls for the invading Americans to use against Quebec. The iron works continued, favoured by the accessibility and excellent quality of the ore. Encouraged by the venture, a company of English and Americans in 1773 anticipated the twentieth century by pursuing in the solid rock north of Lake Superior a hopeful vein of copper. Perhaps fortunately for them it petered out after thirty inches.[40]

It was hoped for a time that a by-product of Canadian timber could be turned to profit. Potash was required for bleaching British textiles and the annual production of wood ash in the province promised an ample supply of raw material. The experiment was not a success, the freight charges being too heavy for any but potash of the finest quality, and the unskilled manufacturer being "capable only of turning gold into dross," according to one who had lost more gold than he could afford. Unfortunately, ashes from every little village along the river had been collected with great efficiency, providing a tangible and depressing monument to the temporary failure of the enterprise.[41]

The great object of every merchant was to meet the bills on the goods shipped out each spring by sending back in the fall furs, oil, wheat, staves, lumber, iron, and anything else that would sell. A modest little trade which yielded some profit was carried on throughout this period by Canadian merchants. "Capillaire" was a syrup made from extract of maidenhair fern, sweetened and flavoured with orange blossoms. The London merchants who received it from Quebec, no doubt in the form of leaves, reported that it sold very well, and urged their correspondents to maintain and if possible increase the supply. This export links Canada pleasantly with contemporary culture, for Dr Johnson was among the many gentlemen in England and France who used it to enhance the flavour of their port wine.[42]

In exchange for their few staples Quebec merchants imported not only the bulk of the goods for the Indian trade, but all the luxuries and many of the necessities of the Canadian community – sugar, wine, spices, coffee, wax and window glass, shoes, including the solid working shoe technically described as "diablement fort," blankets, woollens, cottons, and, in small quantities, the silk stockings and other costly and fashionable articles of dress desired by both sexes and by a variety of classes. As the years went by and it was known that every thrifty farmer had his bag of coins tucked away, it was worth some time and trouble to the merchants to bring in such goods as would draw them from their hiding place. This feat was not to be accomplished without honest effort: " . . . the inhabitants up here are not such a fool as a menny thinks," reported a local storekeeper, complaining of the quality of the goods consigned to him.[43]

There was also considerable profit to be made in handling the increasing trade within the province. Every fall apples, pumpkins, melons, and nuts, as well as wheat, went down the river, while great barrels of cod, green and dry, salt salmon, eels, and oil, went up. Frequently, too, a reliable shipmaster would be entrusted at Quebec with a little barrel of oysters for some favoured merchant or churchman in Montreal, and would bring back perhaps on his return voyage choice pears from the celebrated orchards of the Seminary. Hay and peas were always in demand down river, and bearskin blankets for the long winter. In good years there was a sale in Quebec for the chairs of pearwood or elmwood sent down from Montreal, Quebec sending up in return homespun material, the everyday wear of the great majority of the people. As a trade article it was also used to make the sacks much in demand for the transport of wheat and flour.[44]

After 1760 all these potentially profitable exchanges had to be reorganized and developed in a country still primitive in many ways, impoverished by war, and suffering all the shock and dislocation attendant on a sudden change of government and laws; in a country, moreover, accustomed to paternalism and now turned over without preparation to a considerable measure of free enterprise. The organizers of trade and industry met most of the usual obstacles, some in an unusual form.

There was a shortage of labour, skilled and unskilled. In 1762 in the city of Quebec, with a population of over seven thousand, Murray counted only seventy servants, male and female, a very small proportion for that time in a centre of government and trade. For his own farm he determined to import negroes, for "the Canadians will not work for anyone but themselves." Many people did use slaves. A number of negroes and panis (Indian slaves) were in the country at the time of the Conquest and more negroes were imported. The community, however, was not adapted to slavery. Murray proposed to bring in suitable wives for his negroes. Pierre Guy in Montreal, owning a pretty young panise, on whom he set a high value, and a strong and reliable negro lad, who handled his merchandise, was apparently unable to provide matrimonial happiness for them, and, in despair at their licentious tendencies, finally sent the girl to board at a convent until she could be sold, and the boy up country as a labourer on the portage service organized at Niagara to expedite the passage of trading canoes. Negroes were used as mill hands, and it was proposed to carry out the unpleasant but necessary duty of sweeping chimneys in Quebec by a contractor employing slaves. The number of slaves in the province was never large, however, and there seems to have been no thought of relieving the shortage by any large-scale importation.[45]

It was indeed free and skilled labour that was most needed, and there is evidence of considerable pressure to secure it. St Ours, a seigneur in the district of Montreal, wrote his neighbour, Mme La Corne, that if she did not settle her miller's debt to him she would see the man in prison and her mill closed down. Another man was released from a

Quebec prison by employers who settled his debt of £60 on condition that he go up country three years as a wintering trader.[46] On a somewhat higher level, it was difficult to find for the river schooners captains who were at once honest and competent seamen, and sufficiently literate to deal with bills of lading. Where the captain was unreliable it was not unknown for the wine to turn to water in the casks as the ship proceeded to Montreal. Confidential clerks essential to merchants who did business, as so many did, in both cities, posed another problem. Samuel Jacobs and Benjamin Price both lost money, Price very heavily, from absconding clerks. The incompetence of the managers was blamed, no doubt with some justice, for the failure of the potash works and the slow progress of the distilleries. As in the other colonies where a labourer could so easily be a farmer, and a clerk a storekeeper, there was no easy remedy. In Quebec, where the seasonal nature of employment imposed a hardship on all wage workers and many independent craftsmen, the problem was particularly intractable.[47]

Mere physical obstacles as well as human inadequacy complicated the merchants' task of moving things. The rivers alone made possible a generous exchange of goods along the slender threads of settlement, but the St Lawrence was no easy road. Below Quebec the channel was notoriously difficult, and a first concern of government and merchants alike was the proper apprenticeship and training of pilots. Under the French regime the Jesuit college, now closed, had helped meet this special need by classes in hydrography. Later in the period government gave encouragement to the fixing of buoys and other markers, and to the improvement of charts. Transport along the upper river to Montreal also presented problems. Although small ocean-going vessels, drawing no more than sixteen feet, could go to Montreal, in the early years most goods from abroad were cleared at Quebec and forwarded by the river schooners. There were constant complaints from Montreal at the charges of forwarding agents and at their delay in forwarding goods entrusted to them when more profitable freight appeared. Nor was navigation above Quebec easy. Schooners missing the channel could be wrecked on the rocky ledges that came very near the surface, especially when wind and tide happened to be contrary.[48]

Most of the freighting was done by water in summer, but trains of sleighs with goods for the upper country might set out from Quebec to Montreal in the early spring by the main road north of the river. A "postal service," for forwarding not only letters but travellers along this road, was established between Quebec and Montreal during the military regime, and later extended to New York by way of Skenesborough and Albany. Letter carriers made the round trip between Quebec and Montreal in a week. This service was organized by Hugh Finlay, a land agent from North Carolina, who, perhaps, welcomed the appointment in the first place as a means of extending his land business in Quebec. Compelled to cut his American connections after 1775, he became prominent in Quebec as a merchant and as a member of the council.

Finlay found himself pressing hard, and for long in vain, for the establishment of a monopoly in public transportation. Under his administration, post houses were established at regular intervals along the road, and the postmasters were obliged to maintain horses, carriages, and, where necessary, canoes for forwarding letters and their carriers, and travellers. They often failed to meet their responsibilities because, as Finlay insisted, they were not given the monopoly which alone would have enabled them to do so with a reasonable profit to themselves. As it was, in busy seasons on the farm, and in bad weather, all traffic was left to the postmaster, whereas when work was slack and the weather good, his neighbours would move in and undercut his prices. Although Finlay's appointment depended on the postmaster general in Great Britain, the council alone was competent to give him the authority needed in his office. In spite of all his representations he was left to cope with the forces of free enterprise as best he could. The result was that many letters, including some government letters, went by private hands.[49]

Postal services necessarily depended on roads and ferries. It was the complaint of postmen (that is, of the keepers of post houses) that their horses were ruined by being driven hard in bad weather over bad roads. In theory the roads should have been well maintained. Under the military regime they had been the responsibility of the captains of militia. Murray early appointed as *grands voyers*, or surveyors, two Canadians in whom he had confidence, and who also served the government in other capacities, F. J. Cugnet and Hertel de Rouville. For these men he recommended an annual salary of a hundred pounds each, because in addition to attending to roads they could "furnish government with intelligence from the distant parts of the province." The surveyors were authorized to exact from every man eight days' work with cart and tools, defaulters being reported to the justices' sessions to be punished by fines. The system did not work perfectly. The surveyors were accused of levying fines arbitrarily on their own authority; the deputy surveyor, John Collins (an imperial, not a local, appointment), complained that these expensive appointments deprived him of his work and of his legitimate fees. Nevertheless Murray's decision that labour exacted from Canadians should, if possible, be under the direction of Canadians was politically wise, and the roads were probably no worse than they would have been under Collins' immediate supervision.[50]

The operation of ferries, unlike the postal service, was maintained as a monopoly. The exclusive right of the seigneur to operate a ferry within his own domain was recognized, on condition that the ferry be kept in good repair. In other places private persons were given ferrying rights for three years at a time on condition of maintaining an efficient service.[51]

In this country of water transport, wharves and landing places were a primary consideration to all traders and merchants. By customary law land along the river between high and low water marks was the king's domain. As the smallest boat must have somewhere to tie up, and as freight ships required good berths and solid wharves for unloading, there was much debate as trade increased about how this portion of the king's domain could best be used in the interest of his subjects. In Quebec, where river and ocean shipping mingled, crowded together along the edge of the strip of land that made the lower town, the best use of available space became a bitter issue between Murray and the merchants, and also between Canadians and English. The controversy affords an early example of a clear-cut division on an economic issue between English merchants and the Canadians.

English merchants, and at least one Canadian, were soon securing from the governor and council grants of land for houses and wharves along the St Charles River, and around the headland into the St Lawrence. Over the area under Cape Diamond, the King's Wharf and the adjoining dock or *cul de sac*, there was a prolonged and bitter dispute. The wharf with its slip for building and launching ships was in a ruinous condition and, along with the dock, required considerable expenditure to make it serviceable. An early proposal of English merchants to construct a new and smaller wharf a little distance down river was opposed by Canadians on the ground that it would encroach on the beach reserved for the unloading and sale of firewood, and that such interference would raise the price of that essential commodity. The merits of the case cannot be determined at this distance of time, but the pattern of the dispute is familiar, the English believing that the Canadians were inimical to trade and "progress," and the Canadians that the English in the pursuit of private profit were indifferent to the interests of the consumer. The matter was debated sharply in petition and counter-petition in 1764. A wharf was erected at this place eventually, but perhaps not at this time.[52]

The debate over the King's Wharf and the adjacent dock continued. It was obvious to everyone that they should be repaired and made fit for government service and for commerce, but mercantile jealousy and rivalry and, it must be added, weakness on the part of the government, caused prolonged uncertainty and delay. The matter was complicated by personal issues. Thomas Ainslie had come to Quebec frankly hoping that he would profit by Murray's advancement. Murray, having first put Ainslie in charge of the king's posts, later appointed him collector of the customs that he proposed to levy. Ainslie perhaps was given the use of the King's Wharf for private as well as public purposes, for Murray's conduct in "giving away and turning the King's . . . docks and wharfs into private property" was attacked by the grand jury in 1764. Later Ainslie petitioned the council formally for the use of the wharf on condition that he keep it in repair. Other merchants counter-petitioned, complaining that wharves and landing places in Quebec were the worst of any city on the continent and offering to raise £2,000 rather than see the King's Wharf go into private hands. Collins, the deputy surveyor, supported the merchants, stating that the proposed alienation of the wharf was contrary to the king's interest.

During Carleton's regime, Ainslie's petition was rejected, and after some complicated negotiations, the wharf was leased to Alexander Johnston and others for thirty years, the lease terminable on a year's notice with compensation; included were detailed provisions on the repair and upkeep of the wharf, the clearing and maintenance of the dock and the approaches to it, and a fixed tariff of the maximum fees that could be charged for the docking and unloading of ships.

As Ainslie was Murray's friend and Johnston a protégé of Carleton it might be suspected that each governor did his best to serve his own friend regardless of the public interest. Such suspicions may be groundless. The only alternative to public maintenance, impossible for want of public funds, was private management under public regulation, and each governor may have done his duty by favouring the man or group that seemed the most reliable personally and financially. In this, as in other matters, the merchants appear to have been unduly factious and self seeking. They did, however, have a right to complain that, under governors powerful enough to ignore factions if they chose, it took ten years to arrange for the maintenance of the principal wharf of the principal trading city in the province, the meeting place of ships from two thousand miles across the ocean and goods from two thousand miles inland. For this exhibition of incompetence Murray and Carleton must share the blame. The merchants might be excused for thinking that an assembly would have done better.[53]

Warehouses and storage facilities of all kinds were much needed and could be costly because of the nature of the goods and the seasonal character of the trade. Woollens arriving in the fall and furs sent down in the spring might have to be stored for months, and both needed special protection against the perils of damp, moth, rats, and mice. Wheat, weighty and bulky in relation to its value, represented a different kind of problem. Overloaded sheds were liable to "open" or collapse; damp wheat heated and sprouted, causing serious loss. For furs and trade goods there was a great demand for stone-lined vaults in houses along St Paul's Street in Montreal, but ordinary cellars and sheds might have to serve. In Quebec new granaries and storehouses were going up along the waterfront.

One special danger to stored goods, especially in Montreal, was fire. The frequent fires, sometimes widespread and disastrous, added one more hazard to the merchants' calling. Ill-constructed or "false" chimneys choked with soot, hot ashes stored in wooden boxes, careless smokers, sparks on the highly inflammable wooden shingles heated by the brilliant spring sun, caused numerous outbreaks which occasionally got beyond control. The fire of May 1765 destroyed a large quantity of merchandise, as well as many houses, in Montreal. Fortunately it occurred after the spring boats had gone up country and before the bulk of the furs had come down, or the loss would have been much greater. The returns of losses from this fire show a number of men operating in rented storage space, selling goods on commission for merchants in New York or Boston, an illustration of the way in which some with scanty capital were trying to establish themselves. To protect against the constant danger of fire, ordinances were passed forbidding false chimneys, enforcing regular sweeping, and forbidding the use of wooden shingles. Voluntary associations of merchants organized fire watchers, a better water supply, fire engines, and pumps. The fires continued, but peace and prosperity enabled more Montreal merchants to build houses of stone, with relatively fireproof vaults, and storehouses for their own use and for the accommodation of their correspondents in Quebec. One commodity was not acceptable in any private house. Gunpowder was probably stored by the army until 1771 when the merchants, English and Canadian, prepared to build a magazine of their own.[54]

Merchants in the two cities were dependent on one another for the adequate storage and forwarding of goods, and also for numerous and varied services of debt collection, credit, and exchange in a province where there were few professional lawyers and no banks. For such services there seems to have been no charge. They went on each other's errands with diligence and patience, confident of a return in kind.

One chronic problem weighed on all alike, and appears with wearisome frequency in the correspondence of merchants and officials. Quebec, a debtor province under England as under France, was always short of specie. Every effort was made to export enough goods to maintain a balance, but every fall bills of exchange in London were at a premium if they could be secured at all. This problem, common to all the colonies, was complicated in Quebec by two special circumstances: the continued circulation of pre-Conquest paper money, and the difficulty of establishing a uniform currency for the province.

The existence in Canada of quantities of paper money of doubtful value in notes and bills of exchange at the time of the Conquest was a cause of embarrassment to the new governors and to the holders. The attitude of the government altered with the times. Military governors, anxious to cut all ties with France, at first assured Canadians that the money was quite value-less, and forbade its circulation. As it became clear that the colony would be retained by Britain the attitude changed. The British government under-took to negotiate for the payment of France's obligations to those who were now to be British subjects, and instructions were sent to Quebec that all paper money in the hands of Canadians remaining in the province was to be registered. Inevitably, speculation in the money was going on, buyers offering small quantities of hard cash for paper that had long been idle and fruitless in the hands of the owners. Murray received orders from Britain to check this speculation and he gladly obeyed, revealing that he had him-self been invited to share in it, denouncing those who would thus defraud the Canadians, and urging all holders of paper money not to part with it. Murray acted rightly according to his knowledge, although it seems that the suddenness of his announcement embarrassed some who had been using paper money surreptitiously for normal trading purposes. As it turned out, it would have been better for the Canadians whom he wished to protect to sell the paper for what it would bring. After long negotiations France agreed to redeem the money at a considerable discount, not with cash, but with bonds bearing interest at $4\frac{1}{2}$ per cent. In 1771, the French govern-ment declared itself bankrupt and all payments ceased.

Meanwhile in the province and abroad, in spite of Murray, speculation by merchants and others, Canadian and English, Jew and Gentile, went merrily on. In 1764 buyers advertised for paper money in the Quebec *Gazette*, offering 15 per cent of the face value; others in the country were taking it at 10 per cent or less, giving goods in exchange, and this when it was being negotiated at 20 and 30 per cent in England and France. Al-though some individuals no doubt suffered severely, much of the ultimate loss must have been distributed widely among the various people through whose hands the money passed over a period of some fifteen years.

It has been suggested that losses on the paper currency handicapped Canadian merchants in their competition with the English, and must be accepted as one of the reasons why big business in Quebec eventually moved into English hands. No doubt some Canadian merchants lost money, but it is safe to assume that some, at least, profited from the speculation in which they certainly took part. As few had much reserve capital, what paper money they purchased would be turned over promptly to firms in London and Paris who handled it, and who would suffer the final loss. There is, indeed, no reason to suppose that the Canadian merchants had any serious difficulty, as merchants, in adjusting to the British rule. They transferred their accounts to French-speaking merchants who were already resident in London, and they had no difficulty in getting reasonable credit. It was indeed not easy to get from Britain drygoods, wines, and other beverages exactly suited to Canadian tastes, but here the English merchants suffered as much as, or perhaps more than, their Canadian rivals. The controversy over the management and use of wharves and docks at Quebec does suggest that by 1770, at least, Canadian merchants were less immediately interested in wholesale trade than the English. The general trade situation, no doubt, reflected conditions already observed in the fur trade. Business which had been in the hands of the capitalists retired to France now passed into those of Englishmen with capital or large credit. Smaller Canadian merchants continued to operate as they had before. They were not able to step into the shoes of their departed Canadian rivals but, far from being worse off than before, they shared in the general prosperity.[55]

Such hard money as there was in the province was of a bewildering variety: French crowns and livres, Spanish piastres, Portuguese "Joes," and British pounds, shillings, and pence. Murray followed the colonial practice of overvaluing all coins in relation to sterling in order to keep them in the country. Unfortunately, the values adopted by other colonies differed. As military governor Murray had used the Halifax valuation in Quebec; as civil governor he introduced New England currency for the whole province, attaching to the ordinance a table of equivalents which named twelve different coins from five different countries. New England currency had the practical advantage of equating the livre, in which Canadians did their thinking and accounting, with the English shilling. It was, however, disliked by Quebec merchants, who continued to keep accounts in Halifax currency, and it was ignored by Montreal merchants whose close links with Albany and New York made it almost essential for them to use the low-value New York shilling. Thus in practice and on paper, while pounds and shillings were legal tender, business men had to struggle with four different shillings – sterling, Halifax, New England, and New York – to say nothing of the mysterious "Michilimackinac currency" of the up-country fur trader.

In Montreal Canadians naturally continued to do business and keep accounts in livres and sous. As the livre contained twenty sous, its equation with the shilling of twelve pence was confusing for small transactions. There was also such a dearth of small coins that many retailers took to making change in their own paper in notes of very small denomination. To add to the confusion, clipped "Joes" (worth four pounds at par) appeared, so that merchants when they balanced accounts had to state the weight as well as the denomination of coins transferred. The Ursuline convent in Three Rivers, receiving the bill of a merchant at Quebec for 1,055 livres, 8 sous, sent back a bag containing 17 "Joes," 7 guineas, a gold piece valued at 36 livres, a piastre, a shilling, and 4 sous. With all this rich variety, coins were in short quantity. Much business was done by barter and promissory notes expressed not in pounds or livres, but in minots of wheat, were circulated.[56]

Under French rule, the Canadians had grown accustomed to a paternal government which accepted the responsibility for maintaining, by expenditures in the colony, something like a balance of trade. Shortly after the establishment of civil government Canadian merchants sent in a memorial explaining that between 1749 and 1755 Canadian exports had paid for about a third of the necessary imports, the remainder being made up by the pay of the troops. As troop payments were now greatly reduced by the peace, they suggested that the inevitable deficit be covered either by permanently stationing much larger detachments of troops in the province, or by commissioning the building of ships of war to be paid for by bills of exchange on London. Other representations from Canadians and from Governor Murray, while not supporting these unrealistic proposals, did insist that government loans or investments of some sort must be employed to correct the imbalance of trade. The British government did not respond to these suggestions, satisfied, no doubt, that with peace and low taxes, the economic development of the colony could be left to private investors.[57]

This challenge or opportunity had been taken up by London investors and merchants, English and American, who moved to Quebec. The fur trade, the seal fisheries, wheat, and lumber all offered opportunities for speculative investment. They attracted men, often men of little capital, who were anxious to make their way. Whether their investments were large or small they were generally risking all they had, and sometimes more. They were adventurers in an alien country, responsible to supporters in London who were not prepared to subsidize the incompetent or the unlucky. To succeed they needed to be patient, diligent, and resourceful; perhaps also hard and unscrupulous. Many of them were aware that the only alternative to speedy success was complete failure. They convinced themselves that, forced as they were to incur very heavy risks, if they were not allowed to manage their own affairs with English laws and an English assembly, the government imposed on them should be prompt to understand, and efficient to cope with, all barriers to trade, all deficiencies in communications, in public facilities, in currency, and in the laws which regulated commercial dealings. These considerations may not excuse their unjust accusations against Murray or their seeming indifference to Canadian interests and susceptibilities. They do make it possible to understand why the merchants insisted with such vigour and sincerity that essentially their interests were identical with those of the province.

CHAPTER 7

Subordination from the First
to the Lowest

The English merchants looked hopefully on Lieutenant-Governor Guy Carleton when he arrived to take up his duties in September 1766. In 1768 he was to succeed Murray as governor. Although Carleton, unlike Murray, gave an impression of coldness and reserve, his was not a calm nature. He was ambitious, proud, sensitive, and markedly resentful of any affront to his office or person. Benevolent, humane, competent, a man of wide interests and large views, he was an imperialist of the school of Warren Hastings rather than of Burke. With all his ability it was his weakness that he saw in himself more of the insight of genius than he really possessed.

Carleton already knew something of the divisions in Quebec, and was determined not to be discredited by them. He intended to be designated governor, successor to Murray who, he hoped, would not return to Quebec. He was not the man to be long content with a subordinate role on a narrow provincial stage.

Carleton had, indeed, many advantages over the unfortunate Murray. He came directly from London, he had been personally briefed by officials there, and he had had access to many of the papers dealing with Quebec affairs, including the complaints against Murray.[1] He knew Fowler Walker, the merchants' agent in London, and had learned from him something of the merchants' point of view. Two senior officials who reached Quebec about the same time, the new chief justice, William Hey, and the attorney general, Francis Maseres, were able men, of sound training and satisfactory character. Carleton was assured of such competent advice and respectable behaviour as would give a new authority and dignity to government. Finally, Carleton, in addition to his appointment as civil administrator, had been accorded the necessary power and prestige vainly demanded by Murray. He was commander-in-chief of the troops in the province. He could thus arrive at the city of Quebec with something of the dignity of a French governor. With no intendant, and no independent ecclesiastical authority, only the power of the council and the independence of judges prevented him from enjoying an authority unknown to his French predecessors.

In spite of these advantages Carleton did not underestimate the difficulties of his position. The Canadians were recently conquered, and France had not forgotten her former colony. The law and the constitution remained an unresolved dilemma. The merchants were dissatisfied. In the colonies to the south the dispute over the raising of revenue for imperial defence was causing increasing bitterness. A vain request from Britain for voluntary contributions in 1764 had been followed by Grenville's Stamp Act in 1765. Angry groups in the colonies had resisted to the point of non-importation agreements against British goods. The Stamp Act had been repealed early in the current year, 1766, but many in the colonies still resented and denied the accompanying statutory declaration that the British parliament had a right to impose taxation on them. In Quebec merchants had submitted to the Stamp Act but some were certainly infected with the radical views of Massachusetts.

A slight indication of sympathy for the Americans was discernible in some of the loyal addresses offered to the Lieutenant-Governor on his arrival. Carleton noted this, but his attention was more particularly engaged by an address signed by the magistrates of Quebec and some others. All these were, of course, nominees of Murray, and they included Mabane, Irving, and others who had served Murray on the council. Carleton immediately identified this group as "the party of opposition." He may have been influenced by his new secretary, Cramahé, Murray's former protégé, despised by the Murray party as a turncoat. The Lieutenant-Governor was soon plunged into a contest with this group which threatened to rouse all the old animosities, and to endanger his own career. He emerged from it if not with honour at least with complete success.[2]

It all began with George Allsopp, one of the first of the English merchants to reach Quebec after the Conquest. Allsopp was a man of ability and some education. He had angered Murray by making trouble over the "lantern order" of the military government which compelled private soldiers and all civilians, but not officers, to carry lanterns when they went abroad after dark. He had approved of the hostile address of the Quebec grand jury in the autumn of 1764. He had protested against Murray's maintenance of the monopoly of the king's posts and, in general, he had acted as a leader of the opposition. He was energetic and enterprising. He suffered loss from the early experiments in distilling and potash-making, but was sufficiently successful in the fur and the wheat trade to keep his head above water. In the spring of 1766 he had secured from Henry Ellis the right to act as deputy clerk of the council and deputy provincial secretary. Murray had refused to install him in these offices, giving as his reason Allsopp's factious and disrespectful behaviour. Irving, as administrator, had refused to alter Murray's decision.

Irving had also thwarted Allsopp in the matter of the king's posts. The merchants opposed the lease on the ground that by Murray's own proclamation of 1765 the fur trade was free and monopolies illegal. Allsopp and his partners in 1766 sent goods down river for the trade, and erected buildings near Chicoutimi to shelter goods and traders. Murray was in doubt about the law, but determined to protect the lessors for that year and ordered Allsopp to cease trading. After Murray's departure, as Allsopp persisted, Irving consulted Suckling about the proper means of coercing him. Suckling, too, had doubts about the monopoly, but advised that as Allsopp had no right to acquire land or erect buildings in Indian territory, his buildings could be destroyed. This was ordered by council in August 1766.

On Carleton's arrival in September Allsopp appealed to him against this decision. Carleton, knowing him to be a man of some standing and believing him to be a victim of Murray's personal resentment, was inclined to consider his case favourably. Having called together some members of the council, he referred the question to a committee under Chief Justice Hey. The committee, after careful consideration, reported in favour of Allsopp's claim to the right of free trade. Carleton, therefore, ordered a stay of proceedings against Allsopp. It would have been more prudent for Carleton to have referred the case to the Board of Trade or the Treasury, but this was not his way, and it would have cost Allsopp and his partners, whose claim he believed to be justified, the profits from a year's trading.[3]

The issue of the king's posts was unimportant compared with the political and constitutional dispute of which it was the immediate cause. To deal promptly with Allsopp's complaint Carleton had called the council meeting hastily, summoning the official members only – Irving, his immediate predecessor, Cramahé, his personal secretary, Hey, the Chief Justice, Thomas Mills, the Receiver General, and Goldfrap, Secretary of the Council. There was a good practical reason for this. The matter seemed urgent; the official members could be called at a moment's notice and were free to work continuously in committee. The exclusion of the mercantile element on an issue such as this simplified proceedings, especially as Thomas Dunn was a directly interested party. The procedure, however, was irregular, the arrangements being entered in the council book as a regular meeting to which all members should have been summoned. This error of Carleton's accentuated another grievance of the opposition, the views of the Lieutenant-Governor on precedence in the council. Carleton said that precedence must go to all members appointed by royal warrant or mandamus according to the date of their appointment; and after them, to those appointed in the province by the governor, in virtue of his instructions, but without a mandamus. This meant that Mabane, and other non-official members appointed by Murray, must take the lowest place; one of them might even be denied a place because, owing to the return of Cramahé and to the new appointments, he stood thirteenth in a council officially limited to twelve. The situation was the more irritating because Cramahé had received a mandamus so dated as to preserve his original seniority on the council.

The partial council was taken as a sign that Carleton might be planning in practice to exclude members who would later be eliminated by the arrival from England of mandamuses for nominees of the Lieutenant-Governor. Probably Carleton had in mind only the practice later followed by him and by Haldimand of using the small official group for certain executive and administrative duties. Whatever his intentions, Mabane assumed the worst and determined to challenge him directly. With three of the excluded members he sent, through the sympathetic Irving, a verbal protest to the governor, who answered reassuringly that the meeting had been "no council." To show his goodwill he then invited them all to come to dinner two days later. Next day, however, they presented him with a written remonstrance on his conduct, demanding by implication a written reply.

The remonstrance was a declaration of war. Carleton was rebuked for calling a partial council, but excused because this was said to have been "accident not intention." He was further informed that his views on precedence were entirely erroneous, and that precedence in the council must depend on seniority and not on the king's mandamus. The Lieutenant-Governor was not asked to reconsider his views. He was told bluntly that he was wrong.

As administrator of the province, and military commander-in-chief, Carleton's power was great and his responsibility proportionately heavy. Practical good sense as well as custom required that he be approached with deference, and that any necessary reflections on his principles or policy should be insinuated obliquely, not hurled directly. The presentment of the grand jury, which had so angered Murray, although more abusive, was less arrogant than this "remonstrance" of Mabane and his friends. Although the communication was private, Carleton must have known that all of the Murray party and many more would have read the remonstrance before he received it. Had he been a more experienced administrator, secure in control of a peaceful and undivided community, he could have afforded to make light of the matter. While rebuking the councillors for their blunt and disrespectful language, he could have acknowledged an error of form in summoning the council, and have agreed to refer the question of precedence to his superiors at home. He could even have offered to request mandamuses which would preserve the seniority at least of men like Dunn and Mabane who had served the province faithfully in difficult circumstances. But Carleton, still a "new boy," relatively ignorant of provincial affairs, found himself sharply called to account by the two best informed members of his council, men on whom he ought to have been able to rely to cover his early mistakes and build up his reputation, but who apparently were anxious to take advantage of his mistakes in order to keep him in tutelage. He had no choice. He must either repudiate the remonstrance and subdue the ring-leaders, or he must renounce his hopes of succeeding where Murray had failed, and hand himself over to the party of Mabane until Murray's return reduced him to the shadowy existence of a lieutenant-governor when the governor is present. Carleton had no difficulty in making his choice. He decided to crush the opposition by every means in his power, although he must have been uncertain for a time what the means would be. When his critics came to dine with him on the following day, he gave them to understand that he would consult such councillors as he chose, and maintain the precedence that he believed to be right. As for the remonstrance, they would receive a written answer in due course.

The answer was long in coming. Carleton knew that in his verbal answer he had evaded the issue of the right of all councillors to be summoned to a formal council. To give Mabane anything in writing, or to summon a council, would be to start a long constitutional brawl which would echo unpleasantly across the Atlantic. He summoned no council through the rest of October and November. During November the *Little William* from London brought letters to Murray's friends which led them to assure everyone of his vindication and speedy return. Carleton meanwhile wrote home, emphasizing the issue of precedence on which he was technically right, telling a deliberate falsehood over the affair of the council, casting a mean and false aspersion on the respectable Irving, and speaking slightingly of the others. He had been hoping that, feeling his displeasure, they would resign voluntarily, or offer their submission and make their peace. The news brought by the *Little William* made that improbable, and he bided his time.

Toward the end of the month the Walker case, now two years old, flared up again. Both Carleton and Hey knew that they were especially charged to clear the matter up. Therefore, when Walker produced dubious evidence that six people, three officers and three others, had been implicated in the outrage, the case was taken up by the law officers and Hey issued warrants against all six. It was not quite impossible to believe that officers might have been involved, but when it was learned that warrants had gone out against Judge Fraser, St Luc de La Corne, a leading seigneur and merchant of Montreal, and Joseph Howard, another well-known merchant, the credulity of the inhabitants was overtaxed. Walker's charges were supported by only one person, a private soldier of such character as to be a barely credible witness.

Why Hey decided to issue the warrants is not quite clear. When Carleton authorized execution of the writs by armed soldiers who took the men from their homes at dead of night, carried them down to Quebec, and lodged them in the common jail, the populace was divided between pleasurable excitement that such news should break at the beginning of the dull season, and a genuine sense of horror and sympathy at such harsh treatment of respectable men. Hey added to the resentment by refusing bail because Walker refused his consent, alleging that his life would be in danger. Hey's decision caused surprise even in England; he was a timid man and lacked the courage to take responsibility for Thomas Walker's much-threatened life.

In the city of Quebec, for once, there was an astonishing agreement among all classes, English and Canadian, merchant and soldier, reviling Walker and inveighing against Hey. Someone started a petition to the governor to interfere and secure bail. On Sunday, November 23, after much hurrying in and out of taverns, up and down the steep streets of the city, the petition, signed by large numbers of reputable people, was carried to Carleton. He received it courteously and correctly, refusing to interfere. The decision was Hey's, and it was not for the Lieutenant-Governor to question the law of the Chief Justice.

Others, including Mabane, were less scrupulous. The town was buzzing with criticism of Chief Justice and Lieutenant-Governor; the prisoners received constant visits of respect and sympathy. This was the sort of agitation that had ruined Murray. Carleton determined to stop it; he realized that, fortunately for him, his opponents had overreached themselves. He let it be known through the Attorney General, Maseres, that petitions with over twenty signatures were illegal. Some who had signed were rebuked personally and offered their apologies; others took the hint and called to make their peace with the Lieutenant-Governor. Irving and Mabane, insisting that a petition signed by magistrates was legal, gave no sign of submission; on Thursday, four days after the petition had been presented, they were notified of their dismissal from the council. The following day a reconstituted and submissive council was informed of the dismissal. No reasons were given, but the remonstrance and Carleton's belated written reply were now entered in the council book.

Carleton's action was constitutionally indefensible. The royal instructions allowed suspension of a councillor only by vote of the council after specific charges had been laid, and the accused had been heard in his own defence. Only if there were reasons "not fit to be communicated to the council" could the governor act on his own authority. When he did so he must report to the Board of Trade "his reasons at large" for the suspension, and for the failure to consult the council. It was no wonder that Irving and Mabane were utterly astonished and cast down, assuming as they must have done that their dismissal was a practical impossibility.

If Carleton's conduct was constitutionally and even morally indefensible, it can be argued that the policy of the government and the reckless conduct of Irving and Mabane created a kind of political necessity. Carleton had good reason to believe that under a system where the honest and painstaking Murray could be left without instructions, advice, or support, a victim of local jealousy and malice, the governor who wished to survive would have to serve himself, and not be too dainty in his methods. The event seemed to prove that he had been right in ignoring the letter of his instructions in order to maintain his authority. His dispatches over the council quarrel, to a careful reader obviously inadequate and disingenuous, met with no suspicious inquiries. Only in the following spring there came warm letters from Shelburne, the minister, commending "your prudence and conduct in remedying the disorders and allaying the heats which had prevailed in your government."

Although Irving and Mabane were victims of harsh and unconstitutional conduct, Carleton was not quite wrong in accusing them of factious behaviour. He had the right to expect that they would at least have consulted him before meddling in the delicate and dangerous Walker case. Mabane even allowed himself to speak with contempt of Carleton's supposed pretensions to succeed Murray and to accuse him of stirring the dead embers of the Walker affair to get himself a reputation at home. On hearing this Carleton, as commander-in-chief, announced in the orders of the day that if Mabane, as surgeon of the garrison, did not govern his tongue he would be dismissed. To Mabane this was "the utmost malice of party rage." He was apparently unaware that his own party rage was engaging him to use his considerable social and political influence to dislodge the Lieutenant-Governor, and that he hardly had the right to be surprised if Carleton fought back with such weapons as were at his disposal.[4]

Carleton was careful to be consistent in his policy. Although needing support and inclined to favour Allsopp, he avoided creating an Allsopp party. Only after a reference to the Board of Trade and an investigation by a committee of council was Allsopp installed as deputy in the offices that he had purchased. Carleton's comment was characteristic; even if Allsopp had suffered hardship it was well to demonstrate publicly that his disrespect to Murray as a royal governor was an offence not to be condoned.[5]

Having defied his opponents and consolidated his position, Carleton turned to the routine work of his administration. Although hampered by want of funds, he characteristically paid some attention to the material surroundings and setting of his government. He was impressed with the magnificent site of the capital city, and with the public buildings, religious and secular, "large and even magnificent," though many had been damaged in the siege. The Château St Louis was repaired and fitted for Carleton's reception, a work which would commend itself to his natural taste for pomp, and to his humanity, as the ruinous walls were threatening to fall over the cliff to the danger of His Majesty's humbler subjects living below. To the left of the castle and slightly down the slope stood the spacious and dignified bishop's palace. Repairs to this building were completed by the energy of the bishop. It was then rented to government to the mutual advantage of church and state. The bishop secured much needed revenue and Carleton enjoyed a fine set of government offices in a splendid situation, and conveniently close to his residence.[6]

In the council Carleton introduced a number of useful procedures impossible in the experimental years of Murray's government. The standing rule passed by council that there should be submitted for its approval French translations of all drafts of ordinances presented in English introduced a necessary measure of bilingualism. Much business was referred to committees presided over by Chief Justice Hey. Freed from routine work, the Lieutenant-Governor could give more attention to the province at large, especially to the second capital, Montreal, where he spent a part of every year in a house retained for his use. Another advantage of the committee method was that, fully informed of deliberations but taking no part in them, he might influence discussion indirectly, while avoiding the rough and tumble of debate, or any premature expression of his own opinion. A further departure from Murray's informal paternalism was ordered by the Treasury Board. One of the demands of the grand jury of 1764 was granted by the institution of a regular half-yearly audit of the provincial accounts, which were laid before council and entered on the record.[7]

If Murray's accounts, as Carleton not very charitably pointed out to the home government, had been in some confusion, they reflected a complete confusion in public finance which harassed both men. The problem was a double one: What were the legitimate sources of provincial revenue, and by whom should the revenue be collected and administered?

Before the inauguration of civil government Murray had continued the duties of the French regime on imported wines and spirits. After 1764, believing that under the civil government he had no taxing power, he depended on bills drawn on London. By 1766 the duties were levied again, the British law officers having declared them legal. All merchants complained. They had obeyed the Stamp Act, but insisted that these duties were unconstitutional. The government having no storehouse, they were allowed to clear goods directly from the ships, giving notes for the amount of the duty. These notes they refused to honour. When Irving, following instructions, attached them for debt, some protested by spending a few hours in prison before arranging bail. Carleton on his arrival had to cope with this modest version of the American no-taxes campaigns. He ordered prosecution of the merchants. Chief Justice Hey instructed the jury that they were to determine only the fact of the promise to pay, not the legality of the duties. The jury, no doubt instructed by other authorities that juries had before now corrected the tyranny of law, dealt with fact and law together, returning a verdict for the defendants, who were discharged.

Not content with this, the merchants were also suing Murray for having collected duties contrary to law under the military regime. Perhaps from F. J. Cugnet, who was in charge of French records, they were led to believe that there was no evidence of what the French levies had been. The local authorities did try to stop the suits by offering to guarantee the return of any money collected without authority. The merchants, however, carried their case to London where the missing evidence appeared. Murray, always impulsive and informal, had carried off with him certain records, including the customs books, which he was now happy to produce for the confusion of his former foes. The merchants did, however, get a partial refund as Murray had compromised his legal position by raising the duty on West Indian rum in order to favour the British product. Following this decision in 1768, merchants in Quebec, far from paying any taxes, were being paid £2,000 in all, a refund of excess duties with interest at 5 per cent.

The Treasury Board was still bent on the last word. They proposed to collect the duties, recognized as valid, and to make them retroactive to 1766. Carleton wisely pleaded against any such move. It would, he insisted, ruin some merchants. He also made it clear that the merchants were wholly unconvinced of the legality of the duties. How, they argued, could anyone interpret French taxes on French West Indian goods as meaning English taxes on British rum? The Treasury Board finally yielded. Carleton, like Murray, met his expenses by drawing bills on London, bills which by a special ruling dating from Murray's time would be his personal responsibility should his expenditures be disallowed.

The very important question of taxation had been fought on legal grounds. It is clear the motives and the final decision were political. The merchants favoured public revenue and public expenditure, but they objected to a revenue derived chiefly from the customs duties, and they were determined to demonstrate the necessity of an assembly. The government yielded, partly no doubt on Carleton's representations of political expediency, and partly because, the entire system of law and government being under consideration with a view to new legislation, it was hardly worth while to risk disorder in a hitherto loyal colony for the sake of the annual five or six thousand pounds that might be collected.[8]

Compared with the complicated wrangle over the French duties, the question of the administration of the revenue in Quebec was simple. It is worth noticing because it offers a good illustration of the confusion of imperial, local, and deputed authorities in the eighteenth-century colony. Customs duties were collected by an imperial officer, and they, with all other crown revenues, were paid over to a receiver general appointed by and responsible to the Treasury Board. Under Murray a temporary deputy had acted as receiver general. In 1766 Thomas Mills, appointed in England, came in person to the province. He had precise instructions to deal with all revenues and, having paid the current provincial expenses, to turn the surplus over to the Treasury Board in return for the money paid by Great Britain during the previous two years of Murray's administration. The Treasury Board required Mills to look into revenues from crown lands, from quitrents and seigneurial payments, from the king's posts, and from ecclesiastical property, it being assumed that at least some of the lands of the secular orders would be sequestrated. Mills took his new duties so seriously that there might have been a conflict of authority in the province. He informed Irving that he was responsible for all revenues and for all crown property, and stated that he expected the full support and co-operation of the council. He implied, further, that he, and not the council, should have the final decision on grants of crown lands for wharves and other purposes. As for provincial expenditures, he would personally contract for all necessary services, but he would need no warrant from the governor to spend money, nor would he account for his disbursements to any provincial authority.

The surprising thing is that Mills's instructions, drawn by the Treasury Board independently of the Board of Trade, did almost warrant this generous interpretation, which would have given him the power of the purse so completely as to reduce the governor and council to mere ciphers in civil affairs. Fortunately Mills was not a powerful character and Irving was tactful. He reported the matter to the Board of Trade and in the meantime he seems to have conveyed to Mills that he could collect no money at all in the circumstances without the co-operation of the governor and council and the law officers. Mills made no attempt to dictate to Carleton, presenting his accounts in due form in the spring of 1767. That year he returned home, and thereafter, for many years, his work was done by a deputy, first by Cramahé, and then by a series of other deputies, none of whom magnified his office unduly.[9]

Carleton had a special reason for regretting the want of a regular revenue. A reform which he had much at heart was an alteration of the method of paying officials partly or wholly in fees, to a fixed and regular salary for all. His humanity and his sense of dignity were both outraged by the spectacle of government officials touting for business and receiving their pay too often from those who could ill afford it. The worst scandal was the innocent man held in prison for jail fees, but Carleton believed that the fees in Quebec were generally too high for the wealth of the province, and that they were particularly odious to Canadians, who were unused to this form of taxation.

Not much could be done. If the fees were too high for the province they were probably not too high for the needs of many of the officials, who, according to custom, bought their deputyships for cash down, plus an annual rent. Carleton did do something for the dignity of the Chief Justice, securing him an allowance in lieu of fees. He was also quick to check exactions where he discovered them, sometimes in his zeal for justice going beyond the law. He engaged in a sharp exchange of letters with Ainslie, the customs collector, over supposedly excessive fees. Ainslie had the law on his side, but on being threatened with suspension from office prudently submitted. The fee system, however, remained. It was, perhaps, too much to expect Britain to make an additional allowance for official salaries to a colony which had just successfully asserted its right to pay no taxes at all.[10]

One reform of Carleton's did check an abuse in the exaction of fees. His crowning work before his return to Britain in 1770 was the elaborate ordinance on the administration of justice passed in February of that year. The measure was typical of his general policy, favouring as it did a benevolent and competent bureaucracy, rather than the looser methods of local control typical of English government.

By the ordinance of 1764 justices of the peace were empowered to determine disputes over property to the amount of five pounds when sitting alone and up to thirty pounds when in quarter sessions. This system had not worked well, although Murray had done his best, commissioning half-pay officers and the apparently more substantial and respectable of the English merchants. The abler of these men found themselves overwhelmed with their duties which included not only civil disputes, but also the ordinary criminal and police work of the justice of the peace. The civil jurisdiction was a burden to the conscientious, for they had not the necessary knowledge, nor the leisure to acquire it. Fortunately, in spite of the legendary attachment of the Canadians to suits at law, many minor disputes did not reach the justices, being settled by the priests or the former militia captains. In Terrebonne, near Montreal, there was even a seigneurial court maintained by Colonel Christie and others, with a Canadian judge and attorney. How much business was done there and whether its authority was ever challenged is not known.[11]

There were two very serious objections to the justices' courts. They were empowered, and even obliged, to issue executions against real property as well as against movables, even for small debts. One justice ordered the sale of a house and lot to satisfy a debt of sixty-one livres, or about ten dollars, and "there must have been scores of cases in which for an original debt of two or three hundred livres an habitant and his family were cast homeless into the world."[12] Carleton, indeed, stated that three or four hundred families had lost their homes, their lands having been sold for a fraction of their value, but Carleton in reporting grievances was prone to exaggeration. He was presumably referring to the record, however, when he said that in 1770 he ordered the release of sixteen men imprisoned for debt, owing among them less than forty pounds, and half of that in jail fees.

There was another evil even graver than judicial harshness. Not all the justices were busy men. Some were idle, incompetent, and even dishonest, valuing their commissions for the sake of the fees they might charge, and stirring up disputes in order to increase business. "Not a Protestant butcher, or publican became bankrupt who did not apply to be made a justice," was Carleton's picturesque, if highly coloured, comment. They were accused of scandalous irregularities: giving out blank writs, including judgements and executions, to be filled in by private persons, summoning defendants to come great distances to court without allowing the option of immediate payment, or allowing so short a time for the return of a writ that the defendant must lose by default. All these devices played on the ignorance of the Canadians for the benefit of the justice and the bailiff. The costs for collecting one debt of eleven livres amounted to no less than eighty-four livres.

Complaints of these abuses coming to the council from the district of Montreal led to an investigation and to a request to the justices there to establish proper rules for the regulation of their court. The justices returned a somewhat defiant answer, perhaps resenting the criticisms of official Quebec. The result, probably already determined, was the ordinance of February 1770. All civil jurisdiction was taken from the justices and confided to the court of common pleas, the "Canadian" court, which, as Carleton observed with approval, interpreted the reference to "equity" in the ordinance of 1764 to mean Canadian law. To enable the common pleas to deal with the greatly increased load of work, two courts were established, one for each of the districts of Quebec and Montreal. The English term system was abolished for these courts. They were to sit, as judges had under the French regime, continuously except for brief vacations, and for the periods when, for the convenience of suitors, they were to go on circuit through the country districts. Small cases of twelve pounds or less were to be heard every Friday and in such cases there would in no circumstances be an execution against real property; where it was thought desirable to avoid any execution at all the judge might order payment to be made by instalments.

Carleton's reward and vindication for this humane measure came nearly a year later, after he had left the province, in the form of a petition from Robert MacKay, keeper of His Majesty's jail for the district of Montreal, praying to be allowed a salary, "the late ordinance . . . having operated greatly to his disadvantage by reducing the number of prisoners that had usually been committed to the said goal."[13]

The English merchants sympathized more with MacKay than with Carleton and the debtors. They believed that the effect of the ordinance would be to give too much protection to the careless debtor, making the trader and storekeeper fearful of giving credit to anyone, and so doing injury to the economy of a province which operated so largely on credit. Having tried and failed to stir up an agitation among the Canadians, they presented a memorial of their own, signed by fifty names. They received a sharp rebuke from Carleton. Suggestions for improvement of the law, properly presented, he would welcome, but "if in tumultuous meetings, or by dint of numbers only, laws were to be made or abrogated, the lowest dregs of the people, and the most ignorant among them, would, of course, become the law-givers of the country."[14]

The rebuke was accepted meekly enough, but this encounter and exchange between the merchants and Carleton is significant. Carleton was thinking not only of the merits of the law; he resented, as always, any attempt to influence government by the weight of numbers. On the other hand, the merchants were thinking of more than credit and the collection of debts. They objected to a law that made the few common pleas judges "sole arbiters of the whole property of the province." To put such power into the hands of officials dependent, as several were, on salaries, and looking to the governor for other favours was to introduce a state of "slavery and dependence" unsuitable to a trading colony. This was the real issue. The merchants understood very well that Carleton, remedying an abuse, was also bringing the government nearer to his ideal of a benevolent despotism. They could not deny the abuse, but they resented this whittling away of the most English institution in the province.[15]

In fact, for nearly four years the merchants had been discovering that Carleton's political views were very different from their own. No doubt he had come to Canada well briefed by the merchants' correspondents in London, and bent on redressing their grievances. Over the vexed question of the duties he had acted with tact and moderation, working for conciliation while supporting the authority of Britain. The grievances of the fur traders and seal fishers he had taken up warmly, and with a considerable measure of success. Carleton fully shared Shelburne's view that Britain's imperial strength depended on creating and vigorously exploiting new areas of trade. In 1768 he was sending home a picture of Quebec merchants and fur traders spreading out over a vast fur-trading kingdom in the heart of the continent, a kingdom which would provide bases for the advance of exploration parties over the Rockies to the Pacific coast, where they would make contact with traders from the East Indies. There was nothing parochial in Carleton's outlook. He saw the trading empire as a whole; he thought not in terms of provinces and rivers, but of oceans and continents. With these large ideas on commerce, however, he gradually revealed a political viewpoint which to the merchants was narrow and reactionary.[16]

Carleton never forgot that his first responsibility was the security and well-being of the province of Quebec. Apart from the restoration of order he had certain special responsibilities. As commander of the troops in the province he had to examine and report on the defences of the colony, a question which caused anxiety in view of the critical relations with France and the American colonies. He was aware of the possibility of an attack through either of the two great entrances into the province, the inland waterways that linked New York and Albany with the St Lawrence by way of Lake Champlain, and the passage from the ocean through the gulf and up the St Lawrence. He found no adequate preparations for the defence of either route. He recommended repair of the forts on Lake Champlain and the erection of a strong citadel on Cape Diamond. These measures would deter any but a full-scale invasion from France; and they would enable Carleton, co-operating along the Champlain route with Gage at New York, to contain possible outbreaks in New York and New England and to isolate both from possible areas of disaffection in the southern colonies.[17]

Knowing, however, that only a serious emergency would persuade Britain to heavy expenditures on defence works, Carleton also gave his attention immediately to a civil responsibility inseparable from defence. He had to maintain obedience and loyalty to government in a province inhabited almost entirely by representatives of the very people who might soon be in arms against Great Britain, the newly conquered children of France and the newly arrived immigrants from the American colonies. It was believed that many officers, Canadians and others, who had seen service in Canada were being maintained on army pay and rations in France, awaiting the time when they might be sent to Canada to lead the Canadians once more against Britain. Clearly, to win Canadians over even to a passive submission and loyalty would be worth as much as a citadel. Through a wise system of government and laws, Carleton hoped to do this and much more.

In the spring of 1767, Shelburne, too, was considering the Canadian question. He favoured the usual pattern of American government, a governor, council, and assembly. As a man of liberal outlook he was prepared to meet the special conditions in Quebec by admitting Roman Catholics, although limited to a minority, into both council and assembly. The provincial legislature, thus constituted, should, he thought, proceed immediately to "assimilate such of the French laws as it may be necessary to retain to the standard of the English laws."[18] Shelburne had thought of effecting this constitutional change by a simple alteration of the governor's commission and instructions. There were, as has been seen, serious doubts about the legality of this course, and in June 1767 the opposition put through the House of Lords a resolution bringing the whole matter before Parliament.

The Privy Council having examined the pigeon-holed instructions of 1766, the report of Yorke and de Grey,[19] and other material available, found the evidence before them so inconsistent that in preparation for legislation they decided to order a formal reinvestigation on the spot by the Lieutenant-Governor, assisted by the Chief Justice and the Attorney General. Apparently believing that there was something in the very air of Quebec that bred contention among otherwise reasonable people, the Council decided to send over an official to take part in the discussions and bring back the report. Shelburne chose Maurice Morgann, at one time his private secretary. Morgann was to proceed to Quebec to bring back the report, and also to explain and criticize it. It was hardly surprising if the professional lawyers, fully understanding his role as their critic and the confidential agent of government, should look on him coldly.

> Mr. Morgann the legislator as we are to call him [wrote Maseres] . . . is a well-bred agreeable man but not a lawyer; and he has a pompous way of talking that seems borrowed from the House of Commons cant about the constitution without having precise ideas of what he would say.[20]

Shelburne and the Privy Council were justified in the expectation that they might receive too many opinions from Quebec. Before Morgann's arrival, in the leisurely fashion of the time almost exactly a year after the order had been issued from the Privy Council, the cordial unanimity of opinion which had united the Lieutenant-Governor and the law officers was dissolving. Carleton had moved rapidly away from the views of the merchants' party; Hey and Maseres were cautiously inclined to favour many, although not all, of their views.

Carleton, from the beginning, responded as Murray had done to the courtesy and tact of the Canadians, and to the ready assurance of loyalty and of gratitude for favours done which accompanied their requests for the redress of grievances. As a soldier and a gentleman he had special sympathy for the seigneurs whom he saw also as soldiers and gentlemen, now by the fortunes of war deprived of their employment and of other royal favours which had helped to maintain their prestige in society. Even while engaged in crushing "the opposition" in the fall of 1766 he had represented to the home government the plight of the seigneurs and their need for the favours of government. By November 1767, when he first addressed himself to the task of briefing the government on the constitution and the law, he had come to the firm conclusion that the seigneurs were the key to the whole Quebec question.

> I take it for granted [he wrote] that the natural rights of men, the British interests on this continent and the securing the King's dominion over this province must ever be the principal points of view, in framing its civil constitution and body of laws.

The last, the securing of the king's dominion, must be "the foundation of all." If British rule could not be maintained, they could do little either for the rights of men or for British interests elsewhere on the continent.

Having repeated his statement of the need for defence works, Carleton spoke of the inadequacy of the troops in the province. The new subjects could put into the field eighteen thousand men, half of whom had already seen service. These people "are greatly to be influenced by their seigneurs." Although many seigneurs were now in the service of the King of France, there remained in Canada about a hundred men of seigneurial rank, seventy of whom had seen active service; yet "not one of them is in the King's service, nor one who from any motive whatever is induced to support His government and dominion." They had been "deprived . . . of their honours, privileges, profits and laws," and instead had been exposed to "much expense, chicanery, and confusion with a deluge of new laws unknown and unpublished." As things stood, the best to be hoped from them was passive neutrality and respectful submission. These they had shown in spite of attempts "to engage them in parties by a few whose duty and whose office should have taught them better."

As for the English in the province, the harshness of the climate and the poverty of the soil gave little hope of their numbers being increased by agricultural immigration. Those now in Quebec were chiefly retired officers, disbanded soldiers, and "adventurers in trade" who, discouraged by their small profits, were gradually leaving the province. On the other hand the Canadians were multiplying rapidly, so that ". . . barring a catastrophe shocking to think of this country must to the end of time be peopled by the Canadian race. . . ." A month later he wrote again abusing the ordinance of 1764 and recommending the restoration of Canadian laws and the former judicial system.

> This system of laws established subordination from the first to the lowest which preserved the internal harmony they enjoyed until our arrival, and secured obedience to the supreme seat of government from a very distant province.[21]

This, Carleton's first answer to a request for advice and information, was essentially his last. His clear, vigorous, and eminently quotable prose is typical of a clear and vigorous mind. Unfortunately these merits concealed grave intellectual and moral limitations, a tendency to oversimplify, an unwillingness to balance alternatives, to admit doubt, to acknowledge and correct an error or a false impression. It would be grossly unjust to suggest that Carleton thought of nothing but military security or that "the rights of man" were not important to him. There is ample evidence that he had in mind the total good of the community entrusted to him. There is also evidence that he was to some extent the victim of his own quotability and that he allowed himself to be imprisoned within the rather narrow conclusions of an early brilliant dispatch, conclusions which should have been verified by futher observation and information. It was this attitude of mind which gradually alienated him from the party of the merchants, until each became entirely distrustful of the political views of the other.

Carleton's assertion that the English trading colony was leaving the province was not supported by events. His own trade returns show that imports had dropped somewhat in 1767 after a very sharp increase in 1766, but his estimates of possible revenue from import duties show no expectation of any permanent decline in trade. He might, no doubt, have believed that trade would pass into Canadian hands; that he did not is shown by his statement a year or two later that it was hopeless to attempt to levy duties because of opposition from the English merchants. Moreover, his comments on the fur trade show that he expected that the trade would grow and that English merchants would play a major part in it.[22]

If he underrated the influence and the prospects of the English merchants, he attributed to the seigneurs a consequence that they had never enjoyed. Referring to them commonly as "nobles" he implied that they combined the skill of military officers with the local knowledge and influence of the ideal English country squire. He mentioned as "men of the first property and consequence in the country" a number who lived in or near Montreal. It is probable that he had met them and others on easy social terms during his stay in Montreal in the spring of 1767, and that he accepted literally their political and social pretensions. The seigneurs, however, had no monopoly of ability or social competence. Misled perhaps by an illusion of aristocracy and by the tastes of the professional soldier, Carleton did not observe that, in Quebec and Montreal, Canadian society could boast merchants and notaries abler and better informed than most of the seigneurs.

Carleton could not know that his determined patronage of de Léry, for whom he secured a pension as the first seigneur to kiss the hand of George III, caused contemptuous amusement among Canadian merchants. He should, however, have realized from the returns annexed to his own dispatches that Canadian seigneurs could not well exercise the general influence throughout the countryside that he attributed to them. Of one hundred and four mentioned in his returns, sixty-eight lived in or very near to the towns of Quebec, Three Rivers, and Montreal, leaving only thirty-six in the small towns and villages, and of these three were up at Detroit. It was to be expected that the Canadian seigneur, like his French counterpart, should prefer town life and should choose rural isolation only when compelled by poverty to do so. It was also understandable that Carleton should accept at first his pretension to represent the country as a whole. It was unfortunate that four years in the country should not have enabled Carleton to correct the false simplicity of this early impression of Canadian society.

Carleton was, however, convinced that the seigneurs would support the kind of government that he thought best for Quebec and for the British Empire as Canadian merchants and lawyers would not do. He also believed that they needed only social and political recognition to give them control of the community. Through them he would conciliate the "national spirit" resentful of the exclusion of Canadians from all responsible government posts. Through them also he would equip the province for defensive and perhaps even offensive warfare.[23]

While Carleton was arriving at his solution to the Canadian question, the Chief Justice and the Attorney General, although with less assurance, were coming to different conclusions. At first they and Carleton had been in full agreement. Carleton may even have learned from Maseres to believe that government by council, a revival of the French judicial system and, with a few exceptions, of the whole of Canadian law, was the wisest course. Exactly why the lawyers changed their minds is uncertain. It is likely that daily experience of commercial and other cases in the courts and association with the mixed English-Canadian society in Quebec and Montreal had convinced them that the mere fact of conquest and the inevitable mingling of laws as well as of population made a complete return to the former system less simple than they had supposed. They discovered that what they had thought of as a very simple set of local customs was a highly complex body of law, and that it was so closely bound to the law of France as to make it difficult to dispense with French legal records and French legal opinions.

They were helped to this conclusion, as it happened, by Carleton himself. In the summer of 1767, before receiving any inquiries on the laws, Carleton had charged the French secretary of the council, F. J. Cugnet, to prepare a digest of the civil law.

> I believe it was very ably performed [wrote Maseres] . . . yet it was very difficult for Mr. Hey and me to understand from the great conciseness . . . of the French law language. I remember we were about four hours understanding the first five pages of it . . . though we had Mr. Cugnet at our elbow all the time to explain it to us. In short it was like a lecture on a chapter of Justinian Institutes. When I did understand it I thought the several propositions neatly and accurately expressed.[24]

This hardly fulfilled Carleton's intention of a short and simple statement for the guidance of the amateur. There were other objections. Cugnet's work was shown to Mathurin Joseph Jacrau of the Seminary, an experienced lawyer, and to several others. They praised it highly, then acknowledged one or two little omissions and faults, then drew up a digest of their own so totally different as to be in turn repudiated by Cugnet. Both documents were then submitted to another group of Canadian gentlemen who decided that any sort of code was in itself objectionable as being exclusive, and that the law of the country should continue to rest on the original authorities.[25]

These experiences undoubtedly gave Hey and Maseres a new view of the legal question, of which Carleton was unaware. In the spring of 1768, following the instructions received from England, he ordered Maseres to draft a report on the laws to be presented to Morgann "the legislator" when he should arrive. Maseres with infinite care and at great length suggested four possible methods of reconciling the conflict of laws. He refused to state his own preference, believing the matter sufficiently important and difficult to engage the best legal minds in England. It was clear, however, that the general retention of Canadian law would be his last choice.

Carleton, when presented with this report early in 1769, angrily rejected it and asked the newly arrived Maurice Morgann to draft one. Later, perhaps persuaded by Hey that it would be unseemly to reject the views of lawyers who knew the country in favour of those of a layman who did not, he accepted reports from Hey and Morgann as the basis for one of his own. In fact, whatever document he used, Carleton's report recommended a judicial system already sketched for him by Maseres, and the revival of Canadian law that he had recommended as early as 1767.[26]

Carleton's plan would have carried further the change already in contemplation, and effected the following year by the ordinance of 1770.

He proposed three judicial districts instead of two, a judge and an assistant in each one, and the appointment of seigneurs and militia captains as justices of the peace. The king's bench would be a criminal court only, all civil cases being settled by Canadian justices of the peace and the Canadian court of common pleas. As for the law, Carleton recommended the continuation of Canadian civil law which, he suggested, had been abrogated only through a misunderstanding. He favoured English criminal law and the right of *habeas corpus*. In spite of the lessons of experience he recommended a republication of Canadian law which would make references to French authorities unnecessary.

Hey signed his name to this report; perhaps he thought that the proposals for judicial reform justified his signature. On the question of the law he agreed with Maseres. Both lawyers believed that justice could be done to the Canadians and inconvenience avoided by accepting English law as the law of the country, retaining specifically Canadian laws of real property, alienation, and inheritance. An ordinance to effect this had actually been drafted during Carleton's first year of office but he had decided not to present it to the council,[27] perhaps because he was already bent on a much more sweeping change.

Carleton's report, Morgann's, and Hey's, with the dissenting opinion of Maseres, were sent home with Morgann, reaching Britain in January of 1770.[28] Carleton himself went home on leave the following summer. Leaving the administration in the hands of the faithful Cramahé, assisted by Hey as senior councillor, he went to assist in the completion of the scheme of government that would, he hoped, without neglecting the rights of man or the British interest, ensure that "perfect subordination from the first to the lowest" which he believed to be essential to "the King's dominion."

CHAPTER 8

Freedom as Far as the Laws Permit

One man already in London when Carleton arrived there was a determined critic of the views of the Governor of Quebec. In the fall of 1769 Francis Maseres had received Carleton's permission to go on leave. Carleton reported to Hillsborough, now Secretary of State for the Colonies, that Maseres had an antipathy to Canadians as Roman Catholics, and that he had been "so indiscreet I judged it highly proper to yield to his entreaties and let him depart the province." He hoped that Maseres might find at home a position "where the fervour of his zeal can be of no essential disadvantage to the King's service."[1]

The truth was that Maseres's ability to defend his strongly opposing views made him disagreeable to the Governor. It was a relief to be able to send him home with a convincing smear on his character. Maseres, though unimaginative, was able and fair minded, rated by the great Bentham the most honest lawyer he had ever known. His frankly stated belief that the right policy for Quebec would be to anglicize and protestantize the population was to prove unpopular with nationalist romantics of the nineteenth century and nationalist zealots of the twentieth. In his own day it was not extraordinary, and it implied no dislike of Canadians, with some of whom Maseres was undoubtedly on friendly terms. On the strength of Carleton's comment Maseres has been dismissed as a bigot. He was not a bigot; if he had a religious deficiency it was his inability to comprehend with sympathy the fact of religious faith. With many enlightened thinkers of his day he trusted to the power of rational and humane laws to bring about a more rational and humane society.

In thinking, as he did, that the people of Quebec would ultimately find increased well-being under English law and within the Anglican communion, Maseres was at one with James Murray, whose affection for the people he called "my Canadians" no one doubted. His ideas, in principle, were also accepted by every significant Englishman who concerned himself with Quebec, except Guy Carleton. Carleton was determined that Canadians should remain French, because he believed that the only possible alternative was the hateful and dangerous one of their becoming American.

Carleton, however, was right in believing that religious considerations had played their part in determining Maseres's views on the laws of Quebec. He had come to the colony opposed to the general introduction of English law and a year later he still spoke of the error of taking away Quebec's "innocent, useful, compendious laws." [2] During the next six or eight months he changed his mind, but not from dislike of Canadians, or from religious bigotry in its usual meaning. His experience of the confusion in the courts was reinforced by his conviction that the Canadian law gave too much political and social power to what, politically, he considered a "dangerous . . . and treacherous religion." [3]

Maseres became familiar with the Canadian law and custom which gave the Church, through the parishes, considerable powers of taxation in the levying of tithes and the raising of money for the building of churches and presbyteries. In the summer of 1768 when Jacrau of the Seminary produced his revision of Cugnet's code, Maseres noted that it "raised much ecclesiastical law and privilege unfit for an English colony." [4] The control of marriage by the Church gave it considerable indirect control of property, and, in fees paid for dispensations, provided a modest source of revenue. Altogether Maseres, politically opposed to Roman Catholicism and hoping for eventual assimilation of the Canadians, was profoundly dissatisfied with the privileges that the Church was then enjoying. He was most reluctant to confirm and extend them by a wholesale introduction of Canadian law, although he acknowledged that justice required the retention of many parts of it.

The Church, however, was already consolidating a doubtful position. Canadians had always been given reason to hope that the somewhat ominous clause of the treaty granting freedom of worship "as far as the laws of Great Britain permit" would be interpreted generously. There was one serious cause of anxiety. Canadians could be prepared for the priesthood in the Quebec seminary, but, since the death of Bishop Pontbriand in June 1760, no one in the province had authority to ordain them. For this reason, and for many others, the Canadian church needed a successor to the Bishop. This could be secured only from Rome. And yet one of the laws of Britain expressly stated that "no foreign . . . prelate . . . shall . . . exercise any manner of power, jurisdiction . . . spiritual or ecclesiastical" within any British dominion, and, as everyone knew, the foreign prelate referred to was the Bishop of Rome. It was, therefore, a nice question whether, under the laws of Britain, the Church could maintain the necessary minimum link with Rome.

Various plans were considered. The suggestion that priests, French-speaking but not subjects of France, might be brought from Europe, after screening by the British government, was not acceptable to the Canadian church. The proposal that Canadians could be trained in Quebec and sent abroad for ordination also met objections: it would be difficult to arrange, costly, discouraging to some, and only too attractive to others who might go and not return. A plan which found favour in Quebec was that of the Abbé de La Corne, an expatriate Canadian, a member of the Quebec chapter living in Paris.[5] He suggested that, as appointment by the French king was henceforth impossible, and any formal appointment by the British monarch clearly undesirable, the Church might revert to the ancient custom of election. A candidate after selection by the chapter in Quebec could, with the consent of the British government, be presented to Rome for consecration. La Corne pressed for a titular bishop with full powers as preferable to a bishop *in partibus infidelibus* or a grand vicar, as at once more useful to the Canadian church and, because more independent of Rome, more acceptable to Britain. He pressed his plan on the British government during the winter of 1762-63, discreetly securing the help of the French ambassador and of diplomats of other Roman Catholic powers. By June he had apparently secured an unofficial consent.

At the same time Canadians in Quebec were working toward a similar end. The Grand Vicar, Briand, proposed to Murray that the leading clergy hold an election with his consent, and, if necessary, in his very presence, thus securing "the interests of the state and of religion, and the formalities observed toward the court at Rome."[6] Murray agreed to forward Briand's suggestion to London if he would put it in writing. Even as he did so, petitions to be carried to London by a Canadian layman were being prepared in Quebec, Three Rivers, and Montreal.

On September 13, the day that Briand delivered his petition to Murray, letters arrived from La Corne reporting his negotiations, and giving the impression that the substance of Briand's petition had already been granted. At this time Montgolfier was in Quebec on his way overseas on business for the Montreal Seminary. As members of the chapter urged him to do what he could to further their cause, someone, it seems, suggested that much time would be saved if Montgolfier could name the man favoured by the chapter.

The idea was found acceptable. On September 15, without informing Murray, but assuming, no doubt from La Corne's information, that they were acting "sous le bon plaisir des supérieurs civils et ecclésiastiques,"[7] the chapter met and chose Montgolfier. A more natural choice would have been Briand, president of the chapter, Grand Vicar of Quebec, and on excellent terms with Murray. Briand, however, was unwilling to serve. He was considered a timid man, he was not a good speaker, he was without private means, and he had no claim on any church endowment. Montgolfier was an able man, with an excellent personal reputation, and enjoying the prestige and support of the wealthy Montreal seminary. He was informed of his election and he proceeded to England charged now not only with the interests of his seminary but with those of the whole diocese.

This action of the chapter, however well intentioned, was ill judged. The members must have realized that no one could succeed in the difficult role of ruler of the Church without the ready co-operation of the governor. Murray distrusted Montgolfier, and he would certainly be affronted when he learned of the secret election. It is true that Murray's appointment as civil governor of the whole province was not yet known in Quebec. Possibly the chapter counted on the appointment of his rival, Gage, or of a third party. It is still difficult to understand why, in order to save a few months' time, they ran the risk of adding to the other difficulties of the new bishop that of a hostile and suspicious governor.

The outcome was even worse than might have been anticipated. Rome refused to recognize any right of local election to a bishopric, proposing instead to confer on Montgolfier the office of grand vicar with power to ordain priests. It was generally agreed that more authority was needed to preserve unity and good order in the Church. At this juncture the Canadian bishopric was unwittingly saved by Murray. He refused absolutely to approve the election of Montgolfier. The British cabinet, suffering from the weakness chronic during this decade, and mindful of the mob spirit which some fifteen years later was to show itself capable of throwing all London into confusion with a "no-popery" cry, would not take the risk of imposing a Roman Catholic official on an unwilling governor. The concession unofficially made to La Corne was unofficially withdrawn; a year after his election Montgolfier returned to Quebec, and gave the chapter his resignation.

The chapter following his advice, selected Briand for "presentation" to the authorities at Rome. Briand went first to London where, with the support of Murray from Quebec and of his good friend Cramahé on the spot, he patiently lobbied for an office that he did not want. Cramahé urged that Briand needed no state or dignity but only the permission of government to perform necessary episcopal functions. A change of government in the summer of 1765 caused delay and there was the usual reluctance to make definite or formal commitments. By the end of the year, however, Briand learned that he might proceed to France; and Rome, ignoring the election, conceded the full status of bishop. Consecrated at Suresnes on the outskirts of Paris on March 16, 1766, Briand reached Quebec at last on the evening of June 28, after an absence of nearly two years. Early the next morning all the bells of the city rang as the people hurried out rejoicing at the news, ". . . congratulating each other as they met in the street, and saying again and again, 'It's really true, we have a bishop. God has had pity on us.' " [8]

Maseres was not in Quebec to witness this moving scene. When he arrived two or three months later he was shocked to find Briand fully accepted as Bishop of Quebec. He wore the purple habit and gold cross of the bishop, he had walked through the streets under a canopy of state on the occasion of a church festival, and he was addressed by his flock as "Monseigneur." If he had authority for all this, said Maseres, he could not be blamed, but the general understanding given by Cramahé was that the bishop would adopt no ecclesiastical title and would live in complete retirement.

Briand's defence against any suggestion of ill-faith would have been the assertion that "la Cour" had instructed Carleton in his presence to see that he was recognized as Bishop of Quebec by old and new subjects alike.[9] That any such formal instructions were given to Carleton is not credible. They would have run directly contrary to the written instructions of the Governor of Quebec, who was expressly ordered to maintain the authority of the Bishop of London. Moreover, a few years later Dartmouth, as secretary for the colonies, explicitly denied that any formal authority had been given for the exercise of episcopal powers.[10] No doubt someone had verbally and informally advised Carleton to see that Briand was respected and to further his work, and this may have seemed to both men sufficient warrant for some relaxation of Cramahé's undertakings on his behalf.

Carleton and Briand were on cordial terms from the beginning, and the complex relations of church and state, thanks to Briand's caution and Carleton's goodwill, were maintained with no serious friction. The Church needed a good deal from the state. An expanding population and the creation of new parishes called for the building of churches and presbyteries, which involved, as Maseres noted, taxation by the Church under the authority of the state. Agreement by a parish meeting, the consent of the bishop, and the approval and authority of the courts were all necessary. Briand believed, even before the passing of the Quebec Act, that the courts could enforce a levy agreed on by the parish assembly, and he contrived to convince the doubting Judge Adam Mabane that such a measure could be justified under that most convenient term "equity." [11]

The association of the governor with the bishop in assigning priests to the parishes was continued. Carleton did not interfere as Murray had done, but gave Briand his support, which was occasionally needed. Both Carleton and Cramahé were consulted at least occasionally.[12] A prolonged quarrel in the district of Three Rivers between Pelissier, who operated the St Maurice forges and demanded services in a nearby chapel for his workmen, and St Onge, the Vicar General, was settled at last only when Briand made it clear to both parties that the Governor was supporting his authority. In a difficult question of the annulment of a marriage between Roman Catholics, when Briand was forced to give bitter offence to one party or the other, he was greatly relieved to find that Carleton was prepared to recognize his full authority to determine such matters in his own flock as he thought best.[13]

Carleton expected the full support of government by every parish priest, even though in a more peaceful period he might have afforded to be less exacting than Murray had been. He revived an old custom by asking for the first bailiff in every parish the special seat and other honours formerly accorded to the captain of militia. In this he showed great wisdom, for these ecclesiastical honours were highly valued social distinctions. Through Briand Carleton enlisted the help of parish priests in maintaining good relations between Canadians and "old subjects," especially the soldiers who might be billeted in their districts. It was thought well, without inquiring too closely into past practice, to remind priests that the proper term to apply to Protestants was "separated brethren." Priests were also asked to assume the rather unpopular task of supporting the governor and the bishop in curbing the evils of the local "cabarets."[14]

Briand very willingly urged priests to show their appreciation of a governor "so well disposed towards priests and so favourable to our holy religion." The Bishop was conscious, however, of an ever-present danger where ecclesiastical interests and the claims of the law overlapped. Church seats, for example, if not property, were a "civil right" which could be defended in the law courts. Disputes over pews were frequent and could be immensely complicated, involving family rights of long standing. They represented a dangerous area of joint jurisdiction of church and state. In 1768 a parishioner sued his priest about a church pew before a justice of the peace and won his case. The priest refused to implement the decision, excluded the claimant from the sacraments, and even threatened not to say mass in the church. The justice reported the matter to Carleton who, following his usual practice, turned the matter over to Briand. Briand promptly informed the priest that the decisions of the courts, just or unjust, must be accepted under English or any other law. If he felt injured he could appeal. As for the refusal of the sacraments, he was exceeding his own authority in imposing such a punishment without reference to his superiors.[15] On the other hand, where civil claims encroached on the sanctuary, or affected the order of worship, Briand instructed priests to accept no external authority.[16]

Missionaries at up-country posts, where the military commandant might be tempted to interfere, were especially instructed to guard the authority of the Church, but with prudence and tact. Priests must never admit the right of the commandant to authorize a marriage forbidden by the Church. If circumstances made it impossible to refer to the bishop, the priest should forestall civil action by himself giving a dispensation. On the other hand he need not stubbornly resist the burial of Protestants in consecrated ground. Yielding to the civil power in this matter involved no sacrifice of principle, as the priest could always privately bless afresh every Catholic grave. "Try always to get along with the commandant, and all the English, and even as far as the altar yield them nothing in politeness and affability" was Briand's general direction to one of the missionaries at the posts.[17]

Even within the boundaries of the province and with the obliging Governor Carleton, there could be awkward moments. Soon after his arrival in the province, Carleton wrote an extremely sharp letter to Father Degeay, a Sulpician accused of attempting to convert English soldiers and of conniving at their desertion. The accusations were apparently exaggerated. Montgolfier admitted that Degeay had been imprudent and sent out a special circular on the matter to all priests in his district. Carleton, on receiving apologies and explanations, graciously forgave Degeay because, he said, of his esteem for Briand; flattering, indeed, but calculated to make Briand wonder how far his credit would extend. He could not, of course, forbid conversions. He did recommend that those wishing to be received into the Church, as for example, a Protestant marrying a Roman Catholic, should be received privately before witnesses who were required to conceal the matter, for "we must not insult our masters, or rather, their religion." [18]

Briand was nearly in trouble himself in the spring of 1767 when Carleton learned that Marchand, as vicar general in Montreal, at Briand's request was sounding out the priests of the district about a possible coadjutor and successor to the Bishop. Carleton promptly demanded why votes were being collected when it was for the bishop and chapter to nominate "with the consent of the government." Briand explained and apologized, and later lamented to Marchand, "I do not know, indeed, who it is that keeps the General so well informed about so many things." [19] Briand learned how difficult it was to take any independent course. Even though Carleton might wish to be indulgent he had to reckon with superiors at home. Not for nearly three years was it possible to name a coadjutor, and then Carleton passed over all French priests and chose the elderly, and perhaps rather worldly Canadian, M. Desglis of the Island of Orleans, whom he must have known would not have been Briand's choice.[20] It was no wonder that

Briand continually reminded his priests of the need for circumspection, occasionally adding mournfully, "Behold I send you forth as lambs among wolves." [21]

Briand, however, would have been the first to admit that many of his troubles came as much from the folly of the lambs as from the cunning of the wolves. Few churchmen of that secular age were passionately dedicated, and the Canadian church was the product of the age. There were many evidences of slackness, worldliness, and of the "new ideas" of the age of enlightenment, which Briand held in horror. Of Briand's three vicars general, Montgolfier, Marchand, and St Onge, only Montgolfier was his equal in ability, integrity, and devotion.[22] As for the parish priests and missionaries, some clearly lived hard and devoted lives. Inevitably these men have left less mark on the episcopal archives than some of their relatively wealthy brethren whose slackness, insubordination, and undue affection for material things caused Briand much anxiety. His letters for the decade following 1760 show that out of about one hundred and thirty priests, upwards of thirty had been formally admonished, some of them several times. Two-thirds of this number had been guilty of serious offences against discipline, or of conduct likely to cause scandal in the parish, such as excessive drinking, notorious avarice, or grave social indiscretions. Even priests who were in no serious trouble needed to be reminded not to gossip, not to meddle in politics, and not to forget the church fasts. Ten priests in this period were temporarily deprived of some or all of their functions. There were only two cases of grave immorality; one of these men and one other were also imprisoned for debt.[23]

On the whole it was not a bad record considering the spirit of the times, the shock to ecclesiastical discipline caused by the Conquest following on the demoralization of a long war, and the years of uncertainty about the future of the Church. Matters were made harder by the relative isolation of the clergy. The Sulpicians, who served the parishes in and about Montreal, and who enjoyed the advantages of community life, had a good reputation, although, as it happened, one of the very black sheep was a Sulpician. It was Briand's wish that parish priests might be helped by frequent visits to the seminaries of Quebec and Montreal. Unfortunately there was some little prejudice to overcome, most of the parish priests being Canadian, and all the members of the seminaries French. Briand, himself a Frenchman, looked forward to the day when such distinctions would be wiped out by something like a national church. ". . . when all are in the same condition and when people don't say, 'That man is French,' and 'That man is Canadian' . . . I think that things will go better and more cordially." [24]

Meanwhile Briand did his best to maintain discipline and morale by personal exhortation. He could never forget that the whole future of his church depended on not much more than a hundred priests, most of them men of no more than ordinary abilities and training. He was also acutely aware of his anomalous position as the ruler of an authoritarian church which found itself officially approaching the position of a voluntary and barely tolerated sect. It was not easy to maintain the loyalty and obedience of the clergy. Nor was it easy to win the obedience of the laity. Briand found there, also, that the duties of his position left him in the unhappy position of complete responsibility with little or no legal power, and this at the moment when people long accustomed to implicit obedience to the one and only church were beginning to realize that they now had liberty to choose another church which might be less exacting. "I thought I knew the Canadians," wrote the Bishop; "I saw them as a people docile, submissive, easy to lead, religious, attached to the faith. . . ." Since his return in 1766 he had found in them "indocility, obstinacy, rebellion, ill-will against everything connected with religion and worship." [25]

Briand was determined not to condone these unhappy traits and he instructed priests not to yield to the defiant. Let people find another church if they chose: "If they must be damned let it rather be in following a false religion than in professing the true one." Very few of the Canadians wished to proceed to such an extremity, but some of them loved to stray on the brink of perdition, remaining defiant, or evading the orders that they could not quite defy. Apart from grave moral offences, there were perennial disputes about church law and discipline. Briand claimed tithes from all the faithful; the habitant had convinced himself that he need pay only when he lived in a constituted parish with a resident priest. He might even object to paying tithes to a priest whom he considered unworthy. Briand dismissed all these pleas as irrelevant. "How many habitants are lost for failing to give a handful of barley !" he wrote sadly.[26] A most fruitful cause of dispute, and one on which the habitant could show extraordinary stubbornness, was the management of church property and the location and construction of churches and presbyteries. Briand insisted on his right to approve the situation of the church and every detail of the construction. The opposition of one parish dragged on for years, causing the church to be laid under an interdict, and the parishioners as individuals excluded from the sacraments until one by one they submitted. [27]

Another common source of trouble with the layman was the enforcement of the strict marriage laws. Marriages, of course, must be celebrated by the priest, and when the couple were within the prohibited degrees of affinity they must have a dispensation from the bishop. They must also always have the consent of their parents. Some young people found their own way out of the difficulty by a pre-conquest custom, marriage à la *gaumine*, after one Gaumin, who devised the simple plan of going with his fiancée and two witnesses to the church, where during the service they privately pledged themselves to each other as man and wife. On such marriages the Church frowned heavily, but after the Conquest it had also to cope with the temptation to go to the Protestant clergyman. Briand enforced the rules, including that of securing permission of the parents, but he encouraged the clergy to endeavour to mediate where they felt that the young people were being hardly used. Montgolfier, who had a sense of humour, once reported that a harassed daughter having taken refuge with an uncle, the angry father declared she should never set foot in his house again. Montgolfier, feeling that he could interpret this as the father's consent, had given permission for the marriage.[28]

A source of keen anxiety from the beginning was the fate of the religious communities, especially the communities of men. Murray had pleaded for the women's orders, arguing in their favour their essential services in the nursing of the sick and the education of young girls. The general intention of government was to forbid the men's orders, the Jesuits and the Récollets, to recruit, and to sequester their property for the use of government. The provision of adequate pensions for all who were members of the orders at the time of the Conquest was considered an adequate fulfilment of the promise to respect private proprty. Briand did what he could to defend the orders without whose members he could not man the parishes and missions of the diocese. Here his excellent relations with government were most useful. Thomas Mills, the Receiver General, who in the summer of 1766 annoyed Irving by his officious claim to supervise the expenditures of the council, had travelled from London on the same ship as the new bishop. He had express orders from the Treasury to take over and administer the property of the men's orders. There is no evidence that he attempted to do so. It is possible that his friendship for Briand, which had time to ripen during their long voyage across the Atlantic, made him willing to procrastinate. It is quite certain that, some years later, Briand's influence with Cramahé saved the Jesuits from public dissolution and the loss of their property. Briand had already interceded for the Jesuits in Rome, but fruitlessly. The bulls ordering the dissolution of the order reached him in 1773 when Carleton was in England. Cramahé was administering the province as lieutenant-governor. With Cramahé's consent, Briand did not publish the bulls but communicated them privately to the Jesuits. The fathers having accepted the decision with suitable submission, Briand went on to inform them he reconstituted them a new order on his own authority and under his direction. He ordered them to continue to live as before, wearing their usual garb, managing their property, and carrying on their duties. In the whole province, apart from themselves, only the

Bishop, the Lieutenant-Governor, and his secretary knew that as an order they had ceased to exist.[29]

This remarkable achievement in favour of a society traditionally abhorrent to English Protestants was perhaps largely due to Cramahé's special favour. Both Carleton and Cramahé gave Briand their support in another of his trials, one which represented a fundamental weakness in his position before the Quebec Act. Ecclesiastical Quebec, although it had lost the single-minded devotion of the pioneer days, had not lost the spirit of individualism which had produced in the colony such a variety of missionary efforts – Récollets, Jesuits, the Montreal mission, and the several women's orders. The authority of the bishop in the colony had always been confronted with the claims of groups older than the bishopric. Briand had to meet an old problem in an exaggerated form when he returned to a community that had been without a bishop for six years. He may have had to face some personal opposition also from "*bons patriottes*" like Gravé of the Quebec seminary who would resent the nominee of Governor Murray.

Apparently a considerable volume of subterranean opposition and criticism found open expression in the prolonged quarrel over the parish church of Quebec. The parish church was also the cathedral, or the cathedral was also the parish church. The precise situation of the bishop and chapter on the one hand, and of the *marguilliers* and parish priest on the other, in relation to the control of the church fabric had never been defined. Briand laid the responsibility on Laval, the first bishop, who had consented to the original ambiguity, and on his own good friend and predecessor, Pontbriand, who, before the Conquest, had failed to prosecute the lawsuit that might have cleared up the matter.

The bone of contention, the actual building, had been almost destroyed during the siege. Some time after Briand's return as bishop he learned that the church, which was being rebuilt, was to be under the formal control of the parish priest and the *marguilliers*. The Bishop would be welcome there, as he would in any church of the diocese, but the members of his chapter would have no privileges, and he would have no voice in the management of the property. Briand represented to the priest, Récher, and to his *marguilliers* that a bishop must have his own church from which to govern his diocese. Without it he even doubted his full constitutional powers as bishop. In particular, he believed that he could not appoint priests with permanent tenure in their parishes, and this he particularly wished to do, for their own sakes and for the security of the Church. To all this it was retorted that Quebec really had no need of a bishop; a grand vicar would have been sufficient. To his dismay, Briand found that some members of the Seminary where he lived and notably the lawyer, Jacrau, were also against him.

In this trying position Briand decided on a course which he pursued with perseverance, if not always with patience, for several years. He refused to quarrel with anyone, greeting his most determined opponents with his usual urbanity. He also refused to go to law; the time for that had passed with the Conquest. On the other hand he declined absolutely to enter the "parish church" as bishop. He would come to the church only when it was recognized as his cathedral. The situation threatened to become awkward for him early in 1771 when, the building completed, the bishop was required either to consecrate it, or, by his refusal to do so, to deprive Quebec of the use of a parish church. Briand was equal to the occasion. He consented to make possible the saying of mass by consecrating a stone from the altar, which could be brought to him, but until his opponents admitted his rights as bishop he would not enter the building, and the chapel of the Seminary would remain the cathedral church of the diocese.

For three years more the *marguilliers* held out in spite of the death of Récher, the priest, and of Jacrau who, said Briand, had led them astray. At last, early in 1774 on the eve of the passing of the Quebec Act, Cramahé brought pressure to bear on the *marguilliers*, the chief of whom, said Briand, was "one of his spies." [30] The status of the church was formally defined in a document satisfactory to all parties. On March 16, 1774, eight years after his consecration, Briand was able to celebrate mass in his own cathedral. It was on this triumphant occasion that he publicly announced the appointment of his coadjutor, consecrated two years earlier on the strength of Carleton's nomination and the bulls from Rome. [31]

Maseres did not stay in Quebec long enough to witness Briand's worst trial or his final triumph in the struggle over the cathedral church. Nevertheless his three years in the province, which nearly coincided with Briand's first three years in office, gave him a very good idea of the weaknesses of Briand's position. In particular, living in the city of Quebec, and able from his command of French to understand and participate in the gossip of the capital, Maseres became aware of the currents of opposition to the Bishop personally, and to the exercise of episcopal power in the Church. Maseres' own view was solidly based on political expediency. He was opposed to any measure tending to perpetuate Roman Catholicism beyond those necessary for the fulfilment of the treaty because ". . . the principles of it have a natural tendency to keep up a perpetual disaffection to our government. 'Tis difficult to be well-affected to a set of governors whom they look upon as enemies of God, deserving of, and destined to eternal damnation." [32]

Maseres met Canadian seigneurs in Quebec who confirmed the view that he wished to hold by assuring him that they, too, disapproved of steps calculated to maintain religious distinctions so injurious to them and to their children. One of them was quoted as saying that since His Majesty and the British government think it a necessary piece of state policy to exclude from all employments of trust or profit those who are of our religion, it is something surprising that they should take a step which leads directly to hinder us from ever deserting those prejudices and errors that render us incapable of ever serving our new monarch. Does he mean to perpetuate our exclusion from the honour of serving him to all generations by thus endeavouring to perpetuate that unhappy religion which is the ground of that exclusion?

The same man went on to say that they welcomed toleration and that many of them would have continued in their religion from conscience and conviction, and others from "that kind of punctilio which makes it dishonourable for a man of grown years to give up his father's religion and his own for worldly advantages"; the speaker added, however, that most of the second group would have been happy to see their children take up the religion of the new government, and that there might even be a third group who would become Protestants from conviction. Such changes, from whatever motives, would have

> tended to an union between the two nations; but now that a bishop is sent to domineer over us with his ecclesiastical authority, none of these things can happen; no man dare stir an inch out of the straight path of the Holy Church whether from conscience or from interested motives, but the bishop will immediately hallo his bigots upon him to denounce him in all companies for an heretic an apostate and perhaps an atheist until he becomes an object of detestation to all his relations, servants, and neighbours.

Maseres also met the priests, Briand's opponents, who were equally accommodating in their views, stating that the Church could very well have been served by a vicar general to ordain priests and by a synod of Canadian clergy which would wield no despotic power, but whose acts, approved by the governor and council, would be binding in conscience on all priests.[33]

There is no doubt that Maseres heard these things; all the evidence indicates that he was a most careful and honest reporter. He was, however, prepared to make the doubtful assumption that they were representative of opinion in the province, and on that ground he regretted bitterly the unfortunate policy but for which, in his opinion, a third of the Canadians might already have been converted. He was convinced that it was still not too late if government would take the proper measures. All the property of the regular orders of men and women should be vested in the Crown by act of Parliament; every member should receive a life annuity, with liberty either to remain in a convent or, having left it, to marry. The former church property should be used for Protestant grammar schools, a college with endowed professorships and fellowships, and a seminary for priests.

The bishop should be prohibited from exercising any episcopal power but that of ordination, and that only by special permission of the governor, on pain of deportation. Priests should be continued in their present parishes by an order from the governor licensing them for one or two years, or during pleasure.

The Church being thus placed absolutely under the state, the governor could "encourage" a gradual conversion. A public proclamation should be made permitting any priest to marry and to continue in his parish for one year. If at the end of that time a majority of his parishioners thought him unfitted for office by marriage, he should be withdrawn; otherwise he should be endowed with the living for life. A priest might also secure endowment for life by agreeing to use the liturgy of the Church of England in place of the mass or in addition to it if his conscience would not allow him to renounce the mass entirely. French New Testaments and Bibles and "other good Protestant books" should be distributed to every parish priest who wished to have them.

No successor to the present bishop should be appointed, but the Bishop of London should place at the head of the Protestant clergy "an Englishman who speaks French extremely well." In general two principles should be followed. First, there should be no overt attempts at proselytism, but only a concerted effort to unite all Protestants as far as possible while disuniting the "papists" and leaving every man to act as he thought best. Second, it was important to "make the parish priests themselves the instruments of the intended reformation." This was indeed essential, for if the priests remained staunch, the laymen could not easily be reached. To send in Protestant clergy would do nothing but provoke hostility. If, however, the priests could gradually be won through a conviction that they could lawfully marry, through use of the liturgy in the vernacular, through a persuasion that those who differed from them were not irretrievably damned, and through the promise that "embracing these doctrines should not be attended with any losses to their ecclesiastical revenues but rather the contrary," the battle might be won, and won with a minimum of bitterness and resentment for, as far as possible, every priest would remain in his own parish.

To any sincere believer in either religion or nationalism, this Machiavellian plan is perhaps more repulsive than a policy of outright persecution. Maseres, however, was convinced that, as the end was right, so were the means gentle and good. His Protestantism was, one must suppose, confined to a rational deism, with a decent respect for the moral and social advantages of public worship. He was proposing not so much to pay the parish priests to abandon their religion as to invite them to consider the merits of another one, with the assurance that a change of convictions would not result in a loss of income. To the accusation of bribery he might well have retorted, with the sufferings of his Huguenot forebears less than a century behind him, that the man who could renounce his religion on so slight a pretext had no religion worth keeping. He stressed the fact that his hoped-for conversions would be gradual and that priests must not be pressed to adopt the full Protestant position immediately,

> because the more honest of them will from motives of conscience refuse, and if they did accept would not be capable of continuing to hold their livings because their parishioners would be outraged. . . . It is better, therefore, to encourage them to think for themselves, and to examine the subject, and to abandon some of the errors of popery as they find occasion, and to persuade their parishioners to abandon them likewise.[34]

Maseres undoubtedly underestimated the solid faith of many Canadians, and the loyal devotion to tradition and custom of many more. He also underestimated the qualities of the Bishop, whom he rightly saw as one great obstacle to his scheme of humane anglicization. Oddly enough, the most vivid picture of Briand, and a very pleasing one, comes from Maseres' pen. Having remarked that Briand was "reckoned by many of the Canadians to be a shallow weak man and very vain and fond of outward grandeur and extremely elated and almost intoxicated with his elevation . . ." – reflections, no doubt, of the kindly gossip of the capital – Maseres adds with characteristic frankness and honesty : "I have seen him but a few times and then for the most part in numerous companies at the Governor's table; and there found him an agreeable well-bred cheerful companion. He has, likewise, the very great advantage of being a very handsome man." [35]

Briand had other advantages which Maseres did not discover, for the Bishop, on principle, did not go into society, accepting invitations only from the Governor. He was, perhaps, uniquely fitted to gather up and strengthen the conscious faith and the unconscious loyalties of Canadians. His advantage over anyone else in Canada at the time was partly accidental. No one else knew the whole province as he did. He also had the great advantage of poverty and obvious disinterestedness. A pensioner at the Quebec Seminary, and for years poorer than many of the parish priests, having, as he said, hardly a cup of wine to offer to a guest, he had no interest beyond that of the Church as a whole.[36]

He had, also, a remarkable combination of the personal qualities needed to make a leader in a difficult time. To his opponents he might seem arrogant, dogmatic, censorious, and over-pious. A reading of his letters suggests that these qualities, in so far as he possessed them, were the defects of his virtues. For the Church he did claim much, and, first of all, obedience to himself as bishop during that period of crisis. On the other hand, he was a man of immense warmth and generosity, a stubborn and vigorous fighter, but always without malice, with a certain humour which took much of the harshness from controversy; and with a boundless and spontaneous affection which extended even to his current "enemies." "He has not yet done enough to extinguish affection in a bishop who glories in never having hated anybody," he wrote of one such.[37]

These were the qualities which enabled Briand to maintain his leadership and control over the priests, and to identify his doctrine and discipline with the Church in the minds of the habitants. Of their loyalty to "the Church" there was no question at all, as Maseres shrewdly noted. It was the social, moral, and spiritual centre of their lives. They were wayward and rebellious against authority, including the bishop's authority, but against the Church as such they would not rebel, or very few of them. And for the few who were defiant Briand showed astonishing energy and suppleness in imposing discipline as and when he could. His means were only ecclesiastical: exclusion from the sacraments and, finally, excommunication. These were blunt weapons, to be used with much caution. Wherever possible the guilty person was persuaded to penitence and, in cases of public scandal, to public confession and penance. Even where genuine faith and piety were weak, it is clear that most people were moved by the traditional terrors of public confession, the penitent kneeling at the door of the church, lighted candle in hand, until, mass being over, the priest approached to reconcile him; to say nothing of the more awful ceremony culminating in the priest dashing his lighted candles to the ground and spurning them with his foot in token of the Church's total rejection of rebellious impenitence.

Excommunication, involving, as it did, complete social ostracism of the guilty person by all the faithful, was indeed a heavy punishment from the purely secular viewpoint, if really enforced. Briand knew very well how quickly the force of his penalties could be weakened by a combination of government hostility, Protestant mockery, and general scepticism. He used them rarely, and he was more than ready to meet penitents half way. In any dispute, with a parish or with individuals, having laid down the law with firmness and described the appropriate penances in detail, he would follow very quickly, sometimes in the same letter, with a compromise, offered not as a compromise but as a merciful concession to rebellious children who were showing welcome signs of repentance.

To the priests, many of whom were personal friends, Briand was tireless in encouragement, advice, and exhortation. He was frank and blunt in speaking of their shortcomings, but with them, too, he could move with astonishing rapidity from severe rebukes to the warmest expressions of affection. To one priest who was setting a bad example by carelessness and neglect of the rules of the Church he sent a detailed remonstrance which concluded, ". . . but I am preaching too much. For the rest it is my old heart, speaking to the old M. P. . . ." [38] To one who, after an accident in which a colleague had been drowned, found travelling by boat very trying: "Are you getting a little bolder in the islands? If your fear continues and I can put you in a better place I will do so with much pleasure." [39] The classic case of a rapid transition of sentiment is the letter written when he was vicar general to a priest who had given some trouble. "It is very difficult not to accuse you of malice, deceit, dishonesty, cheating, bad faith and greed"; having dealt thoroughly with these and other matters the letter concluded, "do not give me any more anxiety in this matter that I may never lose the sentiments of esteem, affection and respect with which I always have been and am still . . .," etc. This is an extreme example, but not untypical of Briand's method. It was his practice to establish the sin, preach repentance and reform, and give absolution, all in one letter. Only when repeated applications of this comprehensive treatment were not effective did he resort to deprivation of powers. In general his attitude to priests and laymen alike is summed up in his advice to a priest on how to deal with his flock. He must, first and above all, join with the bishop in prayer for them, and as for preaching,

> avoid invective. . . . Speak more of the beauty of virtue than of the hideousness of vice. It is not always well to meet vices and abuses head-on; it is well to take them in flank. It is better that sinners should tell themselves that they are sinners than that we should tell them so or give them occasion to think that we believe them to be so.[40]

This was Briand's constant maxim and one which he followed with remarkable consistency, even when caution warned him to fear the worst.

It was not likely that any plan of gradual and imperceptible conversion through the agency of the priests could have had much success against the vigour of such a man and one who, as Maseres sadly remarked, was only fifty, and, from his abstemious life, likely to live long.

Maseres' plan was never tried. It is hardly conceivable that it should have been tried. The British ministries of the day were content to show in varying degrees an attitude of easy-going toleration, combined with a fixed conviction that there must be no "establishment" except that of the Anglican Church, which must ultimately prevail. On the other hand, to think of Maseres' approach to the Church as that of an isolated Protestant zealot is entirely to misunderstand the political-imperial theories of the day. Although no other was so carefully argued, plans for the ecclesiastical transformation of Quebec were constantly appearing.[41] The definition of "freedom as far as the laws . . . permit" remained a question until the Quebec

Act and long after. At no time before 1791 was there official recognition of the rather ample powers, privileges, and property which the Roman Catholic Church actually enjoyed. To assume that these benefits were fully achieved with the consecration of the bishop, or even with the passing of the Quebec Act, is to misunderstand the theory of the right relation between church and state generally accepted at this time. It is also very gravely to underrate the remarkable ecclesiastical statesmanship of Bishop Briand.

CHAPTER 9

A More Effectual Provision: The Quebec Act

The Quebec Act, as the framers modestly claimed, was intended to make "a more effectual provision for the province of Quebec." The statement is accurate enough, but it needs interpretation. The Quebec Act applied to two areas: the narrow parallelogram along the St Lawrence defined as the province of Quebec by the Proclamation of 1763, and the much larger area about the Great Lakes and beyond, claimed by France and yielded to Britain by the Treaty of Paris, but until now no part of the province of Quebec.

The union of these areas in 1774 did two things. It introduced a new and controversial form of colonial government into the St Lawrence Valley and it laid down a new policy for the Ohio country, a subject of contention between Britain and the other American colonies for the past twenty years. These two things were done at a time when the taxation controversy with the American colonies was about to culminate in open rebellion. An act of such a kind, passed at such a time, and applying to such territory, could not be seen merely as the clearing away of unfinished business in the St Lawrence Valley. It was imperial legislation, dealing with a difficult imperial problem at a time of crisis in imperial relations. The act, moreover, was drafted in close consultation with Guy Carleton, in accordance with the plans formulated by him during his administration of Quebec – plans formulated quite frankly with a view to military action on the continent as well as to defence against a French invasion.

Apart from all imperial implications, however, provision for more effectual government of Quebec was long overdue. As has been seen, the British government had practically agreed on an important revision and clarification of the law in 1766. The plan was not executed, and from this time there had been repeated postponements as it became clear that an act of Parliament would be needed. Meanwhile, from the early opinion in June 1765 that the penal laws of Britain against Roman Catholics were not applicable in the American colonies, the views of legal experts slowly accumulated. In 1769, as the reports of Carleton, Maseres, and Hey were about to be brought home by Maurice Morgann, the Board of Trade, newly constituted under Hillsborough as Secretary of State for the American colonies, produced its own report on Quebec. Stimulated by renewed requests from merchants in London, Hillsborough and his board recommended an elected assembly so constituted as to be composed of a nearly equal number of seigneurs from country districts, presumed to be Roman Catholics, and of merchants from the towns who would take the oath as Protestants. The law and the law courts were to be regulated according to the neglected plan of 1766. Detailed proposals were made for ecclesiastical arrangements, Protestant and Roman Catholic, and for raising a revenue. Hillsborough believed that this plan might be acted on during the winter of 1769-70. For this reason he declined to ask leave for Carleton to return to England in the fall of 1769 on the ground that he would be needed in Quebec to inaugurate the new constitution.[1]

Hillsborough had been too confident. His plan was set aside by his colleagues to wait for the arrival of Morgann early in 1770 with the Quebec reports. Later in that year Carleton reached London. Thereafter, while Cramahé in Quebec was repeatedly informed that the Quebec business was on the point of being settled, one year followed another and no action was taken. Not that ministers were exactly idle; they were adding to their collection of expert opinions the lengthy reports of Wedderburn, the Solicitor General, Thurlow, the Attorney General, and Marriott, the Advocate General. By the end of 1773 His Majesty's ministers had at their disposal reports from no less than seven law officers, to say nothing of the amateur efforts of Carleton and Maurice Morgann. And still they hesitated.

It is possible to explain, if not to excuse, the fact that it took seven years to deal with a problem clearly stated in 1766. One reason was the weakness of the successive ministries until after 1770, when the advent of the North ministry gave a certain stability to administration. Once parliamentary legislation was determined on, however, any ministry woud be reluctant to touch so contentious a matter as the government of Quebec. It would clearly be impolitic and unjust to satisfy all the wishes of the English mercantile minority, and yet, on the question of French laws and the Roman Catholic religion, popular prejudice would support the minority. Even apart from popular prejudice, the problem of devising a settlement for Quebec that would combine justice and some degree of satisfaction to new and old subjects without endangering the security of the state was indeed baffling. How could Roman Catholics be tolerated and conciliated and at the same time assimilated to Protestantism? What would be a good law for a former French community, cut off from France, united to England, a close neighbour of American colonies, and now infiltrated with Englishmen and Americans? This difficulty was exaggerated by the fact that the good law-yers who offered their expert opinions were, for the most part, too good to give their unqualified approval either to the French system, which they did not know well enough, or to the English, which they knew too well. As for the constitution, an English colony without an assembly seemed unthink-able, an assembly including Roman Catholics unreliable, and an assembly excluding Roman Catholics unjustifiable. It is not surprising if ministers found it easier to ask for reports than to make any use of them.

It is significant, however, that the lawyers' reports, with many individual differences, show a general agreement on the plan favoured by Maseres as the alternative to a code: a retention of English law as a basis with the Canadian law of land tenure, alienation, inheritance, and wills.[2]

For all this unanimity William Knox, the Under-Secretary for the Colonies, remarked ". . . after all the pains that had been taken to procure the best and ablest advice the ministers were, in a great measure, left to their own judgement."[3] Nothing could have been more unjust than this suggestion that the government had been betrayed by its assistants. The differences between the reports were much less surprising than their substantial agreement on law, government, and religion. The ministers chose to walk by other lights, setting aside the reports, or rather, burying them. When the reports were asked for during the debate on the bill, the government refused to produce them, very naturally, for only Attorney General Thurlow's report gave any support to government policy.

The terms of the Quebec bill in its final form were based almost ex-clusively on the wishes of Canadians as interpreted by Guy Carleton. Evidence of what Canadians had really been wanting since the Conquest exists only in fragmentary form, but is sufficient to illustrate, after a fashion, Carleton's oversimplification.

It is clear that a critical moment in the formulation of opinion was Murray's ordinance of September 1764, followed by the attack on it by the grand jury. Murray had evidently conveyed to Canadians much more clearly than the terms of his ordinance could, that the court of common pleas was to be a Canadian court, a refuge from the rigours of English Protestantism, English laws, and the English language. In practice, however, the English might use it, and the attack of the grand jury, or so the members stated later, was based on their alarm at the thought of a jury of Roman Catholics settling a case between Protestants; the converse, the settling of Roman Catholic cases by Protestants, would, they conceded, no doubt be equally disagreeable to Roman Catholics.

However they might strive later to explain their presentments, or explain them away, in fact the English jurors had cited the English penal laws which would exclude Roman Catholics not only from acting as jurors or lawyers, but from the army and all learned professions.[4] This action, and Murray's public rebuke, encouraged the Canadians to make his ordinance and all that it implied a rallying point for the defence of their rights and privileges. Inevitably the Church had a special interest in defending the civil rights of Roman Catholics. Briand, at this time, was just leaving for England and other churchmen at Quebec apparently attempted to take the lead in something which, for want of a better word, must be called an incipient national movement.[5] A document drawn up for the guidance of Canadian Catholics urged unity for common action. It attributed the attack of the grand jury to Canadian passivity, born of fear, and of the private resentments between members of different social ranks.[6] A petition signed by nearly a hundred names, including those of the grand vicar, Perrault, the parish priest of Quebec, Récher, and Boiret, the superior of the Quebec seminary, asked particularly for the maintenance of the court of common pleas "where all cases between Frenchman and Frenchman could be decided," and for the right to transact their own affairs in their own tongue and "to follow our customs, in so far as they are not opposed to the general well being of the colony, and to grant that a law may be published in our language."[7]

The matter did not end there. Early in 1765 two of the Canadian members of the grand jury asked the Governor and council for permission for Canadians to hold an "assembly" to discuss their common interests. Murray agreed, on condition that the meeting be held at Quebec only, and with members of the council present. There is no evidence that Murray deliberately encouraged this movement, beyond the fact that the English accused him, in words that suggested some specific action, of having fostered division between the two groups. The church leaders did encourage it, although with much secrecy. A circular signed by the grand vicars, Perrault and Marchand, was sent to parish priests, pointing out that such an assembly could be most useful to the Church, and that seigneurs from the country and merchants from the towns were the proper people to represent the community. A list of seigneurs was appended "which will make it easier for the habitants and enable them to come more quickly to unanimity in their choice." The priest was instructed to communicate the letter to no one, but, making necessary and discreet use of the contents, to get all who could write to attach their signatures to the list and to return it by "a safe hand."[8]

Meanwhile, thanks to the energy and enterprise of Rouville, seigneur at Three Rivers and Murray's assistant in the billeting at Montreal, an arrangement was made for a preliminary assembly at Montreal to pass resolutions and send down representatives to the meeting at Quebec which would then constitute "une même et seule Assemblée nationale."[9]

Permission was granted for this. The Montreal assembly met early in 1766 in the presence of Adam Mabane, who was in Montreal co-operating with Rouville over the billeting business. It caused comment and opposition. General Burton contented himself with a mild expression of alarm at some twenty seigneurs, including a number of holders of the Croix de St Louis, descending on a city already in a ferment over billeting and corvées. The English vehemently opposed a representative meeting from which, on the orders of Mabane, they were forcibly excluded. They met later and protested formally. They also induced a number of Canadian merchants to join them in protesting, not at a Canadian assembly, but at one composed exclusively of seigneurs undertaking to speak for all Canadians.

The church leaders had clearly been right in deploring divisions based on social rank. In spite of their suggestion that the towns be represented by merchants, the city of Montreal was to be represented at the meeting by three men only, and those three "vivant noblement." Moreover, the seigneurs were accustomed to resent bitterly any Canadians who opposed them and joined themselves to the English, referring to them in writing to Murray as people of no importance, of mean origin, some of them "even Jews."[10]

There is less information about the Quebec assembly, but it clearly was not so exclusive as the one at Montreal, giving due representation to the merchants. The result of its deliberations was probably the document entitled "Observations . . . by the new subjects to General Murray begging him to forward them to the King with his support." Murray may have made a verbal report but, as far as the evidence goes, he did not place this document in the hands of the king's ministers. It was probably this petition that was later referred to by Carleton as having been sent from Canada and mislaid. It was a lengthy document, clear and well composed, seemingly representative of the interests of all classes. It asked for a bishop, tithes for the parish clergy, equality for all subjects with no distinction on account of religion, an unfettered liberty to go to the upper country for the fur trade, protection for the seal fisheries, control of the brandy traffic, more speedy justice, no imprisonment for debt except for merchants, and for all writs and warrants to Canadians to be sent out in French.

All this would almost certainly have met with Murray's approval. There were, however, certain more doubtful articles. A request for protection to the seminaries, the Jesuits, and all other religious orders was natural, but Murray would hardly feel able to support it. More striking were certain requests clearly emanating from the seigneurs, very lengthy and expressed in a tone more calculated to relieve the angry feelings of the petitioners than to secure the substance of the petition. Along with a demand for the maintenance of seigneurial dues and for *haute, moyenne, et basse justice*, there was a vehement attack on the order for land registration and on Goldfrap, the Provincial Secretary, personally. He was accused of having persuaded the home government to order Murray to institute the register solely in order to increase his fees. A return to the old system of registration of land transfers by notaries was requested. It would certainly be less profitable for the secretary but "his fortune is no concern of ours."[11]

The angry and even threatening tone of these last representations suggests that those who prepared them may have known that Murray was pressing for concessions to the Canadians on the ground that without them they would emigrate, leaving the English with an empty and barren territory. It would not be surprising if Murray decided that it would be in the interests of Canadians generally to suppress the actual document, whatever use he may have made of the contents, in pleading their cause in London. The following year a much briefer and more moderate petition went to London from the seigneurs at Montreal alone, thanking the government for the concession of the bishop, and requesting the continuation of Murray as governor, asking civil equality for Roman Catholics and Protestants, and for "the suppression of the register, the expenses of which exhaust the colony without yielding the least advantage in return." [12]

The seigneurs made no reference in this petition to Canadian law. Up to this time there had been no clear-cut request for the continuation of Canadian law in its entirety, possibly because it was believed that such a request would give offence. The nearest approach to a demand for Canadian law was the resolution from the Montreal assembly asking for the preservation of laws and customs "de la manière la plus avantageuse." This item did not find its way into the Quebec petition.

From the return of Briand and the arrival of Carleton until the eve of the Quebec Act there are no more of these glimpses into the movements of the Canadian community. Briand, not a Canadian, would be less inclined than Perrault or Marchand to put himself at the head of a Canadian movement, even one which was related to the interests of the Church. Moreover, newly returned from London, and with full knowledge of the suspicions entertained there of "meddling priests," he would have been horrified at the idea of the vicars general having enlisted the aid of the parish priests in arranging an assembly of Canadians for political purposes, no matter how useful these might seem to be to the Church. Even in 1773 when Montgolfier, distrusting the ability or the goodwill of Chartier de Lotbinière, who was going over to speak for the Canadians, suggested that he was prepared to use seminary funds to send over "Seigneur Panet" as a more

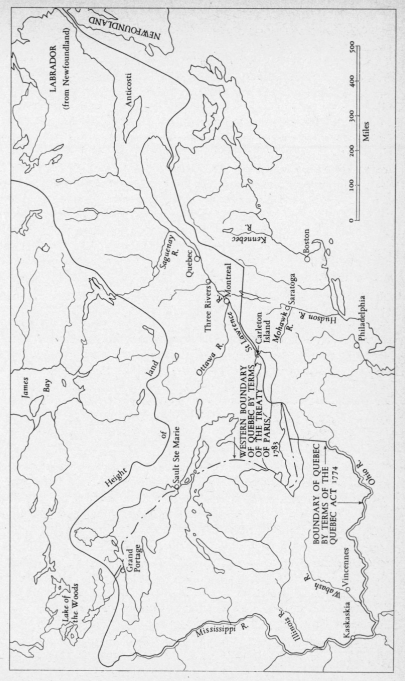

The Boundaries of Quebec, 1774–1783

suitable representative, Briand persuaded him to do nothing, but to depend on Carleton's goodwill.[13]

As for Carleton, he disliked both assemblies and petitions. From 1767 he made himself the spokesman for the seigneurs as representing Canadians. During his regime in Canada there was silence until 1770, the year of his return to England, when, the English once more petitioning for an assembly, some sixty Canadians signed a petition to be presented by Carleton, asking for the first time without any ambiguity to be "restored to our customs and usages administered according to the forms with which we are familiar" and stating their reliance on Carleton, "this worthy representative of Your Majesty, who perfectly comprehends the condition of this colony and the customs of the people," to support their petition.[14]

By 1773, when everyone knew that the act was in the making, there were further signals from Quebec. The English in the city of Quebec prepared to petition for an assembly, and met with eight Canadians, including at least three merchants and a seigneur, to discuss the matter. The Canadians, having first agreed to the petition, later withdrew, to the regret of some of them. An interesting document survives in the form of a draft petition dated 1773, without names, signed only "Les vrais patriotes Canadiens." It states that Canadians were promised the benefit of English law by the Proclamation. This would include an assembly. The writers expressed alarm at their laws and customs being entrusted, as proposed, to the arbitrary authority of a governor and council. It looks as if, in Quebec at least, some Canadians were prepared to join the English in asking an assembly, confident that they could use one to their own advantage.[15]

In Montreal the English also attempted to win Canadian support but failed.

> We were invited [wrote Pierre Guy] a few days ago to an assembly held in the café of our city by the old subjects who communicated to us a letter and memorial addressed to them by the old subjects resident in the city of Quebec, concerning representations to be made for regulating the affairs of the colony, in which they are asking for a House of Assembly. They showed their surprise that we had already made our representation without communicating with them. Our reply was that having learned the division that existed between the old and new subjects in the city of Quebec, which still existed . . . we were determined to make our representation separately, and that in any case their lot was settled, as they were old subjects, whereas ours was not, and that we could not agree to representations which are entirely opposed to our admission to any office [charge].[16]

Guy was not quite fair. The English as late as 1770 had clearly contemplated a purely Protestant assembly, but by 1773, although they would have preferred such a one and thought it practicable, their petitions certainly implied willingness to accept something like the proposal of 1769. At no time, however, did they frankly advocate anything like complete civil equality. The conclusion of Guy and his friends that this attitude forced the new subjects to a separate representation was inevitable and reasonable. Their petition, purporting to come from the province of Quebec, but signed principally, if not entirely, by inhabitants of Montreal, asked for "our ancient laws, privileges and customs," the extension of the province to its former boundaries, and civil equality for old and new subjects. The fervent thanks for the privileges of the military regime, and the eulogies of the House of Hanover, are in sharp contrast to the strident tone of the untutored representations made to Murray nearly ten years before. Carleton's liking for "subordination" had been noted.

With this petition ministers received Carleton's assurance that the seigneurs were the fittest persons to represent Canadian opinion and to lead the Canadian people, and that the seigneurs wanted the restoration of Canadian law in its entirety. Ministers in London could not be expected to know that these demands had achieved precision only under the regime of Carleton and Cramahé; or that if the matter of civil equality for Protestants and Roman Catholics had been cleared up they might have heard much less unanimous opinions from Canadians on questions of law and government.[17]

The triple Quebec question of the laws and the government, of religion, and of the revenue was ultimately settled by two parliamentary statutes. Revenue for provincial purposes was henceforth to be raised, according to Murray's practice and Carleton's advice, by a duty on imported rum and molasses. The duty was to be collected by no doubtful reference to French custom but under an imperial statute, the Quebec Revenue Act. The Quebec Act extended the boundaries of the province of Quebec, as defined by the Proclamation of 1763, to take in that area formerly claimed by the French, which included the Great Lakes, the area south to the confluence of the Ohio and Mississippi rivers, and north to the height of land which separated the lakes from Hudson Bay. New provisions were made for law and government and for religion in the whole of this region.

The ministry had addressed itself seriously to Quebec's problem in the late summer of 1773. The various drafts were produced and discussed during the winter, and the bill was passed through its various stages in Parliament in May and June of 1774. The wording of the preamble caused some slight embarrassment, the first draft saying bluntly that no one knew just what the law had been since 1764. Such frankness seemed superfluous. The final version opened with the extension of the boundary, on the ground that the Proclamation had left without civil government "a large extent of country within which were several colonies and settlements of the subjects of France who claimed to remain there under the faith of the treaty."

In their fury of indignation at the new boundary, the Atlantic colonies overlooked this perfectly accurate statement, and attacked the Quebec Act as one of the "intolerable Acts" of 1774. The extension of Quebec and of Quebec's laws over the coveted Ohio country appeared to the land-seekers even more oppressive than the establishment of the reserve set up in 1763. It was easy to attribute sinister intentions to the British ministries. The suspicions of contemporaries are apparently borne out by a note from Dartmouth to Hillsborough, ". . . nothing can more effectually tend to discourage [settlement] . . . which in the present state of the country it is impossible to prevent."[18] Dartmouth's meaning is, however, quite clear. This clause of the Quebec Act would make it possible to carry out the policy of a western reserve envisaged by the Proclamation.

Setting aside the question of sinister motives, there were plenty of arguments in favour of the enlarged boundary. In this respect the Quebec Act was not, indeed, an intolerable act but an inevitable one.[19] Since 1763 the Canadians on the Illinois and at Detroit had had no effective law for the protection of their property, guaranteed by the Treaty of Paris. From time to time military governors had made ineffectual attempts to get them to move, which they had successfully resisted.[20] As a result there had been sporadic efforts to devise some sort of civil government. Gage proposed a civil constitution for the Illinois but the people of Kaskaskia rejected it and presented themselves with a republican one. Detroit, also, was a chronic storm centre, constantly drawing up lengthy memorials to the government in London about the depredations of the commandants and others on habitant rights. More serious offences than these were committed at Detroit, including the very dangerous ones of attacking and murdering Indians. There was no system of justice there, or anywhere in the upper country, apart from the control of the military commanders. Yet, somehow or other, Detroit provided itself with a "judge," one Philip Dejean. He performed judicial functions, and, presumably, charged fees, for he was neither commissioned nor salaried by the government. In 1772 Cramahé reported his useful activity in charging and sending down a man accused of murder; the man had been tried in Quebec and ultimately executed at Montreal. Dartmouth replied, in general approving the execution of murderers but, adding that Detroit was outside any civil jurisdiction, inquiring upon what authority Cramahé claimed jurisdiction there and "by whom the magistrates there are appointed."[21] Dartmouth might well have believed that, failing any other practicable plan, these scattered Canadian communities which were increasing in number and population must be united to their original centre.

There were even more powerful economic reasons. Effectively, the fur trade of the area had fallen into the hands of the merchants, traders, and voyageurs of the St Lawrence, who alone were capable of meeting the rivalry of the French on the Mississippi. They had achieved astonishing success, establishing fleets on the lakes which gradually superseded the Ottawa as the route from the west, and drawing the furs from Louisiana as well as from the far west. It was clear that this rapidly expanding trade, involving complicated relations with the Indians and increasingly centred on the St Lawrence, must be brought under a central regulation. As the choice lay between Quebec and New York, it was inevitable that Quebec should be chosen. It is notable that Canadians and English alike in the fall of 1773 were petitioning for the province to be restored to its "ancient limits," the one point on which they were in complete agreement.[22]

The most contentious and difficult clauses of the Quebec Act were the simple statements that "in all matters of controversy relative to property and civil rights resort shall be had to the laws of Canada as the rule for the decision of the same" and that "the criminal law of England . . . shall continue to be administered, and shall be observed as law in the province of Quebec." Although this was roughly what Carleton had recommended in 1769 he had apparently changed his mind in accordance with the wishes of some of the seigneurs. The earliest draft on the laws revived the whole law of Canada as it had existed at the Conquest. As no statement was made about what law had existed since 1764, this threatened to confound the confusion already existing. Wedderburn, who was employed to prepare the drafts, persuaded Dartmouth and the cabinet to accept the advice of Chief Justice Hey, which was to ignore the past, accept "the laws and customs of Canada" for future civil suits, and continue English criminal law. Carleton consented to this, but his Canadian witness, the seigneur Chartier de Lotbinière, noted his very strong private reservations. He feared that Canadians might somehow be deprived of some part of their properties or privileges; he stated that the legislative power of the council should be so restricted as to make it impossible for Canadians to be deprived of the administration of justice according to their own custom which, he stated, had been one of the conditions of their capitulation and their later decision not to leave the province. He expressed a strong and reasonable preference for French criminal law without benefit of jury; by this law a man was not exposed to the whims of twelve ignorant men, but was tried by the ablest judges and condemned only on "proofs as clear as day." Although he omitted to explain that the accused's confession under torture might be needed to clinch the matter, Lotbinière's reasoning was not necessarily invalid. Marriott, the Advocate General, preferred English procedure, but deplored the severity of the English punishments under a law "dipt in blood." Both systems were badly in need of the reform which was to be effected a generation later.

The objections of the Whig opposition in Parliament were very different from those of Lotbinière. The question of criminal law did not come up in the debates. Opposition speakers attacked specifically the elimination of *habeas corpus* and trial by jury in civil suits, but they were also unwilling to renounce English civil law, or to vote for Canadian law without knowing more of its nature. North insisted that the Canadian law merely furnished a "general basis" of laws "to be amended and altered as occasion shall arise." [23] Carleton, should he return to Quebec, would thus be cast in the role of mediator between Lord North's "general basis," which would be susceptible to amendment, and Lotbinière's conviction that Canadian law must be rather more sacrosanct than Magna Carta.

In spite of the last-minute petitions sent from Quebec by the English merchants, and of a further representation drawn up and presented on their behalf by Francis Maseres in London, it was a foregone conclusion that the new constitution would not provide for an assembly. Apart from Hillsborough's plan of 1769, which would have introduced distinctions between town and country members completely unrealistic in the melting pot of a society so very near the frontier, no plan had been suggested except for an exclusively Protestant body. Even the unreformed House of Commons would not consider such a travesty of representative government. On the other hand, not the most ardent advocate of representative institutions would have suggested that, fifteen years after the Conquest, when there was strong suspicion that France had not forgotten her old colony, the assembly should be turned over to the Roman Catholic majority. Yet the decision that "it is at present inexpedient to call an assembly" was not reached easily, so deep-seated was the sense that representative institutions were the birthright of all British subjects, and that to deny them was to support despotism. The evidence of a determination to cling to some vestige of parliamentary government is a clause which appeared in the first draft of the bill only, providing that copies of all the ordinances of the council and of the provincial accounts should be laid before both houses of Parliament as soon as possible after being received in England. Failing an assembly, the Act provided for a council of not more than twenty-three or less than seventeen members, to meet at any time on executive business and to pass ordinances with the consent of the governor during the first four months of every year. This arrangement made possible the return of ordinances to London by the first ships in the spring so that, if necessary, they could be disallowed before the next session. The council was not authorized to pass ordinances on religion, or to levy direct taxation. Ordinances imposing any punishment greater than a fine or three months' imprisonment could not be enforced until approval had been signified from London.

The English merchants, disappointed at the refusal of an assembly, were far from satisfied with the arrangements for the council. They asked that it should be larger, up to thirty-one members, and that the act provide for the due representation of all parts of the province. They also requested particularly that the power of suspension or removal of councillors be taken from the governor and reserved to the king by the terms of the Act. They would have been even more disturbed had they known that not only was the governor not deprived of the usual powers of suspension or removal, but that the rigid safeguards contained in the instructions issued to Murray and to Carleton under the Proclamation[24] were to be entirely omitted from the instructions under the Quebec Act, leaving the governor with power to do again what, contrary to his instructions, he had already done in the dismissal of Irving and Mabane.

The merchants had one more strong criticism to make of the council. They had argued that if Roman Catholics should not sit in an assembly, no more should they be members of the council. They wished, therefore, an exclusively Protestant council, or at least one including "only a few of the more moderate sort of Roman Catholics." In the final draft of the bill, however, following the clauses granting freedom of worship, was included a special form of oath to be taken by Roman Catholics, making no reference to the doctrine of transubstantiation or to the royal supremacy over the Church, and referring to religion only in the repudiation of all "pardons and dispensations" which might offer a release from the obligations of the oath.

The publication of this innocuous oath, seen in the context of the opinion of Yorke and de Grey of 1765 that penal laws did not apply in the colony, implied that any Roman Catholic would be eligible for a seat in council, or for other offices under the Crown. The merchants protested that, with no formal protection in the Act, they were liable to be placed under a council wholly composed of Roman Catholics.

Their professed fears are generally dismissed today as either totally insincere or the product of selfish fanaticism. Whether or not they were fanatic, they were sincerely convinced that Roman Catholics were unreliable citizens, rendered incapable by their religion of offering full and single-minded loyalty to the state. The best twentieth-century parallel is the conviction that a member of the communist party must be a bad citizen. The concession of complete civil equality to Roman Catholics in the Quebec Act is remarkable not for the opposition of their fellow-citizens, the Protestant merchants, but for the ready acceptance of the principle by the tolerant aristocrats of the British Parliament, to say nothing of the consent of the King. George III must somehow have convinced himself that his coronation oath did not include Quebec.

The clauses on religion in the Quebec Act had been the subject of much thought. Originally it seems to have been taken for granted that a separate statute would be required. Perhaps because it entailed less publicity, the necessary clauses were included in the constitutional act and elaborated in the private instructions. Concern for the status of the Church had already caused an amendment in the legal clauses. The second draft of the bill gave Canadians "their property, laws, customs and usages." It may have been Hey or Maseres, drawing on local knowledge, who pointed out that this could revive a large body of ecclesiastical law. In order to avoid such a possibility the concession was limited to "property and civil rights." "The free exercise of the religion of the Church of Rome, subject to the King's supremacy" was conceded. It was natural for the ministry in an age when a voluntary church was almost a contradiction in terms to believe that freedom of worship must include for the clergy "their right to a decent and moderate maintenance under the sanction of a British act of parliament." Therefore, tithes from Roman Catholics to their own clergy were enforceable by law, without prejudice to the king's right to levy them on Protestants for a Protestant clergy. This provision for Protestant tithes earned the warm approval of Edmund Burke, who stated his willingness to endow Roman Catholicism but not to reward atheism.

So much for the Quebec Act. It has often been said that those who criticize it as a reactionary measure, a repudiation of the pledges made to English merchants in 1763, ignore the accompanying private instructions in the light of which alone it can fairly be judged. The instructions on the civil law were indeed of the first importance. They would have gratified the merchants as much as they would have offended Chartier de Lotbinière. Carleton was required to consider, with the legislative council, the wisdom of introducing by ordinance, entirely or in part, English law "in all cases of personal actions grounded on debts, promises, contracts and agreements, whether of a mercantile or other nature; and also of wrongs proper to be compensated in damages." He was also practically ordered to see to it that the common-law right of *habeas corpus* was introduced by ordinance.[25]

Had these instructions been followed the legal arrangements would have been approximately the same as those recommended by Maseres in one of the four possible plans contained in his report of 1769. There would have been some delay, and, no doubt, a good deal of contention and confusion for a time, but given competent legal officials, any real mercantile grievances over the laws could soon have been removed and the English in Quebec would have suffered no more injury than the slight one which English pride must suffer in living under French law. Moreover, as North had said in debate, there was nothing to prevent the legislative council from proposing changes in any parts of the civil law.

On the basis of these instructions modern historians have been inclined to praise the Quebec Act as a very liberal measure, a reasonable compromise, generous to the majority of conquered Canadians and fair to the small minority of immigrant English.

Unfortunately, those who call the Act "liberal," in the sense of classic nineteenth-century liberalism, do not read, or at least do not mark, the instructions on religious matters which profoundly modify the apparently generous provisions of the Act.[26] If these instructions had been followed to the letter, the bishop would have been prohibited and prevented from corresponding with any official at Rome; he could have exercised no authority in the church except what was "indispensably necessary" to the free exercise of religion (presumably ordination, confirmation, and, possibly, necessary marriage dispensations); and he could do none even of these things without a special licence from the governor. Only Canadians would have been appointed to parishes, and all appointments would have been made by the governor. Any priest who wished would have been free to marry. The seminaries would have been allowed to retain their property and to admit new members, but the governor or his representative would have been their "visitor," with power to make regulations for them with the advice and consent of the council. The Jesuits would have been immediately dissolved, their members pensioned, and their missionaries withdrawn from the Indians and replaced by Protestant missionaries as soon as this could be done with safety. The Récollets would have been forbidden to recruit; the women's orders might, for the time, have been allowed to go on as before. The Protestant religion would have been protected, encouraged, and endowed under the special authority of the Bishop of London who, with the governor, was to exercise all ecclesiastical authority in the province. In short, it was clearly the hope and intention of government that under a system of rigid state control, but without harsh persecution, the Roman Catholic Church in Quebec would gradually wither away.

If, then, the Act is to be taken with all its accompanying instructions, it cannot possibly be called "liberal" from any modern viewpoint. If the instructions are forgotten and the Act stands alone, it is a charter for French Canadians, no doubt, but it ignores the reasonable requests of English merchants, to say nothing of past promises, and is, indeed, a strange piece of legislation for a victorious commercial empire. If the instructions are emphasized, then the concessions to Canadians become a simple protection to property and custom, and in no sense a recognition of community or "nation," since the instructions contemplated the undermining of the one remaining institution which elicited genuine loyalty from all Canadians.

In short, if the Act and all the instructions are read together and thought of as equally expressing the policy of the ministry, that policy can be seen only as one of gentle but steady and determined anglicization. The recognition of "the liberty of non-English people to be themselves" as an imperial principle was discovered by historians in the Quebec Act after this principle had necessarily been developed by Britain in relation to the other and truly alien peoples which were to become part of the empire during the next century. If this principle is in the Quebec Act, it got in without the knowledge of the men who framed it.

It was, however, the Act that was binding and not the instructions. It would be unrealistic not to recognize that the responsible ministers knew that their essential policy must be expressed in the Act, and that instructions were secondary. By 1774 it is clear that the government, having procrastinated too long, was dominated by one idea. In view of the crisis in America some definite settlement must be made immediately for Quebec and for the upper country. That being so, it was desirable that the plan be simple and clear cut. It was also important that it be agreeable to Carleton, who was trusted to produce in Quebec the desirable results that he had promised.

Carleton, it seems certain, intended from the beginning to ignore what he did not approve. Briand, really alarmed not only by the reference in the Act to the royal supremacy but also by what he knew or suspected of the instructions, was reassured by Carleton both by letter and personally after the Governor arrived in Quebec. Briand was given to understand that the king wished his subjects to have the full and complete enjoyment of their religion. Carleton had indeed already given the ministers notice of his attitude to the instructions on religion. A memorandum in the Dartmouth papers runs as follows:

> General Carleton wishes that on the head of ecclesiastical arrangements, he may be left as much to himself as possible – *he has no objection to having every idea and proposition of government* in regard thereto *suggested in his instructions*; but he disapproves the suppression of any religious communities except the Jesuits, and begs he may be left at liberty to use his own discretion in this very delicate business. [Italics are the author's.] [27]

The deferential conclusion does not conceal the unconscious arrogance of this communication. To Carleton, instructions were not much more than suggestions. In view of his past record it can hardly be supposed that the ministry which sent him to Canada to inaugurate the new constitution considered its own instructions as a primary part of its policy.

It is, therefore, difficult to praise the Quebec Act without reservation either as a solution to the current problem or as an instinctive act of statesmanship anticipating the nationalist feelings of the modern world. It seems clear that a less complete revival of Canadian law would have been satisfactory to the great majority of the Canadians, and would have met the reasonable wishes of the merchants. It might not have satisfied the seigneurs, but they were a minority even smaller than the merchants, and apparently even less popular with other Canadians. The special regard for their wishes was dictated by a political purpose which failed. From the viewpoint of political expediency it is probable that more could have been gained by conciliating the American waverers among the merchants. Certainly the exasperation of the merchants did nothing to improve relations between English and French in Canada.

The Quebec Act has been tormented into a pattern of nationalist motives and implications alien to the time and to the men who framed it. In 1774 recognition of Canadian nationalism would not have been good, and a plan of humane anglicization was not bad. Nationalism was not yet a moral issue. The real moral issues were respected. All speakers in the House of Commons on both sides showed a concern for human rights, placing them, ostensibly at least, above any special interest. The reports of the law officers, without exception, were rational and humane, remarkably free from national prejudice. There was a concern to stress the limitations on the rights of the conqueror. "Can . . . the conqueror impose such laws as he pleases?" asked Wedderburn. "This proposition has been maintained by some lawyers who have not distinguished between force and right." Nor was it forgotten that Canadians were persons: "I am free to say," said Charles James Fox, who opposed the bill, "that the Canadians are my first object; and I maintain that their happiness and their liberties are the proper objects, and ought to be the leading principle of this bill. . . ." [28]

Undoubtedly the British wished first to conciliate and then to anglicize Canadians, and both for their own convenience. But in none of the correspondence or reports on the Quebec question is there any sign that they failed to accept these moral principles as fundamental.

CHAPTER 10

Carleton's Catastrophe

Carleton returned to Quebec on September 18, 1774, with every prospect of success and happiness. He was by his new commission governor-in-chief of a large and valuable province. His quick observation and vivid imagination had fully appreciated its possibilities for trade, settlement, and further expansion into the wilderness. He was about to introduce a system of government which would, he believed, make it a model for all North American colonies. He also had a new source of private happiness in the young wife who accompanied him to Quebec to be the first mistress of the Château St Louis since 1759.

Carleton was soon reminded that the public arrangements which gave him such satisfaction had aroused anger and defiance in Boston and New York. The extension of Quebec over lands claimed by the other colonies for themselves, combined with the provision for alien laws and arbitrary government over the whole area, appeared to the colonists as one more deliberate and flagrant act of tyranny. Armed rebellion seemed inevitable. Carleton and his family were still on the Atlantic when Thomas Gage, Commander-in-Chief of the army in America, was writing to him from Boston to say that he was sending transports up to Quebec for reinforcements. He begged they might be dispatched immediately. He also suggested that Carleton should think of raising a force of Canadians and Indians to operate on the inland frontier.

Carleton received this dispatch the day after his arrival. He saw in it no evidence of the "catastrophe shocking to think of" that had occupied his thoughts seven years earlier; still less did he perceive any omen of his own personal catastrophe. He replied promptly that the troops would be waiting for the transports. As for the Canadians, rejoicing over the Quebec Act, "a Canadian regiment would complete their happiness." [1]

To Dartmouth in London the Governor wrote that all ranks of people among the Canadians were vying with each other in expressions of grati-

tude. He could not say as much of the English merchants. They were form-
ing what he called "cabals" which shortly produced separate addresses to
king, lords, and commons praying for the repeal of the Act. In Quebec, the
seat of the government, only twenty-five signatures could be secured from
the prudent merchants, but in Montreal, richer and more radical, one hundred and sixty-two signed. The Canadian counter-petitions could not muster
so many, but those who signed assured the authorities that they spoke for
all; if any Canadians had joined the English cabals "their hearts were not in
it." Meanwhile Dartmouth had replied to Carleton expressing his gratifica-
tion at the Canadian response. He reminded Carleton that he must take
pains to convince the English that their interests had also been attended
to by the enlargement of the province, and in the plan for "the adoption of
English laws as far as it was consistent with the just claims and moderate
wishes of the Canadians." [2]

Carleton ignored this plain directive. At no time did he give the English
merchants a hint that their representations had even been noticed. Much
of his attention was given to gratifying Canadians in their natural wish for
offices that had been closed to them since the Conquest. Pensions and
sinecures had been secured or promised to a number of the leading seigneurs
but many hopes were still unfulfilled. There was, inevitably, competition to
gain the Governor's ear. A Montreal merchant regretted "the persistence
of the N[oblesse?] in paying court and the tendency of the G[overnor?]
to listen to them." [3]

The position was a difficult one. There were many applicants to claim
the very few offices at the Governor's disposal. Apart from the judgeships
of the common pleas, the big prizes were seats in the council. As the members were named in Carleton's instructions, which he received only in April
1775, hope and disappointment alike were deferred during the winter. It
was known, however, that the lieutenant-governor, the chief justice, and
officials like the receiver general and surveyor general would be *ex officio*
members, and that the English with seats on the existing council must be
considered. Moreover, to appoint many Canadians would be to give them
a possible majority in the council, should English members be absent; it
was unlikely that London would be ready to run such a risk. In the end
places were found for eight Canadians, seven of them Roman Catholics and
seigneurs, the eighth a Protestant merchant, a member of the existing
council.

While disappointments were preparing for many of the grateful upper-
class Canadians, propaganda from the colonies to the south was pouring
into a community not unwilling to receive it. In October an address to the
people of Quebec from the Continental Congress assembled at Philadelphia
was published. It spoke of the Quebec Act as a flagrant violation of human

rights and invited the province to send representatives to the next meeting of the Congress in May. The Quebec *Gazette*, the only newspaper in the province, dared not print the message because its proprietors sustained themselves, with difficulty, on government printing contracts. Every other colonial paper printed the message, and it circulated freely in Quebec. All kinds of other radical or seditious communications, long and short, in French and English, were finding their way in, including the terse message dropped during the spring of 1775 at innumerable houses in the district of Montreal: "Onie soit qui mal y pense. A qui suivra le bon chemin," signed "Baston." [4]

At the same time a young lawyer, John Brown, was commissioned from Boston to make a personal appeal. After a difficult journey during the early spring thaw by the Lake Champlain route, he reached Montreal in April, and was welcomed at an enthusiastic meeting of English merchants at the Montreal Coffee House. Noble things were said about the cause of liberty, but in the end nothing was done. Some merchants were willing to correspond with Philadelphia, but they could not forget that, far more than any of the thirteen Atlantic communities, they were an economic colony of Great Britain, entirely dependent on London for carrying on their business. However bitter they might be, the merchants could not afford a complete break, even if they wished it. John Brown went home and no delegates went from Montreal to the May meeting of the Congress.

Thus, in spite of Carleton's angry talk of "cabals," and the knowledge he had of radical views and some seditious correspondence among the merchants, it was not the English who caused him increasing anxiety as the winter advanced. It was the mass of Canadians on whom he had relied implicitly. He gradually became convinced that they were not only indifferent but hostile. In February he showed something of his mind to Gage when he hinted in a letter that to organize the Canadian militia at that time would be distasteful to Canadians, and would reinforce the argument put about by "the sons of sedition" that the Quebec Act had been passed merely to serve the purposes of government. Time and discreet management would, he said, be needed "to recall [the habitants] to their ancient habits of obedience and discipline." [5]

Carleton did not report half of what he must have known. If he had acted on his knowledge he would have written frankly to London admitting that, having stripped the lower part of the province of troops in order to reinforce Gage, he now needed reinforcements for himself. Canadians were falling into a dangerous state of discontent and disaffection. Many of the seigneurs had grown arrogant and insolent. They were congratulating themselves not merely on a revival of former distinctions, but on being about to achieve a power and prestige which they could never have claimed under France, either personally or as a class. ". . . too much elated," said Chief Justice Hey, ". . . [they] gave very just offence as well to their own people as to the English merchants." [6] The habitants showed in return their "contempt and detestation" of the seigneurs and their resentment at these new pretensions. And, naturally, they were attracted by the new gospel from the other colonies. They had heard the English boast of English liberty; they were now being offered it by their American neighbours. They could hardly be expected to rally in gratitude for the grant of the religion which, as far as they knew, had never been threatened, or for laws of which they had never been completely deprived. As for the oath they had taken, the American agents explained to them that what they had done was to promise not to fight the English, the same English from Boston and New York who now offered them liberty and who, should the offer be refused, would, regretfully, have to treat them as enemies. [7]

What made the situation dangerous was that the habitants, accustomed to obedience, were also accustomed to see the province garrisoned adequately with regular troops who could be used at any time to enforce obedience. Anyone could see in the winter of 1774-75 that the troops were gone. Letters of Canadian merchants passing between Montreal and Quebec in the spring show the alarm felt by men who were in a position to know a good deal of what went on in the countryside. In April François Baby wrote:

> I have not been unaware . . . what a fateful time this has been for our unhappy colony. For three months I have seen the storm coming and some of your gentlemen in Montreal have contributed to it not a little. They are monsters who should have been smothered in the cradle. I fear that before long Canadians will be sorry that they asked for the new form of government. I won't . . . go further into a matter the very idea of which makes me tremble.

Guy answered from Montreal on May 1, the day the Quebec Act came into force. "Your observations . . . are very sound . . . as a good citizen you must mourn the lot of our province, but at least you are free whilst I am tied by a family which keeps me in the country." [8]

Baby's "monsters" may have been those who favoured the Americans. His reference to the Canadians regretting the new constitution, however, suggests that, like Hey, he was made anxious by the arrogance of the behaviour of the seigneurs. What is certain is that these two merchants, knowing the country well, were genuinely alarmed by the turn of events.

Although it was reported that the new councillors in Montreal were eagerly waiting for May 1 and their summons to Quebec, Carleton took no steps to summon the council or to establish the new framework of government beyond issuing six commissions to judges, including two French Canadians, J. C. Panet of Quebec and Hertel de Rouville of Montreal. Their duties were to begin on May 1 "unless they burst with pride," wrote the merchant Perras cheerfully.[9] Carleton was waiting for the arrival of Chief Justice Hey, who had spent the winter in England. Before Hey arrived, however, he received news which put all thought of constitutional arrangements out of his head and sent him hurrying up to Montreal to look to the defence of the province. On May 19 a letter from Gage announced the beginning of hostilities in Massachusetts. Next morning came news that the Americans were invading the province by way of Lake Champlain.

Carleton was now forced to call on the habitants for service. He could count on the goodwill and support of the Church. Montgolfier at Montreal on May 30 sent a circular to the priests of his district, ordering them to remind the habitants that religion, honour, and interest required them to obey all orders of government. Briand sent out a general mandamus to all districts early in June. With few exceptions the priests gave their full support.[10] The seigneurs also were eager to show their devotion. Carleton, therefore, ordered out the militia.

He soon was confirmed in his fear that ancient habits of obedience were lost. The habitants refused to follow their seigneurs and they defied the Church, saying that Briand and Montgolfier were paid to preach for the English. In vain the sacraments were refused to the contumacious. Some may have been indifferent; most, no doubt, planned to make their peace at a convenient season. On June 21 Carleton reluctantly proclaimed martial law as the only regular method of coercing the habitants. All militia captains who had been commissioned during the military regime were ordered to get their men out. Seigneurs and government officials offered supervision and assistance, only to meet strong resistance. Hiding their precious firearms in the woods, the habitants in some places armed themselves with wooden clubs and refused enrolment. Judge Mabane and a seigneur were rescued from mob violence on the Island of Orleans only by the intervention of M. Desglis, the Bishop's coadjutor. Near Three Rivers the habitants threatened to kidnap young Lanaudière, Carleton's Canadian aide-de-camp, and send him to the Americans. In some places they said they would fight under English officers but not under the seigneurs, perhaps an ingenious evasion. In the Chambly district they sent a hurried message to the Americans on Lake Champlain: Were they really coming? If not, the English might have to be obeyed. At Lévis [11] an "assembly" with representatives from a number of parishes met to organize continuous resistance to impressment.[12] In the circumstances Dartmouth's order to Carleton in July to carry out his own favourite plan of raising two battalions of Canadians of three thousand men each must have seemed a very poor joke.[13]

Carleton could have raised fighting men at this time. In this same month fifteen hundred men of the Six Nations offered to aid the British by raiding the back settlements of the colonies, but the Governor refused to authorize this brutal warfare. It was resorted to only after he had left the province.

All this time the Americans were on their way. The invasion was not, at the beginning, a planned campaign. It was an unauthorized raid. The whole affair was over before the Declaration of Independence offered some sort of justification for the invasion by colonial troops of a colony not represented in Congress. Judged as a raid, or a series of raids, the invasion was a remarkable demonstration of skill, enterprise, and endurance. As a regular campaign for the conquest of a province, however, it was too weakly organized to support success. Congress was not equipped to maintain a considerable army in such a remote area, still less to give orderly government in conquered territory.[14]

The affair began with a plan to secure artillery for the colonial levies. Someone remembered the cannon at the Lake Champlain forts, Ticonderoga and Crown Point. Benedict Arnold, who had served in the Seven Years' War, was commissioned by Massachusetts to attempt their capture. As these forts were the key to the water route from Montreal to Albany, Gage had already ordered Carleton to reinforce the garrisons. Even if Carleton had had the force to do so, it was too late. On May 10-11 Arnold with Ethan Allen and a force from Vermont secured the forts and captured a hundred cannon.

Arnold's mission was accomplished with such ease that he was encouraged to take the obvious next step. Lake shipping, including an armed sloop, was laid up for the winter on the Richelieu at St John, the northern end of the inland water route. On May 19 Arnold, in another raid, possessed himself of the sloop, a number of bateaux, and some stores, and made off again up the river to Lake Champlain. His rival and colleague passed him as he returned. Ethan Allen planned to capture and hold the post at St John. The scheme was too ambitious. Major Preston in command at Montreal was already on his way to St John with a superior force. Allen and his men were warned and retreated just in time.

Carleton now had to address himself to the task of preparing for an invasion along the route by which he had hoped to take the offensive. The key point was St John, where navigation ended. Down river, below the rapids, was Chambly, a post surrounded by a stone wall and containing valuable stores of food and gunpowder. Lower still, where the Richelieu flowed into the St Lawrence, was Sorel. The obvious course for an invading force was to pass down the Richelieu and, holding St John and Chambly, to establish itself at Sorel. With a few guns mounted there, it would be possible to cut off Montreal from Quebec, and to advance on either place, or to retreat, as circumstances directed.

To forestall any such move Carleton needed to strengthen the post at St John, and to establish effective control over the triangle of flat, fertile land, with its apex at Sorel and its base resting on St John and La Prairie, opposite the Island of Montreal. The post at St John consisted of a stone house belonging to Colonel Christie, Murray's old enemy, with some barracks and other buildings a short distance away. Around them Captain Marr, the engineering officer, was setting up two square palisaded enclosures protected by earthworks and connected by a covered way, the whole surrounded by a ditch. There was nothing that a soldier would call a fort there, or anywhere in the province, but the earthworks would resist bombardment for a time. While this work went on, a sloop and boats were being built to replace those captured by Arnold.

Carleton made less progress in establishing political control of the all-important triangle. This was the district from which messages had already been sent to say that if the Americans were coming, the Canadians need not obey the English. The disaffection was unfortunate, for this was the granary of Quebec. Had the habitants here consented even to maintain a hostile neutrality, refusing to sell and conveying away supplies, the invasion might have bogged down in their swampy meadows.

Carleton was given time to prepare St John because Congress had decided to sponsor a regular invasion, and elaborate preparations were under way. Benedict Arnold was refused the command and retired from Lake Champlain. The leader in the field was Richard Montgomery, an Irishman, formerly a British officer and a capable one, married to one of the wealthy New York Livingstons. By September Montgomery and his men had reached the Richelieu, and were swarming over the strategic triangle and around St John. The habitants welcomed them, sold them supplies and services, and a number took arms on their side.

In Montreal the militia, English and Canadian, were mustering on the Champ de Mars and taking guard duty. Nor were the women idle in the land of Madeleine de Verchères. The widow Benoist got down her husband's old sword "to defend her family" and so alarmed a passing English officer with a demonstration of her skill that he retreated hastily, assuring her that he was not an American. On the whole the spirit in Montreal, Canadian and English, was so good that Carleton felt able to arrest the egregious Thomas Walker, who had corresponded with the invaders regularly, but who defended his house like a citadel until carried off at last, still protesting the outrage to liberty.

The invaders on their part were soon in some trouble. There were difficulties of transport and of supply. Many were sick from camping on swampy ground. Almost all were ill disciplined. Ethan Allen, sent out to recruit Canadians, found himself at Longueuil on September 25, and took it into his head to capture Montreal but succeeded only, after a brief engagement, in getting captured himself along with forty others. St John's fortifications were standing up well and the besiegers, like the besieged, were running short of supplies.

The tide turned when the Americans battered down the wall at Chambly and secured the gunpowder and stores which should have been destroyed. Major Preston, having put up a gallant resistance with his garrison of English soldiers and a few Canadians, yielded St John on November 2. This disaster compelled Carleton to evacuate Montreal immediately. It was indefensible and he must not be cut off from Quebec. He retreated only just in time. The Americans captured his ships, delayed by a contrary wind at Sorel. Carleton, with the aid of Canadian boatmen, reached Quebec in a whaleboat, safe but without troops.

In his absence Cramahé and the ranking military officer, Colonel Allan McLean, had been preparing for the expected siege. They had a numerous but motley garrison – McLean's own regiment, the Royal Highland Emigrants, recruited under the very noses of the patriots; militia men, English and Canadian; sailors from naval ships detained by Cramahé; and a few scores of Irish fishermen recruited at Newfoundland – some twelve hundred in all. The supplies were adequate, but no more. The morale of the garrison was doubtful. Large numbers of people unused to such labour had been cutting pickets to strengthen the rotten palisade to landward by day, and taking turns at guard duty by night. Some were eager and excited, others sullen and unwilling. Carleton's position was intensely disagreeable. He had spent the summer enduring reverses and humiliations, nearly all the result of his own errors of judgement. Although he could assert that the seigneurs had "behaved well," he almost certainly knew that one had flirted with the Americans, and had drawn off only when they demanded a large sum of hard money for Continental paper; and that Lanaudière, his aide-de-camp, was so unpopular that he had to be excused duties that would take him among Canadians.[15]

On the other hand, he had become unexpectedly indebted to the Canadian merchants whom he had neglected and the English merchants whom he disliked. He had to use Canadian merchants, François Baby in Quebec and St George Dupré in Montreal, to organize such militia and transport services as could be made available. As for the English,

The Governor, [said one] finding all his efforts vain to . . . give proof of his influence over the Canadians through his friends, the nobles of the province, was obliged to have recourse to the English who had been represented as few in number, of little consequence, as not worthy even of the notice, and much less the protection of the government.[16]

It was true. Not only had Carleton generously praised the English of Montreal for their courage; when he led his little force to meet Ethan Allen he sustained only two serious casualties, one a veteran officer killed, and the other, the merchant Alexander Patterson, a leader of the "cabal" for the repeal of the Quebec Act, dangerously wounded. Cramahé, stubbornly clinging to the anti-English party line, still maintained that it would be better if all old subjects showed their true colours and declared for the rebels immediately. Carleton now understood that political distinctions were not so clear cut. During the siege he had to depend on the service and loyalty of many strong critics of his policy who, as he knew, blamed him for their troubles.[17]

If Carleton's thoughts were depressing, they were not paralysing. His calm and cheerful manner, his energy and confidence were remarked on from the moment he arrived at Quebec. He achieved an immediate personal ascendancy over Cramahé's hastily assembled garrison. The writer of an anonymous journal which gives a day-to-day account of life within the walls made Carleton the central figure and the hero of his story.[18] Carleton dealt immediately with the problem of slackness and insubordination in the ranks of the militia by announcing that all able-bodied men who would not serve willingly must leave the town. They were required to leave behind any provisions or stores in their possession. These would be purchased for public use. Some Canadians withdrew, and some English merchants. Like the habitants, some merchants wished to be neutral; others favoured the Americans. All were aware that if the British were driven from Quebec the merchants who had given them active support would probably be ruined.

As Carleton took over from Cramahé and McLean and prepared for the advance of Montgomery from Montreal, the siege of Quebec had, after a fashion, already begun. Benedict Arnold, rejected on Lake Champlain, had no thought of withdrawing from a project which he had some right to regard as his own. Lake Champlain was not the only inland waterway to Quebec. There was a route from New England, up the Kennebec and by the Dead River over to the Chaudière, which flowed into the St Lawrence a little above the city of Quebec. This way was used by the Indians, and was practicable enough for experienced woodsmen travelling light. It was not designed for an army and baggage train. Arnold, however, with the patronage of Washington and the support of Massachusetts, gathered eight hundred men and set off, the men wading upstream as rowing became impossible, pushing the loaded boats before them. That most survived the journey and arrived was a miracle.

> For forty days I waded . . . in freezing weather . . . an allowance of half a pint of flour a man for a fortnight and half of that time no meat; climbing hills, passing through morasses, cedar swamps . . . wading creeks and rivers . . . [wrote one].[19]

Some turned back, but most struggled on, reaching St François on the Chaudière famished and exhausted. The kindly Canadians there, full of pity and admiration, sheltered and fed them and sent them on down river to Ste Marie where the habitants, not to be outdone, offered them a feast at the home of the loyalist seigneur Taschereau, who had left for Quebec to help defend the city against them. The ragged force reached the St Lawrence in the middle of November, just before Carleton's arrival at Quebec. They possessed themselves of Henry Caldwell's farm and mills on the Lévis side, then slipped across the river and defied the city with a parade on the Plains of Abraham. After this they prudently retired up river to Pointe aux Trembles to mend their shoes and get winter moccasins.

The siege which followed throughout the winter, though grim and painful enough to both sides, had its elements of absurdity. Even though Montgomery promptly descended from Montreal to join Arnold with supplies and additional men, the besieged occasionally outnumbered the besiegers. But Carleton's force – "a wretched motley garrison" Arnold called it [20] – was much too raw and undisciplined to risk a sortie and an engagement, with a hostile population in the background. How hostile, no one could know; Bishop Briand, better informed than most, remarked that everyone in the province hoped the Americans would win.[21] As for the besieged city, it was no fortress, but at best an armed camp in a position strong enough but, because of the sharp slopes running down from Cape Diamond, exposed to cannon fire from several directions. This would have been serious, perhaps fatal, had not the cannon brought up by the besiegers been so much lighter than those mounted about the city that the total casualties within the walls were one non-combatant, and a turkey whose leg was broken. Cold, sick, and short of supplies, the Americans were at last reduced to the desperate plan of storming the city.

They chose the bitter stormy night of December 31. Under cover of a blizzard Arnold moved from the suburb of St Roch on the north, while Montgomery from the south passed along the narrow strip of land about the foot of Cape Diamond. Had both these parties succeeded they would have had possession of the Lower Town. It is unlikely that they considered the nearly impossible task of storming the heights from the river side; the best they could hope for was that with all the mercantile wealth of the Lower Town in danger of looting and destruction, the citizens would force a surrender. As it turned out both attacks on the Lower Town failed. Montgomery was killed by a shot from an outpost as he approached the town, and Arnold went down with a painful leg wound at the beginning of the fighting. Arnold's men pressed on for a time through the barricades, but were surrounded and forced to withdraw, with a loss of a hundred killed and over four hundred prisoners. Carleton ordered a "genteel coffin" for his former friend, Montgomery, regretting the "infatuation" of "a genteel man and an agreeable companion." Meanwhile, some of the prisoners, recollecting that their contract with Congress ended on December 31, asked if they might enlist under His Majesty for the coming year.[22]

In spite of their reverse the Americans maintained the siege throughout the winter, but their problems were multiplying. General Wooster, successor to Montgomery, was neither an agreeable companion nor a "genteel man." He deeply offended public opinion when, on a suspicion of unneutral conduct, he arrested Judge Fraser and a number of other citizens and sent them south as prisoners. He failed to win the friendship of Canadians because he did not hide the fact that he despised them and their church. Many of his own men were going home, having completed their period of service. His cash was getting short, and throughout the country resentful habitants were being compelled to accept the paper money they had such good reason to distrust. The Americans, in short, were now compelled to act not as liberators but as conquerors. Many Montrealers must have compared them unfavourably with the conquerors of 1760, Amherst and Gage. Matters were not mended when, late in April, Congress sent three representatives, including Benjamin Franklin, to discuss terms of union. They did not bring cash with them, they could not win over public opinion, and they soon went back to Philadelphia, leaving the army once more in control.

As the spring drew near it became obvious that the army was losing its control. Numerous enough still, the men were discouraged and many were ill. Smallpox was endemic in Montreal. Some went down with the disease, others disabled themselves by use of the current preventative, inoculation, a formidable measure. Moreover if, as seemed certain, Carleton should receive adequate reinforcements from overseas when the river opened, the Americans must either organize a rapid retreat or be caught in a trap.

Rumours of the expected reinforcements, eagerly looked for by the weary garrison in Quebec, reached Quebec early in May. On May 6 the frigate *Surprise* appeared in Quebec basin, the first ship of a British fleet, bringing ten thousand men with ample equipment, supplies, and money. The Americans before Quebec who had already determined on a retreat, withdrew immediately in disorder, leaving many stores behind them.

General Thomas, who had succeeded Wooster in command, at first fell back on the key position of Sorel. Then, learning that he, too, was to be re-inforced by way of Lake Champlain, he advanced once again as far as Three Rivers. The approach to this town, north of Lake St Peter, was difficult, and his army, led astray by a Canadian, bogged down for a time in the swampy land. When he did reach Three Rivers he was dismayed to find waiting for him on land a far larger force than he had expected, while ships coming up river with yet more troops threatened to cut him off from Sorel.

The result was another retreat, hasty, ill-organized, even panicky, but astonishingly successful. From up river and down, the Americans con-verged on St John, destroyed their stores, secured the necessary boats, and made off up the Richelieu to Lake Champlain, to be seen no more on the St Lawrence for the duration of the war. The invasion was over.

The departure of the invaders left Carleton once more in possession of the whole province, a welcome change after his humiliating retreat from Montreal and his miserable winter in the dubious stronghold of Quebec. His firm and effective stand at Quebec was duly praised, and won him as reward the red ribbon of the Knight of the Bath. But George III and the ministers who honoured him were not entirely blind to the fact that the success of the American retreat added one more to the list of Carleton's errors and miscalculations. He had misunderstood Canadian society and especially the outlook of the habitant. He had rashly stripped the province of troops and, by failing to report his predicament in time, he had taken upon himself the responsibility for the success of the American invasion. Finally, with ample reinforcements at his disposal he had failed either to trap the American army or to get possession of its supplies.

Carleton's own dispatches to Dartmouth on this last failure [23] were un-communicative. It is, however, clear that British and Americans were both present in force at Three Rivers on June 8, and that not until June 19 did Carleton reach St John, the last, but not the only point on the water route at which he might have cut off their retreat. Although contrary winds delayed the ships, there were roads of a sort on each side of the St Lawrence, and the habitants could now be effectively coerced. Even had it not been possible to engage the enemy earlier, it need not have taken eleven days for Carleton to cover the hundred miles or so between Three Rivers and St John.

This final military blunder meant that the British army, ready for immediate advance along Lake Champlain to Albany and the line of the Hudson, was deprived of the boats without which it could not move. There was a whole year of delay before Burgoyne could begin his advance, late in the summer of 1777, a year when valuable troops were idle, consuming much-needed supplies. The most plausible explanation of Carleton's error is the extreme difficulty of distinguishing between a rebellion, which may be most effectively dealt with by caution and moderation, and civil war, where the classic rules of warfare come into operation. Carleton, only a few months earlier, had bought a coffin for his former friend Montgomery; he had seen men enlisted under Congress offering overnight to transfer to the service of George III. He had also taken the trouble before he left Quebec in May to try to gather in the Americans, "His Majesty's deluded subjects," who had been left sick and wounded about the city, in order to care for them and send them home, having taught them, he hoped, to be better subjects in future. His whole policy was one of compassion and conciliation, reasonable enough, perhaps, as Congress had not yet issued the Declaration of Independence.

Carleton also wanted to get the Americans out of the country. He did not want to have to keep thousands of men, many of them sick, in a disaffected province, where he had no adequate means of feeding them or of sheltering them against a rigorous climate. It is not, however, clear why he did not force a formal surrender. He might have secured the supplies, and the boats from the lakes, before arranging for the men to go home with a cartel of exchange. One of his junior officers had already followed this course after a minor engagement with the enemy above Montreal.

As Carleton's private papers have not survived, there is no clue to his own explanation of the action which caused adverse comment in Britain and might even have brought about his recall. His official dispatches, while full of his problems after the American retreat, avoid the critical month of June.

Whatever Carleton's motives, by the end of June the province was clear of Americans, but with the boats at the wrong end of Lake Champlain Carleton had to spend the rest of the summer frantically constructing fighting-ships and transport. In October his little fleet was able to venture along Lake Champlain where it encountered and defeated the American naval force. By this time the Americans were so strongly reinforced at Ticonderoga that Carleton dared not attack that fort. Nor, because of the shortage of local supplies, did he venture to take up winter quarters at the recaptured Crown Point. He retreated down the Richelieu and wintered in Canada.

Meanwhile it had been decided in London that Carleton must not command the invading army from Canada. The decision was originally based on military etiquette, Carleton being senior in the service to General Howe, who had succeeded Gage as commander-in-chief in America. Its wisdom seemed to be confirmed when news of Carleton's apparently lethargic conclusion of the 1776 campaign reached London. The dispatch with the news failed to reach Quebec before the river closed in 1776. Only in the spring of 1777 did Carleton learn that he was to turn over the command of the invading force to his junior, General Burgoyne, while he attended to the organization of civil government in the province of Quebec.

Carleton had confidently expected to take the field with the army in the spring, leaving Cramahé to administer the province. He was bitterly disappointed, angry, and humiliated. He did, however, offer loyal support to Burgoyne as he set out on his ill-fated expedition. Burgoyne got his army over the familiar water route without difficulty. His troubles began when he attempted the land journey over to the Hudson. The country was unexpectedly difficult and the inhabitants unexpectedly hostile. As early as August 20 he was writing of the advisability of a retreat. Unhappily he had not the courage to use his own discretion. He pressed on until on October 17 he found himself at Saratoga on the Hudson; surrounded and cut off, he was compelled to surrender his whole army.

The plan of strategy worked out by Carleton in 1767 had been put into operation and had failed dismally. Had he been in command, he might not have met Burgoyne's disaster but he could hardly have hoped for success. His plan assumed that the Canadians would be armed and eager to engage the enemy, instead of remaining as he found them, with few exceptions, either passive or hostile. Henceforth he knew there would be no more invasions from Quebec. Unless the war took a turn most favourable to the British he might expect instead a repetition of the events of 1775-76. Meanwhile, he was civil governor of Quebec and it was his duty to bring into being the constitution of his own devising.

CHAPTER 11

The System of the Generals: Carleton

The Quebec Act, disappointing as it had been to the merchants, was a flexible instrument. In the hands of a liberal and tactful governor it might have afforded the basis for a settlement reasonably satisfactory to Canadians and English alike. Instead it fell into the hands of two governors, each with enough experience of the "turbulence" of American colonies, to use their own expression, to be distrustful of any semblance of popular government. Moreover, for eight years after the Act came into force, the province was either occupied by enemy troops or on the alert for an invasion. During the whole of this time there was reason to think that American invaders would receive open help from some Canadians and sympathy from many others too honourable to break their oath. Neither the men nor the times encouraged a liberal interpretation of an apparently illiberal act. The form of government that was evolved by Carleton and his successor, Frederick Haldimand, was called admiringly "le système des généraux." [1]

The expression would have been found apt enough by the many who resented the system. The generals took the conciliar form of government and developed its autocratic possibilities to the limit. Neither man meant to be harsh, but each believed that circumstances justified the arbitrary rule that he preferred.

Even before Quebec was clear of Americans, Carleton had addressed himself to the task of restoring law and order in the province which had suffered from incipient revolt as well as from invasion. Two weeks before the British confronted the retreating Americans at Three Rivers, he had begun to deal with the district of Quebec. On May 22, François Baby, colonel of militia for the district, set out with Taschereau, seigneur of St Mary's on the Chaudière, and Jenkin Williams, a lawyer, and soon to be clerk of the council, on a seven-week circuit of the parishes, beginning in the neighbourhood of Quebec and the Island of Orleans, then up river to Three Rivers on the north shore, over to the south shore, and down river as far as Kamouraska. Their stated purpose was "the establishment of the militia in each parish and . . . the examination of those who have aided the rebels. . . ." [2]

The procedure was everywhere the same. There was a preliminary interview with the priest, and perhaps some others, to amplify or correct the information that the commissioners already possessed. This was followed by a public muster of the militia. Officers who had co-operated with the rebels were cashiered, and new ones appointed in their places. In flagrant cases men might be declared forever excluded from public office, and even from parish assemblies. Those who had accepted commissions from the rebels were required to burn them publicly, being told that they were performing this office for the public hangman. This ceremony was followed by an "harrangue" in which the habitants were enjoined to be loyal and submissive and to perform faithfully their work on the roads. After this everyone was encouraged to shout "Vive le Roi." In Seigneur Taschereau's parish five men who ostentatiously refrained were required to make public confession and apology before the church on the following Sunday, the seigneur himself remaining behind to see that they did so.

The records of the circuit show abundant evidence that the habitants had aided the Americans with food and other supplies, and with information and espionage services. Some were accused of playing the informer against loyal neighbours, and of inviting the invaders to coerce their priests, and even to detain them and plunder their property. Many had been indifferent, yielding to the threats and promises of the invaders. Some had served only under duress, others very gladly. In two parishes a woman bearing the nickname "la reine d'Hongrie" [3] had been particularly active against the British. In several other places the activities of women were particularly noted. The commissioners, when ordering the newly established militia captains to arrest those who indulged in seditious talk, stated specifically that women were to be detained as well as men.

Most of the parishes visited had suffered more or less severely from the British invasion only sixteen years earlier. No doubt there was general resentment, especially among bereaved women, at the renewal of war, and it was understandable that the British should be blamed. The report of the circuit suggests that Briand's statement that everyone wished the defeat of the British was somewhat exaggerated; on the other hand, much of the information came from the parish priest who would naturally wish to be as favourable as he could. Militia officers, many of them appointed by Carleton in the fall of 1775, were cashiered in thirty-seven out of some fifty parishes visited; only in two places was the militia captain fully exonerated. In one parish where the Americans had been served without resistance, as no one would "talk," the establishment of the militia had to be deferred. In another the habitants complained of the revival of the system of militia captains; they preferred Murray's bailiffs who, being changed every year, were less likely to be oppressive.

The only punishment recorded, apart from the cashiering of militia officers, was the confiscation of guns from notorious "bad subjects." The complaint that this punishment was meted out unevenly was probably too well founded. From this time forward, however, individuals and parishes could be coerced by the destruction of their property if they failed to co-operate in the necessary *corvées*, which might involve being sent up country to assist in military transport in the district of Montreal. One parish, at least, continued for a time armed resistance, but yielded by the end of the summer.[4]

There is little doubt that in his measures to pacify the countryside and to secure submission Carleton acted with the help and advice of Bishop Briand. The circuit could not have been conducted without the co-operation of the parish priests, and it was Briand's special desire that it be completed as quickly as possible. On his instructions all sacraments, including those for the dying, had been withheld from those who persisted in repudiating their oath of allegiance. In one place where, during divine service, an unseen listener had interrupted a patriotic exhortation from the pulpit by shouting *"C'est assez prêché pour les Anglais!"* Briand had laid an interdict on the entire parish. Now that the crisis was over reasons of mercy and of policy urged him speedily to forgive and restore "those poor souls whose blindness merits all our compassion and . . . our tears." The habitants, he said, ". . . are religious, are good at heart, but have been led astray." He would, however, make no move toward a general reconciliation until the government had conceded a general pardon and amnesty.[5]

Baby's circuit in Quebec, and a similar one which followed in Montreal, left Briand free to forgive and restore all who were prepared to give evidence of penitence. The inquisitorial procedures were unpleasant by certain standards, then and now. They were, however, an integral part of the French system, entirely familiar to the habitants. They seem to have been applied with mildness and sympathy for all who had acted under coercion. It was necessary to take some disciplinary measures, to identify disaffection, and to demonstrate that government once more had power to protect the loyal and obedient. Carleton had been severely criticized by observers in the province for not having terrorized the habitants into submission in 1775. He had refused brutal methods of coercion then; in 1776 he avoided vengeful punishment even when he had the power.[6]

By August of 1776 Carleton was able also to undertake some reorganization of the law courts. Of the six judges appointed in April 1775, two were now prisoners of the Americans. Filling their places by temporary appointments, he established a bench of three judges in each of the districts of Quebec and Montreal to try civil cases. He also issued a number of commissions of justice of the peace, Canadian Roman Catholics being included for the first time.[7]

For the next two or three years there was some confusion over judicial and other appointments in Quebec. Carleton assumed not only that he could recommission men who had served before May 1775, but that he had the power to make new appointments without even reporting them to London for confirmation. Lord George Germain in London assumed the usual power of filling colonial offices. The result was that Carleton found himself for a time with more judges than he needed, in addition to a surplus attorney general. The slowness of communications complicated the problem. Fortunately some of the English appointees, especially those who spent their first winter shut up by the Americans in Quebec, found prospects in the new colony less attractive than they had expected, and returned to England.

In the end, five out of the six judges in the common pleas who remained were Carleton's appointments: Adam Mabane, Thomas Dunn, and Pierre Panet who in 1778 replaced J.-C. Panet in Quebec; John Fraser and Hertel de Rouville in Montreal. Three of these, Mabane, Fraser, and Dunn, had already served ten years on the bench. Of the new appointments, Pierre Panet had been a lawyer in Montreal; Rouville had filled a minor judicial post at Three Rivers before the Conquest. Although Murray had employed Rouville, Carleton had at first distrusted him as "having dangerous views" but later came in part to share Rouville's own "exceeding good opinion of his own abilities."[8] Edward Southouse, the only English appointment, was a needy and unsuccessful English attorney. These six men were responsible for the entire administration of civil justice under the Quebec Act. Of the six, only Panet was professionally qualified. The advice of Hey and Maseres that only able lawyers should be appointed judges was forgotten, or was found impracticable.

By January 1777 at the opening of the regular legislative season Carleton was ready to summon a full council for much necessary work. This was not, however, the first meeting of the council under the Quebec Act. In August 1775, during the lull in American activity, the twenty-two members of this new and enlarged council had been summoned to the Château St Louis. Chief Justice Hey had arrived with the draft of an ordinance to set up the law courts and to give some definition to the new system of law, the first and most essential task.

It was at this council meeting that Carleton adopted the policy from which he never swerved, and which he passed on to Haldimand. His instructions required him to communicate to the council the articles of his instructions dealing with matters "wherein their advice and consent are mentioned to be requisite,"[9] and to do so "forthwith." That is, he was to let the councillors know immediately, for their guidance, the opinion of the ministry at home on what would be desirable legislation. If he had done this he must have recommended to them the introduction of English civil law in commercial cases "if not altogether, at least in part." The original instruction, watered down perhaps at Carleton's request, had been "as nearly as possible." He must also have recommended protection for personal liberty by a writ of *habeas corpus*; the original draft had required *habeas corpus* "in its fullest extent." Finally he was required to let the council know not all, but a part, of his instructions on ecclesiastical matters. He was ordered to consult them about the suspension of priests, the regulation of seminaries and women's convents, and, possibly, about the suppression of the Jesuit order.

It was the opinion of James Monk, who came to the province later as attorney general, that if these instructions had been read in council the English would have been largely reconciled and much of the anxiety caused by English disaffection removed. Monk may have been right in this judgement, but there can be little doubt that Carleton was prudent in suppressing part of his instructions. By August 1775 he was realizing his dependence on the clergy, the only substantial body of men in the province which was both loyal and influential. It was hardly likely that Carleton would disturb them at this critical moment by letting them know that he was to associate the council with himself in disciplining priests and in regulating the seminaries and the convents. Carleton, however, went much further. None of the instructions on legislation was communicated by him to the council then or at any other time. Carleton's first act on meeting the council was to deny to it, implicitly, the assistance and authority in legislation to which it was entitled.

At the meeting in August 1775 Carleton's decision to conceal his instructions had a decisive effect. At that time there could be no question of *habeas corpus*, but English commercial law was suggested by Chief Justice Hey, who fully expected to carry his point. The seven Canadian seigneurs were, however, unalterably opposed. To his arguments they answered only, "*Je me renferme dans le Bill.*" They gave him to understand that the "bill" was not, as Lord North had suggested, "a general basis," "a law . . . ready to be altered and amended as occasion shall arise," but rather, as Lotbinière had maintained, a fundamental law, guaranteed by Great Britain and subject in Quebec only to the most trifling modifications. The council was prorogued after a few meetings, no business having been completed.

Whether Carleton had encouraged the seigneurs in their view of the law, or only, by concealing his instructions, failed to discourage it, it became the chief plank in the platform of "the French party," the most powerful party bloc in the council for the next fifteen years. It is impossible to say whether it did represent the views of the majority of the Canadians. Not for several years did a French-speaking member show much initiative in the business of the council. The seigneurs for the most part acted as an obedient official party, following the will of the governor, and looking hopefully for loaves and fishes.[10]

Two men led the party, Cramahé, and Adam Mabane, once more on the council. Cramahé had served successively as secretary to Murray and Carleton and as administrator of the province for four years. Carleton's return in 1774 obliged him to step down, but as secretary to the Governor and chairman of the council, he was powerful. Diligent, methodical, and unimaginative, he had developed a natural liking for authoritarian government, and a suspicion of everything American. Mabane, having been dismissed by Carleton in 1766, had served only two years on the council. He had, however, been Murray's right-hand man during those two years, and he had been on the bench in Quebec since 1764. He was an able man and, like Cramahé, strongly anti-American. It was perhaps through Cramahé's influence that this useful man was restored to favour. Mabane and Cramahé were unrivalled in their experience and knowledge of the province. In 1779 John Fraser, released from his American prison and able to take up his duties on the bench and in the council, made a third in this inner group. These three, with the seigneurs, were at the service of Carleton and, for a time, of Haldimand. They could generally command a majority.

The other members of the council were the chief justice and the provincial secretary *ex officio*, the deputy surveyor general, John Collins, two merchants who were also officials, Thomas Dunn, the judge, and Hugh Finlay, deputy postmaster general, two English seigneurs, and several other merchants, one a Canadian Protestant. The officials were not obliged to vote with the official party and they did not always do so. Life was, however, pleasanter for them, and for the merchants too, when the governor smiled on them. Apart from Cramahé, Mabane, and Fraser, the English-speaking members did not vote as a group.

The merchants, except for the judge, Thomas Dunn, tended to represent the radical or "American" element favouring less arbitrary government and more English law. The most militant member of the group was George Allsopp. Another was Hugh Finlay, the postmaster, milder but persistent. Both were able men, of long experience in the province.

When Carleton summoned the council, in January 1777, he still expected to set out in command of the army of invasion in the spring, leaving

Cramahé once more to administer the province. When he learned of Burgoyne's appointment he persuaded himself that Lord George Germain, whom he suspected of being pro-American and whom he had already accused of deliberately stirring up trouble in the province by "American" appointments, was personally responsible for his having been passed over.* He offered his resignation immediately, in one of the many angry and even insolent dispatches sent to Germain in the course of the year. The resignation was accepted, no doubt with relief, but Carleton could not be replaced until 1778. He remained as governor of Quebec until June of that year. It was during the years 1777 and 1778 that he established the form of government he had always favoured, a benevolent, but barely disguised, despotism.

When the council met in January 1777 for its first effective legislative session, it had no legal member. Hey, returned to England in 1775, had resigned, and no successor was yet appointed. The council was dependent for guidance on the Attorney General, William Grant, an appointee of Carleton and not long resident in the province. This was unfortunate, as there were passed that winter, along with about a dozen ordinances on such familiar subjects as fire, ferries, roads and bridges, bakers, currency, and the sale of strong liquor, two especially contentious ones. One of them regulated procedure in the courts of justice, the other regulated the militia. These two laws affected closely the liberty and property of every individual in the province. Over them political opposition developed, and continued for a decade.

In the constitution of the new law courts there was little change from the ordinance of 1770. The judges of the courts of common pleas were to deal with all civil cases, sitting weekly in Quebec and Montreal, with an additional special weekly sitting for cases under twelve pounds, and two circuits every year throughout the district, for the determination of small cases only, by one judge. The fundamental change from the old system was the disappearance of the superior court of king's bench as a civil court. The king's bench had applied English law, the common pleas

* Lord George Sackville (1716–1785) took the name Germain in 1770 and was created Viscount Sackville in 1782. A military career of some credit was cut short when he was cashiered and disgraced for apparent disobedience to orders at the battle of Minden, 1758. He entered Parliament, proved himself as an able speaker, attached himself to Lord North's party, and became President of the Board of Trade and Secretary of State for the Colonies on November 10, 1775. The latter position he held until February 1782. His official manners were haughty but in private life he was genial. He had been called "the gayest man in Ireland except his father" (who was viceroy). His difficulties with Carleton may be partly explained by some still unknown Irish feud. Officially he seems to have done nothing to provoke Carleton's furious dislike. A. L. Burt says that Carleton resented having to take orders from an officer cashiered for disobedience and suspected of cowardice.

Canadian; henceforth the Canadian court alone would have jurisdiction. From the common pleas an appeal lay directly to a court of appeal composed of the governor, the lieutenant-governor, or the chief justice as president, and any five members of council.

It was the ordinance regulating procedure in the civil courts that was complicated and contentious. Roughly, English procedure was used to get the parties into court and Canadian and French procedure thereafter. During the debates on this ordinance the merchants moved for optional jury trials and English law in commercial cases. The English merchants argued strongly, sometimes overstating their case, but pressing the sound argument that the London merchants on whom the province depended for credit would have more confidence in a system familiar to them and to their own legal advisers. The only concession they could win was the use of the English law of evidence in commercial cases.[11] The motion for optional juries was defeated by no more than seven votes to five, and then not until an announcement was made by the Lieutenant-Governor that the Governor would not assent to an ordinance which should include a provision for juries. This ordinance was passed for two years only, the opposition being left with the hope that they might secure something better next time.

If the ordinances on courts of justice were objectionable to the merchants, the militia law bore hardly on others who could not well speak for themselves, in council or elsewhere. The general purpose of this law was reasonable enough. The government had the right by English law to embody all able-bodied men in the militia for the defence of the country. Canadian custom gave the additional right to exact *corvée* services in the shape of transport duty, provision of firewood, and other services to the army. From the Conquest to 1775 most, if not all, of these services had been paid. The militia ordinance was passed at a critical moment – a few months after the purging of disloyal militia officers effected in 1776 and in the midst of the preparations for Burgoyne's advance to the Hudson. The obvious intention of the ordinance was to assert the authority of a military hierarchy – the commander-in-chief, militia colonels in Quebec, Three Rivers, and Montreal, and a captain with one or more lieutenants in each parish. On the authority of the commander-in-chief, militia captains could require services from the men. Specific punishments in the shape of fines and imprisonment, and confiscation of firearms, were prescribed in the ordinance for disobedience or evasion. Payment, however, which had been discontinued since 1775 was resumed.[12]

Unfortunately, everything in the ordinance but the duty of enrolment and the punishments was left very vague. The intention seems to have been that all orders for militia should be sent from staff officers to district colonels and from the colonels to their own militia captains. In practice it was dangerous for any man even to question the order of his captain, however partial or tyrannical. It was also dangerous for the captain to refuse an order from any regular officer. For using strong language about a German officer, who, without any notice, had commandeered his horse, a militia captain was imprisoned and beaten. His own colonel at Montreal could do no more than write to Baby, adjutant general at Quebec, who would speak to the governor, who would perhaps remonstrate with the offending officer.

The German mercenary troops engaged to supplement Britain's small army created a special problem. They were employed on garrison duty in the lower province, freeing the British troops for active service elsewhere. The Germans were likely to be more peremptory and exacting than the British, and the British commander-in-chief, recognizing the delicate problem of handling foreign troops, would intervene only with caution on minor matters. These troops, and later the loyalists cantoned through the province, made the life of militia men in many parishes burdensome. Transport to the up-country posts they were accustomed to. It was very heavy during the war years with large garrisons at the posts, and still larger groups of dependent Indians to be maintained. This work, however, was organized under a special transport officer, the merchant St George Dupré, who was competent, and who seems to have treated the men justly, protecting them as far as he could from abuse of power. Within the province the German detachments, some used for garrison duty because they were not considered fit for service in the field, were a constant course of irritation. The habitant might have to build barracks for them; when the barracks were built he must supply them with firewood. If there were no barracks he must billet them. He must also be ready at any time for special work on roads and bridges and for aid to troops or convoys of prisoners passing up or down the river. At times, apparently, groups of parishes were organized to provide a conscript labour force for fuel contractors.[13] Payment for all this work was in theory fixed by the commander-in-chief, in practice by the officer and department requiring it. Casual labour such as transport of men or goods from parish to parish was often unpaid. In their ignorance, and pushed from above, militia captains took it upon themselves to levy arbitrary fines on unruly or disobedient militia men. In general, it seems that English regular officers respected the rights of militia officers; the Germans tended to assume the right to ignore them and to discipline militia men as they did their own soldiers, inflicting punishments not included in the ordinance.[14]

The chief complaint about the militia law was its vagueness about what services might be required, whether these were to be free or for payment, by whom the payment was to be fixed, and how infractions of the law should be dealt with. François Baby, as adjutant general in charge of militia for the whole province, and the channel through which complaints to the governor had to pass, stated in 1785 that he did not know all the services that had been required or what pay had been given.[15] In spite of this he was prepared to express his conviction that there had been no hardship or injustice.

Others thought differently. Hugh Finlay who, as postmaster, had personal acquaintances in many parishes along the river tried in vain to modify the proposed ordinance in 1777. In the session of 1778 after the law had been in force for a year, the English seigneur, Caldwell, suggested revisions, with the object of securing a precise definition of obligations, and also effective publication of the regulations throughout the parishes, where few men could read. Although Caldwell's motions were voted down by large majorities, Finlay brought the matter up again a few weeks later in a general motion stating that "the Canadian peasants have cause for heavy complaint," and proceeded to retail the grievances mentioned above. "Let us endeavour to avert the fatal consequences that may attend their spirit of disgust, which is but too general and rankles in the hearts of our fellow subjects of this country."[16]

Not only in council, but privately to the Governor, Finlay urged that Canadians should be shown that the recent ordinances had been intended not to punish but to protect. The belief had become general that the militia regulations were a punishment for bad behaviour in 1775-76, and yet nothing had been done to recognize those individuals who had distinguished themselves by loyal conduct. Now "everyone commands the poor ignorant habitant who reluctantly obeys and inwardly curses the government which sets so many taskmasters over him." Finlay, like Caldwell, urged more specific regulations which might be read once a month at the church door. Knowing their rights and their duties, the habitants would be assured that government was not going to make slaves of them.

As a reward for this move Finlay was dropped from Carleton's inner circle of advisers. The militia law was renewed by the council without change every two years until 1787. Allsopp, Finlay, and Henry Caldwell persistently urged amendment and clarification. No Canadian supported them. François Baby, a member of the council from 1778, refused to support any change and the seigneurs voted with him.

The attitude of the seigneurs, if not admirable, is comprehensible. The insubordination of the habitants had shown how groundless were their pretensions to be leaders of Canadian society; it had also been the means of depriving them of the opportunity of serving as regular officers in Canadian regiments, with some prospect of retirement on half pay at the end of the war. Carleton's refusal to consider the claims of justice is more surprising. The habitants had, however, from his point of view, injured him deeply. He hoped in time to return them to "the condition of obedience and deference" which he believed to be their natural disposition, and he seems to have thought that collective severity, if not collective punishment, was a suitable means to that end. Moreover, as Carleton and Finlay both knew, the habitant hated any form of forced labour, no matter how well paid, and exercised an endless ingenuity in evading his obligations, no matter how well defined.[17] Finlay's pleas for recognition of the rights of all and some reward for past services made no impression, or rather impressed Carleton as an expression of American radicalism. Merchants who spoke for the habitants were supposed to be endeavouring to discredit the government for their own private interests. Caldwell's association with Finlay was dismissed as inexplicable, and Carleton's comment on it is revealing of his efforts to keep the seigneurs voting as a bloc: " . . . Caldwell by his strange motions had no settled policy of a disturbance in view, he neither saw their evil tendency *nor would he listen to advice.*"[18] [*Author's italics.*]

The one man who might have influenced Carleton to a kinder and juster policy was Bishop Briand. There is no evidence that Briand made any representations, although, as the years went by, more than one parish priest wrote to the authorities on behalf of his flock. Briand would, however, hesitate to move except with extreme caution in such a matter, and Carleton left the province too soon after the abuses of the ordinance became clear for him to have much time to act. Moreover, there was another matter at issue for which he felt a more direct responsibility. This concerned not the ordinances that Carleton had passed, but the very important one that he had not passed or even initiated.

Probably neither Briand nor his friend and colleague, Montgolfier, in Montreal, had any precise knowledge of Carleton's ecclesiastical instructions, although it is pretty certain that rumours about them would have reached the province. Briand, however, was disturbed even by the reference to the king's supremacy in the Act. Carleton had already offered his re-assurances. The King, he said, understood perfectly that the Pope was spiritual head of the Church: "Just keep quiet and believe anything you like," was his advice.[19] Now Briand, in correspondence with Montgolfier, was trying not only to forestall any move against the seminaries and the Jesuits, but to secure permission for the seminaries to recruit in France as they had been used to do. Carleton, however, told the Bishop frankly that he could not, with or without the council, move in this matter. If Briand was also aware that the Governor had been ordered to give close supervision to the Roman Church while exalting the power and prestige of the Church of England, he would certainly have been reluctant to cause irritation by bringing up the touchy matter of the militia ordinance.[20]

While busy with judicial appointments in the summer of 1776 and legislation in 1777, Carleton had not forgotten the executive branch of the government. Engaged as he was in military business in 1776, he did not attempt to summon a full council meeting. Instead he constituted the Lieutenant-Governor, Mabane, Finlay, Dunn, and Collins a "privy council" to review public accounts and to do other necessary business. The personal favour of the Governor evidently reconciled Mabane to the institution that had so shocked him in 1766. It was indeed eminently practical; it was inevitable that executive business should be done for the most part by members living in or near Quebec. Montreal members came down in the summer only for urgent meetings. Carleton's plan allowed him to select from the Quebec group the most efficient, loyal, and pliable. Mabane, however, had been right in 1766; there was no authority for a privy council in the instructions, beyond the bare statement that a quorum of five was sufficient for executive business.

By mid-summer of 1777 Carleton's situation as benevolent despot was rendered uneasy by the presence in Quebec of two new law officers, both nominees of Lord George Germain. James Monk, the Attorney General, arrived in May. Born in Boston of parents who had later moved to Nova Scotia, he had succeeded his father there as solicitor general. Having shown some administrative and reforming zeal in that post, he had proceeded to London where he supplemented his legal training by several years of study in the Inner Temple. Monk was commissioned, or at least permitted, by Germain to send him confidential reports on civil affairs in Quebec. Peter Livius, the new chief justice, had been a judge in New Hampshire and had been dismissed for criticizing the governor for financial irregularities in his administration. He had arrived in Quebec in the autumn of 1775 and had spent the winter there before proceeding to Montreal, where he had been appointed to the court of common pleas. Promoted to be chief justice in 1777, he came down to Quebec and was sworn in *ex officio* member of the council in July. Neither Monk nor Livius had any responsibility for the ordinances of 1777, as they took up their posts after the legislative session was over.

Livius from the moment of his arrival at Quebec offered a series of challenges to Carleton's system of government. He found in Monk, who was not a member of council, his silent supporter. It was a reckless course, and if Livius had examined Carleton's record and Cramahé's, he would have seen how dangerous it was. Cramahé had strongly resented Hey's efforts to introduce English commercial law in August 1775. As administrator in Quebec during the autumn months, while Carleton was with the army near Montreal, he treated Hey with a studied rudeness and neglect which the Chief Justice, although easy-going as a rule, resented strongly. It is even possible that it was Hey's realization of Cramahé's hostility, and of his influence with Carleton, that caused his unexpected departure from Quebec by one of the last boats in 1775.[21]

Livius, in Quebec, had been a witness of Cramahé's treatment of Hey, although he may not have realized its significance. During his year in Montreal he had had time to reflect on the situation in the province, on the need for a chief justice, and his proper role under the new constitution. Although the system of law courts was English rather than French, Livius conceived his position to lie somewhere between that of the chief justice in an American colony, who was often the adviser and confidential assistant of the governor, and the French intendant, who exercised a civil and judicial authority almost entirely independent of the military governor. Able as he was, Livius was not acute. He had not reckoned on the personalities opposed to him. Cramahé would resent any encroachment on his special position as Carleton's assistant, and Carleton, with some reason, would repudiate the conception of a chief justice in the role of intendant.

When Livius arrived at Quebec in 1777, Carleton was again with the army at Montreal. Cramahé and his subordinates were conspicuous in their lack of respect and consideration for the new chief justice, as they had been for his predecessor. Livius, unable and unwilling to retreat from this uncomfortable position, soon found himself opposing Cramahé in the court of appeals and, a much more serious matter, challenging his right to detain civilians in the military prison without showing any cause. This second dispute over the right of *habeas corpus*, which Livius believed to exist by common law, even though undefined by ordinance, caused personal bitterness between the two men, and involved other officials in a defiance of the Chief Justice. Carleton, however, settled it promptly on his return by releasing the prisoners, and requiring the lesser officials to offer their apologies to Livius.[22]

Livius was encouraged by this to call on the Governor, apparently to remonstrate with him on the "privy council," and the withholding of his instructions. In the course of the conversation he revealed his theory that the chief justice was the equivalent of the intendant, and that the governor should, at least, pay particular attention to his advice. He even urged Carleton, knowing that he was to leave the province in the spring, to recognize the special position of the chief justice in order that the matter might be cleared up before Haldimand arrived. Carleton snubbed him, and began to reflect on another way of settling Livius' position.

The legislative council in 1778 was not summoned until late in the spring, on March 23. Carleton made it clear that he wished to have an ordinance regulating official fees, and not much else. Other business was discouraged, or shelved; Caldwell's motion on the militia was decisively rejected. When the business of the fees was well under way Livius, on April 8, moved

> that this Board not having hitherto had communication of His Majesty's instructions for . . . passing laws . . . His Excellency . . . be humbly requested to communicate . . . such royal instructions as . . . he may think are proper to be disclosed to us.[23]

So far the wording was tactful enough but the concluding part of the resolution implied that Carleton, if he failed to comply, would be thwarting the royal intentions for the province. The motion came up three days later and was rejected by eleven votes to five. Some days later Livius introduced a motion of protest against Carleton's privy council with a considerable speech. Under Carleton's order of August 8, 1776, Livius said, five people had repeatedly undertaken to act as a council for the affairs of the whole province "in opposition to the . . . [Quebec Act] and in exclusion of His Majesty's Council . . . legally constituted and appointed according to the said Act." He went on to mention particularly the examination of accounts by the privy council, later approved by the Governor in presence of the council, and entered in the minutes "by some accident" as if the whole council had given its consent. These proceedings

> if not timely remedied will give opportunity . . . to future peculation, and perversion of public money under any future governor.[24]

This was a direct indictment of the Governor's conduct, based on the law which was unambiguous, and on facts well known to all. It was a defiance even more open than that offered by Mabane and his friends ten years before, and all the more damaging because this time Carleton had openly persisted for years in the practice which on the former occasion he had half repudiated. Carleton had perhaps been not unwilling to provoke a defiance. He prorogued the council almost immediately without waiting for the passing of the ordinance for the regulation of fees. A few days later Livius received a note from the Provincial Secretary. "I have the governor's command to signify to you that you are no longer chief justice. . . ."[25] The note, in its studied rudeness, ignored even the form of law, for Carleton could do no more than suspend the chief justice. He could not cancel a royal patent.

After a delay of nearly two months Carleton wrote to Germain reporting the sessions of the council and the dismissal of Livius. Many councillors, he said, saw how necessary it was to regulate the fees, but they had been continually interrupted by "motions and speeches . . . quite new in this province, and more suited to the popular assembly of Massachusetts than to the King's council for Canada."

> Mr. Livius, chief justice, took the lead, greedy of power, and more greedy of gain, imperious and impetuous in his temper, but learned in the ways and eloquence of the New England provinces, valuing himself in his knowledge of how to manage governors. . . .

And so, said Carleton, he had at last prorogued the council and dismissed Livius, being compelled to restore order as he had done once before by an "act of severity." He trusted there would now be an end to cabals. There had been none in the province "until your Lordship's arrangements and new system of politics brought them forth." Carleton's report to his superior thus excused his arbitrary action on the ground that it was necessary to check the mischief which Germain had, it was implied, deliberately started by his American appointments. Meanwhile Carleton's confidants were saying that Livius was dismissed not for his motions in the council, but for his conduct from the very beginning which was "to perplex, involve, and render unhappy, not only the officers in their duty, but the measures of government."[26]

Livius may have been overbearing and self-seeking, but Carleton's system could not tolerate any chief justice who took his duty seriously. Hey had been made to feel superfluous. The ordinance of 1777 had deliberately excluded the chief justice from all civil courts, the ones where his knowledge and skill were most needed. The council, where the chief justice sat *ex officio*, was deprived of its executive functions, limited in its legislative activity, and grudged even the freedom of debate which the governor by his instructions was expressly ordered to allow. It was no wonder that Livius, insensitive to Carleton's attitude, should have appealed to him, as the author of the Quebec Act, to establish his own constitution on a sound basis before he was replaced by a successor whose experience was wholly military. Carleton's refusal, his summary dismissal of Livius, and his defiant letter to Germain, reveal more than personal resentment. This was the system in which he really believed: an all-powerful governor, the sole channel of communication with Britain and sole interpreter of his own instructions, with all officials, including councillors and judges, in a proper condition of subordination.

Carleton's arrangements had already caused some concern in Britain. Richard Jackson, counsel to the Board of Trade, invited to offer a legal opinion on the ordinances of 1777, remarked that parts of several of them could be defended only by "the existing state of the province" and "the confidence that is justly due to the known disinterestedness and humanity of the present governor." The ordinance on the courts of justice, he said, gave a power to the governor and council

> which, together with that which they hold as the legislature and supreme executive of the province is such as is scarcely possessed by any body of men in Europe or America, far beyond the power of the governor and council while the province belonged to the Crown of France.

Jackson regretted the absence of juries to determine matters of fact, and he recommended that the presence of the chief justice should be "essentially requisite to a determination of an appeal in council." The militia law he described as "very rigorous."[27]

This report was noted in London but no action was taken until after Carleton's departure. Carleton, therefore, was able to pass his system on to Haldimand with his personal explanations and recommendations. Haldimand found the system well adapted to his disposition and purposes. He accepted Carleton's decision to suspend the Chief Justice, in spite of Livius' pleas for a hearing. Livius, therefore, carried his appeal to England and, although immediately reinstated by the Privy Council, he never returned to the province. His office for eight years was in commission, executed by two common pleas judges and the clerk of the council, "with what jurisprudent ability or public satisfaction will no doubt be stated to your Lordship," wrote Monk to Germain.[28] Carleton and Haldimand together contrived so to interpret the Quebec Act as to make it the instrument of a dictatorship not exactly approved, but tolerated by the home government.

In the summer of 1778 Carleton left the province that he had governed for twelve years. Although he had, seemingly, championed the Canadians and slighted the English, English citizens of Quebec and Montreal, along with Canadians of Quebec, presented the usual complimentary farewell addresses. When, however, the address came down from the Montreal Canadians, the signatures were so conspicuously few that François Baby wrote to Pierre Guy urging him to join himself to the most respectable citizens of Montreal to thwart the efforts of a cabal formed by two or three : "our future interest necessitates this step." Guy was not encouraging, and later reported failure. Perhaps still irritated by seigneurial pretensions, or resenting the militia act, Montreal refused any general expression of gratitude. Not even "interest" would prevail.[29] Even the most respectable citizens may have been infected by "that spirit of licentiousness and independence" which Carleton had been striving to reduce to "a proper subordination."[30]

CHAPTER 12

The System of the Generals: Haldimand

Frederick Haldimand, Quebec's new governor, arrived at last in June 1778. A French Swiss by birth, after some years of service with other foreign forces, he had secured a commission in the British army, where he served his adopted country with a loyalty proud and tenacious, if not passionate. He already knew Quebec, where he had acted briefly as military governor of Three Rivers in 1762-63. Like his two predecessors, Haldimand was strictly honest and personally disinterested, a notable fact in an age when venality was not disgraceful, and success too often depended more on influence than on merit. He was also a competent if not a brilliant soldier, zealous and diligent. Personally, he was simple, affable, and benevolent, with a capacity for personal friendship not limited to his brother officers. In Quebec he came to live on terms of intimacy with François Baby, the merchant. Even closer was his friendship with Adam Mabane, who came near to making himself indispensable to every governor of his time, but to no other so entirely as to Haldimand.

Haldimand had, unfortunately, the defects of his merits, defects which had a profound influence on the community over which he ruled for more than six critical years. He was rigid and obstinate, "a man of narrow mind," incapable of seeing beyond the code of behaviour instilled during long years of military service. Knowing himself to be disinterested and loyal, he could not but believe that all who opposed his views must be disloyal and self seeking. As an officer kind and sympathetic to his juniors, he was in other respects totally unimaginative except in an ability to believe the worst of the designs both of the enemy without, and of the potential enemies whom he discerned within the province.

Not much imagination, however, was needed to tell Haldimand that as governor of Quebec he was in an intensely uncomfortable position. He was responsible for civil order and military defence in a huge and sprawling province. Geography, so favourable to traders, explorers, and conquerors, joined forces with the enemy as soon as the province, as now, itself lay open to invasion. Haldimand had to be prepared to defend the whole line of the lakes as far west and north as Michilimackinac and southwest to the Illinois country. He had to watch with even more vigilance the familiar Champlain-Richelieu route, and the equally dangerous line of the St Francis River which flowed into the St Lawrence from the southeast, just below Sorel. He also had to do what he could to protect the lower river and the gulf, the route on which he now depended exclusively for supplies and reinforcements.

The restoration of the ancient boundaries of Quebec in 1775 would, at the best of times, have placed a heavy burden on the governor at Quebec. The royal instructions, taking account of this, had provided for a number of local governments on the periphery of this vast area: a lieutenant-governor and a judge for civil causes at Gaspé in the gulf, and in each of the four up-country posts of Kaskaskia, Vincennes, Detroit, and Michili-mackinac. The American invasion, together with the totally inadequate provision for the judges' salaries, had rendered the project abortive. Only two lieutenant-governors had reached their posts by 1777, Henry Hamilton at Detroit and Edward Abbott at Vincennes. As they and the men in charge of the other posts were all army officers, administration proceeded much as before, civil duties being almost forgotten in the military responsibilities for which each one was answerable to the governor and commander-in-chief at Quebec. The posts where they found themselves were on the vague borderland of the province. Even though Quebec dominated the trade, numerous traders from the American colonies had been used to mingle freely with each other and with various Indian tribes in the great triangle of territory between the Mississippi and the Ohio. The officers at the posts were now uncertain about the policy to be pursued towards Indians and Americans alike. During the years 1776 and 1777 they had been writing anxiously to Carleton for instructions. Hamilton had even come down from Detroit to Quebec in 1777, but found the Governor absent on military duties. To all the letters he received Carleton made the same answer. He refused to give any order which might seem to relate to the conduct of the war, explaining that all this had been taken out of his hands when Burgoyne was appointed by Germain to his command. He agreed only to relay inquiries to London, small comfort to men who believed that immediate action against the enemy was needed to win over the Indians as allies, and to forestall offensive action from the colonies.[1]

Haldimand took over this difficult command from Carleton on the eve of an event which caused a grave deterioration in the whole situation. France had come to the aid of the colonies, and declared war on Great Britain. It was to be expected that her powerful fleet and her army would reinforce American efforts to reduce the former French colony. As it happened this new threat brought safety; Quebec if conquered must go to the American Colonies or to France. Congress dreaded the restoration of French power on the St Lawrence, and France did not want to see Congress so powerful in North America as to be able to dispense with French aid. The two dangers thus cancelled each other, but neither Haldimand nor anyone else could know this until much later. From his arrival in 1778 until the summer of 1782 he heard countless rumours and received many official notifications of invasions planned by the Richelieu route, or by a French fleet from the Gulf of St Lawrence. From November to May the gulf was secure, but only during the brief period of the spring thaw could he relax his vigilance on the Richelieu and the St Francis.

Haldimand was also unhappily aware that many Canadians, including some, at least, of the clergy and seigneurs, were rejoicing at the new turn of events. In October of 1778 the French Admiral D'Estaing issued an able and eloquent proclamation recalling Canadians to their ancient loyalty : "Vous êtes nés Français, vous n'avez pas cessé de l'être." He made a special appeal to the clergy as well as to the soldiers among the seigneurs, reminding them that only a Roman Catholic power such as France could be relied on for full and permanent protection to the Church. Although Haldimand had evidence of a number of printed copies of this message being posted on the doors of parish churches, a fact which could not be unknown to the clergy and seigneurs, only one parish priest reported the fact and sent in the paper. Bishop Briand, many years later, recalled the unpopularity that he had incurred among his own people for refusing to countenance loyalty to France at this time.[2] Many Canadians undoubtedly wished the restoration of French rule. What Haldimand needed to know, and what he could never tell with certainty, was how many would work actively to bring about the fulfilment of their wish. It was probably safe to assume that, apart from certain of the seigneurs and merchants, fully committed to the British service, few would be bound by the scrupulous observance of the oath of allegiance, enjoined though it was by the church. Haldimand relied completely on Briand and Montgolfier. He could not tell how far they could control the priests and their flocks. He would certainly be able to name one or two in the Quebec seminary, and perhaps in Montreal also, who "had not ceased to be French."

Apart from the danger of invasion and internal revolt, the entrance of France into the war threatened to cut the essential supply lines. Losses from the French navy and from American and French privateers were inevitable. When news of these reached London fresh supplies were immediately dispatched, but the provision fleet, anxiously watched for from the opening of navigation, might be delayed until the fall, or not arrive at all. Assured that the ships were safely up the river, the Governor breathed more freely, but his own responsibility was only beginning. The supplies must reach posts a thousand miles away in time, or his inner defences would collapse. He constantly urged that the fleets leave England earlier in the spring, that they allow him one year's provisions in advance, that they leave a frigate to winter in the gulf to protect shipping and fisheries from American privateers in fall and spring. These pleas were courteously dismissed in London as counsels of perfection.

Equally vain was his plea for adequate reinforcements of first-class British troops to replace the few thousands of German mercenaries, fit only for garrison duty in the lower part of the province, and somewhat difficult guests, who were prone to desert and steal over the border to join their cousins in Pennsylvania. London's reply was that the best troops could not be spared to a province so remote from the centre of action. As this dispatch was preceded and followed by warnings to be on the alert for threatened invasions, it is not surprising that Haldimand's reports, though uniformly courteous, occasionally showed the effects of overstrain. Any special weakness, such as a shortage of troops or provisions, was known to all the province and therefore to the enemy. Indeed, Haldimand's not very loyal Quebeckers, Canadian and English, were better informed on many matters than he was. His official news travelled uncertainly from New York to London and across the ocean again to Quebec, perhaps by way of Halifax. For the rest, he must rely on rebel newspapers. His fellow citizens got their news straight from the centre of action by innumerable channels which he searched for, but could seldom find.[3]

In spite of difficulties Haldimand addressed himself to his task of defending the province cheerfully and even with zest. For the first year or two he had much anxiety over the western posts. Without instructions and practically unsupported, Lieutenant-Governor Abbott had retreated from Vincennes on the Wabash early in 1778. Kaskaskia on the Mississippi was captured by George Rogers Clark with a small band of Americans in July. Even distant Detroit was now exposed to the enterprising Clark. While Haldimand was considering whether forces could be spared for a counter-attack, Hamilton was making one, marching six hundred miles to Vincennes with a mixed force of British troops, Canadians, and Indians. He occupied Vincennes, but got little co-operation from the local inhabitants, who wished to be neutral. Two months later he was forced to surrender to Clark, who sent him, a prisoner in irons, to Williamsburg in Virginia. The news of the disastrous ending to this courageous but rash undertaking, which stripped Detroit of many needed men and supplies, reached Haldimand in the spring of 1779.

Haldimand, unlike Carleton, had no hesitation in issuing orders to the men at the western posts. He hurried reinforcements and supplies up to Detroit, and instructed officers there and at Michilimackinac to incur any expenses necessary for retaining the Indian tribes as active allies. This meant the issuing of rations of food to warriors and their families, along with weapons, blankets, tools, and such necessary articles as hats, frilled linen shirts, petticoats, gaily coloured cloth, and medals, brooches, and earrings, not by the score but by the gross.

Meanwhile, at Niagara, matters were taking a more favourable turn. Sir John Johnson, the wealthy loyalist from the state of New York, saw his Royal Regiment of loyalists being supplemented by "a ranging battalion" under Colonel John Butler, authorized by Carleton in 1777. The early arrivals among the loyalists, some of whom reached Niagara half starved and half naked, were associated with small parties of Indians to bring over from the Mohawk Valley others who wished to leave. The loyalist troops, numbering several thousand before the end of the war, were used by Haldimand on destructive raids along the Mohawk, in the country about Lake Champlain, and wherever they could penetrate into rich farming country. It was a cruel war of devastation practised on civilians and non-combatants, sometimes, in spite of orders to the contrary, with typical Indian cruelty. The raids continued until ended on the orders of Shelburne in 1782. No doubt they were of military usefulness; all the men were potential soldiers and all supplies might be war supplies. Apparently Shelburne, as well as Carleton, wondered if this advantage might not be outweighed by political, to say nothing of moral, considerations.[4]

By 1780 the western posts were secure. Haldimand might, thereafter, have kept the Indians and loyalists inactive, although their own keen and bitter interest in the war would have made this difficult. What he could not do was to cut off their rations. By this time Britain was feeding and maintaining some fourteen thousand Indians, loyalists, and their families, along with six thousand regular troops, and the number was increasing year by year. As for presents, the Indian appetite was insatiable and Haldimand dared not irritate allies who could be bought by the other side. He had, therefore, to convince the colonial department that his requisitions were necessary and that his officers must not be expected to list the exact price of every article needed. Once the perils of the Atlantic and the gulf were passed, the goods followed the fur traders' route, going by ship from Quebec to Montreal and by bateau to Lake Ontario where they were taken over by the fleet of king's ships with only the interruption of the long Niagara portage in their voyage along the lakes. The lake fleet had been left in good condition by Carleton, and Haldimand maintained and strengthened it.

The weak link in this chain was the freighting along the rapids of the upper St Lawrence between Montreal and Lake Ontario. According to custom, the work was done by *corvées* which inevitably became more exacting with the yearly increase in demands from the posts above. When possible the bulk of the work was done in early spring and in the fall, thus sparing the men for work on the farms, but exposing them to bitter discomfort in what became a hated task. To reduce both labour and risk, Haldimand had his engineering officer William Twiss construct early Canadian canals, small channels which allowed the bateaux to bypass this difficult and dangerous passage. The problem of trans-shipment on Lake Ontario was met by the establishment of a depot with storehouses and a fort on Carleton Island, twelve miles from the present Kingston. In 1781 Haldimand rebuilt the old fort at Oswego to forestall the danger of American occupation of a point vital to the safety of his supply route.[5]

Meanwhile there was the danger of invasion on the St Lawrence. Haldimand dismissed Montreal as indefensible, and Quebec as incapable of being made fully defensible in the time and with the means at his disposal. The Richelieu forts, St John and Chambly, would be useful only for a delaying action. The governor concentrated his attention on the key point of Sorel, commanding the mouths of the Richelieu and the St Francis, easily accessible from every other part of the province, and having the additional advantage of a loyal population. There Haldimand established a strong post with barracks for twelve hundred men, and storehouses, all constructed relatively inexpensively with local materials and with the help of *corvée* labour.[6]

Haldimand, however was interested in more than defence. As the news from the south worsened he reminded London that Quebec, if retained, would provide a foothold for the reconquest of the other colonies should that prove necessary. This consideration he advanced as an additional support to his request for more and better troops. He reported the amazing morale of American prisoners, ill-clothed, often barefoot, but thinking only of escape in order to take the field again. These men could not be matched by German mercenaries or even by the British, unused to the country and pampered, he said, by Canadian stoves. For a time Haldimand took up the old idea of a Canadian corps of voyageurs and fishermen. The difficulties and the dangers, however, were obvious, and the plan was finally dismissed in 1781.[7]

From one quarter Haldimand did not need to fear invasion. The people of Vermont, conscious of dubious claims to the land on which they had squatted, refused to associate themselves with Congress. For some years after 1779 the ubiquitous Ethan Allen appeared again in official correspondence as Haldimand followed the instructions from London to try to win Vermont back to Britain. He had, however, little taste for dealings with those whom he described as "profligate banditti" and the negotiations came to nothing.

They did serve to stave off an invasion threat from Vermont, and they saved Vermont from the border raids of Indians and loyalists.[8]

Haldimand had also to meet the possibility of trouble within the province from those whose seditious or treasonable tendencies might make them a public danger. He suspected that these people were numerous, and he knew that he could identify only a few. He tried, at first, shipping undesirables to Great Britain, with the request that they be detained there. One of these was the Montreal seminarian, Huet de la Valinière. He was by common consent a "turbulent person," and Montgolfier and Briand were quite willing to be relieved of responsibility for his conduct. On his arrival in Britain, however, Jackson, the crown lawyer, doubted whether he could be indicted for high treason merely because General Haldimand reported that he was "a rebel in his heart." Poor Valinière, ill and kept on board ship while his case was considered, solved the problem by "dying" in an Irish hospital.[9] Germain wrote to Haldimand that as *habeas corpus* was in force in England he should send home no more prisoners unless he could lay a charge against them. Haldimand, therefore, detained within the province a number of people, some enemy aliens who had been imprudent or defiant, others, including the merchants Pierre du Calvet and Charles Hay, accused of correspondence with the enemy. Du Calvet and Hay remained in prison without a trial for three years even for a time after London had recommended their release, the danger of invasion being over. Haldimand was severely criticized by Canadian and English merchants. There appears to have been adequate evidence that these men had engaged in treasonable correspondence. Haldimand believed in the usefulness of making examples, although prudence and humanity, as well as the almost total lack of accommodation for prisoners, limited his examples to a very few persons.[10]

On Haldimand's arrival in Quebec he was at first warmly received by the English merchants. They found him, with his easy and amiable manner, a welcome change from Carleton, who, even when gracious, was remote. It was not long, however, before fundamental antagonisms appeared. The attitude of the merchants seemed to Haldimand as objectionable as it was incomprehensible. They still resented the Quebec Act and Carleton's interpretation of it, and blamed it in their hearts for the war and the invasion. They wished the war over, they thought it could have been avoided, and they were not sure that Britain was right. These views, though held by many respectable people in Britain, including Fox and Burke, were to Haldimand pure treason.[11]

The entrance of France into the war a year or two after the invaders left Canada, exposed the merchants inevitably to further losses. It had been hard enough, before, to get the trade ships from Britain off early in the spring; now they had to wait the leisurely convenience of government store ships in order to go under convoy. In spite of precautions, they lost goods to the value of £400,000 in one year.[12] It was natural for them to hope that additional business and inflated prices in the colony would, in some measure, compensate for their losses. Haldimand's mind ran in quite another channel. This, he said, "was not the time for pushing commerce." With little understanding of the country's business, and with much else on his mind, he appeared to assume that merchants in wartime had some sort of equivalent for the peacetime officers' half pay. In 1779 passes to the upper country were strictly limited, and officers were charged to check all traders and goods, not hesitating to destroy any goods, especially any ammunition, that might "by chance or design" fall into the enemy's hands.[13]

The merchants still hoped to make a considerable profit by supplying government with presents for the Indians. They even took some pains to cultivate among them demands for the goods that they were ready to supply. Government policy, however, was to send these goods direct from London as army stores, a policy pursued, with variations, in spite of complaints that the blankets were of a colour offensive to the Indians and the shirts were of the wrong cut.[14] The irritated merchants took full advantage of the situation when Haldimand at Montreal, or the officers at the upper posts, were obliged in an emergency to purchase from them. Haldimand resented their dishonesty and greed, not seeing that his avowed policy of keeping the Indians loyal by making them wholly dependent on the king's bounty was tantamount to taking away the livelihood of the merchants.

In 1781 the Governor was exasperated by the story of a former clerk of Taylor and Forsyth, merchants trading at Niagara. The clerk charged that about 40 per cent of their bill to the government of £35,000 was for goods not supplied by them. Haldimand's source was obviously dubious, and the subsequent condemnation of Taylor and Forsyth in the common pleas at Montreal is not complete evidence of their guilt. Probably they and Guy Johnson, the agent, were making a very good thing out of the Indian supplies, although Johnson's explanation that Taylor and Forsyth had taken on to their books goods actually supplied by him from another source for which he had no vouchers may well have been a true explanation of part of the discrepancy. Haldimand, however, was determined to root out dishonesty and waste. Unfortunately he followed his instinct, to distrust all merchants and to trust all army officers. In fact, while Taylor and Forsyth at Niagara were obliging Guy Johnson with their peculiar book-keeping, his own officers were not neglecting their opportunities. Major A. S. De Peyster was building up "a considerable fortune" at Detroit, and Lieutenant-Governor Patrick Sinclair at Michilimackinac had developed so extensive a trade with the Indians in government presents as to drive his civilian rivals out of business, or so they said.[15]

In spite of the competition of Sinclair's enterprise and government benevolence, the fur trade was carried on even about the posts, and fur production from the far west continued to expand. It was, however, restricted by increased difficulty and uncertainty in getting goods up country. Haldimand was prepared to relax restrictions on passes, but in order to prevent the possibility of trading with the enemy he required merchants to send all goods up and to bring the furs down in government vessels only. No private boats were allowed above Carleton Island. In government vessels precedence was given to all government supplies; after that the merchants' goods were supposed to be forwarded in strict rotation. There were, however, many stories of personal favours to some, while others waited interminably; there were also complaints of damage and loss in transit. Haldimand refused all private favours, but he was totally unable to control from Quebec a system which offered countless opportunities for favouritism and graft. Unaware of the western expansion of trade, the Governor believed that the merchants' large consignments must be intended for the enemy. He sent home as evidence the statements of Sinclair who, even as he wrote, was busily engrossing the trade himself. The merchants sought a poor consolation, and further impaired their reputations, by failing to pay the government freight bills. The restraints on their shipping were continued throughout the war and were not immediately lifted at the conclusion of peace.[16]

Haldimand's distrust of the merchants in the western trade was probably sharpened by his conviction that some of them were deliberately causing exorbitant prices, if not actual famine, by engrossing wheat. To the chronic uncertainty of the Quebec wheat market there was now added the inevitable fluctuation caused by the wartime necessity of prohibiting export from the closing of navigation in the fall until late in the following summer, when it was possible to estimate the amount of the new crop. In 1779 Haldimand, who opened and read at least some of the merchants' letters, learned that Drummond and Jordan, and others, were planning "to engross wheat and to enhance the price of flour." No doubt his information was correct. What he did not know was that almost everyone in the province had been in the wheat game for years, and that habitant, priest, *marchand des côtes*, agent, and merchant were all bent on engrossing and hoarding for a rise in price so far as their capital and the limited storage facilities of the province allowed. In view of the very shrewd bargaining that went on at every level, it was unlikely that any one firm would get a corner on the wheat, nor would any engrosser want to leave much wheat in the hands of the habitants, who were notoriously careless in the handling of grain. Haldimand was, however sufficiently alarmed to propose, after a short crop in 1779, that the council impose on the habitants a forced sale at a fixed price. Cramahé joined the merchants in opposing the plan, assuring Haldimand that it would cause serious trouble among the already unreliable habitants of the Richelieu Valley. Had Haldimand been on better terms with the merchants, he might have been able to understand that there was no plot. War had merely intensified the wheat gamble and the fluctuation of prices from month to month, and between one city and another, which was a regular feature of Quebec's commercial life.[17] As it was, Haldimand did not forgive Cramahé or the merchants. In the spring of 1783, when there was no shortage and the province was in no danger, he maintained the embargo on export, keeping merchants waiting as long as seven weeks for permission to ship biscuit to the gulf fishing-stations.[18]

These issues between Haldimand and the merchants were reflected in intense political strife followed by smouldering resentment. Courageous as a soldier, and patient in enduring the trial of prolonged anxiety and the threat of disaster, Haldimand had no gift for civil government and no suspicion of his limitations. Before he left London in 1778 he had shown his approval of Carleton's system by suggesting to Germain that he should be empowered to nominate to all colonial posts, including places on the council, and that all officials, even lieutenant-governors and Indian superintendents, should report to London through him alone.[19] Having thus confidently demanded powers far beyond those possessed by any official under the French regime, he readily accepted Carleton's system on his arrival at Quebec. He continued the "privy council," which now included François Baby, the most able and energetic of the Canadian councillors. He continued to withhold from the legislative council the instructions on legislation which were by this time an open secret. The Governor's wishes, however, were obvious. In 1779 the ordinances on the civil courts and the militia were renewed without change for two years, in spite of attempts at amendment on the part of the merchants.

Haldimand was now free of the legislative council until 1780, but he was not to enjoy a long political vacation. The decision of the Board of Trade that Chief Justice Livius' dismissal was unwarranted had drawn unfavourable attention to the whole system of government. Germain and the Board of Trade, therefore, endeavoured to induce Haldimand to accept London's interpretation of the Quebec Act, rather than Carleton's. In the course of 1779 the Governor was ordered to bring to an end the "privy council," to communicate all instructions on legislation (apart from those on the Church, which were tacitly ignored), and to recommend to the council a specific revision of the court system according to a plan of the Board of Trade. It appeared to the Board that, confined as he was to the criminal court of king's bench and the court of appeals, the chief justice was giving very little service for his ample salary of fourteen hundred pounds a year. The Board was also dissatisfied with the constitution of the court of appeals. This court was composed of the lieutenant-governor or chief justice with any four councillors, but not necessarily the same four at successive sittings, even on the same case. The Board therefore recommended, in some detail, an ordinance which would give the chief justice cognizance of every civil case by making him a member of the court of common pleas in each district. The court of appeals, it was suggested, should be made a permanent body, composed of the chief justice as president and four other councillors, nominated by the governor.

Although all these instructions were unpleasing to Haldimand, who wanted no change, he could not but be conscious of increasing restlessness and discontent in the province. Monk, and the growing number of other professional lawyers, English and Canadian, were critical of the new common pleas courts and their judges. It was difficult for the judges, most of them not trained to the law, to wrestle with the problem of applying Canadian custom to commercial cases between English merchants, accustomed to English usage. Mabane in Quebec had always taken his responsibilities seriously, and before many years had passed showed considerable complacency about his knowledge of law, French, Canadian, and English. In Montreal, however, although Rouville could nearly match Mabane in experience and self-confidence, he was not his equal in character or in diligence. Moreover, the new needs of the time were putting a strain on old laws. Already there was complaint about the use of a Canadian custom, dubiously rooted in French law, which allowed a creditor to demand a court order for the sequestering of his debtor's effects before trial. In rash or careless hands such a procedure could cause involuntary and groundless bankruptcy.[20]

By the autumn of 1779, therefore, Haldimand found himself harassed by instructions from London and complaints in Quebec. After blandly announcing to Germain that he had to consider whether obedience to his instructions was consistent with the king's service, he solved the privy council problem by summoning no formal executive meetings at all. Practically all business, including the examination of accounts, was done on the Governor's personal authority. He did secure advice and assistance but the operations were not recorded in the council book.[21] No instructions were communicated to the legislative council, except the one on the revised constitution suggested for the law courts. Taking advantage of certain defects in the plan which most members admitted, the Governor's party blocked all change: "in the present critical state of the British Empire . . . innovations . . . might be improper." [22] George Allsopp, the merchant who led the opposition, entered a very long and violent protest including not only criticisms of laws and law courts but personal reflections on the judges, for which he was later induced to apologize.

Haldimand waited until the last mails in the autumn of 1780 to admit to Germain that the proposed ordinance had not been passed, and that he had still not communicated his instructions. He was reluctant to do anything to alter the "sacred charter" of the Quebec Act which was keeping the Canadians loyal (or, by his own account, partly loyal). He hoped Germain would see "how necessary it is that government should be supported. I confide in your Lordship's zeal for the King's service to give me every assistance...." [23]

Haldimand's political principles exhibit, with a naïveté that has a certain charm, that recurrent phenomenon in Canadian history, a loyal party, "*plus royaliste que le roi*," preserving the empire by defying the imperial government. Germain appreciated the defiance, but not the charm. Telling Haldimand, in effect, that he could choose between obedience and dismissal, he added bluntly that only "interested people" could have induced him to conceal from the members of the council "how ill they had been used." [24]

The result was that in 1781 the council was finally told officially what they ought to have been told in 1775. By this time, however, Haldimand need fear no ill effects. It was well understood that co-operation would be suitably rewarded and that disobedience was not safe. Cramahé, who by his single vote had killed the wheat ordinance favoured by Haldimand and Mabane in 1780, was sent home in 1781 and relieved of office in 1782. [25] In the summer of 1782 Henry Hamilton, released from his Williamsburg prison, arrived as Cramahé's successor. In December at a meeting of the executive council he joined Allsopp in a vote which, by implication, accused the Governor of stretching his instructions to oblige a friend. [26] Haldimand noted the danger. In the previous session Allsopp had secured eight votes to ten on a motion to introduce an ordinance providing for *habeas corpus*. He would not meet a session of the legislature, on the eve of the peace treaty, with Allsopp and his group receiving the countenance and support of the Lieutenant-Governor. As he could not well suspend Hamilton, he suspended Allsopp, ostensibly for his protest in council of three years before. Evidently feeling that such a reason wanted support, he added to his report home a detailed indictment of Allsopp which covered the past twenty years. He need not have been alarmed. The suspicious Germain had been replaced as secretary by Thomas Townshend, amiable, a little stupid, and comfortably reactionary. London could not have cared less about the fate of George Allsopp.

Although Haldimand now had his council under adequate control he was, by the spring of 1783, deeply involved in the *cause célèbre* which was the climax of his war administration, the case of *Haldimand* vs. *Cochrane*. Hon. John Cochrane was the agent sent out by a London firm of merchants, Harley and Drummond, who were employed by the Treasury to see that the commander-in-chief in Quebec was supplied with the large amounts of ready money that he needed from time to time. The cheapest way to do this was to draw in all the spare cash in the colony by selling bills on London to the merchants who every fall had to make remittances amounting to hundreds of thousands of pounds. So far the system was simple. Cochrane, as remitter's agent, sold bills in Quebec, and turned the cash over to the Governor and commander-in-chief; the bills were sent by the merchants to their correspondents in London and honoured by the Treasury there. The cost and risk of sending gold across the Atlantic in wartime was avoided.

The snare lay in the practice, not introduced by Cochrane but accepted by him on his arrival in 1779, of selling some bills on credit, to be paid off in the course of the year. The practice had its advantages. The agent became in a small way the provincial banker and, as such, found it relatively easy to raise cash during the ten months of the year when almost no one wanted bills on London. Without the influence and the goodwill secured in this way this task would have been much more difficult. On the other hand, there could easily be a dangerous expansion of credit in a province where some merchants were already being carried year after year by their London firms. It was also politically dangerous to increase indebtedness to government in a province open to a successful invasion which might be used as a pretext for wiping out the debts.

Whatever their reason, when in 1780 Harley and Drummond learned from Cochrane of the system, they immediately wrote ordering him to give no more credit from the day he received the letter. Realizing his difficulty, they did send out some gold, but not enough for his needs. Cochrane was perplexed. He managed to roll off responsibility by telling Haldimand that he could not undertake to provide the necessary money without the credit system, but that, in view of his orders, he could now use this system only on the personal orders of the Commander-in-Chief. Haldimand, although anxiously and reluctantly, agreed to lend his authority to the procedure.

By the late summer of 1782 the Treasury as well as Harley and Drummond were expressing their strong disapproval of extending credit on bills, and all pretext for it was removed by the arrival of an adequate supply of gold. Haldimand then approached Cochrane about collecting the outstanding debts to government for which he had made himself responsible. Cochrane, however, was unwilling to press the merchants, arguing that they needed a little time to adjust to the inevitable postwar recession. When Haldimand, desperately anxious to be relieved of his responsibility, insisted, Cochrane gradually revealed the whole of a story hitherto only partly known or suspected. He had neglected the somewhat impracticable safeguards insisted on by Haldimand in extending credit, he had continued to grant it with no authority whatever through the fall of 1782, and, as the Attorney General was able to discover, he had been adjusting his books in such a way as to make the Governor responsible for debts contracted during this period.

Haldimand was both angry and disillusioned. He had liked and trusted Cochrane and had even recommended him, as a safe man, for a seat in the council. Now he found him guilty of disobedience and dishonesty, crimes which he found unpardonable. He informed Cochrane that he intended to sue immediately for the debts in the court of common pleas. When, with Cochrane cheerfully urging that there was no hurry as the debts would all surely be paid in time, he restated his intention, he received the final shock: the debts were not technically due to the Crown at all, but to Cochrane personally, and Cochrane refused to sue unless Haldimand would include all bills issued on credit at any time. Any other course, he said virtuously, would be unfair to Harley and Drummond.

Haldimand could not even stop to consider that Cochrane's advice was probably sound. He wanted no more dealings with a man who had deceived him, he wanted to go on leave to England as soon as possible, and he would not leave Quebec with, as it appeared, £70,000 owing to government for which he was responsible. He first consulted Monk, as attorney general, who told him that legally he had no redress. [27] Then he turned to Adam Mabane. Mabane was only too glad to put his legal learning at the disposal of the Governor. It was unfortunate that he forgot that he was not a consulting lawyer, but a judge – or if he remembered, the implication made no impression on him. He suggested a plan which commended itself to Haldimand and to Jenkin Williams, the Solicitor General. By English law Cochrane alone could sue the merchants, who had given their notes to him, personally. Haldimand, however, could sue Cochrane, or so it was assumed, for the money for which he had been made responsible and, suing Cochrane, he could by the Canadian custom of saisie et arrêt secure writs which would immediately, before trial, attach all monies due to Cochrane in the hands of the debtor merchants.

This procedure was followed. Merchants owing money to Cochrane were forbidden to make any payments, or to transfer any goods except for cash, until the conclusion of the trials. The trials proceeded with expedition, and the first judgement was given for Haldimand in August 1783. As Cochrane had expected, many merchants, especially the smaller ones, went bankrupt as a result. Haldimand, convinced that everyone involved had been deliberately deceiving him and defrauding the government, felt no remorse. In fact, nearly all who had received credit had been steadily paying in the money, so that an indebtedness of something over £450,000 on January 1, 1782, was reduced to £102,000 by the spring of 1783. Of this sum over £70,000 was owed by the single firm of Shaw and Fraser. This firm was prepared, without a lawsuit, to make an assignment of their assets which, properly handled, would have been sufficient to meet all their obligations. As it was, they lost heavily by the sudden departure from the province of a number of their own debtors who went out of business, and by the ultimate throwing on the market of £100,000 worth of British brandy which sold for less than two-thirds of its cost price. [28]

The treatment accorded to the other merchants was not only harsh; it was in some cases positively unjust. At least two Canadian merchants, who had given Cochrane negotiable notes, were compelled to pay the amounts without receiving back their notes. Only after much delay and expense were they given security against a second payment. In their anger at what they deemed general wrong-doing Haldimand and Mabane felt justified in a kind of indiscriminate severity.

What they unintentionally achieved was a public demonstration of the apparent truth of the radical charges against the whole system of government and administration of justice. Cochrane was undoubtedly unscrupulous, although not necessarily personally dishonest. There is no evidence that the merchants had intended to evade payment of their debts, or even that many of them had been granted excessive credit. To extricate himself from an embarrassing position, however, the Governor with Mabane, his "prime minister," arranged to employ, in the service of government against an English official, a very doubtful application of French law. He did this knowing that Mabane would try the case as judge, one of three judges, but accustomed to impose his views on the others. More than that: the defence was refused the protection that French law would have provided. Mabane, challenged on the bench for having already given his views on the case, in effect relied on the privileges of an English judge. The entire resources of the constitution appeared to be concentrated not on protecting the majesty of the law, but on making sure that right prevailed over wrong, Haldimand over Cochrane, government over the greedy merchants.

While the *Haldimand* vs. *Cochrane* cases were being tried, the war, as everyone knew, was drawing to a close and peace terms were being discussed on the basis of British recognition of the colonies which had revolted as an independent power, the United States of America. The treaty, signed in Paris on September 3, 1783, gave to Quebec yet another boundary line, the third since 1760. The inevitable retention by Britain of the New-foundland and gulf fisheries, with certain fishing rights continued to Americans, was the beginning of a century of dispute and negotiation. It also required nearly a century to complete and define the land boun-dary sketched in the treaty. Starting from "the north-west angle of Nova Scotia," this hypothetical line found its way to the forty-fifth parallel, and along the parallel to the St Lawrence River, some little way above its junction with the Ottawa. From there the line went west along the river and through the centre of the Great Lakes to Grand Portage.

This was indeed a revolution. The critical Ohio country, the triangle between the lower lakes, the Ohio, and the Mississippi which has played so large a part in this story, was surrendered to the United States. There was no doubt that Britain had a better claim to it than her former colonies had. Britain had paid the cost of expelling the French in 1760 and of policing and defending the country thereafter. The Indians who claimed it were her allies and many had fought through the war. The colonial claim was, however, energetic. Virginia, Pennsylvania, and New York were accus-tomed to think of their western boundaries as flexible although they had, in fact, been defined by agreement between Britain and the Indian tribes in 1768. They had, however, another powerful claim. They, and only they, were ready to go in and possess the land, not as passing traders but as settlers and cultivators. Their demands were also favoured by Britain's wish to defeat the diplomacy of France by a speedy and liberal settlement with her former colonies. Having shrewdly detected this, Benjamin Franklin demanded for the United States the whole of Quebec, a demand which gave to the ultimate surrender the flattering air of a compromise. Moreover Shelburne and many others with advanced views on free trade were willing to give to others the cost of administering this remote territory, confident that Indians and white men alike would continue to buy British manufactures.

To Haldimand and the officers up country this was a narrow and selfish view which ignorance alone could excuse. Britain could not thus unilater-ally repudiate her treaty with the Indians who had been faithful, if some-what costly, allies during the war. The Indians, themselves, as the news of the treaty leaked through, indignantly maintained that they were allies, not subjects. They had never ceded land to anyone. If the English without consulting them had given their land to the Americans they had committed an act of injustice and cruelty that only Christians were capable of. [29] It fell to the reluctant Haldimand and his officers to tell them that this was exactly what the English had done, and that they could no longer look to the English king for help but must make their peace with the United States of America.

The Americans at first wished to begin to take over the British forts even in the summer of 1783. The British resistance to this proposal was attributed with partial, but only partial, truth to the desire to favour the British fur trade. Haldimand staved off the American commissioners, saying that he was waiting for instructions. He feared that a precipitate British withdrawal might be the signal for a general onslaught of the Indians against any men who spoke English, Britain's loyalist allies being among the first sufferers. The result was that for a decade Britain continued to occupy Detroit, Michilimackinac, Niagara, and other posts on what was now American soil. Fortunately the failure of the United States to enforce fulfilment of obligations undertaken to the loyalists gave a plausible excuse for this breach of the treaty, a breach which commended itself as wise and necessary for a time to men on both sides of the border. [30]

Meanwhile, Haldimand had to attend to the settling in British territory of the militant loyalists of the west, and the others from all states who followed them at the close of the war. Britain's interest and obligation were equally clear, and Haldimand devoted himself to the business of transport and settlement with his usual zeal and benevolence. The loyalists might remain in the Atlantic colonies or Gaspé, or be settled up country. They were not to be permitted in the area which came to be known as the Eastern Townships and which he wished to maintain as a *cordon sanitaire* between Quebec and the rebels, nor were they to settle with compatriots on English seigneuries. The lower St Lawrence was to be preserved for the Canadians. So Haldimand said, but his comments and those of Mabane make it clear that the Canadians were not his only concern. He was also intent on "hiving the Grits," up the river or down, anywhere where they would be adequately provided for away from those English who were already giving him so much trouble, in the council and out of it. [31]

While the immediate problems of the peace were being solved, happily enough for the loyalists, less happily for the Indians, the political cost of revolution and war to the colony on the lower St Lawrence was clear enough. While the mass of Canadians resented the burden and irritation of militia duty, the seigneurs were courted by the Governor. It was, however, observed that not even these privileged persons had power. Canadians never made up more than a third of the members of the council, and, as a number of these came from Montreal, they could hardly attend except for the winter legislative session. Out of six civil court judges only two were Canadians. Apart from the commissions of the peace and a salaried colonel of militia in each district, there were almost no offices of dignity and responsibility open to Canadians. Mabane promoted the claim of François Baby to succeed Cramahé as lieutenant-governor, but, although Haldimand counted Baby as a personal friend, there is no evidence that he recommended the appointment.

It seems so strange that neither Carleton nor Haldimand pressed the claims of Canadians to office that one is inclined to think them wholly cynical in their exaltation of the Quebec Act as the Canadian charter. This view did occur to some Canadians at the time. They were unjust. The governors might have controlled the British penchant for finding jobs for the needy in the colonies, but they did not dare to put Canadians into key positions. Whatever may have been French policy before 1778, there is no doubt that after that time France was putting pressure on Canadians to remember their origin. As long as there was any chance of the colony being reconquered or surrendered it would have been neither safe nor generous to put a Canadian into a position where, in such a closely knit community, he might be subjected to unbearable pressure. It was nonetheless unfortunate that, while most Canadians were forced to render grudging war services, those who might have been their leaders, while denied all real power in the community, were encouraged to satisfy their national pride by joining the governor in defending the distorted Quebec Act as their people's charter.

From the viewpoint of the governor this had the double advantage of securing to him a safe bloc of council votes and preventing Canadians from fraternizing with the dangerous American element. Unhappily the same process, attaching the seigneurs always to the governor, accentuated their division from the habitants and, because it killed the whole council as a working body, deprived the members of the political and administrative experience needed as preparation for the representative institutions which could not long be denied to any North American colony.

CHAPTER 13

The Spirit of Innovation

Haldimand's hopes of leave in England in 1782 were not gratified. It was at the request of the Colonial Secretary, Townshend, soon to become Lord Sydney, that he remained for two more years to help carry the province through the difficult period of transition from war to peace. While attending to the dispatch of thousands of German troops, now on their way home, the Governor was also increasingly concerned with the settlement of the loyalists, and with the delicate problems of Indians, and American relations. Sydney, with good reason, confided in his experience and integrity, and also in the tact and caution with which he handled these difficult problems.

Sydney, with less reason, placed confidence in Haldimand's political judgement. For nearly twenty years Quebec's military governors had been forced to view the province primarily as a strategic factor in an American war. It was unfortunate that in 1783, although the danger of military invasion was over, Haldimand still saw his task primarily in terms of defence against Boston, New York, and Paris. So long as pernicious ideas were creeping in from the south, inspiring committees and petitions, tending to "innovations," he believed it to be his duty to maintain the autocratic system of the generals. He recommended, therefore, a military form of government for the new loyalist settlements, confident that men who had suffered so much from committees and assemblies would want no more of them. He resumed the old plan of a post road to Halifax, that dispatches might go safely through British territory. When Finlay, as postmaster, suggested that it was also important for commercial reasons to maintain the posts by Albany and New York, the official response was one of surprise and hostility. [1] The remnant of British North America might eventually be useful as a political and military base for repairing the rent in the Empire. Meanwhile, the less fraternization the better.

One concession Haldimand was prepared to make to the innovators.

Peace being concluded, there could be no reason for refusing to define the right of *habeas corpus* as his instructions required. Since he was at that time facing civil suits from two merchants for false imprisonment, there was, indeed, every reason for proving that he was not hostile to the guarantee of civil rights. Yet he wished to proceed with caution. The ordinance introduced to council by Mabane at the beginning of the legislative session of 1784 was so restricted as to be immediately pronounced by its critics to be only a mutilated version of the sacred English birthright. With the opposition led by Finlay and William Grant, the merchant, and under the sympathetic eye of Lieutenant-Governor Hamilton, who presided, the members of council expended themselves freely in debate, motion, and counter-motion.

The opposition pressed for a clear statement that *habeas corpus* was to be enjoyed "in the most ample manner," as it was by British subjects elsewhere, whether by statute or common law. The official party retorted by insisting on a special exemption for religious communities in the name of religious freedom. At this point the ladies of the convents, clearly well informed on the progress of the debate, petitioned against any such exception, and the Bishop, when asked for an opinion, tactfully, but decidedly, supported the nuns. Clearly neither Briand nor the sisters were flattered at the suggestion that religious communities must dissolve if the members should be exposed to the privileges of a free society. Eventually a compromise was reached on an ordinance which granted approximately the privileges as defined in the famous British statute of 1679.

The argument over *habeas corpus* proved to be only the prelude to a full-dress constitutional debate. Both parties were conscious that their contest had been waged against the background of political agitation throughout the province. In the autumn of 1783, stimulated, no doubt, by the decisions in *Haldimand* v. *Cochrane*, English merchants and others had prepared and sent over to England a petition asking for the repeal of the Quebec Act, and the grant of an elected assembly. Canadian law governing real estate, dower, marriage settlement, and inheritance they accepted, but they claimed, along with *habeas corpus* as a part of the constitution, English commercial law and optional juries. The petition was urgent in tone, and the more irritating to the official party as it mentioned the need for "men of jurisprudent learning" on the bench. [2]

In answer to this, and to a resolution by William Grant in the council supporting the aims of the petition, the official party in the council proposed to enter on the books an address to the King thanking him for the blessings of peace and good order, the fruits of the Quebec Act, and begging him to maintain in its integrity that "precious charter" by favour of which Canadians "will in a short time be indissolubly incorporated into the British nation." [3] The radical party, outvoted, had to see this address entered as the opinion of the whole council, over the signature of Henry Hamilton. Their own views were forwarded to London in the shape of dissenting opinions also entered on the books. The Quebec Act, it was argued, framed with a noble intention, had indeed secured Canadian privileges; but if the statute alone were to stand as an unalterable charter, it must deprive them of liberty. Indeed, in practice, it was in no sense a "charter." Members of the legislative council, who had the power to alter and amend the laws, were removable practically at the will of the governor. Further, as a bare majority of the minimum membership of the council was considered to be a quorum, (nine members, the minimum being seventeen), a party of as few as five members had the power of determining the law for the entire province. So much for the "charter." The Canadians, like the English, it was urged, needed protection from arbitrary government. [4]

At the same time public interest in political affairs had been showing itself by protests against the secrecy which, in theory, shrouded council debates. Six English and five Canadian merchants had offered a joint request for admission to the debates on *habeas corpus*. In spite of protest from the radicals, the official majority ensured the rejection of the request, but Haldimand wrote home gloomily of the "spirit not unlike to that . . . of the public assemblies in the other colonies at the beginning of the late troubles." There was indeed a growing interest in politics. Even a modest seigneur on the Island of Orleans, having reported on the spring sowing, asked his Quebec correspondent what was going on in the council, "for great things must be happening, particularly for *La Beash Corpus*." [5]

In November 1784 Haldimand at last sailed from Quebec, leaving the administration of the province in the hands of Henry Hamilton. He was far from satisfied with this arrangement. The Governor was deeply disappointed in Hamilton. He had generously tried to help him during his imprisonment at Williamsburg, in spite of his irritation at the unauthorized expedition against Vincennes. Hamilton's conduct as a leading member of the radical party would seem to him disloyal and even indecent, for he had associated himself with this party almost immediately after his arrival. In 1782, however, when Hamilton arrived to take up his duties, the Governor's full confidence was given to Mabane. Hamilton, as president of the council, learned the Governor's wishes from Mabane's motions, and soon found that those who voted against them were considered factious, if not disloyal. A man of independent spirit, he was naturally drawn into opposition, especially as he found that the views of Finlay, Monk, and their friends coincided with his own.

Haldimand, distrusting and apparently disliking Hamilton, felt as if he were turning over the ship to the leader of the mutineers. He did all in his power to limit the mischief that they might do. The lieutenant-governor being now a civilian, the military authority passed automatically to the senior officer in the province, Barry St Leger. Haldimand, who hoped to exercise supervision through Sydney from London, felt free to entrust St Leger, and others whom he named, with much of the business relating to the loyalists and the Indians. He also left orders to continue all wartime restrictions on private shipping on the lakes, thus, he hoped, guarding against illicit trade with the American colonies, and putting it out of the power of Hamilton to remove a major grievance of the merchants.

To Hamilton, personally, Haldimand gave no information and no instructions until the morning of his departure, when he turned over to him a set of formal instructions and thirty-three bundles of papers. These last did not include copies of his dispatches to London. The unlucky Hamilton did not even know the usual form of a governor's dispatch, nor had he, taking over as he did at the time when the governor was accustomed to report at leisure on events of the past year, any idea of what had already been communicated. While Hamilton struggled with his problems in Quebec, Haldimand was advising Sydney to secure harmony in the province by removing from office the Lieutenant-Governor, the Attorney General, and almost the entire opposition party in the council. In spite of his sense of the need for these additional precautions Haldimand stated, privately, that he had left the province in a much better state than it had been in at Carleton's departure. [6]

Haldimand's apparently ungenerous conduct showed the result of the years of strain during which he had carried heavy burdens of anxiety and responsibility. Rigidly honest himself, he had suffered repeated shocks at revelations of every degree of dishonesty in wartime profiteering by men whom he had trusted. Depending, as always, on the purity of his own motives, he was now completely persuaded that the radicals who wished to alter his scheme of government were enemies of domestic peace. The most charitable explanation of his behaviour to Hamilton is that he hoped to force the Lieutenant-Governor in his ignorance to have recourse to the knowledge and experience of Mabane, and so to find political salvation in spite of himself.

Hamilton, however, had no intention of maintaining a mayor of the palace. He believed that the charter conception of the Quebec Act owed at least part of its support to those who willingly emphasized the despotic aspects of French law, in order to disgust Canadians with British rule and turn their hearts back to France. His own conviction was that the impact of the American Revolution on all the people of Quebec, Canadian and

English, must be understood and accepted. Wise legislation would show Canadians that they might have American liberty under English rule without the heavy taxation of which Americans were, at that moment, complaining. [7]

Legislative reform had to wait for the leglislative session which would open in the new year. Meanwhile, on November 24, eight days after Haldimand's departure, there occurred an event of great significance in church and state. Hamilton received the resignation of Bishop Briand, who requested that his coadjutor, Bishop Desglis, might be allowed to take the oath and assume the duties of office. As Briand had been very ill all summer and was now much better, the move astonished everyone, including his successor, who called it a "revolution." With Hamilton's consent, however, the two immediately took steps to secure bulls of consecration for the one who seemed the obvious choice as the new coadjutor. Jean-François Hubert was a Canadian; he had been successively secretary to Pontbriand and to Briand; he had shown his loyalty to Britain in 1775, and had been especially approved by Haldimand to serve at the difficult post of Detroit during the war. Hubert had also the essential advantage of comparative youth. He was not yet fifty.

Although Hubert was an unexceptionable candidate, and one who had been specifically nominated for such a post by Haldimand before he left Quebec, it was two years before the British authorities agreed to his consecration. During this time the succession to the bishopric continued to hang on the lives of two old men. Haldimand was responsible for the delay. He could not forgive Briand for choosing to resign his office to Hamilton rather than to himself. He therefore induced Sydney first to nominate the aging Montgolfier for the position, and then to consider the possibility of sending out an Englishman. This policy was approved by Mabane, Haldimand's faithful Quebec correspondent, as guarding against "the least appearance of recognizing or encouraging any claim of the people, or of any set of men, to elect to offices. . . ." [8]

Haldimand's intervention in church affairs from London, although it looks like an act of ill-nature or even malice, was consistent with his general policy. Still feeling responsible for Quebec, he wanted to discourage all independent action and to maintain the necessary supervision over the Church. He was also persisting in a scheme which he had promoted during his term in Quebec and which he honestly believed would benefit church and state.

The Canadian church was in urgent need of more priests. Briand and Montgolfier had presented this need to Carleton before the recent war with France. They were convinced that the Church must be recruited by French priests, not to serve in the rural parishes, where Canadians were more acceptable, but as professors in the seminaries, missionaries to the Indians, and assistants in the immense parish of Montreal. Haldimand, on his arrival, fully agreed that recruits were necessary. A man of intellectual interests, he went further, and regretted the rather low standards of learning that Briand was forced to accept in the parish priests. The Canadian church needed new blood, he said, but not from France. He would write to the British government to send to the colony priests from Savoy.

Briand found such a plan objectionable from every viewpoint. Since 1760 he had devoted himself to maintaining the integrity of his church in the British state. The task had not always been easy, and he had earned criticism from fellow-churchmen for being too complaisant. He believed, however, that he had retained control of "l'intérieur." Now Haldimand was proposing that a secretary of state, a layman and a heretic, should choose priests for his diocese, men for whose conduct he must be responsible, men whose authority he must maintain. The first might be difficult; the second he knew would be impossible. Canadians could be rebellious enough to their own Canadian priests; and there was already some feeling against the superior airs of Frenchmen. Priests from Savoy, even if they were the best of men, would be difficult to assimilate – and they would not be the best of men. Engaged in this way they could only be "mercenaries." What he needed was priests of a missionary spirit, carefully chosen in France by men whom he knew, and who knew Canada. [9]

It would have been difficult for Briand to explain all this to Haldimand and to show him that, for all their shortcomings, the Canadian priests were bound to the people by complex and subtle relationships not readily achieved by an alien. If he had explained, Haldimand would not have understood. To him a priest was a priest and, like a soldier, he should be apt for service anywhere. "Provided government secures to Canadians the enjoyment of their religion, the country from whence the priests are brought must be a matter of indifference to them." [10] And so he ordered priests from Savoy, guaranteeing them parishes worth a minimum of £200 a year, unless they should find themselves more desirably accommodated in the seminaries. He was not going beyond what his instructions allowed him to do, and the home government approved. Priests were engaged in 1781 and sailed for Quebec the following year. Providence, however, ruled that their ship should be captured, and they found themselves back in France. Nothing daunted, Haldimand ordered more, and in 1784, on the point of leaving the province, he was still, apparently unconscious of offence, promising Montgolfier the first choice among the expected arrivals for his seminary. [11]

It seems clear that the seminary at Montreal had not been quietly waiting for priests from Savoy. In the spring of 1783 two priests from

France had arrived at Quebec and contrived to reach Montreal without Haldimand's knowledge. Montgolfier was probably taken by surprise. Haldimand, himself, was inclined to blame Brassier, the bursar at Montreal, and Gravé, the principal of the Quebec seminary. Montgolfier, correctly, wrote immediately to report to Haldimand that the priests had been admitted to the seminary. He begged to be allowed to accept them as members, and his entreaties were warmly seconded by the Bishop in Quebec and by a numerously signed petition from the citizens of Montreal. Haldimand refused courteously but firmly, and shipped the priests back to France. He probably could have done nothing else. London entirely approved of his action. [12]

The decision, however, produced, in Briand's words, "great fermentation among laity and clergy." Briand, who had formerly referred gratefully to the many signs of kindness shown him by the Governor, now entertained the feelings which later led him to compare Haldimand unfavourably with a Turkish despot. He accepted the decision, however, without protest. The seminary and the people in Montreal, on the contrary, "elected," privately and discreetly, deputies from "the three estates" to carry to London a petition for French priests. Money was collected from the parishes by a circular letter to all captains of militia, and, to avoid all appearance of conspiracy, Haldimand was informed and asked to approve. Not only did he not approve, he insisted that the money be returned and, pronouncing the elections illegal, he consented to pass over the offence and to allow the deputies to leave only because the purpose was a petition to the king.

The deputies, Adhémar and de Lisle, both fur merchants of Montreal, made their way to London in the fall of 1783. Although Briand had declined to support the movement, which he believed had the appearance of an imprudent defiance of the Governor, he privately sent warm recommendations to Carleton and welcome financial assistance to the deputies. Montgolfier also wrote to Carleton privately, begging him as an old friend to enable him "standing on the edge of the grave" to secure a successor as superior of the seminary. With some hope of success at first, the deputies blamed their ultimate failure on the unceasing hostility of Haldimand, who reached England about a year after they did. It is unlikely that Haldimand was entirely responsible. Sydney, although he allowed them, with Quebec's English vicar general, Thomas Hussey, to recruit freely anywhere in Europe, was, from the beginning, determined to allow no subjects of the House of Bourbon into Quebec. When Adhémar pledged that the Church would take full responsibility for their conduct, he was reminded, correctly, that Montgolfier had not even been able to control the French priests who, during their brief stay in Montreal, had preached in public, in spite of a pledge to the contrary. Probably, however, Adhémar's persistence during his two-year mission did succeed in convincing Sydney, if not Haldimand, of the impossibility of imposing alien priests on the Canadians. The new bishop, Desglis, accepted, in principle, priests from any country in Europe, chosen by him or his agents. One, Edmund Burke, did come from Ireland to the Quebec Seminary. For the rest there seems to have been little recruiting abroad until after events in France had effectively put an end to English fears of the House of Bourbon.[13]

Adhémar's mission was inextricably involved with the lively movement for constitutional change, made possible by the peace, and encouraged by Haldimand's departure. His petition and the supporting memorials show an increasingly self-conscious Canadian community learning to interpret the past in the light of the present needs. Religious freedom, "a natural right" and promised by the capitulation and the peace treaty, implied, it was maintained, freedom in the choice of priests, without which Canadians must remain "inferior citizens." The fact that whatever might have been promised in 1763, the freedom of secular deputies of any community to choose its priests was as unknown to the British state of that day as it was to the Roman church, was conveniently overlooked. Had Britain granted the privilege requested, it would, no doubt, have been exercised by the bishop through his English and French vicars general. The words of the petition, however, show clearly the inspiration of the independent non-conforming American colonies.[14]

The same spirit was leading the same people into secular politics. In 1783 Haldimand blamed Adhémar's mission for stirring up the English to prepare their petition for an assembly.[15] In the spring of 1784 Adhémar, writing confidentially from London to Gravé in Quebec, remarked that his want of success had convinced him that there must be a change of government, including an assembly. "Our only hope is in this change."[16] By the fall Canadian and English committees were at work in Quebec and Montreal. After a public meeting at the Récollet convent in Montreal on November 24, a petition following closely the pattern of the English petition of 1783 was prepared. Copies of the petition were carried about the country by messengers who urged everyone who could to sign. Gravé, as vicar general of Quebec, circularized the parishes, telling the priests that they must not sign, but making it clear that he favoured a neutrality of active benevolence.[17]

The French and English versions of the petition were delivered to Hamilton to be forwarded to England on January 7, 1785. He received them courteously while reminding the committees that only a nearly unanimous petition could be expected to bear fruit. Although signatures were being collected through 1785 it was all too evident that there was no unanimity among the Canadians. There is interesting, though fragmentary, evidence of eager debate among those who signed the petition, on the details of the desired constitution. Some, with their English colleagues, looked to the American colonial models, others wished a closer approximation to English or French tradition. Thus, the seigneur Juchereau Duchesnay wanted an upper house, composed of seigneurs and gentlemen sitting by right of birth, as more dignified and respectable than an appointed body. He opposed, however, any formal representation for the Church beyond an *ex officio* place for the bishop. If "the gentlemen of Montreal" (the Seminary) made any difficulty, they might, he suggested, be reminded of the danger of arousing the fanatics of London.[18]

Such discussions, as might be expected, did cause division among Canadian reformers.[19] Meanwhile their official opponents were not idle. Mabane was indignant with Hamilton for, as he said, promoting the petitions. There is no evidence beyond his word that Hamilton did this; but undoubtedly the attitude of the Lieutenant-Governor was well known and would encourage the petitioners. François Baby wrote Haldimand that, situated as they were in Quebec, "the friends of government" hardly dared to oppose the petitions.[20] In Montreal government friends showed more courage, producing and circulating to the habitants an elaborate answer to each article of the petition, but concentrating on the request for an assembly. An assembly, it was asserted, could not put an end to *corvées*, and must inevitably impose taxes, cogent arguments for the habitant who did not trouble himself greatly about the rights of man. The friends of government then produced their own petition, asking fuller representation for Canadians on the council, and freedom for the bishop to bring over priests from Europe. The second request, stealing the opposition thunder, was shrewd; and also disingenuous. Baby, sending a copy to Haldimand in London, begged him to support it, but added that he might explain away such parts as he found undesirable :

> You know that unless we had taken up the cause of priests and religion people of good will could not have induced the public to oppose these talkers who have employed all kinds of fanatic means to secure the adoption of their ideas for a new form of government.[21]

The efforts of "people of good will" prevailed so far that the second petition gained many more signatures than the first, although, said the reformers, many were in the form of crosses and "much could be said about the way that they were obtained." Much, no doubt, could have been said about the way signatures on both sides were obtained, but it was obvious that Canadians were not united. Lord Sydney was glad to agree that the time for a change was not yet, and Adhémar in the summer of 1785, preparing to leave London, wrote sadly that Canadians would not enjoy English liberty until they could form "a body . . . united . . . to establish solidly our religious and civil rights." Hugh Finlay, favourable as he was to an English form of government, agreed that the time had not come. He believed that of literate English and Canadians, the majority wanted an assembly. The habitant, however, thought chiefly of escaping both taxation and the *corvée*. The only remedy, Finlay said, was education "from the pulpit."[22]

The demand for an assembly on the part of Canadians, beginning as it did immediately after Haldimand's departure, coincided with Hamilton's first months in office. What proved to be his only session with the legislative council took place against the background of political agitation, which helped to introduce even more than the usual acrimony into the debates. The official party, feeling that the Lieutenant-Governor was in sympathy with "the spirit of innovation" abroad in the province, was sternly on the defensive.

Hamilton was personally responsible for one innovation. For the first time since the passing of the Quebec Act, the council received formal communication of the king's instructions on new legislation, along with a recommendation that the royal intentions be carried out. The inevitable result was to raise the whole vexed issue of ten years' standing: whether the clause in the Quebec Act on "the customs and usages of Canada" was expected to preserve an entire system of jurisprudence with its own peculiar social and political philosophy, as Chartier de Lotbinière had desired and as Carleton and Haldimand had insisted; or whether this clause was intended to ensure full protection to property rights and family obligations of Canadians, while leaving the door open for change, as Lord North in the debate had explicitly stated. Hamilton, and the royal instructions, were undoubtedly on the side of Lord North.

With this encouragement, Hugh Finlay moved to amend the ordinance on civil procedure by the introduction of English commercial law and juries in commercial cases at the option of either party. Thomas Dunn, merchant, common pleas judge, and a political moderate, moved, in addition, the specific prohibition of the writs of *saisie*, experience having shown them to be "frequently attended with very dangerous consequences and . . . very detrimental to the commerce of the province." Later, the Lieutenant-Governor, obeying another neglected royal instruction, invited the council to consider again the reform of the court of appeals recommended by the secretary of state in 1779, and rejected by the council in 1780.[23]

The system of the generals was thus attacked along a wide front. English merchants claimed their own commercial law as a recognition of the fact that they were an essential element in the life of the province, and not mere passing birds of prey as the governors had frequently suggested. The demand for limited jury trial in civil causes went even deeper. Although the judges opposed it with weighty practical arguments, both sides recognized the jury as the thin end of the wedge of popular government, a check on the arbitrary decisions of judges who were hand in glove with the executive. In the same way, the attack on the *saisies*, while it could be supported by strong practical arguments, was also a protest against Haldimand's victory in the suit against Cochrane, a victory gained through the use of the *saisie* in a non-jury trial.

It was not surprising that the council spent some six weeks in debate on these proposed judicial reforms. In the end, although English commercial law was rejected, and the court of appeals remained as before, jury trials in commercial cases and cases of tort were conceded. François Baby, writing a report and *apologia* to Haldimand, confessed that on this matter he and his friends had voted against the judges, Mabane and Fraser, because "the whole body of merchants English and Canadian wished it," and, he added, the concession might keep the merchants quiet in future.[24]

Finlay blamed the influence of the judges over successive governors for the long delay in granting jury trials. There is no doubt that after the passing of this ordinance the judges, deliberately or through negligence, contrived to support their contention that jury trials would not work well. Having rejected a proposed clause which would have obliged them to give a written charge to the jury, they failed to deliver adequate explanations in their verbal charges. William Smith, after his arrival as chief justice in 1786, complained of cases sent to the jury "upon loose pleadings and without any precise point in issue," making it almost impossible to do even substantial justice to the case on appeal. Mabane and Fraser, the two judges most responsible, by setting their faces against change of any sort at so favourable a time, were building up against themselves a store of bitterness which was to bring upon them a punishment far beyond their deserts, deficient though they were in some respects.[25]

An important ordinance introduced in this session but not carried through to completion dealt with the vexed question of land registration. Merchants thought it necessary for security in business, at least for all traders and merchants; Canadians maintained their firm opposition to a regulation contrary to their customs, and one which involved them in trouble and expense.[26] The chief significance of the proposed ordinance in this session was that it became involved with the perennial debates over the militia law, which this year became an issue not only in council but throughout the province.

Early in the session Hamilton sent a message to the council reminding them of the need to renew the militia ordinances. To Lord Sydney he wrote his own conviction that amendment was much needed.

> Imperfect regulations and a rigid observance of them may pass with tolera-tion in a time of war or internal commotion . . . but a peaceable time should dictate the propriety of lenient measures upon legal and constitutional principles.[27]

In response to Hamilton's message Finlay moved for permission to bring in amendments. The motion was defeated, and the ordinance was renewed, unchanged. Hamilton confessed his "real mortification" at the council's decision.[28]

The news of the refusal of the council even to consider a change in the militia law stirred to renewed activity the Canadian committees at Quebec and Montreal, still collecting signatures to the petition for an assembly, and resentful at what they considered the unfair tactics of the official party in their counter-petition. Although these committees were composed of townspeople who were not much affected directly by the *corvées*, Montreal suffered indirectly when good farmers were taken from their work. If the townspeople were not moved by motives of humanity and abstract justice, they were moved by the sense of a law offensive to their "nation" and by the conviction that a protest against the militia law was a first-class "cry" to combat the argument that an assembly would mean taxation.[29] The committees prepared and presented to Hamilton a strongly worded petition. Acknowledging the obligation of every man to contribute to the defence of the country, they urged that the emergency of war alone justified the *corvées*, "odious and tyrannical in time of peace," as had been clearly shown by certain "illustrious authors." The committees supported their position with specific statements of hardships suffered, statements which suggest not so much flagrant acts of injustice or harsh-ness as innumerable cases of petty injustice and minor hardship.

Hamilton placed the petition before council, expressing regret for the somewhat hostile tone, but showing clearly his sympathy with the sub-stance. Once more, proposals for a precise regulation of the *corvées* were fully discussed in legislative and executive sessions. It was urged that, especially as some services imposed were not justified under the ordinance as it stood, there should be a definition of statutory services, of pay, and of punishable offences, as well as a proper provision of food and even clothing for men on duty.[30]

During the discussion, so many dissenting opinions were entered on the minutes, and so fully and frequently, as to leave a fair record of the debate. Judge Fraser led, very ably, the opposition to any change. This unnecessary revival of old grievances, he argued, amounted to an unfair

attack on army officers, a number of whom, including Carleton and Haldimand, had since left the province. He was supported in this position by
Colonel Henry Hope, formerly quarter-master general, who published in the
Quebec *Gazette* an indignant denial of supposed aspersions on himself and
his brother officers. He was also prepared to support Fraser in the charge
that this ill-timed agitation could imperil the up-country posts by encouraging the habitants to refuse transport duty. Fraser succeeded, too, in
showing that opposition to the militia law had been skilfully blended with
opposition to the registry ordinance, and that some, at least, of the citizens
of Montreal who had signed the petition, later repudiated it, protesting that
they thought they had been petitioning against the registry ordinance only.
Fraser further quoted St George Dupré, the Montreal militia colonel in
charge of transport, as saying that transport service pay was now sufficiently
attractive for him to draw on voluntary labour, a dangerously two-edged
argument. Fraser's final point appealed strongly to the official party: the
petition was not largely signed by "respectable people" but was the work of
"certain rich folk of low birth who seek to rise in society by causing a
change in the province."[31]

Fraser was adequately supported by Mabane, Baby, and their party, and
the petition was tabled. Hamilton reported to Sydney his disappointment
and disapproval and, although he did not mention Hope by name, his
belief that, but for Hope's public retort and the contemptuous attitude
of the council, the petitioners would have been content to wait until
the next year for the necessary amendments. Apart from the bitterness
of party spirit it is difficult to understand such obdurate refusal to consider
a reasonable clarification of the law. During Burgoyne's campaign in 1777,
a British officer, Major Powell, had said that the Canadians would work well
and cheerfully for the precise duration of a stated term of service. If kept
after that time they either deserted or became entirely useless. He had
recommended to Carleton scrupulous adherence to definite undertakings, a
counsel repudiated by the system of the generals.[32]

The official party in the years after 1785 believed the remedy lay in the
old plan favoured by Carleton and the seigneurs of embodying two battalions of militia to be selected by lot from the parishes. St George Dupré
protested vehemently that this would cause "a terrible revolution." The
plan "was intended for the private support of a class that always wishes to
command others." He flatly refused to have anything to do with it; he would
rather "dig the earth with his bare hands." His colleague, Colonel
Sevestre, warned that discontent with the militia law could make "the
chamber" inevitable.[33] In 1787 a general militia law was separated from a
law defining *corvées*, and with the enrolment of English and Canadian
companies of militia one grievance was removed. Although plans for em-

bodying Canadian battalions were carried forward even to the requisition of uniforms, they remained in the paper stage. As the troops were withdrawn from the province and the Americans took over their own territory, the *corvée* problem settled itself.

During the summer of 1785, however, the militia controversy and Hamilton's policy caused much agitation among members of Haldimand's party. The two senior military officers, General St Leger and Colonel Hope, although they disagreed with Hamilton's liberal views, retained their friendship for him, St Leger remarking that the spirit of innovation might make it difficult to get men for *corvée* work, but that he counted on Hamilton's co-operation.[34] Mabane, Baby, and the brothers George and Alexander Davison, merchants who enjoyed Haldimand's confidence, were less moderate, urging Haldimand to return before Hamilton gave them away to the Americans. "It's high time the Big Chief came back," wrote St George Dupré.[35]

But Hamilton's time was running out. Although he had had clear indications of Sydney's want of confidence in him, and of an opposition in Haldimand that could even be called enmity, he seems, optimistically, to have counted on a change of mood in London. Finlay, who served as his secretary, had contrived in the previous year to open a private correspondence with Evan Nepean, Sydney's under-secretary, sending home reports which set forth, in a moderate tone, the views of the reform party.[36] On the other hand Colonel Hope, with friendly intentions, warned Hamilton that he was going too far.

It was immediately after the militia business was concluded in May that Hamilton took the last fatal step. He renewed the lease of the king's posts to the firm which had held it since Murray's day, now represented by Dunn, William Grant, and Charles Stewart. Haldimand was opposed to Grant's politics, and believed that he had tried to cheat the government when he had acted as deputy receiver general. He had decided to transfer this governmental favour to George and Alexander Davison, in whom he had confidence. Before leaving Quebec he had forbidden Hamilton to renew the lease. On his arrival in London, he advised Sydney to offer the lease to the Davisons without giving Dunn and his friends the option of renewal. Dunn and his friends, it was true, had no legal claim. Although their rent had been regularly paid and accepted, the lease had expired, and had not been renewed. It was, however, customary to give the lessees the option of renewal, and they could reasonably have expected the year's notice to which the lease would have entitled them. Sydney, however, accepted Haldimand's advice and in the spring of 1785 sent orders to Hamilton to offer the lease to the Davisons.

Before receiving the official dispatch, Hamilton learned the news from private gossip. The Davisons' friends had sent on the good news. Indignant at what he thought a flagrant injustice, for Dunn and his friends were hoping to recoup losses suffered during the war, Hamilton immediately renewed the lease, contriving to complete the transaction a day or two before he received Sydney's letter.[37]

This act of near defiance – for a whole flight of angry letters assured Sydney that Hamilton had known of his orders – was the last straw. Late in the fall Hamilton received a letter of dismissal which, in its curtness, ranks second only to the one sent by Carleton to the unlucky Livius. Hamilton was ordered to leave the province as soon as he could hand over his charge to Hope, who was appointed his successor. Indignant and hurt, as may be imagined, he obeyed his orders to the letter. The sailing of the last ship left him no time even to dispose of his furniture. Borrowing the money to settle his accounts and pay his immediate expenses, he returned to two years of poverty in England. He was finally appointed governor of Bermuda, where the capital city still bears his name.[38]

It may have been some consolation to Hamilton in his disgrace to know that Hope, his successor, still remained his good friend, and that General St Leger, who found his policies so alarming, continued to esteem him. No solicitations were needed to elicit the warmest addresses of farewell. Young Nicholas Boisseau found relief in verse, very bad verse, but showing clearly his admiration and regret. Most significant of all was the tribute of Samuel Holland, a convinced political opponent, who had known the country since 1760: "No governor nor lieutenant-governor before him ever acquired so much popularity." The comment raises once more the teasing question of how many Canadians were devoted to the charter theory of the Quebec Act.[39]

The party of Haldimand, delighted at Hamilton's overthrow, found little else to please them. Their plan, formed apparently with Haldimand's approval, was that the old governor should return and restore order with the help of Adam Mabane, who was to be appointed chief justice.[40] Mabane, since 1778 one of the commissioners for executing the office of chief justice in criminal matters, and long the senior judge in civil cases, thought, understandably, that the appointment would be no more than a reasonable recognition of services which had brought him much power, but no wealth. Unhappily for him and for his party the ministry, while accepting and even following Haldimand's advice on local matters, had long since had different plans for the future government of Quebec. These plans were being completed in August 1785. About the time that Sydney wrote Hamilton's letter of dismissal he was preparing to tell Haldimand, much more courteously but without much more warning, that he was to be retired. Haldimand, unwilling to retire, was not consoled for his disappointment by a pension and knighthood. To his credit, however, he did all in his power to dissolve the hard core of his Quebec party and reconcile the members to the new regime.[41]

For eighteen months and more the British government had been working on a scheme to draw together the British North American provinces under one governor who should preside as a kind of viceroy with lieutenant-governors under him. At the same time, they had not been entirely unmindful of the petitions from Quebec, reinforced as they were by representations from London merchants, and from Francis Maseres, still perseveringly intent on the laws and constitution of Quebec. Someone was needed to give the right answer to the Quebec question, and at the same time to devise a general government for the imperial remnants on the St Lawrence and about the gulf.

By August 1785 the man had been found and, after much bargaining, his terms had been met. Sir Guy Carleton had consented to return to Quebec as Lord Dorchester, to preside from that ancient city over all of British North America. He was to take with him the friend and adviser who had been with him during the British evacuation of New York, William Smith, the most celebrated if not the most single-minded of the American loyalists.[42] It had been hoped that Dorchester could reach Quebec by the fall of 1785. This proving impossible, Hope was left to administer the province, following his own taste and common prudence by avoiding all innovations until the arrival of the new dignitaries.

CHAPTER 14

Chief Justice Smith
and the Grand Design

On Sunday, October 22, 1786, the frigate *Thisbe* with Dorchester and William Smith on board appeared in the basin at Quebec. The following day the new governor landed. While the guns of the frigate and the batteries of the town exchanged volleys in greeting, the members of the council made their way along the streets, lined with troops and crowded with people, to the wharf. There they welcomed Dorchester, who proceeded, bareheaded and bowing right and left in acknowledgement of greetings from every side, up the Côte de la Montagne to the Château. Governor, councillors, and the principal citizens made their way to the council chamber where Lieutenant-Governor Hope, in uniform, bareheaded and clasping in his gloved hands the seal of the province, seated himself on a dais. Lord Dorchester, seated in an armchair before the dais, rose and bowed. The councillors took their seats at the council table. The clerk rose, read the Governor's commissions, and administered to him the oath of office. The Lieutenant-Governor bowed, descended from the dais, and handed the seal and the commissions to Dorchester. The Governor then mounted the dais as cannon without roared in salute, and all within bowed deeply.[1]

There is little doubt that the plan for this elaborate ceremony, with the new representative of the monarch arriving in state, greeted by the populace, acknowledging majesty in the person of the lieutenant-governor, and himself enthroned in the presence of councillors and commoners, came from the careful hand of William Smith, the new chief justice. No abler man had been sent from Britain since 1760; no other had come with such elaborate plans for the right ordering of this somewhat intractable province; and yet no other with such power and purpose apparently achieved so little.[2]

Smith was born in 1728, the oldest child of a New York lawyer who had left England for the colonies at the age of sixteen. Prominent as a lawyer and landowner, active also in journalism and politics, the younger

Smith was known in New York as a whig opposed at once to the Anglican establishment and to the taxation of America. He was, however, a whig, not a radical. To the end he believed that on the taxation issue Britain had been wrong. Striving to impose taxation over the authority of colonial parliaments, British statesmen had sinned against constitutional and natural right. On the other hand, he condemned the Declaration of Independence as wrong also because it broke what he thought of as an indissoluble covenant between the mother country and the colonies.

For some time after July 1776 Smith lived quietly in the country, hoping for a reconciliation, or, perhaps, undecided whether to maintain the covenant at the risk of losing his considerable property. In 1778, having been forced to make a choice, and having decided to retain his allegiance, he found himself back in New York sharing the diminishing fortunes of the British. In 1779 he was appointed chief justice, a nominal appointment as no courts were held. In 1782 Carleton, in semi-retirement on a comfortable sinecure since his quarrel with Germain in 1778, was sent to New York as commander-in-chief, charged with evacuation of loyalists and troops. Carleton was at his best when, in a crisis, he could assume supreme direction, confident that even the ablest subordinate was glad to accept his authority. Smith, like others before him, succumbed to his spell and became a warm and even a humble admirer.

In political ideas the two men were far apart. Carleton frankly favoured authoritarian government and Smith was a parliament man. They were united by their sense of the importance of the role of monarchy and aristocracy in the British parliamentary system. Smith confirmed Carleton in the view he had expressed years before, that representative institutions had gone astray in the colonies because, necessarily elected on a wide suffrage in those equalitarian societies, they had lacked the balance between the power of the monarch, representing the total community; the influence of the aristocracy, representing ability, education, and wealth; and the will of the majority. The democracy of numerous small assemblies unbridled by monarchy or aristocracy had, Smith believed, resulted in a distortion of the British system.

The remedy lay in a union of the colonies with a revival of the monarchical and aristocratic principles. Smith wanted a federal union with a constitution which would adequately represent American wealth and power. He had no idea of belittling his own country. He conceived of one continental parliament to deal with Britain for all the colonies. This parliament, recognizing Britain's paramount power, would make itself responsible for raising by taxation such reasonable contributions as were agreed to be necessary for imperial defence. Smith had circulated this plan among his fellow countrymen during the years of hesitation before he openly declared himself a loyalist. It was already too late. He took it with him to New York, where he confided it to Carleton, who was temperamentally attracted by large ideas and bold plans. From Smith's further deliberations and his conversations with Carleton in New York, and after their return to London, there emerged his grand design for a new and greater British North America. Like many others he did not believe that Congress could produce a viable republican constitution. He was sure that the colonies must eventually find order and unity under a monarch.

All this time loyalists from the port of New York and by way of the inland routes of Lake Champlain and the Mohawk River were moving into Quebec and Nova Scotia where virgin lands awaited them. The new imperial policy should be based on these facts. The remaining British colonies must be made fit for loyalists to live in; fit, too, for other Americans, weary of republican disorder, who might wish to come in; fit at last, perhaps, for the reception of disillusioned republican states. British North America must be made "a showcase for the continent."[3] Even without the United States it could become the centre of an immense dominion. The former colonies had no treaty claims beyond the Mississippi. Britain, on the other hand, still held the generous claims of the original charters and, by right of conquest, the claims of France in the northwest. The new empire could be continent-wide, extending, as Carleton had dreamed, to the Rockies and beyond.

The government of this greater Canada must be, Smith insisted, "liberal." There should be the nearest possible approach to British parliamentary government, with the added improvement of "the admission of all, whether French or English, to office, honour and popular suffrage and trust without any contracted preference or religious discrimination."[4] Liberalism would be prevented from degenerating either into an excess of democracy or into undue subordination to the British Parliament by a strong central government, headed by a man fit in person and in power to enhance the monarchical part of the constitution. A "governor general" should link together lieutenant-governors in each province on the one hand, and the British government on the other, by being himself "the reservoir of all information and the sole conduit of communication."[5] The governor general would also be the commander-in-chief of the army; he would have full powers to appoint and suspend all officers; and he would be in charge of public lands and Indian relations.

The man cast for this role by Smith was Carleton; and Carleton, as the idea commended itself to him, fixed on Smith as his chief justice and confidential adviser. Meanwhile, Sydney and his colleagues were quite ready to believe that Carleton would be a good man to succeed Haldimand in Quebec. He knew the country, he knew the Canadians, and he was fresh from dealing with the loyalists. It was, however, hardly to be expected that the timid Sydney, who in 1785 was loyally supporting Haldimand in his opposition to all "innovations," would go into raptures over Smith's wide-ranging plans. Apart from this difficulty, Carleton was claiming his peerage and there were some natural doubts about Smith as a loyalist. The British government resisted and delayed. At last, after two and a half years spent in conferring, bargaining, and lobbying, both men got substantially what they asked for. Smith was appointed Chief Justice of Quebec. Carleton, now Lord Dorchester, was commissioned as governor (not governor general) and commander-in-chief of British North America, with powers of correspondence and general supervision over the lieutenant-governors of the maritime provinces. He was authorized to visit the other provinces and even to assume the powers of government there if he thought it desirable.

So much for the grand design. Sydney was more immediately concerned with the ever-present Quebec question. He required of the new governor the full information and advice that would enable the government to proceed to such constitutional changes as might be needed to meet the demands of the merchants and the loyalists. The petitions of 1783 and 1784, and the corresponding counter-petitions, and innumerable other communications were before him. With each succeeding year of peace there was less excuse for putting off the awkward issue.

In these circumstances it was unfortunate that Smith with his energy, ability, and experience should cross the Atlantic bemused with his grand design, seeing Quebec chiefly as a means of repairing the "rent" in the Empire, the road to "communion" if not to union with the United States. Quebec needed a dispassionate attention to its diverse and now rapidly changing elements in order that a system might be contrived just to the individual and favourable to the general prosperity. Neither Dorchester nor Smith, able and informed as they were, could approach the problem in this way. Dorchester was embarrassed, even paralysed, because he could neither forget nor frankly acknowledge his distortion of the Quebec Act into "the system of the generals." When Smith asked him how the ordinance on the courts of justice had come to be drawn without attention to the royal instructions, he pretended to have forgotten the circumstances. While Dorchester, compromised by his past, was inclined to remain politically passive, Smith was hurried into action by his dream of the future. With his eyes on Quebec but his mind on New York, he pursued a course which did nothing to mend the rent in the Empire, and not much to improve conditions in the province.

Even if Smith had been the most modest and cautious of men he must have found his first years in Quebec difficult. The senior council members in Quebec and their friends, Lieutenant-Governor Hope, Adam Mabane, François Baby, and Major Mathews, Haldimand's former secretary, all lamented Haldimand's retirement and feared any alteration of his policy. Prudence and a sense of duty enforced respect for Lord Dorchester, but Smith, an American, a dubious loyalist, and almost certainly an innovator, had thrust himself into Dorchester's confidence and occupied the place that Mabane claimed as his. From the beginning Smith encountered Mabane's strong personal resentment.

All personal feelings apart, Mabane and his friends maintained a doctrine the very antithesis of the one that seemed to Smith so obviously right. They might grudgingly agree to some concessions for up-country loyalists, but they saw no need for change in Quebec proper. The six thousand loyalists settled there who had borne arms for the king had accepted their lands knowing the Canadian laws that went with them. No change was needed for them. If "late loyalists" must be admitted they should go to the maritime colonies where their own kind of government was established and where the British fleet was available to protect and, if necessary, control them. Quebec ought to be considered a frontier province, its alien religion, laws, and government serving as welcome protection against noxious infiltrations from the United States. The people who had, it was believed, increased from 75,000 to 113,000 in a quarter of a century could easily occupy all the available lands in another thirty years.[6]

Mabane soon had an opportunity of explaining this policy to Smith. In obedience to his instructions to gather and forward information to London, Dorchester, shortly after his arrival, cast four committees of council on justice, commerce, agriculture and settlement, and defence and communications. Smith and Mabane were on the justice committee, with several others, of whom two only, Finlay and St Ours, attended. Smith, according to his custom, confronted the committee with a draft report proposing certain changes in the court system, and asked their approval. Mabane answered with a point-blank rejection. No concessions should be made to English-speaking settlers, and no changes should be made. He and St Ours, voting consistently against Finlay, rejected all proposals for the amendment of the judicial system. Smith, undisturbed, noted in his diary that Dorchester, with whom he dined almost every night, had agreed that the committee reports would probably be unsuitable and must be turned over to a general committe for revision. Meanwhile necessary legislation could proceed independently.[7] For all his whig principles, Smith was prepared to use Dorchester's support to impose his views on the members of council, for most of whom he had little respect.

In December Smith made a critical move in delivering judgement on a complicated case before the court of appeals. Alexander Gray, the Solicitor

General, was conducting a cause of his own against William Grant, the merchant. Gray, as curator, under Canadian law, of the estate of his late uncle, the merchant John Gray, sued Grant in the common pleas for a debt owed to the estate. Grant did not deny the debt, but questioned Gray's right to sue him. Grant lost the case in the lower court and appealed. The judgement, given on December 29, was prepared by Smith and concurred in by the English-speaking majority that happened to sit that day. Smith sustained Grant's appeal, finding Gray's curatorship invalid because granted to him under Canadian law. He decreed that when both parties were English the proceedings must be governed by English law.

The Chief Justice dwelt at some length on the principle of his decision as being at once good law, and desirable for the well-being of the province. Whereas Quebec courts since 1775 had assumed that under the Quebec Act Canadian law was in force for all residents of the province, Smith argued that the whole of the enacting sentence must be assumed to relate to the opening clause, which referred to "Canadians" only. The Proclamation of 1763 had offered English law to all; as the Canadians preferred their own laws, these had been specifically confirmed to them in 1774. It was not intended, however, in this general fashion and without an express enactment to take English law away from English subjects. Smith added that Gray's curatorship was not, in his view, valid under Canadian law, but this he did not stress. He rather used the opportunity of showing how wrong, how injurious to commerce, and how discouraging to loyalists was the current interpretation of the law.

Smith's interpretation was not altogether new in Quebec. Monk had argued for English law in a suit where both parties were English in 1781, and William Dummer Powell, a loyalist lawyer, had done the same in 1783 in Haldimand vs. Cochrane. A recent judgement rendered in the Privy Council in Britain seemed to lend support to this view. On the other hand, when Smith's decision was referred by Sydney to the English law officers, their opinion was that the wording of the Act would hardly bear the interpretation. They suggested, with professional calm, that the doubt be resolved by taking a test case to the Privy Council.[8]

Even though justice would have been satisfied by declaring Gray's curatorship invalid under Canadian law, Smith no doubt conceived that his duty as chief justice required him to state the whole law as he saw it. Mabane promptly offered his defiance. From the bench in the court of common pleas he repudiated Smith's interpretation as erroneous, and announced that it would not bind the lower courts. At the same time he privately boasted that "he had driven away three lieutenant-governors and chief justices and should think it strange if he could not do so again."[9]

Smith scoffed at the threat, naturally; he was equally ready to scoff at

Mabane's law. He did not realize that, however a lawyer might regard his decision, the announcement, and the deliberate effort to publicize it, was a political blunder. His ignorance of the province made him insensitive to the alarm that must be felt by all Canadians at this sudden announcement that law was not territorial but personal, and that it was government policy henceforth to attract to the lower part of the province as many English-speaking people as possible. This was too sudden a reversal of the system of the generals. It was bound to arouse strong resentment from the exponents of the charter theory of the Quebec Act and vague fears among others, even those favourable to some modification of the law. Petitions protesting the judgement were presented to Lord Dorchester from Quebec and from Montreal. The Quebec petition referred to Canadian law as having been confided to the people by their ancient sovereigns, "une loi et édit perpetuelles et irrévocables." Montreal in more moderate language referred to the good faith of the monarch and to his sense of justice to preserve property and law according to "le vœu unanime et invariable de la nation." [10]

When these petitions were laid before the council Smith openly doubted their authenticity. He believed that Hope and Mabane had promoted them with the help of Rouville in Montreal. [11] He ignored them in favour of the presentations from the merchants of Quebec and Montreal to the committe on commerce. These two groups agreed in expressing great dissatisfaction with the administration of justice and with parts of the substantive law. Only in Quebec, where no Canadian merchants signed, was there a demand for English commercial law as a whole, but in Montreal Canadians and English were united in asking for certain changes and were clearly not dedicated to the principle of a "perpetual edict." [12]

The chief justice, therefore, proceeded confidently with his program. The ordinance on the courts of justice, amended in 1785 by the addition of the clause permitting optional juries, fell due for renewal again in this year, 1787. Smith presented an entirely new ordinance. He proposed important practical changes. The English term system, changed in the common pleas to weekly courts by Carleton's ordinance of 1770, was reintroduced in modified form. The weekly sittings, most useful for certain purposes, had never been suited to complicated commercial cases and had been a burden to the merchants who had cases in court during the intense pressure of business which coincided with the arrival of the first ships in spring and the final departure of the ships in the fall. Smith also proposed safeguards against the abuse of the *saisies*, which Dunn had tried to abolish in 1785, and certain additional powers to the court of appeals.

The essential purpose of the bill, however, was a fundamental reinter-pretation of the law which would confirm the decision handed down in *Gray* vs. *Grant*. A lengthy preamble stated that the Quebec Act was a temporary measure and that the interests of the loyalists must now be consulted. Henceforth, all suits in which both parties were English were to be tried and determined "as if the same had been begun and prosecuted in Westminster Hall." Canadians were protected; they could secure their own law by pleading their descent.

Three days later another bill was laid on the council table by Paul Roch St Ours. The exact terms are not known. It apparently renewed the old ordinance with two important changes: the elimination of optional juries, granted in 1785, and of the English law of evidence in commercial suits. The English law of evidence had been the one concession made to the merchants in the original ordinance of 1777. It was obvious that a major political contest was impending between the now clearly defined parties of Smith and Mabane. The two bills were tabled for a time as the council turned to other business. In March, while Smith was absent in Montreal at the assizes, Mabane and his party threw out his bill and proceeded to debate St Ours's. The war was now in the enemy's country. Back in Quebec Smith found himself on the defensive.[13]

The next move of Smith's party was to call on public opinion by printing the Chief Justice's bill and circulating it among the merchants. St Ours's bill was not printed but the intention of abolishing jury trial and the English law of evidence was known. The merchants, therefore, asked to be allowed to appear with their lawyer to make representations to council on the bill, as it concerned their interests. The request could hardly be refused. James Monk, for ten years a power in the merchants' party, secured Dorchester's permission to act as their counsel. On the appointed day, Saturday, April 14, Monk, his clients, and a crowd of merchants, officers, and others pressed into the council chamber and Monk was given permission to present his case.

The speech that followed was a landmark in the political history of the colony. Monk addressed the council from half past ten in the morning until a quarter to five. As had been expected he pleaded for the retention of the jury clause and the English law of evidence, and he urged more consideration for the needs and interests of the loyalists. He went on, however, to a vehement attack on the laws and the law courts, and to a personal attack on the judges, especially Mabane and Fraser. He charged that the laws as they administered them were confused and contradictory, the courts lacked "order, rule . . . and certainty," and that they, personally, were partial and arbitrary. He supported his arguments with numerous examples, citing sixteen specific cases. For six hours his eloquence flowed on while Mabane and Fraser sitting before him could neither check him nor say a word in their own defence.[14]

Monk hated Mabane. With Mabane's counsel and support Haldimand had rejected his opinion on the Cochrane case, had arbitrarily delayed the payment of his fees for government work and had reduced his income by transferring part of his work to the newly created office of solicitor general, bestowed on the politically reliable Scot, Alexander Gray. Moreover, in almost every court in the province, the common pleas, the court of appeals, and the king's bench, Monk had been obliged to offer humble obedience and respect to Mabane whom he despised as a layman on the bench.

Monk was not a noble figure. He was an ambitious man, probably not dishonest, but greedy for money and power. With all his faults Mabane was his superior in benevolence and integrity, and he was a better public servant. Yet on this occasion, in spite of his violence, Monk achieved a dignity beyond his merits. For ten years Quebec, exposed to all the radical ferment of revolutionary America, had lived under the system of the generals, where there was no place for free political discussion, but only for political gossip and private influence. Now for the first time in the history of the colony public issues were aired at a public meeting of the legislature.

Smith approved of Monk's performance although throughout the session he had urged on his followers the need for tact and caution. Monk's speech was, he said, the longest he had ever heard, but delivered "warmly, from the heart" and not at all wearisome. He shared the hope of the merchants that the speech would have the effect of killing St Ours's bill and clearing the way for judicial reform.

He might have foreseen that there could be no such tame conclusion to the affair. Monk had said too much. Lord Dorchester believed that there must be a formal investigation into the administration of justice. Smith appeared for a time to agree, asserting in council that Monk's "high charges" must be examined. It seems certain that this was pure political manoeuvring. Smith wanted the withdrawal of St Ours's bill and the acceptance of his own, and the threat of an investigation looked like a good bargaining-counter. He was willing even to compromise and modify his own bill. In the end, however, he overplayed his hand. The judges, Fraser and Mabane, held out, knowing that some of Monk's charges could not be proved, and hoping to concentrate attention on them. Finally Dorchester took Smith at his word, and ordered him as chief justice and, being newly arrived in the province, obviously not involved, to carry out the investigation himself. The immediate question of the constitution of the courts was settled by renewing the ordinance of 1785 with some of Smith's amendments.[15]

The investigation, perhaps unique in colonial history and affording a remarkably vivid picture of the operations of colonial courts, did reveal ample cause for complaint on the part of suitors. It became clear that the laws, on commercial matters especially, were confused and uncertain. It could hardly have been otherwise. The custom of Paris, the basic civil law during the French regime, was a guide only, a collection of general maxims developed into something like a practical legal code by the elaborate commentaries of men like Ferrière and Pothier, whose works were used and quoted in the courts.

The custom was not adapted to modern commercial affairs. Louis XIV's law of 1673, the so-called *code marchand*, clarified many matters. The courts, however, did not agree as to whether this law, which had not been registered by the *conseil supérieur* of New France, was a part of the law of Canada. The situation was further complicated by the Canadian custom, already mentioned, of the *saisies*, provisional seizures of goods at the commencement of a suit. These seizures, obscurely rooted in French custom, had been developed in Canada apparently to protect the "last outfitter" against a defaulting trader. There was a reason for them, but there was so much uncertainty about the procedure which should govern them that merchants agreed they did more harm than good. A great source of confusion was the law governing bills of exchange, promissory notes, and other forms of paper money much used in a country always short of· hard money. The usefulness of these instruments of credit depended on the rigid observance of conventions clearly understood. In the Quebec courts it appeared that the laws of Old and New France had mingled with those of Albany, New York, and London, leaving merchants uncertain what rule would be followed.

Finally, there was no bankruptcy law in the province which would enable merchants to release unfortunate debtors and to bring pressure to bear on fraudulent ones. There was also, as has been seen, no effective law for the registration of titles to real property. A man could not do business without lending money or extending credit, but he had no sure means of ascertaining the prior claims existing on real property offered as security. The successful suitor might find himself responsible for obligations strange and embarrassing, as when a stern Calvinist found himself pledged to pay fifty livres a year for life to a young priest engaged to say masses for the soul of a former owner.[16]

Another general cause of complaint was the careless keeping of court records and papers. A man might lose a suit on appeal either because the papers were not to be found or because the judges of the lower court had not seen to it that a proper return was made to the higher court.

The uncertainty of the law was in a sense exaggerated by its complexities. Commercial cases were not simple; nor were the rules formed to govern them. For example, a man approaching bankruptcy might be sued by a creditor who seized and, until the court should pronounce judgement, put a seal on all goods on his premises. The goods seized might very well comprise some to be sold on commission, others purchased on a current account, others on an account rendered and overdue, others just delivered by the consigner and still in their original packages, others already sold and not delivered although paid for. Common sense might say that should the apparent owner go bankrupt, at least the first and last groups should be kept out of the common stock as in no sense belonging to the bankrupt man. In all these groups, however, it could make a great deal of difference whether the judge followed the custom of Paris, the *code marchand*, Canadian custom, English law, or his own sense of what was fair.[17]

Herein lay the merchants' grievance. Some cases might be clear enough, but especially in a complicated case, and especially with certain of the judges, it was not possible to say beforehand what law would be followed. This meant among other things that in a colony where so much business was done on credit no man could depend on his good judgement to tell him how much credit could safely be given and to whom. Recovery of his property might too often depend only on the unpredictable decisions of the courts.

The most important question before Smith was the extent to which the judges were responsible for these conditions. Monk had rashly accused them of partiality; of having by "grace and favour" given to one man what they refused to another. He forgot that the very confusion of law made it difficult to prove this charge. In non-jury trials there was no necessity for the judge publicly to apply the law to a case at all and very often he did not. As Monk's two cases were not exactly parallel the judges were able to retort that they did not come under the same law. There is no question, however, that in fact many people did believe them guilty, at least occasionally, of political or even of personal prejudice.

They also suffered for want of the discipline of legal training. They had not grasped the importance, in view of the confusion of the laws, of requiring scrupulous records to be kept and of stating the reasons for their decisions, thus building up a kind of case law. Failing to do these things, they inevitably seemed arbitrary, and encountering criticism, took refuge in their judicial authority.

Their real fault, however, was graver. Mabane, Fraser, and Dunn were members of the legislative council, and Rouville was apparently in close touch with the seigneurs from Montreal who were councillors. Men competent to sit on the bench at all ought to have recognized the confusion of the law and requested a clarification and even new and appropriate legislation from the council. Instead they steadily opposed all change.

Fraser and Mabane had even voted against Dunn, their fellow judge, when he, a belated reformer, suggested the abolition of the *saisies* in 1785.

Monk and his colleague, a loyalist lawyer, Isaac Ogden, marshalling a mass of evidence, made the investigation a cruel exposure, the more so because Monk was skilful enough to relieve the solemnity of the proceedings by ridicule. The whole province was invited to laugh at the story of how young Thomas Walker, the lawyer, had won a bet with a colleague that he could get from the Quebec bench a writ of *saisie conservatoire* that would seal up all the possessions of the other for an unauthenticated debt of one dollar; [18] and at Rouville, who once settled a suit for damages by discharging the suitors and fixing the blame and the damages on a third man who had dropped in to see the course of justice; and at Fraser, who, waving away the account books offered by James McGill to prove that he did not owe money (a thousand pounds) to a certain retired army officer, and taking from his pocket a letter from the plaintiff, a personal friend, assured the court that Colonel Campbell was incapable of a dishonourable action.

The exposure was, indeed, too complete, and too cruel. It automatically aroused a certain sympathy for the judges, honest and respectable men who had never stooped to profit from their office. It also proved highly embarrassing to Smith and to Dorchester. Smith had not wanted to conduct the investigation and had tried to get out of it. He had the lowest opinion of Mabane, Fraser, and Rouville, who dominated the bench in their respective districts, but he was too good a judge not to know that as their political opponent, and as having had some responsibiltiy for precipitating the investigation, he ought not to pronounce judgement.

He could not, however, offer the obvious defence for the judges by putting the blame where it originally lay, on "the system of the generals"; on Carleton who had suppressed his instructions and dismissed the Chief Justice for demanding them; on Carleton for having advised in 1775 the reappointment of Fraser and Mabane, whose limitations he ought to have known from experience; and still on Carleton for having added to Mabane's power and responsibility by naming him the first of three commissioners for executing the office of the chief justice.

The final result was that Smith gathered up the huge pile of paper which had accumulated in his files between June and November of 1787, and transferred it to the Governor along with an ingenious letter as a substitute for a report. Remarking that the investigation had touched on the conduct of the judges and the system of law and law courts, he reminded the Governor that impeachment of judges, like legislation, was a matter for "government," and not for the chief justice. He, therefore, humbly submitted his letter – and the evidence – "to your Lordship's great wisdom." Dorchester, in his great wisdom, passed on the poisoned chalice. He sent the whole lot home to Sydney, explaining that the lateness of the season gave him no time to read and report on it.

Sydney in reply vented his irritation in a severe letter to Dorchester, reproaching him and the Chief Justice for having failed to send home a proper report. As for the merchants, he said, they must, like traders elsewhere, be content with the laws of the country where they did their business. Although the papers of the investigation were turned over to the crown lawyers for examination, Sydney signified his moderate sympathy with the judges by dismissing Monk for the intemperance of his speech and appointing in his place Alexander Gray, who had acted as counsel for the judges in the investigation.

So ended the investigation. No other action of any kind was taken from London. After the better part of a year spent in political uproar the law, the law courts, and the judges remained much as they had been. Naturally, if not quite fairly, those who had welcomed the investigation became increasingly critical of the way in which it had been conducted; ". . . the battle was not fought with a *thing* as it ought to have been; but it was maliciously fought with *men* as it ought *not to have been*," said the correspondent of the Quebec *Herald*. For this Monk, not Smith, must be blamed. Smith would have avoided the investigation had he been able, and he would perhaps after the initial speech have liked to control Monk's exuberance. He was sharply critical of counsel on both sides for loading the record with masses of detail, but, conscious of his own partisanship, he had not the moral courage to restrain them.[19]

Smith's first year in the province had not, then, resulted in any great benefit to the merchants who had hoped for so much from the new regime. It had, indeed, begun to reveal a fundamental cleavage of interest between him and the merchants. Their ultimate design, as grand in its way as that of the Chief Justice, was widely different. Smith's viewpoint was legal and political; his economic interests were in land. He hoped to repair the rent of the Empire by an English constitution and an appropriate land policy. The merchants, on the other hand, lamented not so much the rent of the Empire as the loss of the Ohio country, which yielded two-thirds of the annual fur export. It was, said a Canadian in Montreal, "like having the right arm torn out."[20] Once the merchants were relieved of the immediate danger of losing the trading posts, their concern was not to repair the Empire but to secure such government and laws in Quebec as would keep furs and all other commodities flowing down the St Lawrence instead of down the Hudson or the Mississippi or out of the Bay.[21]

Political disappointments at Quebec hampered but did not prevent the carrying out of the mercantile design. Although the bulk of the furs still came from the lakes, before 1783 Montreal traders had reached the Athabasca country, seeking the finer furs of the far northwest. They were encouraged, even urged, from London to extinguish the pretended rights of the Hudson's Bay Company, resting on nothing but a charter of Charles II "become extinct by the principles of the Revolution." They should by all means press on through the Bay and up the Nelson River; from there to the Pacific, the distance was, according to their London correspondent, "inconsiderable."[22] In 1793 Alexander Mackenzie was to cover this "inconsiderable" distance and to reach the Pacific, although not by way of the Bay. Thus, only five years after Sydney's irritable remark that the merchants of Quebec, like other merchants, must be content with the laws of the country they traded in, these men had, by their single efforts, sketched the extension of the country they traded in from a province on the river to a continental empire.

These formidable characters did not, however, live like a band of brothers. Rivalry between them was occasionally deadly and always costly. In 1787 Joseph Howard of Montreal calculated that one-third of the goods sent up country every year was wasted by competitive trading. He favoured the old scheme of a government monopoly sold out in shares, the proceeds to be spent on public works. So organized, the trade could be worked, he said, with a thousand men instead of the fifteen hundred currently employed.[23] Long before this, other merchants had been trying other plans. For some years traders in the west had mitigated competition by the use of ephemeral co-operative "pools." In 1779 there had appeared the first of a series of agreements associating a number of individuals engaged in the fur trade, under the name of the North West Company. The company from the beginning included some of the greatest names in the later fur trade: Joseph and Benjamin Frobisher, Simon McTavish, and James McGill.[24] The agreements helped to eliminate wasteful and violent competition and to regulate the relations between "wintering partners," Montreal agents, and London merchants, which grew ever more complicated as the trade lines lengthened.

The advent of the large company saw the beginning of the end of the equal and friendly association of English and Canadians in the fur trade. The English almost from the beginning had been the larger investors, but a merchant was in the trade whether he sent one or twenty canoes up country. The appearance of the large and powerful company, with a limited number of shares all held by individuals or firms active in the trade, tended to eliminate Canadians from this aspect of the enterprise. Of well-known Canadian names in the trade only one, Maurice Regis Blondeau, appeared among the North Westers before 1791; another, Charles Chaboillez, came in in 1794. There were several reasons for the absence of Canadian names. Canadians had less capital; they tended to prefer a one-man or a family business; and the strong instinct for family property made them shun the heavy financial risks involved in trade in the far northwest.[25]

Canadians did not, however, shun the heavy personal risks of the northwest trade. If they had, the trade could not have been carried on. They supplied the majority of the fifteen hundred men who ventured up country or went out with the spring canoes. During the years following 1783, as the Ohio trade declined with advancing settlement, the trade from the far northwest increased; it grew from £25,000 in 1784 to £100,000 in 1794, equal at that time to the combined trade of Michilimackinac, Detroit, and Niagara, then being relinquished to the United States.[26]

The enormous difficulties of the route to the west were overcome not only by endurance and skill, but by careful organization. From the first the large four-ton canoes were exchanged for small ones at Grand Portage before beginning the second lap of the journey, which might be a thousand or even two thousand miles farther. The great problem was food for the journey. The big canoes restocked at Michilimackinac and additional supplies went from there to Grand Portage in bateaux or decked ships. The small canoes leaving Grand Portage for the west could not hope to take adequate food for the journey to the wintering grounds. They had to get some additional supplies on the way or face severe suffering if not starvation. It was, therefore, of the greatest importance that such provisions as they could take should always be available at the moment of their departure for the west. To ensure this, great pains were taken with the organization of transport along the lakes.[27]

Since 1783 the merchants had been pleading for permission to deal with this problem by placing their own boats and decked ships once more on the lakes. Merchants trading to Niagara and Detroit did all their freighting by ship, using canoes, as a rule, only along the difficult route from Montreal to Lake Ontario. The traders to Michilimackinac and the far west used ships to carry provisions from Detroit to Michilimackinac to supply the westbound canoes and to feed the considerable numbers employed at Sault Ste Marie in the summer. Since the beginning of the war, however, forbidden to use their own ships or boats, they had been dependent on the services of the king's ships which accepted commercial freight when there was available space. It has been noted that when Haldimand left the province in 1784 he ordered the commanding officer to maintain the wartime restrictions. Unfortunately the number of government ships had been cut down, leaving a tonnage totally inadequate to meet the needs of the army, the Indian service, and the merchants.

In August 1785, after a series of representations, James McGill sent a long and carefully reasoned letter to Hamilton ridiculing the motive of the regulation, the supposed danger of smuggling with the United States. As long as London offered the cheapest trade goods and the best market for furs, Montreal merchants, living on the high road between London and the west, would be only too glad to see that it was used. Hamilton was sympathetic but powerless. St Leger allowed the use of bateaux on the lakes that year, but, in view of Haldimand's "pointed instructions," he continued to prohibit decked ships. Hope, when he succeeded Hamilton, with the additional power of commander-in-chief, did what he could to improve the government service, but he did not venture to alter the system.[28]

This grievance was immediately brought to Dorchester's attention by the committees of merchants reporting to the council committee on commerce early in 1787. Nothing could be done during the furious session of 1787. The following year the merchants were at last relieved by an ordinance allowing private owners to operate on the lakes any kind of ship up to ninety tons burden, if it was British-built and worked by a British crew. In 1788 also Dorchester settled the vexed question of the arrears of freight owed by merchants for the war years by an ordinance turning the debts over to trustees for collection. He arranged for adequate deductions or a total discharge to merchants who could establish loss or damages from neglect. Thus five years after the peace treaty which had "torn out the right arm" of the merchants, the left one was unshackled, and merchant ships in increasing numbers moved freely along the lakes. The merchants did not forget this relief. When Dorchester left Quebec in August 1791 they sent a cordial farewell address, acknowledging with gratitude his services to commerce, particularly "that part which relates to the Indian or western trade."[29]

The merchants' wish to use the St Lawrence as an outlet for commodities other than furs was partly satisfied by a proclamation of Lord Dorchester in 1787, followed by an ordinance in 1788, opening the Champlain–Richelieu route to many natural and semi-processed products of Vermont : lumber of all sorts, including masts, hoops, and staves; grains, dairy products, meat, fish, and pig iron. In this matter the wishes of the merchants coincided with those of the Chief Justice. Both looked on the trade as satisfactory in itself and as calculated to encourage Vermont, still hesitating, to join British North America rather than the United States.[30]

In 1788, also, the council produced an elaborate ordinance to regulate the operations of pilots on the lower St Lawrence, the first one for some twenty years. The new law depended on an apprenticeship system of five years or more, although apprentices were allowed, on passing an examination, to pilot ships after four years' training. Careful provisions were made for the control and protection of the pilots, on whose unremitting labour during the busy months from May to November the whole commercial life of the province depended. Elaborate regulations to control fires and lights on all ships tied up at the wharves of Quebec, and also to prevent any ship from approaching a wharf with more than a pound of gunpowder on board showed the terror of fire in the ships crowded along the docks.[31]

Another ordinance dealt with the St Lawrence fisheries. Negligible in relation to the fur trade they yet represented an important minor industry operated by local men or, frequently, by Quebec merchants. They consumed about a third of the provincial export of wheat, in the form of flour and biscuit, thus giving encouragement to millers and biscuit-makers. Some of the fishers were a lawless lot, and they had been both corrupted and harassed by the carelessness of the totally uncontrolled ships from the American colonies. The ordinance of 1788 dealt with complaints of long standing. The old rule of "first come, first served" on the beaches was confirmed, with safeguards to those in permanent occupation and to private property. Fouling of waters and damaging of harbours by tossing overboard ballast and offal as the new catch was processed and stored was strictly forbidden. Enforcement was confided to the local justices of the peace, and to the lieutenant-governor, who had been appointed in 1778. Unfortunately this last official needed a ship and small force of men to patrol the beaches. For this, as for so many other desirable projects, there was no money.[32]

This useful legislation was only preliminary to the larger plans of the Quebec merchants for taking over the West Indian trade now, in theory, closed to the United States. The merchants suggested that henceforth they send over to Europe only enough wheat to supply their need of wine and fruit. These desirable commodities they proposed to bring back direct, instead of allowing them to lose their flavour in the roundabout journey from Spain to London and on to Quebec. It was even hoped that Spanish and Portuguese fishermen might bring the fruit and wine to Quebec and then load up with flour and biscuit before going to their fishing grounds. The bulk of the wheat was to go to the West Indies direct, duty free, in exchange for rum and molasses which, in turn, would be admitted to Quebec free or at a reduced rate. George Allsopp, one of the promoters of the plan, admitted that Quebec flour could not, at the moment, rival American flour in quality. It was proposed, however, to instruct the habitants and to encourage them to deliver better and cleaner grain by building public granaries to receive all grain for export. The grain would be classified into three grades according to quality, and stored in separate bins. As a further stimulus to diversified trade the merchants asked for bounties on lumber and encouragement for ship-building, to be carried on in the winter months. This last, it was hoped, would help to solve the seasonal unemployment which caused so much suffering among the poor.

These bold schemes, showing as they did the energy and optimism of the commercial group, bore no immediate fruit. Reduction of duties and payment of bounties were hardly to be expected when the annual cost of civil government was already a charge on the treasury. The obvious remedy of an assembly only raised the larger, still unsolved constitutional problem. It was inevitable that a commerce so far existing chiefly in the imagination should have little appeal to a ministry and parliament moved as a rule only by solid and obvious material considerations. The fundamental obstacle was, however, one that the merchants could hardly be expected to see. The same geographical situation that enabled Montreal merchants to outstrip those of New York and Boston in drawing furs from the remote interior worked against them in the West Indian trade. The colony laboured under the insuperable handicaps of distance and winter ice. Not even the might of Britain's mercantile system could totally defy geography.[33]

One other factor at this time stood in the way of Quebec's taking over the West Indian trade. Although crops in the province might be bountiful, the yield was uncertain, and the want of proper storage facilities prevented the accumulation of such a surplus as could secure a supply for a steady market. Before the war the apparently rapid increase in wheat production caused great optimism. As it happened, not until after 1791 did the provincial yield match the plentiful harvests of the years immediately before the war.[34] In 1788 and 1789 the vulnerable situation of the province was dramatically illustrated by a crop shortage that created a famine. The situation was aggravated by the peculiar agricultural methods of the habitants and their ignorance of the effect of crop diseases. The 1788 crop in Quebec and in the neighbouring states was apparently struck by a disease, smut or rust, that produced heavy straw but unfilled heads. The habitants, unsuspecting, put away their sheaves for the winter threshing while wheat from the 1787 crop was shipped out as usual. Not until the early winter, after the close of navigation, was it realized that the crop was very poor, only half or a third of what had been expected. With no stored surplus in the province, the shortage rapidly became acute. The four-pound loaf rose from sixpence to fourteenpence. The poor in the towns, many of whom certainly went hungry every winter, suffered terribly, and those in the country, for once, were no better off. Public and private relief, generously offered, was too slow to be fully effective because the shortage had appeared so suddenly. Fortunately there was an adequate crop in 1789 which relieved the situation. The need for public storehouses was clearly demonstrated and also for such precise information as would maintain a safe surplus and forestall any such disaster in future.[35]

Meanwhile Smith, although necessarily involved in all council work, was giving his special attention to certain matters very near his heart because related to his North American design. From his arrival in Quebec, one of his principal interests had been the system of land tenure. He had been shocked to discover that Dorchester was instructed to continue making all grants *en fief et seigneurie*. Such instructions, said Smith, "neither invited to the settlement of the country nor to the preservation of it," and might even be made the ground of impeachment to the ministers as a design to throw the colony into the States.[36] Dorchester fully agreed, explained that he had not been consulted, and arranged, as he hoped, for a change of instructions. The home government was willing, but thought it desirable also to deal with the right of converting tenures from *en seigneurie* to English tenure. This matter was necessarily referred to the council. One of the seigneurs, Lanaudière, appointed councillor in 1788, was in favour of such a measure. He wished more freedom in the sale and exploitation of his lands, and he expatiated, inaccurately, on the abuses of the seigneurial system. The others, however, offended by Smith's insistence on English law for the English, by his constant fraternization with newly arrived Americans, and by his large plans for settling and anglicizing the colony, offered successful resistance. No provision was made for conversion to freehold tenure; new grants continued to be made *en seigneurie* with the king as seigneur.

Mabane and the seigneurial party also resisted Smith's effort to introduce an ordinance clarifying and reforming Canadian law on wills and guardianships. Here the English party had a grievance. Although the Quebec Act allowed them to make wills by English law, guardianship was administered, contrary to English custom, by the common pleas court, where Canadian law was imposed on old and new subjects alike. Smith's proposal for an ordinance which would allow each group its own customs was defeated and Mabane's ordinance, confirming current usage, was carried by ten votes to eight in 1790. It was, however, disallowed by Dorchester, who reported to William Grenville, now in charge of colonial affairs, that strife in the council had been so bitter that he had decided to use his constitutional right to "advise upon it." The fact is significant. With all his ability Smith never succeeded in dominating the council. The best that Dorchester could or would do was to give him some protection against opposition.

By 1791 the Chief Justice had done most useful work in revising the court system to meet territorial expansion and population growth. New judicial districts were organized for the loyalist settlements. The district of

Hesse with its centre at Detroit at last received a judge with legal training, the loyalist lawyer William Dummer Powell. The population growth in the lower part of the province was met by the creation of a new district of Three Rivers, which helped lessen the scandal of circuit courts where one judge had been known to determine over a hundred cases in one day.[37] The same purpose was met by the legislative council giving power to the executive to establish "circle courts," local courts presided over by a local judge for the trial of small causes in certain groups of parishes.

All these reforms were very useful. In these and many administrative matters Smith served the province and the Governor well. Apart, however, from the minor changes in 1787, throughout these years he did nothing to redress the grievances of the merchants in commercial matters. That the grievances remained, and were felt, the correspondence in the newly established Montreal *Gazette* and the Quebec *Herald* abundantly shows. Merchants, especially, demanded an adequate bankruptcy law and a registry law. The newspapers, which provided increasingly a forum for the discussion of public issues, expressed the public dissatisfaction. Correspondents complained that the council was ill-informed on commercial matters. Even if the councillors were "God's vice-regents," said one, the public still had a right to expect that they would acquit themselves like honest men.[38] This criticism was almost patently directed at Smith, who prided himself on being well informed about everything and whose somewhat arrogant manner invited the jibe of "God's vice-regent."

If Smith could have been cordial to the merchants and conciliatory to Mabane and the seigneurial party, he might have made himself the representative of an influential group in the province favourable to representative institutions and to a commercial law, French or English, which would be clear, modern, and suited to the needs of the province. Instead, there seems to have developed between him and the merchants mutual misunderstanding and contempt. He found them, no doubt, unpolished and ill-educated. They found him ignorant of the fur trade and unaware of its importance.[39] Absorbed in his schemes for reassuring the loyalists by a guarantee of English law and freehold tenure, absorbed also, and not entirely creditably, with the idea of creating a landed aristocracy by the right use of vacant lands,[40] he neither shared, nor cared to share, the viewpoint of the merchant.

No doubt he felt his increasing isolation. It was said of him that there was not a man in the province "less rich in friends."[41] Bent on his great plans, however, he was insensitive to the needs and interests of his immediate neighbours. He continued to fix his hopes on such an influx of loyalists as would transform Quebec into a New York made safe for democracy.

CHAPTER 15

The Darkest Corner of the Dominion

After Smith had been rather more than a year in Quebec he expressed his gloomy view of the intellectual and political climate of the province by describing it as "the Darkest Corner of the Dominion." His first impressions, more superficial, had also been much more favourable. He had written to his wife, who was still in New York, of cheap and plentiful food in the market – "Fowls ninepence a Brace" – of the comfort of the iron stoves in every passage which supplemented the generous open fires, and of the security of houses roofed with slate or metal in contrast to the "three hundred acres of shingles" in New York. He commended also the comfort of the roomy, closed cariole, and the good snow roads: "the whole distance [between Quebec and Montreal] being a *Street*, makes the winter so agreeable to these French folks, the gayest animals upon Earth."[1]

Gaiety at Quebec flourished on a foundation of material well-being. Internal peace, combined with generous government spending during the American war, had made possible an unusual level of comfort and prosperity. Certain kinds of food had, indeed, always been plentiful. "It is easy," said Smith, "to be a good Catholic in such a Fish Country."[2] Pigs, cattle, and horses were also compelled to be good Catholics in winter when frozen fish was used to supplement their diet.[3] This solution to the chronic fodder problem made meat more abundant than it could have been had the habitants depended on the scanty supply of hay. Potatoes and all other vegetables, including the once rare cauliflower, were now plentiful. The cellars of the Quebec Seminary, glowing like a summer garden with the colours of the carefully stored produce, were spoken of as one of the sights of the city.[4]

Country folk were able to live in much comfort on the produce of their farms supplemented from the nearby forest and stream. They bought little but molasses, snuff, and the brandy which was to be had in any one of the six or seven hundred inns in the province. In town all kinds of exotic luxuries were available for those who could afford them : wines – madeira, port, sherry, and perhaps, by skill or good fortune, the much-loved red wines of France; sugar and spices; lemons and oranges; dried fruits, coffee, tea, chocolate, and sweets. Friends of the nuns, who exchanged gifts with their sisters in the West Indies, might even enjoy that delicious sweetmeat, angélique. Fruit from Montreal was always available in season; the fortunate were able to preserve their cherries in liqueur. Spruce beer, the essential ingredient of which was easy to come by, was a popular drink, at least in the towns.[5]

The houses, whose warmth was so grateful to Smith, were typical of the comfort, the hospitality, and the gaiety of the country. There was no sharp line of cleavage between town and country dwellings. The cities still showed everything from the crude outline of the primitive log house to the stately bishop's palace at Quebec or the enchanting Château Vaudreuil in Montreal.[6] Most people, however, lived in solid habitations which could clearly trace their ancestry back to the farmhouses of Brittany, Anjou, and Normandy. The terror of fire in the towns was encouraging more and more building in stone; country people too were building comfortable and even imposing manor houses with their attendant buildings, stables, storehouses, dairy, and oven.[7] The simpler houses had a large family room with perhaps a separate kitchen on the ground floor, and a half-story above for sleeping quarters, unheated of course, but cosy enough with a warm chimney passing through, and bearskin blankets on the beds. The grander houses would have two and a half stories. Those built for merchants in Quebec and Montreal were constructed with stone-lined vaults below, and a heavily reinforced floor in the garret to allow maximum space for storage.

The houses had a look of comfort and stability. The traditional steeply pitched roof of northern France and the wide chimney at either end were well adapted to the heavy snows and bitter winds of a Canadian winter. For the rest, windows were arranged not to impress the passerby with a sense of their symmetry, but in order to give appropriate lighting and ventilation to each room, large or small. Doors were placed for convenience and for comfort; every good builder as he planned the house was prudently aware of the prevailing winds. The effect of these practical arrangements from the outside was, and still is, pleasing and often delightful, not because it was "quaint," but because Canadian builders somehow contrived to preserve a sound tradition which they developed in their own fashion. They could give a pleasant proportion to the lines of the most insignificant dairy-house or field oven. In more pretentious dwellings they experimented and used their imagination, yet with necessary restraint.[8]

The period following the Conquest was critical in that it limited but did

not eliminate influences from France. It also brought, with the coming
of the loyalists, new ideas and modes of construction to which Canadian
builders responded. Until near the end of the century, however, the building tradition was chiefly French, and most of the houses were unpreten-
tious. In Quebec Smith had some difficulty finding a house which met his
sense of what was fitting for one of his station: two drawing-rooms, a
dining-room and study below, and five bedrooms.[9]

While Smith was looking for a house in the winter of 1786-87, he was
bombarding his wife with letters full of affection, and also full of instructions on the care of his books and the importance of ordering her household
goods from London. Wooden furniture of the more ordinary sort, he admitted, could be got cheaply in Quebec. The now highly valued examples
of the Canadian craftsmanship of that day in fine staircases and mantel-
pieces, as well as in furniture, show that he might have admitted more
than that. He did not even mention another Canadian craft, that of the
silversmith, which was now entering its greatest period. Canadian silversmiths had produced fine work before the Conquest, and had continued
to do so without interruption. Probably the workers depended for a steady
income chiefly on the increasing demand for silver jewellery and medals
used in the fur trade and, during the war, for government presents to the
Indians. In 1781 Pierre Huguet, a wig-maker, moved from Quebec to
Montreal and set up a workshop to supply the trade. It is even possible
that Huguet was encouraged to change his home and his profession by
Haldimand who had to supply himself with these silver articles locally
and who dreaded falling into the hands of unknown Montreal merchants.
It seems reasonable to suppose that it was the large demand for "pot-boilers"
in the shape of Indian silverware that enabled the province to support
artists like François Ranvoyzé, Lawrence Amyot, Huguet himself, and
many others. These men continued the fine tradition of the pre-conquest
craftsmen who were themselves something more than imitators of pieces
imported from France. Although their most elaborate work was commissioned by the churches, they also produced beautiful and distinguished
pieces for the table.[10]

It is easy to believe that there was a market for table silver. During the
long winter months the citizens of Quebec and Montreal appear to have
moved constantly in and out of each other's houses, enjoying quiet hospitality or more boisterous merry-making. "We have had a continual round
of dissipation here, dancing clubs, drinking, etc.," wrote Simon McTavish
from Montreal in 1778.[11] The general report, however, was that Montreal could not match Quebec for gaiety. It was noted rather for card-
playing, indulged in even by the pious, and sometimes for considerable
stakes.[12] Young men from Montreal who could afford it, and who pos-

sessed the necessary stamina, went down to Quebec for "the season." By the end of this period, however, it was maintained that Boucherville was the gayest place in Canada. "Nobody talks of anything but Boucherville. The most beautiful girls . . . the best dressed, the most brilliant are here. The city is nothing to it."[13]

The Château St Louis was the dignified centre of the social life of the province. Although Lady Dorchester had not yet arrived, Lord Dorchester in December 1786 gave a "route," "all English in manner," reported Smith to his wife, "except the ceremony of kissing which my Lord Dorchester engrossed all to himself." As the ladies and gentlemen were ushered in by different doors, the Governor kissed each lady on both cheeks in acknowledgement of her curtsey. Smith on this occasion enjoyed his tea and cards until ten, at which hour the Governor retired. Young William, his seventeen-year-old son, captivated by a major's wife, stayed until midnight.[14]

Formal or informal, the gaieties demanded, or provided an excuse for, appropriate dress. In all ranks of society dress was of absorbing interest to the women, and to some of the men. On ordinary occasions the habitants wore a modified European peasant costume, a short, full skirt and jacket for the women, and a shirt and loose trousers for the men, all made of their own linen and wool homespun. No doubt these garments were dull enough except for the knitted caps in wintertime, and the splendid ceintures fléchées of the men.[15] On Sundays and holidays, regardless of class, all women dressed as expensively as they could afford, and in the latest fashion as far as they knew it. By the late 1780's English and French fashions were regularly reported in the Quebec Herald. From the Herald it could be learned, for example, that in October 1790 French ladies were wearing white hats with red plumes and white dresses with trains striped red and white "à la nationale."[16]

There was sufficient demand for fashionable clothes for the merchants to be able to advertise generous stocks of the picturesque fabrics of the day, brocaded silks and satins, taffetas and moirés, muslins, plain, checked, or "sprigged," for parties; and for more ordinary occasions serge, dimity, calico, and chintz. White silk stockings for men and women were a luxury, becoming more common toward the end of the period. For rough wear women could get shoes described as "everlasting," but they could also have them in satin, velvet, or red morocco. Hairdressers were prepared to dress their hair in the impressive erections of the day, over which English ladies wore caps and lappets, and Canadian ladies from seigneurial families the knot of ribbons called the fontange, the one article of dress strictly reserved to those of their class.[17]

Men on state occasions could outdo their wives in splendour in their fine merino or moiré coats, heavily laced with gold or silver, worn over a waistcoat of cloth of silver or gold, black satin breeches, and the finest of cambric shirts trimmed with twenty or thirty yards of Venetian lace.[18] A matter of serious concern to fashionable men and women was the uncertain supply of hair powder. Until the 1780's it was manufactured in the province sporadically and not always skilfully. The London product cost eighteen shillings a pound, a large sum for this perishable but essential article of dress.

By the time Smith arrived at Quebec the people of the towns had achieved a certain organization in their gaiety. There had aways been dining and drinking and dancing to entertain them, with sleigh rides and races on the ice in the winter and the traditional Quebec picnics to Montmorency Falls in summer. The English seem to have brought with them their clubbing propensities. In the sixties Masonic Lodges appeared in Quebec and Montreal. In Montreal they caused some distress to the Grand Vicar, Montgolfier, who found that the weekly dinner had been shifted from Friday to another day for the accommodation of members of his flock, including *marguilliers* of the parish church.[19] There was also a Greybeards Club, presumably confined to the English, of all who had been in the country in 1760 or earlier. Later there appeared a Veterans' Club, composed of the "gentlemen" who served at Quebec in 1775-76 and who dined together once a year or oftener to celebrate the defence of Quebec.[20]

As time went on organized social activities included both sexes. Respectable people united to provide the fortnightly "assemblies" which opened with the stately minuet, before going on to popular country dances. William Moore, later the editor and publisher of the Quebec *Herald*, appeared in the eighties as the manager of a small theatrical company which presented English plays in Quebec and Montreal to subscribers, and to a limited number of the general public. Earlier, the pupils of the Montreal College had presented French plays to strictly segregrated audiences, ladies and gentlemen attending on separate occasions. Later on, an adult amateur company was formed which played to mixed audiences. To the chagrin of young men, the Church forbade women, young or old, to take any role.[21]

The people of the province knew how to compensate themseves amply for the rigours of winter, and it seems clear that religious differences and political disagreements did not prevent a friendly and mutually enjoyable mingling of Canadians and English. At the same time the gaiety could be touched with anxiety and tension. There was an inevitable social insecurity among certain members of this mixed society at a time when the aristocratic class structure, although crumbling, was still impressive. Who was a gentleman? The Masons once rejected an application for membership from an innkeeper as "a most improper person"; whether it was the inn or the character of the person that was improper was not stated. During the military regime social friction had arisen among the English. The army officers, taking advantage of the casual customs of the day, decided that most of the merchants were not gentlemen, but that nearly all of their wives were ladies, and therefore invited the ladies to parties without their husbands.[22]

There was, however, nothing casual about the customs governing the conduct of young unmarried ladies. Such was the difficulty of achieving a tête à tête with a young man that the long pauses in the country dances must often have been most welcome to both parties. The strong desire to give material support to social status, especially when the status was dubious, made elders very firm on the subject of adequate marriage settlements. Young J. F. Perrault, with little visible means of support, who announced that his fiancée was not beautiful and had no money but that he was marrying her because he loved her, was a rare anticipation of the romantic age. It was more usual for young ladies to sit pensively at home while the bachelors who should have attended them scandalized the censorious by driving about the country with young married women, or indulged themselves in even less desirable society.

As a result the staid parties at the Château St Louis, even if not highly diverting, were welcomed as setting a certain standard of decorum, offering a dignified pattern of life which Canadians appreciated, as Dorchester knew. The English appreciated it too, if one may take seriously the refrain of the poem which celebrated the arrival of Lady Dorchester in 1787: "Virtue, with Dorchester, is come again." Correspondence in the Herald and private letters expressed anxiety about the future of a society condemned as extravagant, wasteful, and self-indulgent, careless of manners and of morals. These sentiments would certainly have been approved by the former Bishop Briand, whose admiration for Dorchester was inspired partly by the regularity of his life.[23]

Life in the country, less sophisticated and luxurious than in the city, was equally gay and probably more stable. It is true that, as Carleton had found to his cost, the seigneur was not the patron of his parish. Chief Justice Hey, Hugh Finlay, and Chief Justice Smith all reported the habitant's dislike and resentment of the seigneurs. This evidence is no proof, as these three could easily be reflecting their own prejudices, or repeating each other. There are, however, many other indications of the habitant's resistance to seigneurial authority in small matters, and of the attitude of seigneurs like Lanaudière, no very favourable specimen certainly, who spoke of the habitants as "canaille."

On the other hand, there are pleasant traces of benevolent paternalism and of a social solidarity among seigneurs, slightly pathetic but not without merit. St Ours in 1788 wrote from Montreal to his friend and kinsman, the seigneur of La Valtrie, who was suing Lanaudière for a debt, begging him to break off the suit. Lanaudière had indeed behaved badly but it was not seemly "now that so few people of good birth are left in the country" for one of his rank to be roundly abused by a lawyer in open court.[24] This same La Valtrie, living alone on his encumbered estate, doing without tea and wine to send money to his wife, who was trying to arrange a marriage for their daughter in France, still contrived in the famine year of 1788-89 to provide food and seed grain for his poorer tenants when some elsewhere were boiling hay for nourishment.[25]

The position of the seigneurs was, however, much too ambiguous to offer any social stability to Canadians, who, for all their independence, were strongly class conscious and addicted to symbols of prestige. They found their frame of reference rather in the parish, the priest, and the Church. Something has been said of the moral and spiritual role of the Church. In that age of widespread scepticism and indifference these were reinforced by, and almost inseparable from, the material reality of the church edifice and the presbytery. Church buildings were a source of absorbing interest and pride to the habitants. Immediately after the Conquest they set about repairing their damaged churches and the next few decades saw the construction of twenty-five or thirty new ones, which represented in a remarkable fashion the distinctive and developing culture of New France.

The building of a church was essentially a community activity, many different people of every class being laid under contribution. No plans for building could be initiated without the permission of the bishop. Once this had been secured a parish meeting would be called to approve the project and to elect syndics who would be responsible for securing the consent of the civil power to make a levy on the parish.[26]

The decision as to where and in what fashion a church should be built rested with the bishop. Briand guarded this prerogative carefully; the mistakes of inexperience or ignorance might well be too costly for a parish to bear. The habitants, however, often had their own ideas and battled for them strenuously, as in the dispute over the site of the church of Ste Rose. Briand learned by experience to yield a little in time rather than provoke a contest because, as he said, once the habitants get hold of an idea, "ils ne s'en demordent guère."[27]

It was Briand's custom to delegate his authority in supervising the building of a church to a priest with special knowledge and experience, perhaps Montgolfier, or Jacrau of the Quebec Seminary, or Conefroy, a younger priest ordained in 1776. The priest would visit the parish to consider such factors as population, wealth, availability of material, and workmen. He had also to determine the site, a most important and often contentious matter. He might also visit the seigneur, who, even if a Protestant, was expected to co-operate. Henry Caldwell provided the wood for at least one church. The architect priest might also summon a local committee of the master mason, the carpenter, and the joiner to agree on the general plan which would, however, necessarily leave something to individual taste and skill.

Most churches after 1760 were built with a transept instead of in the older style popularized by the Récollets. Some had an imposing west end, with two towers, others the simpler wooden steeple moulded to the steep pitch of the roof. This manner of building, with the general direction in the hands of a small group who consulted together and profited by each other's experience, the work carried out by local craftsmen in their own fashion, produced a group of churches with common characteristics but much individuality of style. After 1790 Conefroy, building his own parish church at Boucherville, produced a *devis*, a kind of codification of knowledge acquired in this experimental period.

Naturally when the parish could afford it, and many could, woodcarvers and silversmiths were called on for their contributions. This period saw work from well-known carvers such as the Levasseur, and the Baillargé, who carved for the cathedral in Quebec, and Philippe Liébert in Montreal, to say nothing of the Seminary cabinet-maker, Pierre Emond, who decorated the tiny private chapel of Jean Olivier Briand, using an olive tree as a motif. Carving in Canada had a venerable ancestry. Laval had co-operated with Talon in founding a school in order that the less successful of his seminarians, the "stickit ministers," if they could not illuminate might at least adorn the church. Meanwhile Ranvoyzé, Amyot, and the others were providing some of their most distinguished work in the chalices, lamps, and *bénitiers* which are still the pride of Quebec.[28]

These churches were built by the people. They did not merely pay for them. They participated in the planning, they helped in the building, and they argued and protested endlessly with syndics, *marguilliers*, priest, and bishop. The *fabrique*, entrusted to the *marguilliers*, was in a real sense theirs. There they were baptized and buried, and there they were married in a brief ceremony followed by the most prolonged of all their merry-makings, the three-day country wedding. They learned there on Sunday of the latest laws, of sales of land, of the orders sent through the captains of militia.

Most important of all, on Sundays they sat, or they might sit, in their parish church. Volumes could be written on the church pew. It was the first Canadian social register. Probably no other one subject occupied more space in the voluminous correspondence of the bishop. Not all churches could provide seats for every worshipper. The seigneur, and perhaps a co-seigneur, and the captain of militia each had his special pew by right. Some other officials might have a claim to one. Bishop Briand required all who thought they had a claim to secure a letter from the governor, making the request on their behalf. Pews other than official pews were rented at auction, and no doubt there was keen competition for a desirable situation. There were rules about the right of a widow to retain her late husband's seat, about rights of family succession, and about rights of families who had left the parish and still wished to rent the pew. There were rights dubious and complex enough to afford infinite exercise for the Canadian gifts for disputation and litigation. On one point Briand was firm. Seats were not property, and could not be sold. They were, however, like mediaeval lands, subject to an infinite variety of claims. In the country, and in some measure in town also, the church seat provided a kind of social order visible, enduring, and yet flexible.[29]

The picture of old Quebec distinguished by comfort and gaiety, by beauty and harmony in landscape, churches, and dwellings, is true enough. It is obviously not the whole truth. The writer in the Quebec *Herald* who grieved at extravagance, waste, and self-indulgence had only to look around him to see squalor and misery. Quebec, "very beautifully disposed by nature and not meanly improved," as William Smith said, rather patronizingly, was reached by land along avenues full of "noxious vapours" and "encumbered by heaps of old shoes, cast moccasins . . . broken bottles, tattered britches . . . bones, dead cats and dogs . . . the emptying of slaughterhouses and cleaning of stables." In Montreal public-spirited citizens with houses fronting on the market-place and St Paul's Street had paved both areas at their own expense, but Montreal also suffered from "noxious vapours" emitted by the jail, which was lacking in every amenity and was the curse of the neighbourhood.[30]

There was also poverty. Every day in winter crowds of beggars walked the streets of Quebec with large bags to gather food from the compassionate. Some people suggested that portions of this food were certainly exchanged for drink as the same beggars were occasionally seen drunk in a ditch by evening. The proposed remedy of a licensing system for the truly needy was rejected by the casually charitable. Nor was there any serious effort made to check the poverty caused by winter unemployment. The matter was discussed but funds and organization were wanting.

As servants were so scarce that "best friends" stooped to steal each other's domestic treasures with the bribe of higher wages, it might have been expected that some of the needy would have found domestic employment. The poor, however, preferred their independence. It was notorious that Canadians hated to engage themselves as servants. It is possible that the few hundred slaves and an unknown number of indentured servants in the province created a prejudice against domestic service, and led many to choose freedom with privation.

The scarcity of labour did not ensure good treatment of servants. In Montreal a runaway apprentice lad of seventeen, brought back by his mother, was beaten by his master and the other workmen with such unusual brutality that he at last lost consciousness. This incident did attract the attention of the grand jury and the master was fined ten livres, rather less than two dollars, at the quarter sessions. The *Gazette* was overjoyed at the humanity of the jury in noticing the offence at all. Only six months later the wardens of the Protestant church advertised an orphan boy of eight to be bound out as apprentice : "Any person inclined to have him may apply to Mr Jacob Schiefflin."[31]

Another kind of labourer was attracting public attention as the western fur trade grew, the courageous, unmanageable, and often unfortunate voyageur. Merchants of Montreal were co-operating in an attempt to introduce some regularity and humanity into the trade. As voyageurs always had to have some wages in advance and as too many disappeared before the departure for the west, Montreal fur men agreed among themselves to hire none without a certificate from the priest of the parish where he lived. The demand must have embarrassed some of these wandering spirits but it may have been liberally interpreted. Early in 1791 the Beaver Club started a public fund for the relief of widows and children of voyageurs and of the men themselves when necessary. No doubt much must have been done throughout the years by private charity. This is the first evidence of public concern for the men who pursued the most dangerous and exhausting of callings, but one essential to the trade.[32]

One source of misery to rich and poor alike was sickness, which might destroy life or health, and against which there was little protection. William Smith, boasting of the healthfulness of the climate, said no one was ever ill, and none died except infants and the extremely old. This reckless remark recoiled on the speaker, for Smith himself suffered a good deal of sickness in Quebec and died at sixty-five. There are many contemporary references to sickness among people of all ages, although there may well have been less than in the cities of contemporary Europe. Smallpox was endemic and venereal diseases common. The fear of suffering from venereal disease was intensified by a general belief that it was readily transmitted by any kind of physical contact. In 1785 people were reporting an epidemic; no doubt many were ill, whatever the cause. There was general neglect of private cleanliness, as well as of public sanitation, and "putrid sore throats" were common.

Doctors, although the subject of much criticism and the butt of innumerable jokes, were yet encouraged to do their best, or their worst. One poor lady who broke her arm in mounting a ladder, as a good housekeeper should, to dust the top of a door frame, was treated assiduously by five doctors. The tale of her sufferings over a period of several months can still try the nerves of the twentieth-century reader.[33]

Beyond the British garrison doctors, there were probably few who could boast even the training afforded by the schools of the day. Too many probably were, as one man said, like watchmakers who insist on cleaning the watch in order to ensure themselves a livelihood by weakening the springs. Many did more than weaken the springs. James Fisher, the garrison surgeon in Quebec, reported to the council that in view of the few doctors and the large number of quacks, "it would contribute to the increase of His Majesty's subjects were there not one of the aesculapian tribe in this part of British North America."[34] He advised a strict system of licensing and in the meantime suggested that the ever-useful parish priest be asked to urge people "to avoid the promiscuous use of large bleedings, violent and drastic purgative medicines, and keeping their houses too close and hot." The advice, if given, was probably fruitless. Drugs were consumed in such quantity as to promise the doctor a moderate income from the profits of his dispensary alone. It may well be that the poor who could not afford doctors were better off than the rich.[35]

The sick and the poor, however, were not unprovided for. Apart from private charity and kindness the province had its own welfare institutions. The seminaries of Quebec and Montreal and the Jesuits strove to be good seigneurs. As the number of Jesuits grew smaller they gave away much of their modest income. The Montreal seminary also accepted the privileges of comparative wealth and extended its generosity beyond the district of Montreal.

The active social workers in the province, however, were the communities of nuns, none of them wealthy, some financially embarrassed, but all in some measure fulfilling the intentions of their founders. Poverty and Protestant antipathy at first made their continued existence seem precarious. In theory the British government did not sanction religious communities, and the original intention was to forbid further recruiting and let them die out. The policy was followed for the men's orders, at least for the Jesuits. The seminaries, associations of secular priests, were tolerated and suffered to retain their property because of their services to education and the training of priests.

The continued toleration of the nuns was disapproved in some quarters. Hugh Finlay, moderate and not uncharitable but concerned with the growth of population and the exploitation of untilled lands, believed that no novice should be permitted to take vows before the age of forty.[36] It was hardly to be expected that a Protestant in those days should acknowledge the reality of a vocation. It is, however, strange that Finlay should not have understood the value of institutions which provided so useful and respectable a career for women prevented from marrying by the economic and social rigidities of their society.

The actual number of the nuns was not great enough to give cause for concern to Finlay or to the committee on population. The total membership of the women's communities in 1790 was under two hundred. Although this was not a period of intense devotion, there were devout nuns and there were many useful ones. The general hospitals both at Quebec and Montreal were primarily for the shelter of the poor, especially the children and the aged. They cared also for the sick in body and mind. The nuns of the *Hôtels Dieu* in the two cities were engaged rather in professional nursing, if the expression can be used of this time. The Ursulines at Quebec were a teaching order, instructing girls in reading and writing, sewing and embroidery. The Ursulines at Three Rivers, a later and independent foundation, maintained both a school and a hospital. In addition to these, the Sisters of the Congregation, with their centre at Montreal, maintained small boarding- and day-schools for girls in various parts of the province. Through their efforts and those of the Ursulines many girls received a rudimentary education. As Governor Murray had noted, the women in this respect were more fortunate than the men.[37]

Some of the communities possessed seigneuries, partly cultivated and not a great source of wealth. All suffered from the removal of the care and protection of France, although it seems that gifts continued to come from there. The nuns were also helped by gifts from Bishop Briand, who had not much to give. He could be more generous with advice and financial supervision. These he provided especially for the sisters of the General Hospital at Quebec, who were embarrassed by a somewhat feckless sister bursar and also laboured under a heavy burden of debt contracted for the care of wounded French soldiers for which they could not get compensation. The *Hôtel Dieu* in Quebec had been forced to rebuild after a fire in 1765. All these communities survived in spite of financial problems and political threats. Not only did they continue to recruit, they also received the daughters of Protestant parents who even consented to pay the dowry and be present at the ceremony. Although the nuns, like the Bishop, might be made anxious by the official British policy, they were never in real danger of political or economic extinction.[38]

The communities were able to survive economically partly because they adhered to some of the principles of free enterprise. It was apparently the custom for nuns to receive a minimum diet at the common table of the community; for their clothing and all extras or *"douceurs"* they depended on friends and on their own labour in their spare time.[39] Excelling in the manual dexterity and ingenuity typical of their nation, they turned their rooms into little workshops for the production of all sorts of articles: workboxes, bags, purses, baskets, artificial flowers, shoes, and slippers. They adapted Indian skills and materials, embroidering leather and birchbark with quills and beads. They even catered to a transatlantic demand for Indian curios with little models of birch canoes manned by miniature Indians. They made dolls for the children. They made maple sugar, jam, chocolate, peppermint, and sugar biscuits. They seem also to have supplied merchants with sweet biscuit and perhaps with some of the hard biscuit sent down to the fisheries. Nuns in all three cities learned the art of gilding; the carvings of Philippe Liébert, who occupied an upper floor in the Grey Nuns' premises in Montreal, were gilded by the sisters who lived below.[40]

These otherwise innocent and useful business operations had their disadvantages in so far as they were carried on by individuals for their private needs. The common life was affected and discipline could be weakened. It was typical of eighteenth-century convent life in France that the flesh should not be unbearably mortified, and the atmosphere carried over to Canada. Sister Thérèse Jésus (Ursule Baby) of Three Rivers gave very careful attention to the quality of the serge and linen, to say nothing of the wine and the snuff, procured for her by her brother François in Quebec. Sister Thérèse, however, full of good works, was even more assiduous in reminding François (what he was prone to forget) that he had a soul, and in begging him for cast-off clothes that she might make them over for their nieces, whose father was an impoverished seigneur.

Bishop Briand was, however, seriously concerned at the indiscipline of the nuns of the General Hospital in Quebec in the years following the Conquest. They had asked permission to receive novices. He replied at enormous length, asking, in effect, how they proposed to teach others a rule that they did not observe themselves. They were discourteous to superiors, giving only reluctant obedience, they took their meals in every corner of the house instead of in the refectory only, they indulged themselves in private spending on clothes, especially indulging their fancy in shoes, and they neglected their office, some of them rarely going to divine service.[41] The Ursulines were also taken to task more mildly for "*recherchées*" shoes. Briand considered the practice of private spending a "dangerous liberty." [42]

Because of their private earning and spending, and no doubt for other reasons, some of the communities mingled freely with the outer world. The Quebec Ursulines preserved their rule and remained strictly cloistered. The Ursulines at Three Rivers were apparently not cloistered. They seem to have done their business without much restriction and to have received visits from friends and relatives perhaps even in their private rooms. If their correspondence was censored at all, it must have been with a most indulgent eye, considering what was written. Nor does the novitiate seem to have been severe: "The mother superior tells me that you are better at cards than devotion," wrote Pierre Guy to his sister at Three Rivers.

There is, however, no doubt of the existence of religious ardour as well as of charity even in this worldly period. It was shortly before the Conquest that one of the best-known women's orders in Canada received official recognition. The Grey Sisters were founded in Montreal by Mme Marguerite d'Youville, who, under the sponsorship of the Sulpician, Louis Normant, joined herself with a few other women to serve the poor. At first they had their trials. The charitable townspeople, unable to think of a creditable reason for a few women living together and working among the poor, assumed that the purpose of the association was to sell brandy, provided by the Seminary, to the Indians; hence the name "*soeurs grises,*" given in derision. After some trials they had been put in charge of the General Hospital where they cared for various unfortunates. After the Conquest they took on the care of the numerous foundlings left by the armies, a work which they carried on throughout the period and for which they received a modest grant from the government.[43]

Only some time after the arrival of Briand as bishop in 1766 did this order assume its characteristic habit, not exactly grey, but a more practical coffee colour. Because of the hard and dirty work undertaken by the sisters Mme d'Youville chose a loose sleeve turned back over the wrist. Briand, having seen it, expressed a gentle doubt whether a nun should reveal her wrist to the world. The sisters, therefore, devised a washable undersleeve which they modelled on a doll sent down to Quebec for his inspection and approval.[44] Briand's answer was warm and affectionate, approving the addition and thanking them for their attention to his wishes.

Briand gave much care and pains to advising the nuns whose conduct did not always come up to his exacting standards. Among his numerous letters, however, there is none more attractive or more characteristic than the one to a newly elected mother superior, enjoining on her gentleness and a positive approach: "Do not say to a proud and haughty girl, 'you are proud and haughty,' but rather, 'my daughter, be more humble, you are not sufficiently humble. There is some appearance of pride in what you have said or done.' 'Be more gentle,' you will say to an angry girl, 'Gentleness is pleasing to our Lord. Try to dominate anger. . . . ' " A girl who had not been rebuked enough, he added, would complete her repentance in her prayers. The letter may be taken also as a tribute to the quality of the nun to whom it was addressed. Briand did not cast pearls before swine.

Although in country and town alike it was the Church that provided the general frame of civilized life, Quebec was not outside the rationalist secularizing stream of eighteenth-century thought. There was no printing press in the province until after the Conquest, and no regular publishing house for long after that, but books were available to those who wanted them, and the *philosophes* of the age were read and appreciated by some of the clergy and the bourgeoisie. The seigneurs were not attracted by the ideas of the *philosophes* and few were interested in reading.[45] In 1764 a considerable auction sale of English books suggests that departing officers were leaving small collections behind them. In the same year a modest circulating library offered its patrons, for sixpence a week, a choice of several hundred volumes in French and English. It was a small enough collection for a city of that size but some, at least, were buying their own books. In 1772 François Baby, then a busy and very gay young merchant, asked a friend in London to get him the works of "Voltaire, Rousseau and other good writers." Much later his friend Pierre Guy, in Montreal, sent nine volumes of Voltaire to his sister, now received as a nun at Three Rivers, assuring her that she would enjoy them and that they would amuse the grand vicar if he had not already read them.[46]

The American Revolution brought a flood of ephemeral political literature to the province. It also brought from Philadelphia the printer Fleury Mesplet and his press, and Valentin Jautard, who with him founded the Montreal *Gazette* in 1778. The venture came to an end for a time in 1779 when Haldimand imprisoned them for publishing uncensored and critical material, contrary to orders. Haldimand, however, did concern himself with the intellectual life of the province. He founded a circulating library in Quebec, open to subscribers at £5 a year. This was a fee difficult to collect and was successively reduced until it reached thirty shillings, or little more than the sixpence a week fee of the earlier venture. By the time Haldimand left the province there were two thousand volumes available in French and English. Montreal about this time also founded a subscription library. The young Mezière, emerging from Montreal College, bitterly described by him as "a college entrusted to ignorant clerics . . . the tomb of my youthful years," was still sufficiently literate to be able to celebrate his resurrection by consuming eagerly the books available to him, the works of Rousseau, Mably, Montesquieu, and other *philosophes*.[47]

In Quebec, at least, there were bookshops. Colonel Hope in the autumn of 1784 sent the merchant Perrault, an advocate of an elected assembly, a French edition of Blackstone, explaining that he had "come across it in [his] morning walk." "I promise you that the reading of it will give you a great deal of pleasure," wrote Hope, who received a graceful letter of thanks in reply, another evidence of the pleasant mingling of people of different languages and different political views. By 1787 advertisers were offering a number of seventeenth- and eighteenth-century classics and other works in both languages, including, strangely, "Macaulay's History of England" in five volumes.[48]

From 1785 the reading public was offered the Montreal *Gazette* in French and English and from 1788 the Quebec *Herald* in English. These papers at first followed the example of the Quebec *Gazette*. Their proprietors were printers rather than publishers and confined themselves to official announcements, extracts from overseas and American newspapers, and advertisements. There were no editorials. Gradually, however, comment on local events crept in, beginning cautiously in the "Poet's Corner," but extending rapidly over lengthening columns of letters, signed invariably with pseudonyms. The *Herald* and the Montreal *Gazette* were radical. They encouraged letters on both sides of a given question, but on the whole they presented the *philosophe* side of the constitutional and religious debates which grew continually more animated from 1787 until the passing of the Constitutional Act. The *Gazette*, the more radical of the two, from 1789 drew generously on the contemporary publications of revolutionary France, advocating social equality, public education, and a church which should set aside ecclesiastical pretensions and devote itself to inculcating sound morals by precept and example.[49]

Priestly claims were criticized. Seigneurial pretensions were attacked bitterly and even cruelly. *"Un homme comme il faut"* was represented as a person without brains, education, or wealth, who went into debt in order to dress fashionably and badly, whose religion, a mere superstition, was made an excuse for condemning others, who expended himself in flattery and silly jokes, crawled to his superiors and equals but "looks scornfully on the honest industrious labourer from whom he receives his bread, and the skilful workman who decorates his house, who . . . has sworn to be in opposition to sense and to nature." The same writers, clearly Montreal *bourgeois*, attacked monasticism, suggesting the organization of a band of "anti-monks" to go from house to house telling people to keep their money for their old age, "to love God with all their hearts and never give anything to monks."[50]

Meanwhile the example of France and the prospect of representative institutions was producing in Montreal a mild reflection of French revolutionary clubs. In the summer of 1791, there appeared the Robin Hood Society. It shortly changed its name to the Montreal Society as more suitable to the traditions of French-speaking members. Proceedings began under the sponsorship of elder statesmen, with a debate on "The Duty of

Electors" in July. By September youth was at the helm; ladies were invited to contribute their weekly sixpence and to join with the young men in a debate on the relative merits of marriage and celibacy. This proceeding inspired a mildly deprecating letter to the *Gazette* from one whom the young people identified as a seigneur, and whose ideas – and orthography – they held up to merciless ridicule.[51]

Radical sentiment everywhere in the province was stimulated by two issues which received increasing attention from the time of the arrival of Dorchester: the disposition of the Jesuit estates and plans for a system of public education. Both these matters touched the Church very nearly. As it happened, the Church at the moment was passing through a series of internal crises complicated but not caused by these issues.

Bishop Desglis, elderly and a little indolent, who had succeeded Briand in 1784, continued to reside on the Island of Orleans. He was not, however, content to be a bishop *fainéant*. Hubert, his coadjutor, who undertook a much-needed visitation of the entire diocese, irritated him by seeming to usurp his state and authority. In addition, by 1786 St Onge, Vicar General of Three Rivers, was under a cloud, and in 1788 the Vicar General of Quebec, Gravé of the Seminary, had been "*cassé*." As Hubert warmly supported Gravé, there was some danger of scandal to the Church. It was averted by Briand who, consulted by Hubert, contrived to make peace just before Desglis solved the immediate problem by his death in June 1788.[52]

Hubert, who succeeded Desglis, soon found out what it was to have a difficult coadjutor. Charles François Bailly de Messein, after having studied in France, had returned to Quebec shortly after the Conquest. After ordination he served for a time the Indian missions in Acadia. Back in Quebec he had attracted the favourable attention of Carleton, who had persuaded Briand to allow Bailly to return with him to England as tutor to his children. Carleton now promptly named him as Hubert's coadjutor, mentioning rather lamely in his dispatch to London that in 1776 Bailly had been wounded in the king's service. Bailly had other more appropriate qualifications. He was an able man, probably better educated, and certainly of wider experience, than Bishop Hubert. He was, however, inclined to take lightly the ecclesiastical virtues of humility and obedience, his outlook was not notably spiritual, and he was undoubtedly infected with what Briand called "new ideas."[53]

Hubert, diligent and conscientious, but without social graces or emotional warmth, entered on his duties without thinking much about Bailly. During his visitations as coadjutor he had been impressed by the piety and devotion of the people but had noted with regret the "*relâchement*" of the clergy.[54] He particularly objected to their habit of paying lengthy visits away from their parishes, and he promptly issued a public order to correct the abuse. The order was clearly tactless in its implied criticism, and was also apparently excessively rigid. Bailly, who had a parish in the district of Montreal, rushed to the defence of the clergy. Hubert, realizing perhaps an error of method, then produced what seems to have been a very sensible plan for regular synod meetings of representatives chosen by the parish priests to discuss matters of discipline and to introduce a desirable uniformity in various matters. Having circulated the plan to the priests, he showed it to Dorchester who immediately vetoed it. Dorchester still distrusted representative institutions, and, although willing to translate his ecclesiastical instructions in the most liberal terms for the benefit of the Church, he was not going to increase the Bishop's power by allowing him to speak in the name of an elected synod.[55]

Deprived of the help of a synod, Hubert had to face the opposition of the coadjutor who seems to have seen himself as a kind of deputy bishop at Montreal. In addition to the cause of priests who felt injured by Hubert's regulations, Bailly took up another matter about which there were complaints. Feast days, often celebrated too lavishly, fell with much frequency in the busy periods of a short season, particularly in the month of June. They were harassing to farmers, fishermen, and townspeople. The critical were very ready to point out that they did nothing to further the cause of religion. Hubert was personally willing to make some adjustment but, doubting his authority, insisted on referring the matter to Rome. Bailly made the most of the grievance. On another matter also Bailly had popular sentiment on his side. Hubert, like his predecessors, co-operated with government in requiring priests, according to the custom before the Conquest, to send copies of the parish registers yearly to Quebec for the government records. The priests complained of this as an imposition and Bailly supported them.

Bailly was at last suppressed. Although agreeing with him on certain matters, the priests supported Hubert's authority; and, as Bailly was apparently trading on Dorchester's friendship, Briand intervened with a gentle but unequivocal letter to Dorchester condemning Bailly's insubordination. Rome, appealed to by both parties, also supported Hubert. The contention did, however, add to the Bishop's difficulties in dealing with the two major issues of the Jesuit estates and education.[56]

On these two issues Smith, bent on bringing light and learning to "the darkest corner of the Dominion" through a general system of secular education, had a special interest. Naturally Hubert was no less interested. He felt compelled by his office to express himself as entirely opposed to Smith's secular views. Although the disagreement between the two men was never openly violent, an anonymous cleric left on record his own strong resentment of Smith.[57]

The differences between the Chief Justice and the Bishop reveal the cultural differences and even the antipathy between many of the loyalists and the Canadians. The loyalists were struck by the great degree of illiteracy among the people of the province. The loyalist tradition, whether of Protestant piety or of rational scepticism, tended to apply to culture and to civilization the one basic test of literacy. The charm and culture of some of the Canadian churchmen, their significant if modest achievements in architecture and the arts, could not save them from condemnation, tacit or open, as unworthy pastors who willingly maintained superstition by keeping people in ignorance. To the loyalists the parish school was fundamental to salvation in the next world and to freedom and civilization in this. These sentiments appeared in the correspondence columns of the newspapers, not so much in the form of expressions of active ill-will as of Protestant axioms. Implicit in them was a criticism of the traditions of New France. There were Canadians, influenced by the "new ideas," who understood and agreed in some measure.

This was the background of the double issue of the Jesuit estates and of public education. Before Dorchester left England Amherst had approached him and Smith about his claim to the Jesuit estates. The claim was based on an order-in-council of 1770 granting him all Jesuit property in Canada "except the colleges and chapels."[58] Dorchester, instructed to implement this order, laid the matter before the executive council in 1787.

It is unnecessary to trace the complicated processes by which Amherst's claim was shelved and the "Jesuit estates problem" left to plague Quebec politics for another century. Dorchester and Smith, both disapproving the grant, seem to have been willing to take advantage of the many technical and legal difficulties in the way of determining exactly what property the Jesuits held, what obligations in leases, debts, or mortgages existed, and how much of the property could be considered as excluded from the terms "colleges" and "chapels," both of which might be deemed to include far more than stone and mortar.[59]

Meanwhile, before the council investigation was even well under way, Dorchester received a petition, not from churchmen, but from the Canadian reform groups which had organized themselves with the English in 1784 to ask for an assembly.[60] They now secured English co-operation in claiming the Jesuit lands for the province, on the ground that the Jesuits had received them as a trust for missionary work and for the education of youth. The British government had in law, they maintained, the right to change the trusteeship, but not to divert the property from the purposes for which it had been given.

The petitioners stated that the Jesuits had maintained their college until the Conquest and had continued an elementary school for some years after. Gradually their building had been taken over by the government for a barracks and a repository for the provincial archives. In Montreal, not without some trepidation, the Seminary had encouraged the priest J. B. Curatteau to develop and enlarge his private school into the Montreal College, held in the Château Vaudreuil. The Seminary had applied without success for permission to bring in professors from France.

Canadians could not, therefore, be accused of indifference to education. They now claimed the property of the dying Jesuit community to be used for its original purpose, but in a different fashion. They asked for a nonsectarian university, for the benefit of Canadians and English alike. It was not to be under the management of the Church. As the *fabrique* of a church was entrusted to lay *marguilliers* elected by heads of families, so the university property would be in the hands of trustees elected by the people of the province.[61]

The petition, signed by one hundred and ninety-five names, French and English, was presented to Lord Dorchester late in 1787. Whether or not Smith inspired the petition, he was in touch with the petitioners as they prepared it, offering encouragement and advice.[62] Smith had already been named chairman of a council committee on education. Very much engaged with other business in 1788, he did not summon his education committee until 1789. Possibly he wanted to assure himself that Amherst's claims could be, as in fact they were, subjected to indefinite legal delaying action. When Smith did call the committee in 1789 it was apparent that he was prepared to make up for lost time. Having personally conducted the necessary preliminary investigations, he delivered to the committee a carefully prepared speech and persuaded them to accept it as an interim report.

The report summarized the unsatisfactory state of education in the province and offered a remedy. Apart from the *collège classique* programs in the Seminary at Quebec and in the Montreal College there were a number of small schools in the cities, most of them supported by fees, a few receiving trifling government grants for the salary of the master. The general state of education from the modern viewpoint was deplorable. Although girls, thanks to the nuns, were more fortunate than the boys, the great majority of the inhabitants were condemned for want of elementary schools to live "in a vile state of barbarism." Not half a dozen in a parish, according to Smith, could read or write.[63]

Smith proposed the remedy of an elementary school in each parish, to be supported by rates and fees, and open to the needy without charge. In every county there should be a secondary school to teach mathematics, grammar, and languages, along with such practical subjects as bookkeeping, navigation, and surveying.

The whole scheme was to be crowned with a university for "that improvement of the mind . . . indispensable to . . . every great social community." A university on the splendid scale of those of the old world might be impossible, but Quebec, a meeting place for the two great cultures of western Europe, might hope one day to attract students from the whole of North America. The university should start modestly with a rector and four tutors, men "without prejudices" offering instruction in literature, mathematics, philosophy, and science. Theology would be taught not in the university, by its constitution non-sectarian, but in confessional seminaries. The government of the university would be in the hands of a corporation chosen equally from Roman Catholics and Protestants with the addition *ex officio* of royal judges and bishops. Such an institution by "a union of hearts and hands" could guard against "the illiberality of a contracted and sectarian spirit."[64]

Bishop Hubert, consulted beforehand by Smith, although he tried to express himself tactfully, was squarely opposed to the principles of this scheme. He permitted his objections to be published. He thought illiteracy in the province exaggerated, he did not think many would want higher education while there was still such abundance of uncleared land close at hand, and he suspected that Smith's men "without prejudices" would be men without religion, governing themselves by "natural law," and the enemies of morality and discipline. Hubert's preferred plan was the encouragement of existing schools and the revival of the Jesuit college. This college should, with its property, be taken over by the diocese when the Jesuit Order in Canada, by the death of the few remaining elderly members, ceased to exist: a smooth settlement of the double issue of the Church, but one hardly likely to appeal to Smith.[65]

Hubert, in his turn, was opposed by his own people, the signers of the petition of 1787, and others. In the spring of 1790 this group was encouraged by the bequest of Simon Sanguinet, a Montreal lawyer who had made his own way and acquired a competence, and who now bequeathed what was reported to be a considerable estate in land and money for the endowment of the projected university.[66] The secularists, as they may be called, also received the vigorous support of the coadjutor Bailly who, on this issue more than on any other, stood out as the rational cleric, the exponent of morality and learning, the enemy of superstition, the enlightened priest who does no more than tolerate the simple exercises of piety. Bailly in a long and satirical letter published in May 1790 professed to be unable to believe that the Bishop had written the statements that some unscrupulous person had published over his name. He defended the principle of secular learning, argued that the circulation of the blood could be investigated without a theological preface, and, with more than a touch of malice, said that, rather than lurk in a corner to see whether the weary habitant made the sign of the cross before lying down to rest, he would betake himself to the church and pray for him "in the language of Horace and Virgil."[67]

Bailly's support was welcomed and the secularists continued to express their views throughout the summer of 1790. The Montreal College was criticized for bad teaching. It was proposed that it should be taken over by the *marguilliers* of the parish church and entrusted to lay direction. Priests were criticized for squandering on "trivialities," such as wooden chandeliers, silver vases, candles, carpets, and other luxuries, money that should go to learning. Priests and seigneurs alike were attacked for opposing the university. The clergy were urged to surrender the wealth they owed to the superstition of the people to an institution which would substitute for "a philosophy of words," "a natural philosophy based on sound sentiment."[68]

The debate, a lively illustration of Quebec's ability at least to reflect the ideas of the old world, was academic in both senses of the word. Britain, having recently appointed Charles Inglis of Nova Scotia Bishop of the Church of England in North America, had no thought of renouncing the official policy of religion and education fostered and guided by a state church. The prolonged and bitter controversy, half a century later, over the "godless university" at Toronto is evidence enough that Smith's scheme, although in the best tradition of eighteenth-century rational non-conformity, was far in advance of its time in British North America.

Hubert, although pained and embarrassed by Bailly's sophisticated mockery, was supported by the public. In the midst of its anti-clerical correspondence the Montreal *Gazette* had published a reader's eulogy of the essential work of good priests, naming several who worked in the district of Montreal.[69] More important, at the end of the year Mesplet, the publisher, cried *mea culpa* (in French and English!), admitting that he had displeased the majority of his readers and promising no more reflections on "the fundamental doctrines" of religion.[70]

Obviously the clerical censors had been at work; equally obviously they had the tacit support of the majority even of literate Canadians. Canadians undoubtedly loved anti-clerical jokes. Some were barbed, others genial, as when Pierre Guy comforted the Récollet priest, frustrated because his exorcisms had not deterred the worms that were destroying Montreal's fruit crop, by suggesting that the worms were Protestants who could not understand Latin prayers.[71] Canadians were, however, for a variety of reasons fundamentally loyal to the Church as an institution. They were not prepared to support the insolence of Bailly ridiculing Hubert who had served the community faithfully for thirty years. Moreover one, at least, of the actively radical group shared Hubert's doubts about professors "without prejudices," remarking, "I doubt whether Rousseau ever really thought that the system he planned for Emile would be applicable to a college."[72]

No doubt Smith was right in believing that neither Bishop Hubert nor his secretary and assistant Plessis had a burning desire to spread the light of learning.[73] On the other hand the columns of the Quebec *Herald* show an English-speaking group strongly Presbyterian, to judge by the advertisement of large consignments of the *Shorter Catechism*, and sternly intolerant in their views. Correspondents who discussed theological issues with enthusiasm dismissed the Roman position without examinaton as purely superstitous.[74] There was also a striking lack of intellectual sympathy for French culture and civilization from some of these vigorous but narrow loyalists. When Smith himself, in an address to a grand jury in Quebec, referred to the union in the province of the two great civilizations of the west, he was severely taken to task by those who asked how a civilization founded on despotism and superstition could be great. Smith's rational desire to bring enlightenment to "the darkest corner of the Dominion," if it had not foundered on the passivity of Britain and the opposition of the Bishop, would almost certainly have been wrecked by his own fellow countrymen.

CHAPTER 16

Mr Grenville's Plan

The stormy council session of 1787, and the ensuing investigation into the conduct of the judges and the confusion of the laws, had enabled Dorchester to postpone his report to the government in London on the constitution of the province. The longer he delayed, the more difficult he found his task. He could deal with the problem of merchant shipping on the lakes. He did interest himself in the primitive settlements of the western loyalists, in relations with the Indians, and in the embodiment of Canadian and English militia companies. The more subtle and complex questions of law and the constitution baffled him. He hovered between the superb simplicity of his own Quebec Act and the distant grandeur of Smith's British North American design; he could not bring himself to face and grapple with the crude and complicated political realities of the province that was now his immediate responsibility. It is hardly surprising that after only three years as Lord Dorchester in the Château St Louis he had found that grandeur was not enough, and was asking leave to go home to England.[1]

Dorchester should have known before he left England that his assignment was likely to be embarrassing as well as difficult. Since 1784 joint English and Canadian committees of merchants had been pressing in London the petition of that year, asking an assembly, along with English commercial law and Canadian land law. This petition of 1784, which included also an indirect indictment of the "system of the generals," was the basis of sustained political activity in the province and in London until 1791.

There had, indeed, been a brief pause in 1785, for Haldimand's departure and Hamilton's liberal views had encouraged the hope of immediate reforms. The dismissal of Hamilton, however, as the merchants said, "ended the dream." Fresh representations were sent immediately to London with the result that in April 1786 Thomas Powis, the member who was acting for the merchants, rose in the House of Commons and moved for action on the petition of 1784. The answer of government was that action must wait until Carleton, who had not yet received his new title and who was to leave shortly for Quebec, had made his report. The answer had not satisfied the opposition. Carleton was praised as a soldier, but the political grievances against him, including the concealing of his instructions and his dismissal of Livius, were reviewed. The House, it was suggested, could dispense with his further advice on legislation for Quebec.

Although the resolution was easily defeated and the debate attracted little attention, it must have reminded Carleton unpleasantly of the immediate practical issues waiting to be resolved. Immediately after his arrival, as has been seen, he showed great activity, appointing the four committees of council to make a thorough review of the economic and political needs of the province. The waiting merchants responded with energy to the request of the committee on commerce for advice and information. If the Montreal committee were to send down all the papers they had collected, said an observer, "they would need a hay rack to get them to Quebec."² Before these collections could even be considered, however, the judicial investigation produced such a mass of evidence on grievances that the reports of the committees were set aside.

The merchants, determined to follow up the exposure of 1787, chose Adam Lymburner to go over to London to press once more the petition of 1784, the reasonableness of which they believed was vindicated by the recent revelations. Dorchester, when Lymburner called to ask approval for his mission, most uncharacteristically refused to express any opinion, although he later informed Sydney that Lymburner was "a decent sensible man."³ Lymburner made his way to London and the London merchants brought the matter before the Commons in the spring of 1788, reminding Sydney bluntly that he had now been putting them off for two and a half years on the ground that he had no information.

They were put off again. Sydney had the happy excuse of the immense quantity of papers from the judicial investigation, which had not yet, he said, been sufficiently digested. The matter, however, was debated again in the Commons, and Lymburner was called to speak at the bar of the House. The younger Pitt, engaged in the work of his great peace ministry, turned aside from other cares long enough to make a comment which did scant justice to the intelligence of his toryism. He deprecated any change while the province was "in a state of heat and fermentation,"⁴ not staying to inquire what had caused the heat, or how it might be reduced. His opposition was decisive, but, said Lymburner, "Mr Pitt was as roughly handled and closely pinned down as ever he was in that House," and a fresh consideration of the question based on full information was promised for the next session.[5]

Lymburner, maintained as agent of the Quebec merchants, went over yearly until the passing of the Constitutional Act in 1791. The debate of 1788, however, in committing the British government to action, compelled the hitherto passive Dorchester to take some part in the discussion. Sydney, having discovered late in the summer of 1788 that he still lacked "information," sent out a special ship with orders to Dorchester to send back his report immediately.

The demand was reasonable. Dorchester had now been two years in the province without sending home any dispatch which could match in clarity and vigour those of his former administration. He had sent one substantial dispatch in June 1787, admitting that "the English party" was increasing and that, with the influx of more loyalists, the demand for an assembly must increase. He still doubted the wisdom of introducing it in such a mixed province, adding, unhelpfully, that in the circumstances he was at a loss to suggest any satisfactory plan of government. He did not mention a possible division of the province, which his instructions required him to consider. His one positive suggestion was that, for the sake of the loyalists, authority should be given to grant land in freehold, making substantial reservations, one-sixth of all public lands, for the endowment of suitable persons who might constitute a provincial aristocracy.[6]

In the autumn of 1788 he received Sydney's urgent letter pointing out that the various representations from the province were of "so opposite a tendency" that he must have precise information on the different parties, their distribution in the province, their property, and their influence. Even then Dorchester's reply, dated November 8, 1788, was non-committal. He gave an estimate of the relative numbers of English and Canadians, one to five in the whole province, one to fifteen in the lower districts of Quebec and Montreal. A change of government was desired chiefly by "the commercial element" in the towns. The habitants did not understand the issue, and the clergy had not interfered. The "Canadian gentlemen" were opposed, fearing the introduction of strange laws and "the pursuit and adoption of wrong measures."

There were also serious physical obstacles to the gathering of representatives in a province eleven hundred miles long and with a difficult climate. The division of the province, suggested again by Sydney, he considered objectionable from every viewpoint but he did not explain his objections. He saw no immediate need for new regulations "other . . . than such as are involved in . . . the general jurisprudence of the country." He did not enlarge on this statement.

It was a strange communication, coming as it did from the once fluent and confident governor and on a subject about which it was his first duty to be fully informed. An examination even of the scanty surviving evidence shows how much more he could have said. Dorchester may have thought it unnecessary to enlarge on the position of the English merchants who had stated their own case fully and frequently. He might, however, have done them the belated justice of recognizing that they had suffered, and suffered needlessly, from confused and unfamiliar laws arbitrarily administered. "Hitherto property has stood subjected to a sort of standing arbitrator, walking by the dictate of private discretion," said Smith, and there is no reason to believe that he concealed this opinion from Dorchester.[7] The only reference to the question in this dispatch was the vaguest of references to changes in the "general jurisprudence," although now, after the lapse of a year, Dorchester could not offer the excuse that he had had no time to read the evidence offered in the judicial investigation.

Dorchester gave careful attention to the seigneurs, but he misrepresented them. He showed them as "Canadian gentlemen," alarmed at a too rapid introduction of unfamiliar laws, and afraid of the rash actions of untutored democracy. In fact, as he knew very well, this was not the position of the seigneurs. They did not merely fear sudden or rash change. They objected consistently in the name of the "nation" to any change at all in Canadian law which they presented as inherited from the kings of France, a "charter," a "perpetual edict." Their position was comprehensible enough. They had in mind the traditional royal charter which was supposed to guarantee its holders against the encroachment of other bodies, or of the agents of the king himself. But if Dorchester understood this respectable mediaevalism he could hardly be expected to explain it to the minister of a modern parliamentary state as the philosophy of those whom he still liked to present as the leaders of Canadian society.[8] It had been the contention of the seigneurs in their opposition to Smith's interpretation of the law in *Gray* vs. *Grant* [9] that their views were those of all Canadians, "the nation." In this they were undoubtedly wrong. The political interest aroused among Canadians of many different social levels was a matter of current comment. As Dorchester's council committees on agriculture, commerce, and so forth were at work in 1787, a carpenter who could not write sought out a notary to take down his views, "for the sake of the province," on arts and crafts, and especially on carpentry, which, he said, had been forgotten.[10] What the seigneurs did represent was the concern of Canadians for their laws of real property, but many believed that these could be protected by methods less archaic than the stubborn defence of a "perpetual edict."

"Les Canadiens Vrais Patriotes" already mentioned had, in 1773, maintained that their laws, guaranteed to them, they claimed, by the articles of capitulation, had been unaffected by the Proclamation of 1763 which did no more than guarantee British protection. This group had objected to the Quebec Act because the Act put it in the power of an arbitrary council to change their law. For this reason they had demanded an assembly as their right under British law. They were quite prepared to accept English commercial law.[11]

These views were shared by those Canadians, possibly the same individuals, who had joined the English in the petition of 1784 and sent Lymburner over to London as their agent. Dorchester in his dispatch of November 1788 made no special mention of Canadian merchants, including them, no doubt, in "the commercial element." His words, however, leave the impression that Canadians must be either the "gentlemen" whose views he had explained, or clergy, or habitants. In fact, apart from the clergy, the most vocal and literate group of Canadians were merchants, well-to-do retail traders, notaries, and lawyers. This Dorchester would know very well from ordinary social contacts and from reading the Montreal *Gazette*. Among these merchants were some dedicated advocates of representative institutions. J. F. Perrault, a member of the Montreal merchants' committee, even objected to the voluntary co-operation of the merchants with the council committee on commerce. They would not secure the adoption of their views, he said, but the fact of consultation would be an excuse for delaying the grant of an assembly.[12]

By the fall of 1788 everyone knew that the government in London was to bring in legislation on the constitution and laws of the province during the next session of Parliament. Every party, naturally, wanted to send back one last word on the subject before it should be too late. The result was another open contest between the seigneurial party petitioning for no change, and the party of the merchants, Canadians and English, standing by their petition of 1784. The seigneurs, pleading that an assembly would endanger religion, property, and personal security, represented as usual that they, as the landed proprietors, spoke for "the nation." This bold claim, of course, touched off a counter-petition from their Canadian opponents and from the English. There was, privately and in the press, a hot dispute about the property holdings of the opposing parties, and about how much property it took to represent "the nation." The party favouring an assembly did establish that their opponents could hardly claim to represent the bulk even of the landed property.[13] The advocates of an assembly also challenged the seigneurial methods of collecting signatures. Pierre Guy, the merchant, who was also a commissioner of the peace, received an amusing letter from a friend at Varennes. The local seigneur had recently had a visitor, "a noble emissary M. R. . . . le [Rouville]." After mass the militia officers and other principal habitants were invited to dinner at the seigneur's home. There they were told that Lord Dorchester asked all loyal subjects to sign a petition against taxation. Many cautiously declined, saying they would think about it. The seigneur, however, wrote down their names though some of them were "in a much better condition to do it for themselves than he was." Someone remarking that "borrowed signatures were not legal," their seigneur answered that the procedure was quite regular if approved by a commissioner of the peace.[14] "I was not aware," remarked the writer, "that such a prerogative was attached to your office."[15]

The validity of the signatures to a petition was always likely to be questioned. The seigneurial claim to represent the nation received a more damaging attack in the Montreal *Gazette* from one who recalled that it was Montreal merchants who, in the name of the habitants, had protested against the severity of the militia law.

> The seigneurs regard themselves as the protectors and leaders of the whole country. . . . [These] famous protectors took very good care not to join their voices to those of the oppressed when the Germans, sent to defend the colony, came into it as if it were a conquered country, when undisciplined soldiers gave themselves up to the greatest excesses as if they were the gods of the Gentiles. These protectors had neither mouths nor ears; if there had been a representation of the people the Germans would have been promptly controlled. . . .[16]

At the same time among those Canadians who did favour, or who had favoured, an assembly there were some reservations. The insistence of the seigneurs that their law was endangered might have been disregarded, but the obviously anglicizing policy of Chief Justice Smith and other loyalists, the increasing immigration into the province, and the loyalist demand for freehold tenure were alarming. Attorney General Monk noted at this same time, the fall of 1788, that the English and Canadian committees had so much trouble in agreeing on their directives to Lymburner that the vessel on which he had booked a passage sailed without him. It was finally agreed that each group should instruct him, in its own terms, to continue to press for an assembly. The English confirmed their support of the petition of 1784; the Canadians added to their demand for an assembly and English commercial law a request for the restoration of their general law exactly as it had been at the time of the Conquest, before it had been, as they said, arbitrarily changed by the council.[17]

Another evidence of caution and even of alarm is the statement of Juchereau Duchesnay, seigneur and mill owner of Beauport, who had signed the petition of 1784 and who had been sufficiently advanced in his views for Haldimand to suggest that the pension granted him for serving against Pontiac in 1764 should be discontinued. In 1788 he wrote Perrault, of the merchants' committee in Quebec, saying that he had signed the petition in 1784, not expecting an assembly, but hoping for a reformed council. Even now, he would rather have an assembly than the council as at present constituted, "... but I will never subscribe to the English laws of commerce unrestricted ... [they] attack those parts of our laws which protect helpless widows and children. ..."[18]

Duchesnay had touched on a grave point of difference which derived not from partiality or prejudice but from differing social traditions. Time, patience, and skilled legal advice were needed to suggest a workable compromise between the protection of families and the legitimate demands of the merchants and traders for security. Smith might have been able to show the possibility of compromise if all his thoughts and hopes had not been turned elsewhere.

It is not possible to make a definite statement of the number of Canadians who wanted an assembly. No doubt Hugh Finlay was right when he said that the mass of the habitants wanted only to avoid or at least to postpone taxation. It seems certain, however, that a considerable number of literate Canadians, in keeping with their own traditions and contemporary political thought, favoured an assembly, and that perhaps an even larger number had lost all confidence in the government of the council. At the same time, although aware that at the moment they should be able to count on a majority in an elected assembly, they were conscious that the English had the political experience, and that immigration and natural increase might alter the balance.

Curiously, at the same time that some Canadians were expressing doubts, the English, although hitherto they had demanded an assembly in all confidence, were also hesitating and were willing to delay. Among the various political communications which crossed the Atlantic from Quebec in the autumn of 1788 were private letters from two men, still allies, to their friends in London. James Monk wrote very frankly to the most distinguished of his predecessors, Francis Maseres, and to Brook Watson, the merchant. Chief Justice Smith also wrote to Watson in his usual style, at once vigorous and illusive.

Monk, as has been seen, had reported home the dissensions between the Canadian and English committees over Lymburner's instructions. When he saw the instructions proposed by the Canadians he was alarmed. They demanded that the Church be officially freed from the "royal supremacy" mentioned in the Quebec Act; that the religious communities be confirmed in the full enjoyment of their property; that distribution of offices under the Crown be made to Canadians and English alike in proportion to their numbers; and that officials be appointed and their salaries determined by the assembly.[19] Clearly these Canadians had sufficient confidence in their ability to use an assembly for their own purposes that they were prepared to accept the risks involved in the operation of an unfamiliar institution, especially if they could secure at the same time a constitutional guarantee of the complete independence of the Church.

As a frank exponent of anglicization Monk was bent on frustrating such designs. He told Maseres that Lymburner was well meaning but naïve, far too confident in the power of the commercial interest to ensure an English majority in the proposed assembly. Monk believed that an English majority might be secured, but only through special electoral arrangements for over-representing the predominantly English districts. Failing such arrangements he was opposed to an assembly : "A House of Assembly should *never* be granted nor a legislative council until the majority of members returned would *evidently* be with the old subjects."[20] "A House of Assembly, unlimited in its power, unsecured to the Protestant interest and the King's old subjects, would be a real curse on the colony and what Great Britain ought never to grant."[21]

Meanwhile Smith was writing to Watson. He did not, he said, find that his ideas on government coincided with those of any others in the colony, "Protestant nor Popish Catholic, British nor Canadian, Merchant nor Landholder, Loyalist up the River. . . . " Words could not express his admiration for the British constitution, but one could hardly hope to see such perfection in a British colony. He would be content with "good Judges, good Counsellors, and a good Governor."[22] He continued, having mentioned the Canadian requests to Lymburner, to dilate in a cloudy fashion on the hope of drawing to the province men who had suffered for the constitution and who "by their number will drown all distinctions in the province in a flood of loyalty." In a later letter he mentioned the three necessary supports of political power, "Property . . . Knowledge and Virtue, or the reputation for it."[23]

Monk's and Smith's letters taken together are the key to Dorchester's uncommunicative dispatch. This dispatch was drafted by the Chief Justice and accepted by Dorchester with no material alteration, except that he softened Smith's abrupt dismissal of the importance of the seigneurs.[24] The proposal of an assembly at this moment seemed to Smith irrelevant and inconvenient. He wanted representative government only when Quebec was ready for something like the complete British system. The time for that would not come until the influx of loyalists and other desirable immigrants should make it possible to assimilate the elements of the civilization of France – which, unlike some other loyalists, he sincerely admired – into the secular and parliamentary framework of a British North American state. He was content until that time to work with the council which, with Dorchester's help, he still hoped to dominate, introducing such changes in judicial and financial administration, land tenures, and education as would attract an ever-growing stream of immigrants from the United States.[25]

If Sydney had received from Dorchester the careful analysis of interests and opinions in the province that he had a right to expect, he would probably have learned that the differences of opinion between Canadians and English on the merits of an assembly were attributable less to conflicting traditions than to a natural uncertainty in each group as to whether the institution could be used to its own advantage. Where there was a doubt the English who have put themselves on record were, from the modern viewpoint, quite as illiberal as the most reactionary of the seigneurs. In justice to them it must be said that they would probably have excused their determination to dominate on the ground that Canadians, being generally illiterate, should also be deemed politically incapable.

As it happened Sydney made no use of Dorchester's dispatch or of any other papers. The crisis caused by the temporary insanity of George III and a bitter debate over the Regency Bill was a pretext for postponing the Canada question once again. In June 1789 Sydney resigned and was succeeded by a first cousin of William Pitt, William Grenville. Grenville was conscientious, thorough, and enormously industrious. By the end of the summer he had mastered the materials at his disposal. Dorchester, accustomed to Sydney's leisurely ways, must have been surprised at the bulky packet which reached him early in the new year. A public dispatch announced government's intention to proceed immediately to introduce legislation for a new constitution, including an elected assembly. Grenville enclosed, in addition, a private letter, an exhaustive "paper" analysing the Canadian petitions and the whole constitutional question, with a complete draft of the proposed bill, which required only comments from Dorchester and recommendations on certain details.

It was perhaps as well that Grenville should not have been bewildered by the variety and fluctuation of opinion in the province on the question of an assembly. The essential facts of the situation were clear to him and seemed to admit of only one solution. Obviously the loyalists must be granted the government which they claimed as their birthright, and for which they had risked their lives and sacrificed their property. Nor did it seem to Grenville possible to isolate the Canadians in North America with an apparently archaic constitution, alien to the British tradition and recently repudiated in France. As for the timing of the change, the recent lesson to be drawn from the American Revolution seemed to suggest that it was wise to anticipate demands: " . . . it is a point of true policy to make these concessions at a time when they may be received as matter of favour . . . rather than to wait 'till they shall be extorted from us by

. . . necessity. . . ." [26] The bill sent for Dorchester's comments granted "a constitution assimilated . . . to that of Great Britain," including an elected assembly, an appointed second chamber, and an executive council.

Grenville had examined with scrupulous care the arguments advanced against an assembly. The objection to an assembly as a means of introducing taxation he dismissed easily. Britain could not continue to maintain the government of the colony at a cost, he estimated, of £100,000 a year, apart from military expenditures,[27] and without any provision for local improvements and public works. Whether or not there was an assembly, the province must in future be taxed for the expenses of its own civil government. The other objections to an assembly, the size and shape of the province, and the Canadian fear of injurious or unpleasant innovations, would, Grenville hoped, be removed by the other part of his plan. The colony was to be divided into two new provinces with the four new loyalist districts above Montreal comprising one, and the old Canadian settlements down the river to Gaspé the other. There was a considerable Canadian settlement in the new district of Hesse near Detroit; and there were the vigorous and vocal English down river who, as Grenville must have known, would feel utterly betrayed. He admitted that the solution was not ideal, but, evidently recalling Pitt's remark that the colony was already "in a state of heat and fermentation," he believed it best when introducing representative institutions for the first time to ensure that in each assembly one cultural group or the other should have a clear preponderance. Eventually "the removal of ancient prejudices by the habit of obedience to the same government, and by the sense of a common interest," might make possible another arrangement. In the meantime the Canadians might be relieved of anxiety over their laws and the seigneurs might be less fearful of a loss of dignity.

Grenville did not forget altogether the plight of the merchants in the lower province. As the Quebec Act was not repealed, in spite of the merchants' repeated requests, the whole basis of Canadian civil law remained unchanged. The first draft of the new bill did, however, allow for the insertion of some sort of commercial code. Unfortunately the execution of the plan presented too many practical difficulties, and Grenville regretfully dropped the idea, observing, dubiously, that as the complaints had been chiefly of the uncertainty of the laws "that uncertainty might perhaps be removed immediately by the local legislature. . . ."[28] The only concession to English law in the lower province was the right of receiving grants of public land in freehold tenure.

In setting up new colonial assemblies Grenville could hardly be unmindful of the problems that his father, George Grenville, had encountered in the former colonies. He did acknowledge that it was probably impossible that any colony with an independent legislature should remain permanently attached to the parent state. It was the task of government to postpone the separation as long as possible and in the meantime make the connection "advantageous to the Mother Country without oppression or injury to the Colony."[29] Grenville accepted the current view that in the American colonies the British constitution had been perverted by the excessive power of popular assemblies uncontrolled by the aristocratic and monarchical elements which in Britain exercised so strong an influence. It was his hope that he might encourage in Canada a class of people to provide at once a brake and a steering wheel for the democratic car. He proposed, therefore, life or hereditary baronies for at least some members of the legislative council. As the province increased in wealth even higher titles might be given. He had also some thought of reservations of public lands to provide an independent revenue for the Crown, but he did not pursue this scheme.

Dorchester, favourable as he was to aristocratic leadership, exposed the weakness of Grenville's proposed peerage. It was not a question so much of the amount as of the stability of a man's wealth. "[The] fluctuating state of property . . . would cause all hereditary honours to fall into disregard"; in Quebec a man might be wealthy one day and a beggar the next. Grenville persisted, however; the act as passed envisaged the possibility of colonial peerages for legislative councillors.[30]

The experienced Smith, fully agreeing with Grenville on the dangers of excessive democracy, and with Dorchester on the futility of an artificial aristocracy, took this opportunity of presenting his own solution, a national or "general" government to gather together the petty assemblies in North America. Such a government would give popular leaders a legitimate goal for their ambition and a sense of the responsibilities of power. He sent by Dorchester the detailed scheme of this federal government as a supplement to "Mr Grenville's Plan," recommending it also as a sure means of protecting Britain's remaining possessions from anything "meditated to her detriment by the new nation she has consented to create." These were prophetic words but Smith shared the fate of other prophets in getting no honour at home. Grenville dismissed the plan curtly, pointing out that British North America already had an executive union; a legislative union was "liable to considerable objection." Grenville's bill thus owed nothing material to the knowledge of either Dorchester or Smith. It was introduced in the House of Commons in March 1791 and received the royal assent in June; it was to take effect on December 26 following. One awkward corner was passed in a somewhat awkward fashion. It was not possible to define the boundaries of the two new provinces without specifically either including or excluding the Indian posts to the southwest still held by Britain, although within the territory of the United States.

The new act, therefore, stated only the intention of dividing the province; this was done later by order-in-council.

If Grenville's bill owed nothing to Smith or Dorchester, it owed no more to the collective wisdom of the British House of Commons. Britain was now preparing the third constitution for Quebec since the Conquest. None had been harshly conceived; all three in intention were liberal. In the preparation of neither of the first two had circumstances permitted exclusive attention to the condition and needs of the province. The Proclamation of 1763 had been designed primarily to be a solution of the difficult problem of the Ohio country. The Quebec Act had been passed when all in Britain were necessarily preoccupied with the threatening situation in the Atlantic colonies. The Constitutional Act had, indeed, been planned by Grenville with the most careful attention to the province for which it was intended. By sheer accident, however, the whole course of the debate in the House of Commons was diverted by the painful and public breach which occurred in the House between the two great Whig leaders of the day, Edmund Burke, the elder statesman, and his disciple, the brilliant Charles James Fox.

The affair was touched off by a preliminary reference of Fox to Grenville's plan for giving an aristocratic complexion to the new legislative councils. Fox suggested that elected councils would be more suitable to North American conditions. For this he was accused of republican principles, an accusation that he indignantly denied. Burke, whose *Reflections* had been published a few months earlier, had for some time been growing restless in the company of Whigs who looked indulgently on the political proceedings in France. He therefore chose this occasion to dissociate himself not only from republicanism, but from the whole doctrine of revolution, by a violent attack on the French leaders and the new French constitution, an attack which even Pitt deplored. Fox retorted, accusing Burke of inconsistency, reminding him of his championship of the Americans, and especially of his famous words in vindication of colonial resistance, "I do not know how to draw up an indictment against a whole people." Burke, deeply hurt, repudiated Fox and his principles, announcing to the House that the alliance and friendship of twenty-five years was over. Fox, rising to reply in a house deeply moved, was so overcome as to be almost unable to speak.

It was curiously appropriate that the tragic parting between these two great exponents of American liberty should take place in the House of Commons and during a debate on a bill to extend parliamentary government in America. The event added a touch of distinction, and even of tragic grandeur, to an otherwise arid discussion. To the solution of the Canadian question the Commons debate contributed exactly nothing. Fox made a brief plea for concessions to the merchants in the commercial laws; he also questioned the wisdom of dividing the province. He admitted, however, that his information was inadequate, as indeed it was.

Meanwhile, during the autumn of 1790 the merchants, who would gladly have informed him, had tried in vain to discover the details of the plan.[31] They learned them at last, with surprise and dismay. The Quebec Act was not repealed, there were no legal concessions, and, cut off from the growing loyalist settlements above Montreal, they were once more a minority as insignificant as in 1776. Adam Lymburner fought gallantly for the program of 1784, presenting an impassioned appeal against the bill at the bar of the House on March 26. Remembering that he represented Canadians and English he did not stress the unhappy situation of the English minority. Instead he reviewed the bitter grievances of the past fifteen years: arbitrary government, the tyranny of unknown laws, "the pride and insolence of a set of men whose minds were corrupted by despotic power." Now, having been neglected as well as oppressed, with every public building in decay, the province must suffer the cost of division and the burden of supporting two governments, with no reform assured either in laws or law courts.[32]

Adam Lymburner, that "decent and sensible man," had done his duty; and William Grenville had done his. Neither Lymburner nor Grenville could have foreseen all the consequences of what Grenville had done. In granting Lower Canada an elective assembly he had provided Canadians with a national forum at the very moment when the new phenomenon of nationalism as a mass emotion was making its appearance in France.

It was to France that for the past few years young Canadian radicals had looked for inspiration. The word "nation," however, was not yet a radical term, and the modern concept of nationalism was not familiar to them. The use of the word nation before 1791 seems to have been largely confined to the seigneurs, who used it of themselves along with the community that they liked to regard as a kind of appanage of their class. Perhaps for this very reason it had been avoided by the radicals who by conviction were cosmopolitan as they were equalitarian.

The radical English Quebec *Herald* early in 1789 brought the use of the word under discussion. Attacking the current seigneurial petition against an assembly the *Herald* accused the seigneurs of having had "the audacity to talk of themselves as a nation," speaking of English law as "foreign." They forgot, said the writer, that by conquest their "nation" had become a province of Great Britain. The word here was clearly used in a legalistic sense rather than in a moral or cultural one. The seigneurs were accused of something like sedition, with no thought that offence might be given to Canadian allies in the political struggle then being waged on class lines, merchants and townspeople against reactionary seigneurs.[33]

At the same time there were signs that the loyalists' assumptions of superiority and their careless contempt for Canadian laws and religion were arousing resentment. Even while co-operating with English merchants to secure an assembly, the Canadian committee in Quebec published an indignant announcement in the *Herald* accusing a loyalist lawyer, Isaac Ogden, of having furnished a recent distinguished visitor, Prince William Henry, with information false and injurious to their religion and clergy, and their laws.[34] The word "nation" was not used in this connection. It was however, used significantly by the radicals two years later. A Canadian "gentleman" was reported to have said, disparagingly, that Canadians could not stand together, referring to their co-operation with the English and probably also to the current vigorous criticism of Judge Rouville for disbarring a Canadian lawyer. It was true, said a writer to the Montreal *Gazette*, that Canadians, loving freedom and hating all prejudices, might not wish to stand with that trifling group, the "gentleman" and his friends, "basely enthusiastic lovers of old times." Apart, however, from this small class any patriotic observer could see that, united in their resolution to resist despotism and arbitrary government, the nation as a whole (*"le corps de la nation"*) did stand as one.[35]

Thus unconsciously the seigneurs, fighting a losing battle for their dream of the old days and the old ways, defending Canadian law in the name of "the single unchanging will of the nation," had been preparing the ground soon to be taken over by their radical opponents, who would occupy it with the sincere conviction that it had always been theirs.

The thirty years following the Conquest was a critical period in the history of Quebec and of Canada. During these years the policy of the British government, of British governors, and of English immigrants to Canadians permitted, provoked, and encouraged the development of the instinctive Canadian sense of community into the self-conscious nationalism which was developing by the end of the century. It has generally been believed that only the conciliatory policy of the Quebec Act prevented Canadians from turning the province over to the Americans in 1775. The evidence available seems insufficient for such a conclusion. Assuming that the influence of the Church was decisive, it can hardly be asserted that the Church would have been satisfied with no more and no less than Carleton's personal interpretation of the Quebec Act.

On the other hand it is more than doubtful whether the interpretation favoured by Lord North, and Lords Dartmouth and George Germain, of at once conciliating the Canadians and paving the way for anglicization, would have produced the expected results. The Quebec Act came late in the eighteenth century, at the moment when the American and the French revolutions were about to release emotional forces which must make nonsense of the cold rational calculations of Francis Maseres. If the besieged state of the province had not seemed to authorize "the system of the generals," more, probably, would have been done through concession and compromise to satisfy the demands of the English merchants. Canadians might well have received less consideration, the necessity for conciliating them being less apparent. The danger from France being less, they might, however, have been admitted more freely to senior positions in the government service.

As it was, the "system of the generals" combined a generally just and humane conduct toward a conquered people with the maximum irritation of the potentially radical elements in the towns, both English and Canadian. At the same time, the Roman Catholic community, although conceded in practice a freedom and toleration unexampled at the time, was kept constantly aware of a continuing danger of extinction through the systematic application of his instructions by some future hostile governor.

It would have been difficult for any statesman deliberately to have conceived a policy better calculated to develop a strong and vigorous national spirit than the one accidentally evolved by the generally humane and tolerant principles of London interpreted in Quebec by soldiers who inevitably saw all provincial problems in terms of defence, and of the political future, not of one province, but of a whole continent.

ABBREVIATIONS

A.A.M.: Archives of the Archbishopric of Montreal.
A.A.Q.: Archives of the Archbishopric of Quebec.
A.H.R.: *American Historical Review.*
B.M.: British Museum.
C.H.R.: *Canadian Historical Review.*
C.O.: Colonial Office.
E.H.R.: *English Historical Review.*
P.A.C.: Public Archives of Canada.
R.A.P.Q.: *Report of the Public Archives of Quebec.*
S. and D.: A. Shortt and A. G. Doughty, *Documents relating to the Constitutional History of Canada, 1760–1791.*

NOTES TO CHAPTER TWO

1. R.A.P.Q., 1923-1924, p. 391, Bougainville, Mémoire depuis le 15 Novembre 1758; P.A.C., Murray Papers, I, 26; S. and D., p. 7 and n. 1.

2. Vincent T. Harlow, The Founding of the Second British Empire (London, 1952), I, 162 ff.; William L. Grant, "Canada versus Guadeloupe," A.H.R., XVII (1912), 735-43.

3. J. B. Brebner, North Atlantic Triangle (New Haven, 1945), p. 40.

4. Jack M. Sosin, Whitehall and the Wilderness; the Middle West in British Colonial Policy, 1760-1775 (Lincoln, Neb., 1961), p. 7. I am indebted to this work for the whole of the argument on the reasons for the retention of Canada, pp. 1-26. Theodore C. Pease, "The Mississippi Boundary of 1763 : A Reappraisal of Responsibility," A.H.R., XL (1934-35), 278-86.

5. The policy of the Proclamation of 1763 is discussed in C. W. Alvord, The Mississippi Valley in British Politics (2 vols.; Cleveland, Ohio, 1917). Alvord first showed strikingly the significance of the Proclamation in relation to the whole imperial problem. His theories on the genesis of the Proclamation have been challenged by R. A. Humphrey, "Lord Shelburne and the Proclamation of 1763," E.H.R., XLIX (1934), 241-64, and

by Sosin, Whitehall and the Wilderness, pp. 3-78.

6. Sosin, Whitehall and the Wilderness, p. 46. For the above discussion, see pp. 1-111 and especially pp. 33-51 and Humphrey, "Lord Shelburne," loc. cit. supra n. 5.

7. H. H. Peckham, Pontiac and the Indian Uprising (Princeton, 1947); Charles S. Grant, "Pontiac's Rebellion and the British Troop Moves of 1763," Mississippi Valley Historical Review, XL (1953-54), 75; Bernard Knollenberg, "General Amherst and Germ Warfare," ibid., XLI (1954-55), 489.

8. Peckham, op. cit., p. 72.

9. Ibid., p. 110, n. 11.

10. Grant, "Pontiac's Rebellion."

11. P.A.C., B.M., Add. MSS, 21,682, fols. 54 ff. Another investigation held at Fort Pitt by Colonel Bouquet produced evidence suggesting that Christie had lost his nerve and surrendered before it was clear that the fort must fall. Ibid., fols. 62 ff.; P.A.C., Murray Papers, III, 159; Peckham, Pontiac, p. 170.

12. Criticisms of the proposed regulation of the trade came from new colonies as well as old : R. A. Humphrey, "Governor Murray's Views on the Plan of 1764 for the Management of Indian Affairs," C.H.R., XVI (1935), 162.

NOTES TO CHAPTER THREE

1. P.A.C., Murray Papers, I, 6, Nov. 1759.

2. P.A.C., C.O. 42/24, p. 1.

3. A. G. Doughty (ed.), The Journal of Captain Knox (Toronto: Champlain Society, 1914), II, 309, 311, 312.

4. P.A.C., Report, 1918, App. B, 1, 7, 9.

5. Doughty, Journal of Captain Knox, II, 272; P.A.C., Murray Papers, III, 47.

6. Accounts of the numbers differ, Murray making the discrepancy very high, Lévis reducing it. Doughty, Journal of

Captain Knox, II, 396; P.A.C., Murray Papers, I, 26.

7. P.A.C., Report, 1918, App. B, 13.

8. M. Trudel, L'Eglise Canadienne sous le régime militaire (Montreal, 1956-57), II, 207 ff.; P.A.C., Murray Papers, III, 105; Dartmouth Papers [Originals], V, 2272; C.O. 42/25, 218-23.

9. P.A.C.: Murray Papers, II, 47, 128; C.O. 42/24, 34, 36, 101; 42/25, 77, 79; 42/26, 22; 42/27, 9. Marine Léland,

"François-Joseph Cugnet," *Revue de l'Univ. Laval*, XVI (1961-62), 929.

10. M. Brunet, *La Présence Anglaise et les Canadiens* (Montreal, 1958), p. 39.

11. A. L. Burt, *The Old Province of Quebec* (Minneapolis, 1933), p. 35.

12. A.A.M., Montgolfier to Briand, 16 Mar., 29 Mar. 1761; P.A.C.: Murray Papers, III, 49; P.A.C., *Report, 1918*, App. B, 33, 39, 41, 43, 47, 61, 99.

13. *Ibid.*, 37, 42, 58–59, 102, 122.

14. *Ibid.*, 14-17, 21, 32, 33-34, 48, 54-55, 61, 90, 102-3, 128.

15. P.A.C., Murray Papers, II, 29; III, 52.

16. P.A.C., Baby Collection, Correspondence (hereafter referred to as "Baby Letters"), La Corne, La Valtrie, Lanaudière correspondence, 1763, 1764. There are numerous references in the Baby Letters to the blending of classes, the more natural since most of the seigneurs were by French standards "non-noble." Charles François Tarieu de Lanaudière, whose son, Charles-Louis, wounded on the Plains of Abraham, had returned with his regiment to France, was apparently actively engaged in the fur and the wheat trade at the time of the Conquest. He decided to stay in Canada and received many government favours. The Perrault, prominent merchants of Quebec, were intermarried with the Boucherville family; a Baby married the Sieur de Niverville; François Baby married a Lanaudière; St George Dupré and his brother le Comte, who signed themselves as seigneurs, were both merchants. C.O. 42/24, 72.

17. R. de Roquebrune, "L'exode des Canadiens après 1760," *La Nouvelle Revue Canadienne*, 3 (Sept.-Oct. 1953).

18. Allana G. Reid, "General Trade between Quebec and France during the French Regime," *C.H.R.*, XXXIV (1953), 18-32; Brunet, *La Présence Anglaise*, p. 49; F. Ouellet, "M. Michel Brunet et le problème de la conquête," *Bulletin des Recherches Historiques*, LXII (June, 1956), 92; R.A.P.Q., 1924-1925, p. 94; P.A.C. C.O. 42/24, 72.

19. *Infra*, p. 83, 84

20. P.A.C., C.O. 42/24, 97-98, 141, 147, 159; Baby Letters, Jauge to F. Baby, 14 June 1763, 2022-2027, 17 Apr. 1762, 1873-1875, 15 May 1763, 2010-2013.

21. P.A.C., Dartmouth Papers [Originals], V, 2259, 2261.

22. P.A.C., *Report, 1918*, App. B, 55.

23. For material on the Church in this and later chapters, I am much indebted to Trudel, *L'Eglise Canadienne*.

24. P.A.C., C.O. 42/24, 101; A.A.Q., Evêques de Québec, I. 87.

25. A.A.Q., Copies des Lettres, III, 93.

NOTES TO CHAPTER FOUR

1. P.A.C.: C.O. 42/25, 46; Murray Papers, II, 56, 62, 65, 113, 125.

2. P.A.C., Murray Papers, II, 6, 23, 32, 33, 61, 278; III, 157.

3. S. and D., p. 211.

4. P.A.C.: C.O. 42/25, 148, 150, 154, 156, 160; Murray Papers, II, 142, 152, 154, 158, 248, 276; S, IX, 26; Doughty, *Journal of Captain Knox*, III, 119, 225.

5. P.A.C., Murray Papers, II, 191.

6. *Ibid.*, II, 17, 43, 65, 67, 162, 247; P.A.C., C.O. 42/25, 50, 52.

7. P.A.C. C.O. 42/25, 60, 63, 167; Murray Papers, III, 100, 230.

8. P.A.C., Murray Papers, II, 151, 175; III, 126; S, IX, 26.

9. P.A.C., Quebec Leg. Coun., A, 68.

10. *Ibid.*, 21, 65; P.A.C., C.O. 42/25, 95.

11. P.A.C.: Murray Papers, II, 188; Quebec Leg. Coun., B, 23 ff.; S, X, 56, 57, 61; XII, 37.

12. S. M. Scott, "Chapters in the History of the Law of Quebec, 1764-1767" (unpublished doctoral dissertation, Ann Arbor, 1933), Chap. 4; P.A.C.: Quebec Leg. Coun., A, 51, 52; B, 44; S, I, 133; X, 16; Murray Papers, II, 188; C.O. 42/25, 225.

13. P.A.C., Murray Papers, II, 178; III, 255.

14. Ibid., II, 170; III, 179, 255.

15. Ibid., II, 170.

16. Ibid., III, 47.

17. Ibid., II, 4, 53, 113, 226; III, 157, 211-45; P.A.C.: B.M., Add. MSS, 35915, fols. 133 ff. (Hardwicke Papers); C.O. 42/1, 377.

18. P.A.C.: Quebec Leg. Coun., A, 117; S, XXI, 231; C.O. 42/25, 171; Murray Papers, II, 201. S. and D., p. 212. Perrault, the Quebec merchant, writing to François Baby in Montreal, 8 April 1765, speaks with bitterness of the behaviour of the English and, referring apparently to the grand jury, does suggest deliberate deceit: ". . . without some care on our part we shall be reduced to slavery." (Baby Letters, p. 2212.) Perrault may have been influenced by Murray; if the English merchants were able to hoodwink the Canadians into signing what they did not understand, there would have been no need to make a separate English presentment protesting against Roman Catholic juries.

19. P.A.C., C.O. 42/25, 217, 242; S. and D., p. 232.

20. P.A.C.: Murray Papers, II, 53, 59, 116, 128; B.M., Add. MSS, 35915, fols. 125, 157, 213 (Hardwicke Papers).

21. P.A.C.: Quebec Leg. Coun., A, 97-98; C.O. 42/25, 228 ff.

22. P.A.C., Dartmouth Papers [Originals], V, 2254.

23. A. L. Burt, "The Mystery of Walker's Ear," C.H.R., III (Sept. 1922), 233; P.A.C.: C.O. 42/25, 231 ff.; 42/26, 28; Murray Papers, II, 207; Dartmouth Papers [Originals], V, 2265; Quebec Gazette, Supplement, 23 May 1765.

24. Christie was sued by two merchants, Knipe and Lequesne, for having illegally conscripted their employees. They were eventually awarded £3,599 damages. P.A.C., Quebec Leg. Coun., B, 55 ff.

25. P.A.C.: C.O. 42/26, 49-113; S, I, 149; IX, 49, 63, 94, 95; X, 56, 57, 61; XIII, 50; Murray Papers, II, 258-68.

26. P.A.C.: Quebec Leg. Coun., A, 72, 135, 276-77; B, 64 ff., 68, 69, 114, 116-17; S, I, 80; Murray Papers, II, 201. Among those who associated themselves with the English merchants was the Canadian, Pierre Guy.

27. P.A.C., Murray Papers, II, 248-49, 271, 280-85.

28. P.A.C., C.O. 42/26, 9.

29. P.A.C., Dartmouth Papers [Originals], V, 2266; S. and D., p. 216.

NOTES TO CHAPTER FIVE

1. For material in this chapter I have drawn freely on Scott, "Chapters in the History of the Law of Quebec, 1764-1767."

2. Lord Mansfield in Campbell vs. Hall put it much more strongly: "Articles of capitulation, upon which the country is surrendered, and treaties of peace by which it is ceded, are sacred and inviolate, according to their true intent and meaning." S. and D., p. 526.

3. Supra, pp. 15-16.

4 S. and D., p. 297.

5. Ibid., pp. 205, 249, 250, 401.

6. P.A.C., Quebec Leg. Coun., B, 105-6,

contains a curious account of the complaint of one Pelissier which came before the council. Pelissier found the proceedings in the J.P.'s court (using a jury in a case of assault) so illogical as to endanger all life and property. The attorney general and the council, even the sympathetic Murray, found Pelissier's complaint so intemperate that he was finally ordered to leave the province. He was probably something of a troublemaker, but it is quite clear that, accepting the rational inquisition of the French court, he found the English system of allowing the witness to give evidence, and then allowing the jury to ignore him, so irrational as to be dangerous. See also Baby Letters, p. 2356.

7. H. Neatby, Administration of Justice under the Quebec Act (Minneapolis, 1937), pp. 58-59, 159 ff.; P.A.C.: S, IX, 82; Quebec Leg. Coun., B, 75; Murray Papers, II, 189.

8. P.A.C., Quebec Leg. Coun., A, 19-21; S, IX, 51, 52.

9. P.A.C.: RG IV, "Provincial Secretary, Enteries"; Quebec Leg. Coun., B, 155; S, XIV, 29.

10. P.A.C., C.O. 42/25, 236.

11. P.A.C., S, IX, 88.

12. Scott, History of the Law of Quebec, App. VI; Scott's figures suggest that, with some glaring exceptions, costs were about what they had been under the military government when there had been no complaint. He also gives evidence to show that office-holders, whether patentees in England or deputies in Canada, did not find their office

very profitable. Lieutenant-Governor Irving remarked on the low fees of the court of common pleas. P.A.C., C.O. 42/26, 216; S, X, 16; XIII, 22, 27.

13. S. and D., p. 252.

14. P.A.C., S, XII, 108. By 7 Feb. 1765, at least six Canadians had been admitted barristers in the court of common pleas. Quebec Gazette, 7 Feb. 1765.

15. P.A.C., Monk Papers, II, 147, Deed of Sale, 27 Mar. 1787; S, XIV, 5, Deed of Sale, 1769.

16. P.A.C., Baby Letters, Christie-Magnan Letters, 1770-72.

17. Scott, History of the Law of Quebec, pp. 211-12.

18. W. P. M. Kennedy, Statutes, Treaties and Documents of the Canadian Constitution, 1713-1929 (Oxford, 1930), p. 123.

19. R. A. Humphrey and S. Morley Scott, "Lord Northington and the Laws of Canada," C.H.R., XIV (1933), 42.

20. P.A.C., Dartmouth Papers [Originals], V, 2262.

NOTES TO CHAPTER SIX

1. I am indebted for much material in this chapter to Isabel Craig, "Economic Conditions in Canada, 1763-83," (unpublished M.A. thesis, McGill, 1937).

2. The general impression that the habitant had nothing to do is obviously exaggerated. After his fall plowing he might gather reeds from the river to supplement his fodder supply. As soon as the snow fell he had to get in his winter wood. He had also to thresh his wheat. He might still, however, have a good deal of leisure.

3. P.A.C.: Murray Papers, II, 214; III, 246, 269, 273; Finlay Papers, p. 8. Quebec Gazette, 25 Oct. 1764, 27 June 1765.

4. P.A.C., B.M., Add. MSS, 21681, fol. 1 (report of Burton from Three Rivers endorsed as received by the Board of Trade 31 May 1763; an abridged and slightly altered version is printed in S and D.,

p. 81); Dartmouth Papers [Originals], VI, 2306; VII, 2398; Murray Papers, II, 61, 84. Quebec Gazette, 4 Apr. 1765.

5. P.A.C., C.O. 42/27, 113.

6. P.A.C., Baby Letters, pp. 3045, 3051, 3057, 3076, 3083, 3085, 3086, 3218, 3256, 3277, 3290, 3298, 3313, 3339, 3342, 3346, 3356, 3387, 3429, 3669, 3671.

7. P.A.C., Jacobs Papers, I, 39; II, 18, 47; VIII, 113, 137; IX, 188, 199, 235, 286, 348, 358, 382, 403, 436; X, 466, 626, 751, 758; XI, 962; XII, 997, 1005, 1006, 1018, 1021.

8. P.A.C.: Jacobs Papers, VIII, 63, 77, 105, 120-23, 125, 131, 155; IX, 296; XI, 842; Baby Letters, pp. 3758, 3759, 4159, 4188, 4192, 4218, 4229, 4257, 4264, 4268, 4274, 4284.

9. P.A.C.: C.O. 42/31, 173; 42/49, 383; Baby Letters, pp. 2595, 3096, 3235, 3300, 3659; Jacobs Papers, XI, 962.

10. P.A.C.: Jacobs Papers, XI, 932, 937; S, XV, 47, 50; S. and D., p. 517.

11. Baby Letters, pp. 2602, 3032, 3866.

12. P.A.C.: Jacobs Papers, I, 44-48; II, 9; VIII, 22, 55, 83, 113, 137, 142-46, 154; IX, 191, 195, 271, 368, 379; X, 448, 592, 723; XI, 770, 802-3, 805, 816, 846-47, 852, 861, 870, 890, 895; XII, 1033, 1039-41, 1049; Baby Letters, pp. 2407, 2430, 2434, 2469, 2582, 2607, 2695, 2733, 2754, 2877, 2922, 3235, 3357, 3439, 3601, 3606, 3659, 3674, 3749, 3758, 3796, 3812, 3827, 3858, 3866, 3871, 3885, 4051, 4098.

13. P.A.C., C.O., 42/26, 192; 42/27, 99; 42/28, 262; Quebec Gazette, 28 Feb. 1765; S. and D., p. 270; P.A.C., Montreal-St Sulpice, M, III, 127, Petition of Seigneurs to Murray [1765?]; M, III, 133, Petition of Seigneurs to Justices of Peace, 26 Sept. 1765.

14. The Jacobs Papers (P.A.C.) give vivid pictures of the struggles of smaller men. Samuel Jacobs started after the Conquest with his finger in a number of pies, and business premises in both Quebec and Montreal. A few years later he was confined to St Denis on the Richelieu, a storekeeper and grain buyer, finding much difficulty in meeting his bills. At least two of his associates seem to have had similar experiences.

15. G. O. Rothney, "The Case of Bayne and Brymer," C.H.R., XV (1934), 264; P.A.C.: B.M., Add. MSS, 35915 (Hardwicke Papers), fols. 58, 74, 94, 105, 110, 112, 118, 316; Dartmouth Papers (Patshull), IV, Hocquart to Dartmouth, 22 Dec. 1774; Quebec Leg. Coun., B, 85; S, X, 86, 99, 101; XV, 95, 96. Quebec Gazette, 20 Sept. 1764; P.A.C., 42/24, 49, 173; 42/25, 37, 77, 79, 81; 42/28, 111, 117, 559; Baby Letters, pp. 3914, 3916, 3917, 3922, 3928, 3929, 3932.

16. W. L. Morton, "A Note on Palliser's Act," C.H.R., XXXIV (1953), 33; P.A.C.: C.O. 42/27, 38; 42/28, 55, 58, 60; Baby Letters, pp. 4007, 4012, 4014, 4030.

17. P.A.C., Murray Papers, III, 38.

18. P.A.C., S, IA is composed entirely of copies of leases and other documents relating to the king's posts.

19. P.A.C., Report, 1918, App. B, 120, 126, 141, 155.

20. P.A.C., Baby Letters, p. 2060.

21. P.A.C., C.O. 42/27, 90; 42/28, 165.

22 Ibid.

23. P.A.C.: C.O. 42/26, 355; 42/27, 73, 138, 140, 213; 42/28, 165, 169, 312; Dartmouth Papers [Originals], III, 259, Gage to Shelburne, 22 Feb. 1767; B.M., Add. MSS, 35915 (Hardwicke Papers), fols. 234-46, 322-31; Baby Letters, pp. 2339, 2399, 2486, 2535, 2540.

24. P.A.C.: C.O. 42/27, 138; Baby Letters, p. 2345. R. A. Humphrey, "Governor Murray's Views on the Proclamation of 1764 for the Management of Indian Affairs," C.H.R., XVI (1935), 162.

25. P.A.C., C.O. 42/27, 81.

26. W. E. Stevens, The North-West Fur Trade 1763-1800 (Univ. of Illinois, Urbana, Ill., 1928). M. G. Reid, "The Quebec Fur Traders and Western Policy, 1763-1774," C.H.R., VI (1925), 15. Charles E. Lart (ed.), "Fur Trade Returns, 1767," C.H.R., III (1922), 351; P.A.C.: C.O. 42/25, 201, 202; 42/26, 304, 355; 42/27, 77, 160; 42/28, 159, 165, 178; Quebec Leg. Coun., A, 174-77, 199; S, IX, 34; XIII, 104; XV, 11; B.M., Add. MSS, 35915 (Hardwicke Papers), fols. 228, 247; Baby Letters, p. 32-45. In the spring of 1767 James Morrison, travelling to Michilimackinac by way of Niagara and Detroit and trading on the way, was arrested with his party as he passed along Lake Ontario, but after a short time was able to satisfy the commandant at Niagara who released his goods and allowed him to continue his journey. P.A.C., Lindsay-Morrison Papers, II, 110 ff., 159.

27. P.A.C., Baby Letters, pp. 2209, 2212, 2216, 2251, 2365, 2519, 2524, 2877, 2917, 4433, 4490, 4504, 4521; Ramsay Traquair, "Montreal and the Indian Trade Silver," C.H.R., XIX (1938), 1. In 1765 François Baby complained of the high prices of

one "Alexandre," a silversmith of Quebec, saying that henceforth he would buy more cheaply in Montreal. Alexandre insisted that his prices were fair and that his rivals used an inferior alloy. About ten years later a Montreal silversmith, Schindler, was drummed out of Detroit, accused of selling base metal ornaments as silver. Baby Letters, p. 2212; P.A.C., C.O. 42/38, 247.

28. Lart, loc. cit. supra n. 26; P.A.C., C.O. 42/14, 98, 98a.

29. P.A.C., Jacobs Papers, X, 626. As provincial currency was over-valued, the normal premium for sterling was 11 per cent. In the fall those who had to make payments might pay 12 per cent or more.

30. The Baby Letters give plenty of evidence for the period before the Quebec Act; after this there is very little information on François Baby's business but there is no evidence that he did not continue to work with his brother in Detroit.

31. P.A.C., Baby Letters, pp. 2305, 2307, 2372, 2373, 2377, 2385, 2387, 3305, 3390, 3577, 3971.

32. P.A.C., Lindsay-Morrison Papers, II, 156.

33. P.A.C., Baby Letters, 2373, 3365, 3373, 3590.

34. Ibid., pp. 2060, 2843, 2857, 2947, 2976, 3087, 3231, 3357, 3592.

35. P.A.C.: C.O. 42/27, 140; see also P.A.C., S, IX, 34.

36. P.A.C., Baby Letters, pp. 3150, 3166, 3170.

37. Lart, loc. cit. supra n. 26; Reid, loc. cit. supra n. 26; Brunet, La Présence Anglaise; P.A.C. 42/27, 140. M. Brunet's essay shows the problems of adjustment that faced the Canadian merchant; his suggestion, however, that none could survive unless aided by pensions or government posts, is not, I think, supported by the evidence. François Baby had no pension and no office until 1778. By that time he could boast of a pros-

perous business built up by his own efforts. See also Ouellet, loc. cit. supra Ch. 3, n. 18.

38. P.A.C.: Dartmouth Papers [Originals], VI, 2306; C.O. 42/28, 415, 417; 42/31, 71, 75; Quebec Leg. Coun., B, 150-51; S, X, 23; Baby Letters, pp. 2391, 2551, 3866; Jacobs Papers, X, 455.

39. P.A.C.: C.O. 42/29, 122; 42/31, 176; Quebec Leg. Coun., B, 37, 39; Jacobs Papers, VIII, 106, 150; IX, 319, 391; X, 448, 626, 676.

40. Craig, op. cit., pp. 162-68; P.A.C.: Quebec Leg. Coun., C, 64; S, XII, 129; XIII, 45.

41. P.A.C.: Quebec Leg. Coun., C, 30; S, XIII, 119, 120, 122, 125; Jacobs Papers, IX, 304, 381, 386, 403; X, 448, 465, 467, 493, 500.

42. P.A.C.: RG IV, "Provincial Secretary, Enteries," p. 107; Baby Letters, pp. 2595, 2943.

43. P.A.C., Jacobs Papers, VIII, 46.

44. P.A.C., Baby Letters, pp. 3509, 3577, 3588, 4098, 4118, 5982.

45. P.A.C.: Baby Letters, pp. 2812, 2833, 2860, 2952, 4069, 4407, 4410, 4417, 4473, 5953, 6345; Lindsay-Morrison Papers, II, 150, 155, 170; III, 410. R.A.P.Q., 1921-1922, pp. 120, 121, 123; P.A.C., Hart Papers, 7 Sept. 1779, 23 May 1786. For a general discussion of slavery in Quebec, see M. Trudel, L'Esclavage au Canada Français (Laval, 1960), Vol. I.

46. P.A.C.: Baby Letters, p. 3073; S, XV, 90.

47. P.A.C.: Dartmouth Papers [Originals], VI, 2306; Baby Letters, pp. 2314, 2407, 2429, 2663, 4058, 4111; Murray Papers, II, 15; S, XIII, 54, 103; Report, 1918, App. B, 115; S. and D., p. 34.

48. P.A.C., Baby Letters, pp. 2972, 2989. After the Conquest James Cook, who in the next decade was to achieve fame as the explorer of the Pacific, was employed for a time in surveying the channel.

49. P.A.C.: Report, 1918, p. 144; S, X, 34; XII, 43, 132-35; XIV, 22, 57; Finlay

Papers, pp. 23, 48, 57, 61. Quebec *Gazette*, 23 May 1765.

50. P.A.C.: *Report, 1918*, App. B, 103, 114-15, 122, 139; Quebec Leg, Coun., B, 93-94, 133 ff., 200, 251; C.O. 42/26, 192-213.

51. P.A.C., S, I, 109-12; X, 42, 117; XV, 57.

52. P.A.C.: Quebec Leg. Coun., A, 89, 144; B, 1, 74, 195-96, 222; S, I, 186, 191, 196; C.O. 42/1, 181.

53. P.A.C.: Quebec Leg. Coun., B, 142, 195-96, 215; C, 9, 16, 141; S, IX, 92; XII, 5, 54, 59, 62; XIII, 87, 89, 95; XIV, 23, 122; XV, 77.

54. P.A.C., Quebec Leg. Coun., C, 101; S, XI, 4 ff.; XII, 93; XV, 104; Baby Letters, pp. 2429, 3390; Jacobs Papers, VIII, 177. Quebec *Gazette*, 21 Mar. 1765.

55. Jean Hamelin, "A la Recherche d'un cours monetaire canadien, 1760-77," *Revue d'histoire de l'Amérique Française*, XV (1961-62), p. 24; Brunet, *op. cit.*; P.A.C.: C.O. 42/24, 70, 161, 191; 42/25, 39, 98, 100, 126, 209; 24/26, 15; 24/28, 44; Baby Letters, pp. 2154, 2326, 2375, 2414, 2635, 2642, 2710; Jacobs Papers, VIII, 137; IX, 190.

56. Hamelin, *op. cit.*; P.A.C.: Quebec Leg. Coun., A, 36-37, 40-41, 78, 178; S, I, 120; IX, 73; XII, 96; XIII, 56, 71; C.O. 42/31, 140; Baby Papers, pp. 2434, 3006. Quebec *Gazette*, 7 Nov. 1765.

57. P.A.C., C.O. 42/25, 269.

NOTES TO CHAPTER SEVEN

1. P.A.C., Dartmouth Papers [Originals], V, 2270.

2. P.A.C.: C.O. 42/26, 282 ff.; Murray Papers, III, 203.

3. P.A.C.: Quebec Leg. Coun., B, 162, 206-7; S, XIV, 121; C.O. 42/26, 226-70, 308, 336. Dunn and Gray took their case to the Privy Council and won it; eventually they received remission of rent for the interruption to their trade.

4. S. and D., pp., 276 ff.; P.A.C.: Quebec Leg. Coun., B, 206-10, 216; S, XII, 88; C.O. 42/27, 69, 87, 91, 211; 42/30, 121, 205; Murray Papers, III, 188, 191, 203, 208.

5. P.A.C., C.O. 42/26, 326; 42/27, 209; 42/28, 325.

6. W. P. M. Kennedy and G. Lanctôt, *Reports on the Laws of Quebec, 1767-70* (P.A.C. Publication No. 12, 1931), p. 59; P.A.C., Quebec Leg. Coun., B, 142, 161, 162.

7. P.A.C.: Quebec Leg. Coun., B, 154, 225, 243; C, 21, 95; S, XIII, 14; C.O. 42/27, 61.

8. P.A.C.: Quebec Leg. Coun., B, 194, 240; C, 69, 87, 92; S, XII, 100; XIII, 110, 113, 114; C.O. 42/26, 160, 162, 188, 190, 220; 42/28, 531 ff.; 42/29, 53; Murray Papers, III, 171.

9. H. R. Balls, "Quebec, 1763-1774: The Financial Administration," *C.H.R.*, XLI (1960), 203; P.A.C.: Quebec Leg. Coun., B, 171, 174; S, XII, 29, 110; XIII, 52, 69; C.O. 42/26, 214; 42/28, 514.

10. P.A.C.: Quebec Leg. Coun., B, 159, 236; C, 42, 82, 109; Exec. Coun., D, 54 ff.; S, X, 105; XIV, 109; C.O. 42/27, 123; 42/28, 190, 193 ff., 227, 307, 523, 525; 42/30, 76; 42/31, 24; 42/34, 76 ff.; Dartmouth Papers [Originals], VI, 2303; *ibid.*, [Patshull], IV, undated, ascribed to William Knox.

11. P.A.C., C.O. 42/30, 175 ff.

12. Scott, "Chapters in the History of the Law of Quebec. 1764-1767," p. 227.

13. P.A.C., Quebec Leg. Coun., C, 97.

14. P.A.C., C.O. 42/30, 43.

15. P.A.C.: Quebec Leg. Coun., C, 60, 65, 70; S, XIII, 93; XIV, 35, 51-63; C.O. 42/30, 7, 25, 43, 168, 175, 191.

16. P.A.C., C.O. 42/28, 159.

17. S. and D., pp. 280, 281.

18. Burt, *The Old Province of Quebec*, p. 151.

19. *Supra*, p. 52.

20. W. S. Wallace (ed.), *The Maseres Letters, 1766-68* (Toronto, 1919), pp. 118-19; S. and D., p. 287.

21. S. and D., pp. 281, 288.

22. P.A.C., C.O. 42/28, 86, 90, 98.

23. P.A.C., Baby Letters, p. 2917.

24. S. and D., pp. 281, 288, 299, 325; P.A.C., C.O. 42/28, 68; 42/29, 9, 31, 88.

25. Wallace, *The Maseres Letters, 1766-68*, p. 103; F. S. Cugnet, *Traité abrégé des anciennes loix, coûtumes et usages de la colonie du Canada* (Quebec, 1775); Léland, *loc. cit. supra* chap 3, n. 9, XVI, 107 *passim*, XVII, 64 *passim*, XVIII, 337, 717; XIX, 144, 254.

26. S. and D., pp. 327, 370; Kennedy and Lanctôt, *Laws of Quebec*; Wallace, *Maseres Letters, 1766-68*, pp. 101-3, App. E, p. 130.

27. S. and D., p. 292.

28. *Ibid.*, p. 370 n. l.

NOTES TO CHAPTER EIGHT

1. P.A.C., C.O. 42/29, 98.

2. S. M. Scott, "The authorship of certain papers in the *Lower Canada Jurist*," C.H.R., X (1929), 335; Wallace, *Maseres Letters*, p. 58.

3. Wallace, *Maseres Letters*, p. 58. It may seem like special pleading to say that Maseres was not a bigot; but Cardinal Richelieu, who certainly thought Protestantism "dangerous and treacherous," has never been accused of bigotry.

4. *Ibid.*, p. 103.

5. See Trudel, *L'Eglise Canadienne*, I, 243-334, for the procedures leading to the appointment of Bishop Briand.

6. A.A.Q., Pères Jesuites, I, 1.

7. A.A.Q., Vicaires Généraux, V, 13.

8. Trudel, *L'Eglise Canadienne*, I, 333; R.A.P.Q., 1929-1930, p. 67.

9. Trudel, *L'Eglise Canadienne*, I, 332.

10. P.A.C., C.O. 42/31, 136, 169.

11. A.A.Q., Gouvernement, V, 50; Evêques de Québec, I, 125; Copies des Lettres, III, 266; IV, 227, 307; V, 403.

12. A.A.Q., Copies des Lettres, III, 417, 425; IV, 515.

13. *Ibid.*, III, 361, 571 ff.; IV, 59.

14. A.A.Q., Gouvernement, I, 17, 19-22.

15. A.A.Q., Copies des Lettres, III, 409; IV, 605.

16. *Ibid.*, III, 266-67.

17. *Ibid.*, III, 333, 441; IV, 95, 143, 565.

18. *Ibid.*, IV, 147, 265; V, 103; Gouvernement, I, 18; A.A.M., Montgolfier to Briand, 23 Nov., 21 Dec., 24 Dec. 1766.

19. A.A.Q., Copies des Lettres, III, 251, 353.

20. *Ibid.*, IV, p. 127, 135, 139, 546; P.A.C., C.O. 42/27, 227.

21. A.A.Q., Copies des Lettres, III, 297; IV, 59.

22. *Ibid.*, IV, 547, 639; V, 153.

23. *Ibid.*; A.A.M., Letters of Montgolfier. This statement is based on the evidence of numerous letters to or about priests. In 1775 Briand commented on the imprudence or worse of priests, indulgent to themselves but "so imperious with the habitants . . . [over] even very slight faults." A.A.Q., Copies des Lettres, IV, 552.

24. *Ibid.*, III, 355-56; P.A.C., C.O. 42/27, 227.

25. A.A.Q., Copies des Lettres, III, 503.

26. *Ibid.*, III, 365; IV, 115, 145-46, 177.

27. *Ibid.*, III, 271-76, 429-46; IV, 104; V, 42; A.A.Q., Evêques de Québec, I, 184; P.A.C., Briand Papers, Briand to the Parish of St Francis, 26 Sept. 1782.

28. A.A.M., Montgolfier to Briand, 3 Dec., 11 Dec. 1769; 25 Mar. 1770; A.A.Q., Evêques de Québec, I, 150; Copies des Lettres, IV, 29, 33, 111, 241; R.A.P.Q., 1920-1921, pp. 366 ff.

29. A.A.Q., Copies des Lettres, III, 181; Evêques de Québec, I, 162, 173; A.A.M., Montgolfier to Briand, 28 Mar. 1774. Montreal Collège Ste Marie, Briand to Catherine Briand, 26 Sept. 1776; P. Camille de Rochemonteix: *Les Jesuites*

de la Nouvelle France, (1906), II, 213 ff.

30. A.A.Q., Copies des Lettres, IV, 128. The reference is mysterious. It may mean that Cramahé was now maintaining an intelligence service, or the man may have been employed by him in the winter of 1759-60; Briand would naturally find it hard to forget the sins of those who had been paid to betray their country.

31. A.A.Q., Copies des Lettres, III, 229, 327, 357, 369, 405, 417, 425; IV, 75, 128, 157, 191, 202, 205, 206, 209, 357, 419, 455, 475, 503, 535, 537; Gouvernement, I, 24. A.A.M., Montgolfier to Briand, 24 Sept. 1768.

32. Wallace, *Maseres Letters*, p. 54.

33. P.A.C., MG 23 G II, 5, Maseres to the Reverend Mr. Majendie in Denmark Street, 1768.

34. *Ibid.*

35. *Ibid.*; P.A.C., MG 17.7 Archives St Sulpice, Paris, IV, 41.

36. M. Trudel, "La Servitude de l'Eglise Catholique sous le régime anglais," C.H.A. *Report*, *1963*, p. 42. A gift received in France enabled him to purchase his episcopal robes. He also had an allowance of three thousand livres from the clergy in France. After the Quebec Act the British government allowed him £200 a year.

37. A.A.Q., Copies des Lettres, IV, 194.

38. *Ibid.*, IV, 187.

39. *Ibid.*, 103.

40. *Ibid.*, III, 445; IV, 303, 601.

41. P.A.C.: Dartmouth Papers [Originals], V, 2259; VI, 2232, 2333; VII, 2362; C.O. 42/24, 216. A.A.Q., Gouvernement, I, 23; S. and D., pp. 427-430.

NOTES TO CHAPTER NINE

1. P.A.C., C.O. 42/29, 55.

2. S. and D., pp. 327, 424, 437, 440; Kennedy and Lanctôt, *Reports on the Laws of Quebec*. The exception was Thurlow, Attorney General.

3. S. and D., p. 537 n.

4. *Ibid.*, pp. 212 ff.

5. Although nationalism in its modern sense was not to emerge for another generation, Canadians had, from the beginning, a sense of the integrity of their community, and they did use the word "nation." A nun, for example, deplored the action of a Canadian girl who married an English Protestant as a betrayal of her "nation." Trudel, *L'Eglise Canadienne*, p. 174. The word was used by church leaders probably before it was taken up by seigneurs.

6. A.A.Q., Gouvernement, V, 30, "Mémoire pour servir du [sic] Conduite aux Canadiens Catholiques Romains . . . etc., 1765."

7. S. and D., p. 227.

8. P.A.C., MG 17.7, Archives, St Sulpice,

Paris, IV, 18, Marchand and Perrault to Kerberio, Lataille, Filiau, 28 June 1765.

9. A.A.Q., Gouvernement, V, 23 (n.d.), Inhabitants of Three Rivers to the governor and council.

10. P.A.C.: C.O. 42/26, 22; Quebec Leg. Coun., B, 128-31.

11. A.A.Q., Gouvernement, V, 25.

12. S. and D., p. 270.

13. A.A.M., Montgolfier to Briand, 5 July 1773; P.A.C., Montreal-St Sulpice, Briand to Montgolfier, 17 July 1773.

14. P.A.C., C.O. 42/30, 161; S. and D., p. 421. See, however, Gouvernement, V, 2, 21, as showing a desire to maintain Canadian law on the part of the Church.

15. P.A.C.: Baby Collection, Political Papers, Vol. XL, Letter to Quebec *Gazette*, 21 July 1773; XLVIII, Address to His Majesty, 24 July 1773 (30,938); Baby Letters, p. 3222.

16. P.A.C., Baby Letters, p. 3619.

17. Apart from the draft petition mentioned there is evidence that there was strong division among the Canadians at

Quebec. When Hey left he was presented with an address lauding his work and hoping for his speedy return. François Baby wrote angrily to Guy in Montreal mentioning that Bishop Briand, Rigauville, and a few others had signed from "timidity, fear or stupidity" and that for fear timid souls at Montreal should do the same, Guy was to forewarn his friends. This bitterness against Hey could come only from his disagreement with Carleton over the laws. Baby at this time, hoping for office, was working closely with the seigneurial party. Guy had acted with the seigneurs but had not the same ambitions and was inclined to scoff at seigneurial pretensions. *Ibid.*, p. 3588.

18. P.A.C., Dartmouth Papers [Originals], VI, 2343.

19. Reid, *loc. cit. supra* chap. 6, note 26.

20. P.A.C., C.O. 42/1, 400 ff.

21. *Ibid.*, 42/31, 149, 158. P.A.C., Baby Letters, p. 2943. There is no record of

Cramahé's answer. Dejean continued as "judge" and claimed in 1775 ecclesiastical honours from Briand, who refused them. Hamilton, who went there as lieutenant-governor, accepted him and he and Hamilton together were charged with murder by a grand jury at Montreal as the result of a bizarre trial which culminated in one of those condemned to death, a woman, being pardoned on condition that she execute her accomplice. C.O. 42/38, 243 ff.

22. Reid, *loc cit. supra* chap. 6. note 26; S. and D., pp. 501, 508, 509; P.A.C., C.O. 42/32, 59.

23. Sir Henry Cavendish, *Debates of the House of Commons* (1774) (London, 1839), p. 11.

24. See *supra*, pp. 92, 93.

25. S. and D., pp. 599, 600.

26. *Ibid.*, pp. 602, 606; P.A.C., C.O. 42/14, 138-39.

27. S. and D., p. 568, n. 1.

28. Cavendish, *Debates*, p. 246.

NOTES TO CHAPTER TEN

1. S. and D., pp. 583-84.

2. *Ibid.*, pp. 583-84, 589 ff.; P.A.C.: C.O. 42/34, 13 ff.; Baby Letters, pp. 3740, 3767. Some Canadians were sufficiently alarmed to consider requesting the bishop to instruct the parish priests to forbid the habitants from signing any petition circulated by the English.

3. P.A.C., Baby Letters, p. 3871. Some did very well. In 1786 Charles-Louis de Lanaudière got £500 a year from Pitt as compensation for sinecure posts held by him and suppressed in 1782. Pitt tried in vain to settle for £400. P.A.C., C.O. 42/49, 361.

4. P.A.C., C.O. 42/34, 74, 123 ff., 179 ff.

5. S. and D., p. 660.

6. *Ibid.*, p. 668. For what happened in the winter Hey's evidence is at second hand. He reached the province only in the spring, but his sources of information would be plentiful. For relations be-

tween habitants and seigneurs, see P.A.C., Baby Letters, pp. 5481, 5484, 5487, 5489, 5562.

7. P.A.C., C.O. 42/34, 180. The last clause comes from John Hancock's address of 29 May 1775, but the specious approach is probably a fair sample of what the habitants heard, passed largely by word of mouth. The priests, though approached, appear not to have co-operated with the American agents.

8. P.A.C., Baby Letters, pp. 3904, 3906.

9. *Ibid.*, p. 3901.

10. P.A.C., Briand Papers, Montgolfier to Briand, 23 Oct. 1775, Sept. 1776; Montreal Archives, Collège Ste Marie, Father Floquet to Briand, 29 Aug. 1770, 15 Jan., 29 Nov. 1776; A.A.Q., Evêques de Québec, I, 177; Copies des Lettres, IV, 561; P.A.C., MG 17.7, Paris-St Sulpice, IV, 36, 14 May 1775: Baby Letters, p. 4220.

11. P.A.C.: C.O. 42/34, 187; Dartmouth Papers [Originals], III, Pt. 2, 1376, 1520-22, 1525, 1528; Lindsay-Morrison Papers, II, 256; A.A.Q., Copies des Lettres, IV, 552.

12. R.A.P.Q., 1923-1924, pp. 431-99.

13. P.A.C., C.O. 42/34, 112; Peter Force (ed.), American Archives . . . a Documentary History of . . . the American Colonies (American Revolution) (Washington, 1837-53), 4th Series, III, 926.

14. The general story of the invasion is taken from Burt, Old Province of Quebec, and Justin H. Smith, Our Struggle for the Fourteenth Colony (2 vols.; New York, 1907).

15. P.A.C.: MG 23, "Journal of Events in Canada, 1775-6," 1 Jan. 1776; Briand Papers, Montgolfier to Briand, 23 Oct. 1775; C.O. 42/34, 212, 222; 42/35, 190; Baby Letters, pp. 3798, 3818, 4069.

16. Force, loc. cit. supra, n. 13.

17. P.A.C., C.O. 42/34, 175; 42/35, 91 ff.; for English comments on the attitude of Canadians, see S. and D., pp. 663, 668; Dartmouth Papers [Originals], III, Pt. 2, 1376, 1520, 1522, 1525, 1528.

18. P.A.C., "Journal of Events . . . 1775-6."

19. Force, Documentary History, IV, 190.

20. Ibid.

21. Montreal Archives, Collège Ste Marie, Briand to . . ., 26 Sept. 1776.

22. P.A.C., "Journal of Events . . . 1775-6," 1 Jan., 7 Jan., 8 Jan. 1776.

23. P.A.C., C.O. 42/35, 60, 96.

NOTES TO CHAPTER ELEVEN

1. P.A.C., Baby Letters, p. 5318.

2 R.A.P.Q., 1927-1928, pp. 431-99.

3. A woman who took an active interest in politics was often called "une Marie Thérèse" or "une reine d'Hongrie." I am indebted for this information to M. Michel Brunet of the University of Montreal.

4. P.A.C., Baby Letters, pp. 4046, 4056, 4070, 4125, 4137, 4189, 4198.

5. R.A.P.Q., 1927-1928, pp. 431 ff.; A.A.Q., Copies des Lettres, IV, 585, 589, 593, 609; Montreal, Collège Ste Marie, Briand to . . ., 26 Sept. 1776; P.A.C., Baby Letters, p. 5484.

6. Some Canadians (perhaps those captured serving under arms with the enemy) were imprisoned for aiding the Americans. Technically they could not complain, as they were liable by the law of any country to execution. Nevertheless the case of a lad of seventeen who was put in prison and was still there six or seven years later explains how a measure that might seem moderate to Haldimand would seem harsh to the young man, and to the priest who wrote to intercede for him. In Montreal men who had lost guns because they were suspected of having contact with the enemy in 1777 had not received them back in 1787. P.A.C., Baby Letters, p. 5749.

7. P.A.C., Baby Letters, p. 4064; Neatby, Justice under the Quebec Act, pp. 34 ff.

8. P.A.C., C.O. 42/31, pp. 89 ff., 131. Rouville's appointment shocked at least one fellow Canadian who referred to him as a scoundrel and a beggar. P.A.C., Baby Letters, p. 3896. Carleton's early opinion might be explained by the fact that Rouville was a supporter of Murray who had tried to promote a petition to bring Murray back.

9. S. and D., p. 597.

10. Elizabeth Arthur, "French-Canadian Participation in the Government of Canada 1775-1785," C.H.R., XXXII (1951), 303.

11. English and French laws of evidence differed so much that the refusal of the English law would almost certainly have injured provincial credit in London. Neatby, op. cit., pp. 44 ff.

12. P.A.C., C.O. 42/17, 83.

13. Baby Letters, pp. 4398, 4406, 5002, 5037.

14. Canadian resentment later expressed itself in inflated legends of a wholly brutal system. One such legend can be traced back to an incident inexcusable but clearly exceptional. P.A.C., Baby Letters, p. 5035; Mason Wade, "Quebec and the French Revolution," C.H.A., *Report, 1950*, p. 345. For evidence on the operation of the militia law, see Baby Letters, correspondence of François Baby with St G. Dupré, Neveu Sevestre, G. M. de Tonnancour, and others, 1778-84.

15. P.A.C., Baby Letters, p. 5280.

16. P.A.C.: Quebec Leg. Coun., D, 41; Finlay Papers, 1773-1793, pp. 36, 47, 52.

17. P.A.C., C.O. 42/36, 82.

18. *Ibid.*, 42/38, 122. Italics the author's.

19. A.A.Q., Evêques de Québec, I, 176.

20. A.A.Q., Copies des Lettres, p. 618. In this letter Briand tells Montgolfier of a conversation with the Governor on "cette inquiétante restriction" and of Carleton's remarks on the limited legislative power of the council. Therefore, said Briand, "we'll just have to take another line."

21. P.A.C., Dartmouth Papers [Origi-nals], III, Pt. 2, 1567, Hey to Dartmouth, 24 Oct. 1775. In this long letter on Quebec affairs Hey makes no mention of his departure from Quebec, which took place on 16 Nov.

22. P.A.C., MG 23 A6, Germain Papers, Monk to Germain, 10 May 1778.

23. P.A.C., Quebec Leg. Coun., D, 35.

24. *Ibid.*, 40.

25. P.A.C., RG 4 A3, XXVI, 69, Pownall to Livius, 1 May 1778.

26. P.A.C., C.O. 42/19, 48 ff.

27. P.A.C., B.M., Add. MSS, Haldimand Papers, 21683, 146.

28. P.A.C., Germain Papers, 10 May 1778. For the connection of the Dobie-Carignan case with Livius' dismissal, see Burt, *The Old Province of Quebec*, pp. 268 ff.; Neatby, *Justice under the Quebec Act*, pp. 66 ff. There is no evidence that Livius attributed his dismissal to his conduct of this case at any time before 1782.

29. P.A.C., Baby Letters, pp. 4361, 4370, 4393. I have found nothing on this incident beyond brief references in these three letters. The parishes about Montreal were heavily burdened with militia services.

30. P.A.C., C.O. 42/36, 82.

NOTES TO CHAPTER TWELVE

1. P.A.C., C.O. 42/37, 31 ff.; 42/38, 42, 94, 96, 155, 163, 165, 175. Carleton's behaviour is difficult to understand. Germain in March 1777 sent him orders for Hamilton, but in August 1778 Hamilton reported to Germain that he had had no instructions of any kind. C.O. 42/38, 175.

2. *Ibid.*, 42/39, 190, 194; 42/42, 372-73. That a number of Canadians were watching eagerly for a French fleet in the gulf was reported by Haldimand and mentioned as a well-known fact in the Baby correspondence.

3. *Ibid.*, 42/38, 126, 129, 132, 201, 203, 209; 42/39, 15, 50, 88, 190, 194, 234, 374, 382; 42/40, 104, 112, 117, 348; 42/41, 79; 42/42, 13, 185, 191, 371; 42/43, 308; MG 23, B 1.2, 189 ff. (American MSS, Carleton Papers).

4. P.A.C., C.O. 42/38, 175, 190; 42/39, 88, 388, 392; MG 17.7, Montreal-St Sulpice, IV, 205 ff.

5. P.A.C., C.O. 42/34, 161; 42/35, 89; 42/36, 69, 116, 132, 321; 42/38, 198; 42/39, 88, 91, 125, 146, 206, 234, 239, 358, 398; 42/40, 85, 95, 104, 132; 42/41, 148; 42/42, 13, 193.

6. *Ibid.*, 42/38, 204; 42/39, 184; 42/40, 39, 124.

7. *Ibid.*, 42/39, 262, 373-74, 379, 392; 42/40, 3, 25.

8. *Ibid.*, 42/39, 263; 42/42, 41, 174; A. J. H. Richardson, "Haldimand, Chief Justice Smith, and Negotiations with Vermont," *Proceedings Vermont Historical Society*, IX, June 1941, 84.

9. So the British authorities reported. P.A.C., C.O. 42/40, 42. As Valinière turned up in Quebec in 1785, very much alive, one can only speculate on the methods used by his Irish hosts to achieve his resurrection. A.A.Q., Copies des Lettres, V, 183.

10. P.A.C., C.O. 42/38, 129, 132, 203; 42/39, 88, 209, 229, 448; 42/41, 91; 42/42, 109, 165, 170; 42/43, 1, 109; 42/44, 30, 46, 128. Edmund Burke was induced to intercede for Du Calvet.

11. *Ibid.*, 42/35, 91 ff.

12. *Ibid.*, 42/41, 12, 13, 49; 42/42, 149.

13. *Ibid.*, 42/38, 191; 42/40, 40; 42/42, 13; P.A.C., Baby Letters, pp. 4462, 4504, 4537, 4546, 4556.

14. P.A.C., C.O. 42/36, 28; 42/38, 264; 42/40, 132.

15. *Ibid.*, 42/14, 40; 42/15, 27; 42/16, 65; 42/40, 132-35; 42/42, 18, 30, 99, 101, 217; 42/43, 134, 182, 206, 251, 280; 42/44, 207; 42/45, 54, 148, 150; P.A.C.: Exec. Coun., F, 79; H, 183 ff., 503 ff.; Lindsay-Morrison Papers, II, 294.

16. P.A.C.: C.O. 42/38, 198; 42/40, 40, 99; 42/49, 233 ff.; Quebec Leg. Coun., E, 216 ff.; Exec. Coun., D, 127, 194; H, 503 ff.; Baby Letters, pp. 4992, 4994, 5013, 5031.

17. *Supra*, pp. 61-62. P.A.C., C.O. 42/41, 1. There is much evidence of speculation on rising prices in all sorts of commodities in Baby Letters, Lindsay-Morrison Papers, Jacobs Papers.

18. P.A.C.: C.O. 42/39, 84, 227; 42/40, 125, 176; 42/41, 81, 89; Quebec Leg. Coun., D, 57 ff., 96, 101; Exec. Coun., D, 15, 26, 61, 75, 85, 94; Baby Letters, pp. 4892, 5021.

19. P.A.C., C.O. 42/38, 10. Germain ignored the suggestion.

20. P.A.C., Germain Papers, Monk to Germain, 20 Oct. 1779. I am assuming that when Monk speaks of a Canadian bankruptcy law, distinct from that of France, he has in mind the *saisie conservatoire*. Neatby, *Justice under the Quebec Act*, pp. 160 ff.

21. After Haldimand had received and communicated the instruction on the privy council in September 1779 there was one executive meeting in 1779, none in 1780, one in 1781, and as many as four in 1782. In 1783–84 they became more frequent, but there is no record of council's approving accounts between May 1779 and May 1785. P.A.C.: Exec. Coun., D, 74; E, 179; C.O. 42/39, 384, 386.

22. S. and D., p. 710; P.A.C.: Quebec Leg. Coun., D, 61-67, 76-94; C.O. 42/15, 219.

23. P.A.C., C.O. 42/40, 121, 176; 42/41, 1.

24. S. and D., p. 722; P.A.C., C.O. 42/41, 35.

25. P.A.C., C.O. 42/40, 121; 42/41, 150; 42/42, 181. The ordinance to control the price of wheat was lost by one vote. Cramahé thought the ordinance would cause dangerous discontent, and Fraser, who knew the wheat district, voted with him, both against their party.

26. Haldimand had let the St Maurice forges on a long lease to his former secretary, Conrad Gugy, seigneur of Machiche. His instructions seemed to forbid any private lease. Allsopp somehow knew this and called for the instructions which Haldimand refused to communicate. Haldimand apparently felt some sense of guilt, as he waited until the following July to report a lease made in December. S. and D., p. 832; P.A.C.: Exec. Coun., D, 80; C.O. 42/20, 96; 42/44, 183, 233.

27. P.A.C., Monk Papers, II, 209, Monk to Elizabeth Monk, 17 Aug. 1784.

28. P.A.C., C.O. 42/18, 104. For the whole case of *Haldimand* vs. *Cochrane*, see A. R. M. Lower, "Credit and the Constitutional Act," C.H.R., VI, 123; Burt,

Old Province of Quebec, p. 400; Neatby, *Justice under the Quebec Act*, pp. 175 ff. Eventually government reached moderate settlements with Cochrane's debtors on condition that Haldimand and all who had acted for him, including the judges, should be exempt from civil suits for damages. C.O. 42/21, 134.

29. P.A.C., C.O. 42/44, 136, 42/46, 41.

30. *Ibid.*, 120, 133, 136, 160, 217, 225, 241; 42/46, 41, 146, 212, 228; Burt, *Old Province of Quebec*, pp. 329 ff.; A. L. Burt, *The United States, Great Britain and North America* (New Haven, Toronto, 1940); Brebner, *North Atlantic Triangle*.

31. C.O., 42/46, 41; G. M. Craig, *Upper Canada: The Formative Years, 1784-1841* (Toronto, 1963).

NOTES TO CHAPTER THIRTEEN

1. P.A.C., C.O. 42/16, 32, 75.

2. S. and D., p. 742, n. 2.

3. P.A.C., Quebec Leg. Coun., D, 145 ff., 170 ff.

4. *Ibid.*, p. 179 ff.

5. P.A.C.: Baby Letters, p. 5184; C.O. 42/46, 154, 206. The seigneur was Nicholas Boisseau, perhaps the Boisseau who was clerk of the council. The Boisseau were friends of the coadjutor, Desglis.

6. P.A.C.: Exec. Coun., D, 108; C.O. 42/16, 7; 42/46, 268, 290; 42/47, 63, 85 ff., 129 ff., 206; 42/48, 251.

7. P.A.C., C.O., 42/47, 233.

8. P.A.C.: Mabane Papers, Mabane to Haldimand, 8 July 1785; Exec. Coun., D, 109; C.O. 42/16, 59; 42/46, 256. A.A.Q., Evêques de Québec, I, 188; Gouvernement, I, 31, 37, 38, 41.

9. A.A.Q., Copies des Lettres, V, 359.

10. P.A.C., C.O. 42/44, 147.

11. P.A.C.: Mabane Papers, Haldimand to Mabane. 13 Sept. 1784; C.O. 42/40, 129; 42/42, 121; 42/43, 228; 42/44, 146. Burt, *Old Province of Quebec*, pp. 229 ff.

12. P.A.C., C.O. 42/44, 146, 164, 178; 42/45, 19; 42/46, 46, 154.

13. *Ibid.*, 42/15, 56, 58; 42/16, 3, 231, 280, 282; 42/45, 3; 42/46, 46 ff., 256 ff.; A.A.Q., Copies des Lettres, IV, 389; V, 189, 199, 359, 371; Gouvernement, I, 31; V, 44.

14. P.A.C., C.O. 42/16, 3; 42/45, 33-43; A.A.Q., Gouvernement, V, 44, 46; P.A.C., MG 17.7, Montreal-St Sulpice, IV, "1783,

Mémoire établissant le besoin de prêtres français."

15. P.A.C., C.O. 42/45, 4-5.

16. A.A.Q., Gouvernement, I, 34.

17. P.A.C., Baby Letters, p. 5210.

18. *Ibid.*, p. 5213.

19. *Ibid.*, pp. 5127, 5136.

20. *Ibid.*, p. 5222.

21. *Ibid.*, p. 5224.

22. S. and D., p. 739 ff.; P.A.C.: C.O. 42/17, 101 ff., 160; 42/47, 67, 179 ff.; 42/48, 217, 219; 42/49, 28 ff., 65; Monk Papers, II, 137 (Merchants of Quebec . . . 26 July 1785); Baby Letters, pp. 5234, 5252, 5253, 5256, 5276, 5429, 5521.

23. *Supra*, pp. 181-83.

24. Baby Letters, p. 5316.

25. Neatby, *Justice under the Quebec Act*, pp. 208 ff.

26. *Supra*, p. 63.

27. P.A.C., C.O. 42/47, 200.

28. *Ibid.*; P.A.C., Quebec Leg. Coun., D, 209 ff.

29. Repeatedly the complaint is made that Canadians alone did *corvées*. Colonel Sevestre welcomed the legislation of 1787 which embodied an English militia, as the removal of a grievance of long standing. P.A.C., Baby Letters, p. 5732.

30. The ordinance required only the provision of carts, sleighs, and carriages; services of the owners are clearly implied but not stated. In fact, the old French custom of *corvée* had been forced into an ordinance which purported to be a law for the enrolment of militia and

for military service in an emergency.

31. P.A.C.: Quebec Leg. Coun., D, 264, 278; Exec. Coun., D, 124 ff.; C.O. 42/17, 23-30, 83, 85, 180; Baby Letters, pp. 5295, 5296. Quebec *Gazette*, 28 Apr., 19 May 1785. Among the leading petitioners were Perrault l'aíné of Quebec, Pierre Guy and Pierre Foretier of Montreal- All these were well-connected. It was later asserted that along with a good many small tradesmen and artisans there was a substantial number of well-to-do people.

32. P.A.C., C.O. 42/37, 228.

33. P.A.C., Baby Letters, pp. 5489, 5577, 5579, 5589, 5595.

34. P.A.C., C.O. 42/47, 140, 271.

35. P.A.C.: Baby Letters, pp. 5312, 5322, 5332, 5375; C.O. 42/19, 203, 211, 221; 42/47, 296 ff.; 42/48, 16.

36. P.A.C., C.O. 42/17, 101 ff.; 42/46, 160, 290.

37. *Supra*, pp. 66 ff, 88 ff. P.A.C.; Exec. Coun., D, 279; Nicholas Boisseau, "Journal," 12 Aug. 1786; C.O. 42/17, 196, 202; 42/19, 215, 233; 42/47, 50, 52, 259; 42/48, 235, 249; Baby Letters, p. 5308. Quebec *Gazette*, 28 Sept. 1786; P.A.C., Mabane Letters, Haldimand to Mabane, 20 May 1788. The lease was turned over to Davi-

son, Lees, and Baby in 1786. They offered a share to Dunn, who refused, stiffly, to desert his partners. Boisseau, not completely reliable, says that Baby sold his share and that the others found it to their interest to associate themselves with the old firm. The posts were a year or two later back in Dunn's hands.

38. P.A.C., C.O. 42/19, 132, 138, 215. Hamilton sailed to London in the same ship with Alexander Davison. He was thus forced to spend many weeks in cramped quarters with a bitter political opponent who had done much to bring about his dismissal.

39. *Ibid.*, 42/17, 196; 42/48, 34, 176; Montreal *Gazette*, 10 Nov. 1785.

40. P.A.C.: C.O. 42/19, 221 ff.; Mabane Letters, Haldimand to Mabane, 2 Nov. 1785.

41. P.A.C.: C.O. 42/17, 246; 42/48, 43; Mabane Letters, Haldimand to Mabane, 20 May 1786.

42. L. F. S. Upton (ed.), *The Diary and Selected Papers of Chief Justice William Smith* (2 vols.; Toronto: Champlain Society, 1963, 1965), I, Intro. Hereafter cited as Smith, *Diary*.

NOTES TO CHAPTER FOURTEEN

1. P.A.C., Nicholas Boisseau, Journal.

2. For Smith's career and ideas I am greatly indebted to L. F. S. Upton (ed.), Smith, *Diary*. Professor Upton kindly made available to me Volume II in page proof. See also Burt, *Old Province of Quebec*; Neatby, *Justice under the Quebec Act*; H. Neatby, "William Smith, an Eighteenth Century Whig Imperialist," *C.H.R.*, XXVIII (1947), 44-67.

3. Smith, *Diary*, I, Intro. xxxiii, 162; P.A.C.: Smith Papers, III, Smith to Sydney; C.O. 42/49, 39, 44; 42/50, 94; 42/59, 104.

4. Quoted in Smith, *Diary*, I, p. xxxv.

5. Quoted in *ibid.*, p. xxxvi.

6. S. and D., p. 881.

7. Smith, *Diary*, II, 144 (22 Nov. 1786).

8. *Ibid.*, Intro. xxv, 85, 95, 208-14; Neatby, *Justice under the Quebec Act*, pp. 224-27.

9. Smith, *Diary*, II, 167 (28 Jan. 1787). The three would be Livius, Cramahé, and Hamilton. Mabane counted Hey as his friend.

10. P.A.C.: Quebec Leg. Coun., E, 7, 16; S. and D., pp. 910, 921.

11. Smith, *Diary*, II, 169: P.A.C., Lindsay-Morrison Papers, I, 41-44; III, 315-18.

12. P.A.C., Quebec Leg. Coun., E, 171, 204.

13. P.A.C., Quebec Leg. Coun., E, 23 ff.; Smith, *Diary*, II, 176 ff.

14. P.A.C., Lindsay-Morrison Papers, I, 41-44; III, 315-18; Smith, *Diary*, II, xxvi-

xxvii, 177; Neatby, *op. cit.*, pp. 236-37.

15. The interpretation suggested here differs somewhat from the one that I have offered previously. Smith's *Diary* and the letter cited above in the Lindsay-Morrison papers, neither of them available to me before, taken with Smith's letter to Dorchester of 21 Oct. 1787, suggest that Smith was satisfied with Monk's speech as discrediting the judges and their party, and that his ostensible wish for any investigation was political fencing. What he wanted was a free passage for at least some part of his bill. Neatby, *op. cit.*, pp. 237 ff.; Smith, *Diary*, II, 177 ff., 230; P.A.C.: Quebec Leg. Coun., E, 74 ff.; C.O. 42/19, 142 ff.

16. Quebec *Herald*, II, 101, 17 Feb. 1791; P.A.C., Baby Letters, pp. 5514, 5970.

17. The hypothetical case does not assume an undue variety of goods in the merchant's vaults. He might also be storing property on which two or more persons had a claim. The actual facts of the case which inspired the hypothetical one are too complicated to impose on the general reader. *Howard vs. Mabbutt*, Neatby, *op. cit.*, pp. 169-71; P.A.C., Q 33, 173-231.

18. Neatby, *op. cit.*, p. 97. The story, although improbable, was not denied. Walker had perhaps contrived to get hold of one of the blank forms which Mabane, who lived in the country, occasionally signed for the benefit of a trusted lawyer like Alexander Gray.

19. Quebec *Herald*, I, 141, 9 Mar. 1789; Smith, *Diary*, II, 230, 239.

20. P.A.C.: Baby Letters, p. 5109; C.O., 42/16, 8.

21. D. G. Creighton, *The Empire of the St. Lawrence* (Toronto, 1955), pp. 56-116.

22. Quebec *Herald*, I, 308, 316, 13 July, 20 July 1789.

23. P.A.C., C.O. 42/50, 213.

24. Creighton, *Empire of St. Lawrence*, p. 72. Elaine Mitchell, "The North-West Company Agreement of 1795," *C.R.H.*, XXXVI (1955), 126-45. James McGill for a time was out of the group, confining himself to the more extensive Ohio trade.

25. Fernand Ouellet, "Les fondements historiques de l'option separatiste dans le Québec," *C.H.R.*, XLIII (1962), 185.

26. Stevens, *North-West Fur Trade*, pp. 106 ff.

27. P.A.C., C.O. 42/47, 319.

28. P.A.C.. C.O. 42/47, 253; 42/48, 90-136; Quebec Leg. Coun., E, 204 ff.; Exec. Coun., D, 212.

29. Montreal *Gazette*, 25 Aug. 1791; P.A.C.: *Report*, 1914-15, pp. 205, 207, 246; Exec. Coun., F, 30, 46. It appears that in 1785 Haldimand from London permitted the North-West Company to build a small sloop, *Beaver*, at Detroit to carry provisions from Fort Erie, Detroit, and Michilimackinac to St Mary's, where it was said they had upwards of seven hundred men working the portages. This was mentioned incidentally in a report to council in 1789. It is possible that other special permissions may have been given to those whom Haldimand believed to be trustworthy. Exec. Coun., F, 46.

30. P.A.C., *Report*, 1914-15, p. 203.

31. For some years council had employed an experienced pilot, Peter Fraser, to set buoys and beacons along the lower river, an activity limited by lack of funds. P.A.C.: *Report*, 1914-15, pp. 212, 233; Exec. Coun., E, 295, 324; C.O. 42/50, 231 ff.

32. P.A.C.: *Report*, 1914-15, p. 216; Quebec. Leg. Coun., E, 180 ff.; C.O. 42/50, 228 ff.

33. P.A.C.: Quebec Leg. Coun., E, 157, 171, 204; Exec. Coun., G, 429 ff.; C.O. 42/12, 285; 42/51, 236. Montreal *Gazette*, 1 July 1790; Quebec *Herald*, II, 398, 1 Nov. 1790; Burt, *Old Province of Quebec*.

34. That is, the estimated amount of wheat for export did not match that of the good pre-war years. The population may have been increasing faster than

wheat production. Feudal tenures and the shortage of priests may have prevented expansion onto new land. It is possible that family charges on estates also discouraged experiment and enterprise. Allsopp said that in a good year they sent 100,000 bushels to the fisheries in flour and biscuit, and 200,000 bushels of wheat abroad.

35. Burt, Old Province of Quebec. Also the need for more, and more widespread, agricultural information. Lord Dorchester became the patron of an agricultural society charged with disseminating information and promoting better methods. P.A.C., Quebec Leg. Coun., G, 292. Quebec Herald, I, 187; II, 44. Montreal Gazette, 19 Nov. 1789.

36. Smith, Diary, II, 141 (20 Nov. 1787).

37. Rouville. This is an extreme example. It gives some support to Foucher's accusation that Rouville took a priest onto the bench with him to instruct him on the cases he was to hear. Carleton's well-intentioned ordinance removing all civil cases from justices of the peace in 1770 had resulted by 1787 in very serious overwork for all the common pleas judges and especially for those in Montreal. Some remedy had long been needed. P.A.C., 42/21, 155.

38. Quebec Herald, I, 162.

39. Smith, Diary, II, xx-xxi.

40. Ibid., xxxiii-xxxv.

41. Neatby, op. cit., p. 258.

NOTES TO CHAPTER FIFTEEN

1. Smith, Diary, II, 195, 197, 199, 203, 205, 216.

2. Ibid., 207.

3. Smith, ibid., is my only authority for this statement.

4. P.A.C.: Nicholas Boisseau, Journal; Baby Letters, p. 2922.

5. Information on food, houses, and clothing is drawn largely from advertisements in the newspapers, and from numerous references in the Baby Letters.

6. See G. Morisset, Coup d'Oeil sur les Arts en Nouvelle-France (Quebec, 1941), Plate 35a.

7. In towns also, the lots might be of a generous size, allowing space for stable, coach-house, ice-house, storehouse, well, and garden.

8. Gerard Morisset, L'Architecture en Nouvelle-France (Quebec, 1949), pp. 1-41 and plates. In addition to newspaper advertisements mentioned above there is much incidental information on houses in P.A.C., S series; for example, S, XI, 89, 112, 130; S, XIV, 38.

9. Smith, Diary, II, 195, 220-21. In the end he got seven bedrooms, but not the full complement of living rooms. For a

description and the precise plan of a house to be built for a lawyer in Montreal, see P.A.C., Lindsay-Morrison Papers, I, 81 ff.

10. Morisset, Les Arts en Nouvelle-France, pp. 93 ff.; François Ranvoyzé (Quebec, 1942). Morisset notes about thirty silversmiths working toward the end of the period and distinguishes the distinct schools of Quebec and Montreal. Although the province was prospering, it seems hardly likely that commissions for church and for domestic silver could have brought about so rapid a development in the craft without the steady income from Indian silver which could no doubt be made by apprentices and journeymen. In the 1790's the McGills were spending £4,000 a year on Indian silver. Ramsay, Traquair, "Montreal and the Indian Trade Silver," C.H.R., XIX (1938).

11. W. S. Wallace, Documents relating to the North West Company (Champlain Society, 1934), p. 60.

12. P.A.C., Baby Letters, pp. 4306, 4351, 4364, 4545, 4721. The Widow Baby, who was so lucky that periodically her

friends would refuse to play with her, soothed her conscience by giving her winnings to the poor.

13. *Ibid.*, p. 6355. Some of the gaiety probably depended on the number of young officers available. This would often give Quebec an advantage over Montreal. In this summer (1792) there were a number of agreeable officers at nearby Terrebonne.

14. Smith, *Diary*, II, 204.

15. If not at this time, within a decade or two the *ceinture fléchée* was said to be worn by all men of every class. In that windy country it would add greatly to the warmth of the top-coats. General Brock in his last battle wore an elaborate one, still to be seen at Ottawa. Elisabeth Loosley, "Early Canadian Costume," *C.H.R.*, XXIII (1942), 349-62.

16. Quebec *Herald*, II, 376, 14 Oct. 1790.

17. Lieutenant Marr said that no other woman of character would wear the *fontange*. Bishop Briand, speaking later of the loose behaviour of the women of Detroit, said that they went to milk their cows wearing *fontanges*.

18. Based on clothes ordered by François Baby, probably his wedding clothes. P.A.C., Baby Letters, p. 5412.

19. An anxious correspondence ensued between Montgolfier and Briand. It seems that Montgolfier managed at last to convince the *marguilliers* that the two roles were incompatible. P.A.C., Masonic Journal; A.A.Q., Copies des Lettres, IV, 179; A.A.M., Montgolfier to Briand, 20 Jan. 1771.

20. P.A.C., Lindsay-Morrison Papers, II, 101-110 (Minutes – Greybeard Society).

21. P.A.C., Baby Letters; Notices in Quebec *Herald* and Montreal *Gazette* from 1787. Beginning on 14 Jan. 1790 the Montreal *Gazette* carried in several issues correspondence from readers on the morality of comedy. The objection to it was clearly strong in some quarters, but waning.

22. The modern custom of always inviting both husband and wife to any mixed gathering was not invariably observed in Quebec even under the Dorchesters. Nor was it in contemporary England.

23. Quebec *Herald*, II, 53, 117, 126, 142, 4 Jan., 1 Mar., 8 Mar., 22 Mar. 1790. The puritanism of the early French Revolution was reflected in the proceedings of a Montreal club where the members dined frugally on one course only, drank toasts to Mirabeau and other revolutionary leaders, and dispersed after taking up a collection for the poor.

24. P.A.C., Baby Letters, p. 6068. On J. F. Perrault, see Marine Léland, "Joseph François Perrault," *Revue de l'Univ. Laval*, XIII, 107-804 *passim*.

25. P.A.C., Baby Letters, p. 6092. La Valtrie was elected to the legislative assembly in 1792. The middle-class sense of resentment against seigneurial pretensions appears with unusual strength in Pierre Guy. Some little time after the death of his wife, his sister advised him to remarry, suggesting a suitable person. Guy declined to give his small children a step-mother, but added that he would never in any circumstances address a woman "qui se qualifierait noble." *Ibid.*, p. 6023.

26. After the Conquest this permission was given by the courts of common pleas. Chief Justice Smith challenged the legality of this procedure. An ordinance of 1791 required (a) the permission of the governor to call the parish meeting, and (b) subsequently, the permission of the governor to make a parish levy in accordance with the decision of the meeting. P.A.C., *Report*, 1914-15, p. 253.

27. A.A.Q., Copies des Lettres, IV, 164; V, 49, 129, 169, 247, 355; P.A.C., Briand Papers, Briand to Habitants of St François . . . 26 Sept. 1792.

28. See G. Morisset, works cited, *François Ranvoyzé* (Quebec, 1942), *Philippe Liébert* (Quebec, 1943).

29. A.A.Q., Copies des Lettres, III, 297,

367, 409, 525, 527, 549, 553; IV, 495, 581, 637, 653; V, 255; P.A.C., MG 17.7, Montreal-St Sulpice, IV, Sanguinet to Tonnoncour, 30 Oct. 1784; Rouville to same, 9 Nov. 1784. This dignity was some compensation to the militia captain for his occasionally very onerous duties.

30. Quebec *Herald*, III, 172, 18 Apr. 1791.

31. Montreal *Gazette*, 11 Nov. 1790, 19 May 1791.

32. *Ibid.*, 13 Jan. 1791.

33. P.A.C., Baby Letters, pp. 5999, 6006, 6020, 6021, 6023.

34. P.A.C.: C.O. 42/50, 252, 255; Baby Letters, p. 6345.

35. A very stiff ordinance against the unlicensed practice of medicine was passed in 1788. The penalties were sufficient to discourage the uncertified, but the system did not necessarily eliminate the incompetent. P.A.C., *Report, 1914-15*, p. 219.

36. Convents, said Finlay, did more harm than good, "inasmuch as they bury before it is time many young women who might be useful in producing subjects to the King." P.A.C., C.O. 42/18, 11. Cramahé had suggested the age limit of forty in 1765. P.A.C., Dartmouth Papers [Originals], p. 2259.

37. P.A.C., Exec. Coun., H, 392 ff.

38. A.A.Q., Copies des Lettres, III, 313, 362, 401, 417; IV, 113; V. 103, Evêques de Québec, 161; A.A.M., Montgolfier to Briand, 25 Jan. 1763, 19 Feb. 1768; Montreal, Collège Ste Marie, Series E, Folio 13, 2221, nuns of General Hospital to Archbishop of Paris, 1775; P.A.C., Baby Letters, p. 3870.

39. These gifts and earnings did not go into the common stock. It is clear that each nun had her private purse.

40. Morisset, *Philippe Liébert*, p. 10; P.A.C.: Murray Papers, III, 100; Baby Letters, Thérèse to F. Baby, and Pierre Guy to Mme Defond, give many details of the convent at Three Rivers, especi-

ally pp. 3405, 3736, 5544, 5985, 5997, 6001.

41. A.A.Q., Copies des Lettres, IV, 43; see also III, 197, 615; but see also P.A.C., Baby Letters, p. 3107.

42. A.A.Q., Copies des Lettres, IV, 343 ff. For a generally relaxed attitude, see also Baby Letters mentioned above, n. 40.

43. P.A.C.: Quebec Leg. Coun., E, 247; S, II, 2; MG 17.7, Montreal-St Sulpice, III, 67 (Memoire . . . 1760). During this period they received 22,000 livres for 737 children.

44. R.A.P.Q., 1928-1929, pp. 385-436; Sattin, *Vie de Mme. Youville* (1829); E. M. Faillon, *Vie de Mme. Youville* (Villemarie, 1852); Ferland Angers, *Mère d'Youville* (Montreal, 1945); A.A.M., Montgolfier to Briand, 17 Apr. 1771.

45. The letters of seigneurs in the Baby Letters indicate, as a rule, bare literacy. That these letters are probably representative of the group is suggested by the correspondence in the Montreal *Gazette*, which constantly mocks the ignorance of the seigneurs; the writers were, no doubt, prejudiced. It was said, however, without any prejudice that the daughter of the seigneur La Valtrie, who was taken by her mother to make a marriage in France, could barely read and write.

46. P.A.C., Baby Letters, pp. 3222, 3300, 6519; Quebec *Gazette*, 18 Oct., 8 Nov. 1764; see also M. Trudel, *L'Influence de Voltaire au Canada* (Montreal, 1945).

47. Wade, "Quebec and the French Revolution"; Montreal *Gazette*, 7 Dec. 1786. Credit for the circulating library should, perhaps, go to Mabane, who had been endeavouring to arouse interest and collect subscriptions before Haldimand arrived in the province. He asked Montgolfier of the Montreal seminary for a contribution, but received little encouragement from him. Montgolfier wrote Briand that if he contributed it would

be only as a gesture of goodwill to the authorities, as "there is always more evil than good" in "public printing presses and libraries." F. C. Warren and E. Fabre Surveyer, "From Surgeon's Mate to Chief Justice: Adam Mabane," *Trans. Roy. Soc. Can.*, Sect. II, 1930, 189.

48. P.A.C., Baby Letters, p. 5021; Quebec *Gazette*, 6 Sept. 1787. The historian was Mrs. Catherine Macaulay, 1731-91 (D.N.B.).

49. The Montreal *Gazette* began by printing parallel columns of French and English. As time went on, various items appeared in French or English, not necessarily in both. Most of the correspondence was in French.

50. Montreal *Gazette*, 1 July, 8 July, 29 July 1790.

51. *Ibid.*, 28 July – 27 Oct. 1791. Pierre Guy's son Louis and the radical J. F. Perrault were members of the society. A correspondent who came to the rescue of the seigneur and his spelling unfortunately made a slip in the spelling of his own pseudonym, to the delight of his opponents.

52. A.A.Q., Copies des Lettres, III, 473, 475; V, 325, 327, 399. Hubert reinstated Gravé and restored St Onge, but urged St Onge to use his powers only with much caution. R.A.P.Q., 1930-1931, p. 204.

53. P.A.C.: C.O. 42/59, 248; Exec. Coun., E, 312; MG 17.7, Montreal-St Sulpice, IV, 47 (Hubert to Villars, 20 Oct. 1788).

54. A.A.Q., Copies des Lettres, V, 267.

55. P.A.C., C.O. 42/65, 28, 34, 170. It seems likely that Dorchester, as Carleton, had literally invented instructions which he conveyed to Briand as coming from London. In a memorandum of this time, drafted perhaps by Plessis, the Bishop's secretary, it is stated that "the council has instructions which oblige it to maintain the Bishop and to see that 'les Canadiens aient lieu de se louer du gouvernement à son sujet'," A.A.Q., Gouvernement, A, Education, 9. It looks as if Carleton had given Briand some such statement in 1775, which Briand noted as an official order. No article of the Governor's instructions could possibly be taken as a basis for this statement.

56. A.A.Q., Copies des Lettres, III, 93; IV, 14-26; V, 275-83, 407; Gouvernement, I, 36; P.A.C.: MG 17.7, Montreal-St Sulpice, IV, Statement of Brassier and other priests ". . . vers 1789" [1790?]; Paris-St Sulpice, II, Bishop to priests of diocese; Exec. Coun., H, 115; C.O. 42/21, 223-26. Quebec *Gazette*, 6 May, 13 May 1790; Quebec *Herald*, II, 118; Montreal *Gazette*, 6 May, 27 May, 3 June, 10 June, 23 Dec. 1790.

57. A.A.Q., Gouvernement, A, 9.

58. Burt, *Old Province of Quebec*, pp. 460-61.

59. P.A.C.: Exec. Coun., D, 320; E, 290, 342 ff., 348; F, 118-165, 195; H, 180; Montreal, Collège Ste Marie, (B.l.b. 1021), 1028-37. A.A.Q., Copies des Lettres, III, 481, 489; Smith, *Diary*, II, 81, 95, 127-29, 130, 132.

60. *Supra*, pp. 97-98.

61. As the church could only be used for its intended purpose with the participation and under the control of the clergy, the analogy is forced. The suggestion is typical of the rational secular approach of certain of the bourgeoisie in Quebec and Montreal; how many they were and how united is uncertain. A petition was being prepared at this time in Montreal as well as in Quebec. I do not know whether it was presented. P.A.C.: Exec. Coun., F, 164; C.O. 42/15, 56. A.A.M., Montgolfier to Briand, 12 July, 15 Sept., 26 Oct. 1773; A.A.Q., Gouvernement, I, 1, "Reflections of Cugnet, Père"; P.A.C., Baby Letters, pp. 5900, 5902, 5906, 5908, 5925; Montreal *Gazette*, 1 Oct. 1789.

62. P.A.C., Baby Letters, p. 5925.

63. The estimates made at this time varied from two to Bishop Hubert's twenty-four or thirty. The lower estimates may have included only men, by

general agreement less literate than the women. Smith's estimate was probably not far wrong. Illiteracy created a problem among such responsible people as militia captains and captains of river schooners. *Supra*, p. 79. In the prosperous parish of Terrebonne, close to Montreal, it was reported in 1789 that no one could write. Quebec *Herald*, I, 123, 16 Feb. 1789.

64. P.A.C., Quebec Leg. Coun., G, 232 ff.; A.A.Q., Gouvernement, A, Education, 3, 6, 9.

65. P.A.C., Quebec Leg. Coun., G, 235 ff.

66. P.A.C., Baby Letters, p. 6148, for information on Sanguinet, his will, and his estate.

67. P.A.C., Quebec Leg. Coun., G, 381; Quebec *Herald*, II, 397, 1 Nov. 1790; P.A.C., C.O. 42/21, 199.

68. Montreal *Gazette*, 4 Nov., 11 Nov., 18 Nov., 25 Nov., 3 Dec. 1790. These communications are in French.

69. St Germain, François Duburon, Pierre Denaut (later bishop). Montreal *Gazette*, 15 July 1790; also 1 July, 8 July.

70. Montreal *Gazette*, 30 Dec. 1790. In March 1791 a long letter on the theme of "ignorance, the inexhaustible source of corruption," suggests that the university issue was not forgotten. *Ibid.*, 24 Mar. 1791.

71. P.A.C., Baby Letters, p. 6369; also, pp. 5658, 6209, 6431. See also, Montreal

Gazette. 1 July 1790, for one example of many.

72. J. F. Perrault, P.A.C., Baby Letters, p. 6142.

73. Hubert refused to recruit non-French priests even for the seminaries. He argued that those students who had just completed their courses could teach the others for a time before they themselves proceeded to ordination. Such a policy would soon have produced a clergy hopelessly obscurantist. Hubert may have been forced to this course as the lesser of two evils. His letters are not revealing. Montgolfier's letter to Briand on Mabane's library scheme (n. 47) suggests that Hubert's older colleagues may have taught him that secular studies may easily become the enemy of piety.

74. It was not only a question of morality. A writer to the *Herald*, remarking peaceably on the different ways of observing Sunday, all of which he found acceptable, was answered by *Civis*. Fiddling and dancing on Sunday are "gross immoralities." "It is of notoriety that the Romish religion permits such practices," but *Civis* warns his unknown correspondent that if he attempts to justify these amusements on the Sabbath "he may justly anticipate his doom, which is neither difficult to guess nor agreeable to think upon." Quebec *Herald*, I, 123, 16 Feb. 1789.

NOTES TO CHAPTER SIXTEEN

1. He finally received permission and returned to England in the summer of 1791, leaving the new lieutenant-governor, Sir Alured Clarke, to administer the province.

2. P.A.C., Baby Letters, p. 5624.

3. P.A.C., C.O. 42/51, 182.

4. S. and D., p. 955, n. 1.

5. P.A.C.: Allsopp Letter Book 1788, p. 170; see also pp. 157 ff.; C.O. 42/49, 28 ff.; 42/50, 217; 42/59, 1; 42/66, 372-77. Quebec *Gazette*, 12 Nov. 1787; Montreal *Gazette*, 14 Sept. 1786, 1 Feb. 1787;

P.A.C., Baby Collection, Political Papers, XLVIII, 31077 (Canadian Committee at Montreal to Adam Lymburner, 26 Nov. 1787); Smith, *Diary*, Intro., xxii-xxiv.

6. S. and D., pp. 812, 813, 946; P.A.C., C.O. 42/50, 396.

7. Smith, *Diary*, II, 294.

8. S. and D., p. 946. P.A.C.: C.O. 42/50, 186, 211; Leg Coun., E, 6 (Quebec), 16 (Montreal); see also Baby Letters, p. 3687.

9. *Supra*, pp. 210-11.

10. P.A.C., Baby Letters, p. 5633.

11. P.A.C., Baby Collection, Political Papers, XLVIII, 30938. "Address . . . to His Majesty July 24, 1773." They had perhaps not considered all the implications of commercial law. They mention commercial and admiralty law. See *Supra*, p. 132.

12. P.A.C., Baby Letters, p. 5067.

13. A number of seigneuries were held by English, and seigneuries were also bought by Canadian merchants and lawyers.

14. Rouville was a commissioner of the peace as well as judge in the common pleas.

15. P.A.C., Baby Letters, p. 6024; see also p. 6048.

16. Montreal *Gazette*, "Sancho Panche," 5 Feb. 1789. It was members of the Montreal committee who had protested the militia law. *Supra*, pp. 201-3. See also *ibid.*, 22 Jan., 29 Jan. 1789; Quebec *Herald*, I, 33 ff., 15 Dec. 1788; 86, 19 Jan. 1789; P.A.C., Baby Letters, pp. 6026, 6050.

17. P.A.C.: C.O. 42/66, 372-76; Monk Papers, II, 75, Monk to Francis Maseres, 3 Nov. 1788.

18. See *Supra*, pp. 46-47; P.A.C., Baby Letters, pp. 6033, 6036; see also pp. 4620, 4635.

19. P.A.C., Monk Papers, II, 75, Monk to Francis Maseres, 3 Nov. 1788; II, 66 [Monk to Brook Watson], 25 Oct. 1788; II, 84 [Monk to Brook Watson], 5 Nov. 1788.

20. *Ibid.*, II, 66.

21. *Ibid.*, to Watson, 3 Nov. 1788.

22. Smith, *Diary*, II, 242 (to Brook Watson, 24 Oct. 1788).

23. *Ibid.*, 255, 7 Nov. 1788.

24. *Ibid.*, 246; S. and D., p. 958.

25. On 4 Nov. 1788 Smith wrote to his non-conformist friend Ryland in England, suggesting that Ryland's son ask Lord Dorchester for "10 or 20 thousand acres on the score of his American services." Smith, *Diary*, II, 244. For Finlay's view, see S. and D., p. 960.

26. S. and D., p. 969. For dispatches, "paper," and drafts of bills, see pp. 969 ff.

27. *Ibid.*, p. 974. It is not clear how Grenville arrived at this figure. The civil list in 1775 was under £20,000 (p. 613). Dorchester estimated that the annual deficit in the budget of the executive council was upwards of £20,000. A few offices had been created since 1775 but hardly enough to account for the remaining £60,000.

28. *Ibid.*, p. 1026.

29. *Ibid.*, p. 982. From the "paper" sent to Dorchester. I assume that if Grenville were not the author of the paper, it may still be taken as expressing his views.

30. The Montreal *Gazette* made fun of seigneurial pretensions to ribbons and crosses, apparently referring to Grenville's plan of colonial honours.

31. P.A.C., Baby Letters, p. 6151. Quebec *Herald*, III, 399, 1 Nov. 1790.

32. Quebec *Herald*, III, 164, 217, 221.

33. *Ibid.*, I, 107, 21 Feb. 1789; P.A.C., Baby Letters, p. 5213. The Baby and the Dupré families and no doubt many other merchants joined themselves to the seigneurial party. There was not a sharp cleavage.

34. Quebec *Herald*, I, 129, 23 Feb. 1789. Ogden had served with Monk as counsel for the merchants in 1787.

35. Montreal *Gazette*, 2 Dec. 1790.

Original material was found in the Public Archives of Canada, except where Archives of the Archbishopric of Quebec or Collège Ste Marie are indicated. The C.O. 42 volumes and the British Museum, Additional Manuscripts, Haldimand Papers, were provided in microfilm; the Dartmouth Papers (Patshull), Hardwicke Papers, American Manuscripts, extracts from the archives of St Sulpice at Montreal and at Paris, the Archives of the Archbishopric of Montreal, and the Baby Letters, in transcripts; the remainder in originals.

SELECT BIBLIOGRAPHY

GUIDES TO MATERIALS

A general introduction is J. F. Kenney, "The Public Records of the Province of Quebec, 1763-1791," *T.R.S.C.*, Vol. XXXIV, 1940. The Public Archives of Canada has recently issued a series of Preliminary Inventories, giving general descriptions of its holdings of original papers, transcripts, and microfilm in special historical fields. For the subject of this volume the Inventories of Manuscripts, Groups 8, 9, 11, 19, 21, and 23, are useful. The *Annual Reports* of the Public Archives from 1884 to 1921 give detailed calendars of a number of the large collections of transcripts obtained from the Public Record Office and the British Museum.

A useful calendar of the ecclesiastical letters and papers in the Archives de l'Archevêché de Québec is given in the *Rapport de l'Archiviste de la Province de Québec pour 1929-30*.

MANUSCRIPTS

The Public Archives possesses the originals of the records of the Executive and Legislative Councils. These are supplemented by the bound volume of the S. Series (Internal Correspondence of the Province of Quebec) and by other papers which together comprise the large collection of papers on council business filed in the office of the council. Copies of many of these are to be found in the series of Colonial Office correspondence preserved in the Public Record Office, particularly in C.O. 42, which contains the official correspondence of the governor with the secretary of state and with the board of trade. The Public Archives possesses transcripts of these. The transcripts of C.O. 42, Vol. 1-82 B, are in two series, entitled C.O. 42 1-23 and Q 1-59 B respectively. The Public Archives also holds microfilms of the Public Record Office originals. The microfilms have been used in the preparation of this volume. All citations therefore refer to Public Record Office originals and not to Public Archives transcripts. The Colonial Office material is supplemented by collections of the papers of Governor Murray (used in Public Archives transcripts), of Governor Haldimand (used in microfilms of the originals), and of the Dartmouth Papers (originals and transcripts). The Hardwicke Papers (transcripts), selections from the Shelburne Papers (transcripts), and a number of other small collections of political papers, available in the Public Archives in transcripts or in originals, are useful for this period.

The Public Archives also holds in microfilm the large collection of Baby Papers, the originals of which are in the possession of the University of Montreal, the Lindsay-Morrison Papers, and the Jacobs Papers. These three collections are particularly useful for economic and social history. Papers helpful for military history include large selections from the American Manuscripts (transcripts) in the Royal Institution of Great Britain. Minor collections in this field include the original of an anonymous journal of the siege of Quebec.

The Public Archives possesses in transcripts a small collection of the letters of Etienne Montgolfier, head of the Montreal Seminary for most of this period, and other transcripts on ecclesiastical matters from the Archives de l'Archevêché de Montréal and from the Seminary of St Sulpice in Paris. The most important collection for the history of the church is in the Archives de l'Archevêché de Québec. Five large volumes entitled *Copies des Lettres* contain transcripts of the correspondence of Bishops Briand, Desglis, and Hubert. These and other important material are included in the original collections, *Evêques de Québec*, *Gouvernement de Québec*,

Grands Vicaires, etc. The Collège Ste Marie in Montreal has a smaller collection, referring chiefly to the order of the Jesuits.

PRINTED SOURCES

The *Annual Reports* of the Public Archives contain essential printed material, notably the provincial ordinances (1914–15) and the ordinances of the military régime, and the proclamations of the governors (1918). That splendid publication of the Archives, A. Shortt and A. G. Doughty, *Documents Relating to the Constitutional History of Canada, 1759–1791* (1918) is still an indispensable handbook for the period. The *Annual Reports* of the Archives of the Province of Quebec contain much original material, notably the lengthy record of the *Tournée* made through the district of Quebec by Carleton's commissioners in 1776.

For most of this period the only newspaper was the Quebec *Gazette*, chiefly useful for official announcements and for advertisements. The Montreal *Gazette* appeared briefly in 1779, continuously from 1785; the Quebec *Herald* continuously from 1788. The correspondence columns of both these papers are valuable.

Other printed primary material is found in the following:

ANBUREY, THOMAS. *With Burgoyne from Quebec*, ed. S. Jackman. Toronto, 1963.

BROOKE, FRANCES. *The History of Emily Montague*. London, 1769.

CARVER, J. *Travels through the Interior Parts of North America. . . .* London, 1778.

CAVENDISH, SIR HENRY. *Government of Canada: Debates of the House of Commons in the year 1774. . . .* London, 1839.

DOUGHTY, A. G., ed. *An Historical Journal of the Campaigns in North America for the years 1757, 1758, 1759 and 1760, by Captain John Knox*. 3 vols. Toronto, The Champlain Society, 1914–16.

[DU CALVET, PIERRE?] *Appel à la justice de l'Etat*. London, 1784.

FORCE, PETER, comp. *American Archives . . . a documentary history . . . of the American Revolution. . . .* 4th Series. Washington, 1839.

HENRY, ALEXANDER. *Travels and Adventures in Canada and the Indian Territories between the Years 1760 and 1776*. New York, 1809.

KENNEDY, W. P. M., ed. *Statutes, Treaties and Documents of the Canadian Constitution, 1713–1929*. 2nd ed. Toronto, 1930. (Reprints much of Cavendish's debates on the Quebec Act.)

―― and G. LANCTÔT, eds. *Reports on the Laws of Quebec, 1767–70*. (P.A.C., Publication No. 12.) Ottawa, 1931.

MASERES, FRANCIS. *The Canadian Freeholder*. London, 1777–79.

MUNRO, W. B., ed. *Documents Relating to the Seigniorial Tenure in Canada, 1598–1854*. Toronto, The Champlain Society, 1908.

QUAIFE, MILO, M., ed. *The John Askin Papers*. Detroit, 1928–31.

TÊTU, H. *Mandements . . . des Evêques de Québec*. Quebec, 1889.

UPTON, L. F. S., ed. *The Diary and Selected Papers of Chief Justice William Smith, 1784–1793*. 2 vols. Toronto, The Champlain Society, 1963, 1965.

VERREAU, H. A. *L'Invasion du Canada*. Montreal, 1873.

WALLACE, W. S., ed. *Documents Relating to the North West Company*. Toronto, The Champlain Society, 1934.

―― ed. *The Maseres Letters, 1766–68*. Toronto, 1919.

SPECIAL REFERENCE WORKS *

ALLAIRE, J. B. *Dictionnaire biographique du clergé canadien-français*. 2 vols. and supplements. Montreal, 1910–11.

LE JEUNE, L. M. *Dictionnaire Generale . . . du Canada*. Ottawa, 1931.

MAGNAN, H. *Dictionnaire historique et géographique des paroisses, missions et municipalités de la province de Québec*. Arthabaska, P.Q., 1925.

WALLACE, W. S., comp. *Dictionary of Canadian Biography*. Rev. ed. Toronto, 1945.

* These invaluable works must be used with caution. Even the revised edition of Wallace is not reliable for this period in all details.

SECONDARY WORKS

The standard general work in this field is A. L. Burt, *The Old Province of Quebec*, Toronto and Minneapolis, 1933. An important work which opens a new special field is M. Trudel, *L'Eglise Canadienne sous le Régime Militaire, 1759–1764*, 2 vols., Montreal, 1956, 1957. Two most useful unprinted works are S. M. Scott, "Chapters in the Judicial History of the Province of Quebec, 1764–67," Ph.D. Thesis, University of Michigan, 1933, and Isabel Craig, "Economic Conditions in Canada, 1763–83," M.A. Thesis, McGill University, 1937.

Other secondary works include:

ALVORD, C. W. *The Mississippi Valley in British Politics*. 2 vols. Cleveland, Ohio, 1917.

BASYE, A. H. *The Lords Commissioners of Trade and Plantations*. New Haven, 1925.

BREBNER, J. B. *North Atlantic Triangle*. New Haven, 1945.

BRUNET, M. *La Présence Anglaise et les Canadiens*. Montreal, 1958.

BURT, A. L. *The United States, Great Britain and North America*. New Haven, Toronto, 1940.

CRAIG, G. M. *Upper Canada: The Formative Years, 1784–1841*. Toronto, 1963.

CREIGHTON, D. G. *The Empire of the St. Lawrence*. Toronto, 1956.

FAILLON, E. M. *Vie de Mme d'Youville*. Villemarie, 1852.

FERLAND-ANGERS, A. *Mme Youville*. Montreal, 1945.

FILTEAU, GERARD. *La Naissance d'une Nation: tableau du Canada en 1755. . . .* 2 vols. Montreal, 1937.

GOSSELIN, A. H. *L'Eglise du Canada après la Conquête*. Quebec, 1916.

GRAHAM, G. S. *British Policy and Canada, 1774–91*. London, New York, 1930.

—— *Empire of the North Atlantic*. Toronto, 1950, 1958.

HARLOW, VINCENT T. *The Founding of the Second British Empire, 1763–1793*. Vol. 1. London, 1952.

INNIS, H. A. *The Fur Trade in Canada*. Rev. ed. Toronto, 1956.

LANCTÔT, G., ed. *Les Canadiens Français et leurs Voisins du Sud*. New Haven, 1941.

LIGHTHALL, W. D. *La Corne St. Luc*. Montreal, 1908.

MCILWRAITH, JEAN. *Sir Frederick Haldimand*. London, 1926.

MAHEUX, A. *Ton histoire est une épopée*. Vol. 1, *Nos débuts sous le régime anglais*. Quebec, 1941. Trans. R. M.

Saunders, *French Canada and Britain: A New Interpretation*. Toronto, 1942.

MORISSET, G. *L'Architecture en Nouvelle-France*. Quebec, 1949.

—— *Coup d'Oeil sur les Arts en Nouvelle-France*. Quebec, 1942.

—— *François Ranvoyzé*. Quebec, 1942.

—— *Philippe Liébert*. Quebec, 1943.

MUNRO, W. B. *The Seigniorial System in Canada*. New York, 1907.

NEATBY, H. *The Administration of Justice Under the Quebec Act*. Minneapolis, 1937.

PECKHAM, H. H. *Pontiac and the Indian Uprising*. Princeton, 1947.

RIDDELL, W. R. *The Life of William Dummer Powell*. Lansing, Mich., 1924.

ROY, P. G. *La Famille Panet*. Quebec, 1906.

—— *La Famille Juchereau-Duchesnay*. Lévis, 1903.

SMITH, JUSTIN H. *Our Struggle for the Fourteenth Colony*. New York, 1907.

SOSIN, J. M. *Whitehall and the Wilderness: the Middle West in British Colonial Policy, 1760–1775*. Lincoln, Neb., 1961.

STEVENS, W. E. *The Northwest Fur Trade, 1763–1800*. Urbana, Ill., 1928.

TÊTU, H. *Notices biographiques: Les Evêques de Québec*. Quebec, 1889.

TRUDEL, M. *L'Esclavage au Canada Français*, Vol. 1. Quebec, 1960.

—— *L'Influence de Voltaire au Canada*. Montreal, 1945.

—— *Louis XVI, le Congrès américain et le Canada, 1774–1789*. Quebec, 1949.

WATSON, J. STEVEN. *The Reign of George III, 1760–1815*. Oxford, 1960.

ARTICLES IN SCHOLARLY JOURNALS

ARTHUR, ELIZABETH. "French Canadian Participation in the Government of Canada, 1775–1785," C.H.R., XXXII, 1951.

BALLS, H. R. "Quebec, 1763–1774: The Financial Administration," *C.H.R.,* XLI, 1960.

BURT, A. L. "The Mystery of Walker's Ear," *C.H.R.,* III, 1922.

—— "The Tragedy of Chief Justice Livius," *C.H.R.,* V, 1924.

DELAFIELD, M. L. "William Smith—The Historian," *Magazine of American History,* VI, 1881.

GRANT, CHARLES S. "Pontiac's Rebellion and the British Troop Moves of 1763," *Mississippi Valley Historical Review,* XL, 1953–54.

HAMELIN, JEAN. "A la recherche d'un cours monétaire canadien, 1760–77," *Revue d'histoire de l'Amérique Française,* XV, 1961–62.

HUMPHREYS, R. A. "Governor Murray's Views on the Plan of 1764 for the Management of Indian Affairs," *C.H.R.,* XVI, 1935.

—— "Lord Shelburne and the Proclamation of 1763," *E.H.R.,* XLIX, 1934.

—— AND SCOTT, S. M. "Lord Northington and the Laws of Canada," *C.H.R.,* XIV, 1933.

KNOLLENBERG, BERNARD. "General Amherst and Germ Warfare," *Mississippi Valley Historical Review,* XLI, 1954–55.

LART, CHARLES, ed. "Fur Trade Reutrns, 1767," *C.H.R.,* III, 1922.

LELAND, MARINE. "François-Joseph Cugnet," *Rev. de l'Université Laval,* XVI, 1961–62.

LOOSLEY, ELIZABETH. "Early Canadian Costume," *C.H.R.,* XXIII, 1942.

LOWER, A. R. M. "Credit and the Constitutional Act," *C.H.R.,* VI, 1925.

LUNN, JEAN S. "Agriculture and War in Canada, 1748–1760," *C.H.R.,* XVI, 1935.

[MASERES, FRANCIS] "A View of the Civil Government and Administration of Justice in the Province of Canada While it was Subject to the Crown of France," *Lower Canada Jurist,* Montreal, 1857.

MORTON, W. L. "A Note on Palliser's Act," *C.H.R.,* XXXIV, 1953.

NEATBY, H. "Jean-Olivier Briand: A 'Minor' Canadian," *C.H.A., Report,* 1963.

—— "William Smith, an Eighteenth Century Whig Imperialist," *C.H.R.,* XXVIII, 1947.

OUELLET, FERNAND. "M. Michel Brunet et la problème de la conquête," *Bulletin des Recherches Historiques,* LXII, 1956.

—— "Les fondements historiques. . . ." *C.H.R.,* XLIII, (1962) 185.

PEASE, THEODORE C. "The Mississippi Boundary of 1763: A Reappraisal of Responsibility," *A.H.R.,* XL, 1934–35.

REID, ALLANA G. "General Trade between Quebec and France during the French Regime," *C.H.R.,* XXXIV, 1953.

REID, M. G. "The Quebec Fur Traders and Western Policy," *C.H.R.,* VI, 1925.

RICHARDSON, A. J. H. "Chief Justice William Smith and the Haldimand Negotiations," *Proceedings of the Vermont Historical Society,* IX, 1941.

—— "The Old Province of Quebec and Our Heritage in Architecture," *C.H.A., Report,* 1963.

R. DE ROQUEBRUNE, "L'exode des Canadiens après 1760," *La Nouvelle Revue Canadienne,* Sept.–Oct., 1953.

ROTHNEY, G. O. "The Case of Bayne and Brymer," *C.H.R.,* XVI, 1934.

SCOTT, S. M. "The Authorship of Certain Papers in the *Lower Canada Jurist,*" *C.H.R.,* X, 1929.

TRAQUAIR, RAMSEY. "Montreal and the Indian Trade Silver," *C.H.R.,* XIX, 1938.

TRUDEL, M. "La Servitude de l'Eglise Catholique sous le régime anglais," *C.H.A., Report,* 1963.

WADE, MASON. "Quebec and the French Revolution," *C.H.R.,* XXXI, 1950.

WALLACE, W. S. "The Pedlars from Quebec," *C.H.R.,* XIII, 1932.

WARREN, F. C. AND SURVEYOR, E. FABRE. "From Surgeon's Mate to Chief Justice: Adam Mabane," *T.R.S.C.,* 1930, Sec. II.

THE
CANADIAN
CENTENARY
SERIES

A HISTORY OF CANADA IN EIGHTEEN VOLUMES

The Canadian Centenary Series is a comprehensive history of the peoples and lands which form the Dominion of Canada.

Although the series is designed as a unified whole so that no part of the story is left untold, each volume is complete in itself. Written for the general reader as well as for the scholar, each of the eighteen volumes of *The Canadian Centenary Series* is the work of a leading Canadian historian who is an authority on the period covered in his volume. Their combined efforts have made a new and significant contribution to the understanding of Canada and of Canada today.

W. L. Morton, Vanier Professor of History, Trent University, is the Executive Editor of *The Canadian Centenary Series*. A graduate of the Universities of Manitoba and Oxford, he is the author of *The Kingdom of Canada; Manitoba: A History; The Progressive Party in Canada; The Critical Years: The Union of British North America, 1857-1873;* and other writings. He has also edited *The Journal of Alexander Begg and Other Documents Relevant to the Red River Resistance.* Holder of the honorary degrees of LL.D. and D.LITT., he has been awarded the Tyrrell Medal of the Royal Society of Canada and the Governor General's Award for Non-Fiction.

D. G. Creighton, former Chairman of the Department of History, University of Toronto, is the Advisory Editor of *The Canadian Centenary Series.* A graduate of the Universities of Toronto and Oxford, he is the author of *John A. Macdonald: The Young Politician; John A. Macdonald: The Old Chieftain; Dominion of the North; The Empire of the St. Lawrence* and many other works. Holder of numerous honorary degrees, LL.D., and D.LITT, he has twice won the Governor General's Award for Non-Fiction. He has also been awarded the Tyrrell Medal of the Royal Society of Canada, the University of Alberta National Award in Letters, the University of British Columbia Medal for Popular Biography, and the Molson Prize of the Canada Council.